Poetry Night at the Ballpark

and Other Scenes from an Alternative America

WRITINGS, 1986–2014

ALSO BY BILL KAUFFMAN

Every Man a King

Country Towns of New York

America First! Its History, Culture, and Politics

With Good Intentions? Reflections on the Myth of Progress in America

Dispatches from the Muckdog Gazette: A Mostly Affectionate Account of a Small Town's Fight to Survive

Look Homeward, America: In Search of Reactionary Radicals and Front-Porch Anarchists

Ain't My America: The Long, Noble History of Antiwar Conservatism and Middle-American Anti-Imperialism

Forgotten Founder, Drunken Prophet: The Life of Luther Martin

Bye Bye Miss American Empire: Neighborhood Patriots, Backcountry Rebels, and their Underdog Crusades to Redraw America's Political Map

Copperhead (A Screenplay)

Poetry Night at the Ballpark

and Other Scenes from an Alternative America

WRITINGS, 1986–2014

Bill Kauffman

Front Porch Republic *Books*

POETRY NIGHT AT THE BALLPARK AND OTHER SCENES FROM AN ALTERNATIVE AMERICA
Writings 1986–2014

Copyright © 2015 Bill Kauffman. All rights reserved. Except for brief quotations in critical publications or reviews, no part of this book may be reproduced in any manner without prior written permission from the publisher. Write: Permissions, Wipf and Stock Publishers, 199 W. 8th Ave., Suite 3, Eugene, OR 97401.

Front Porch Republic
An Imprint of Wipf and Stock Publishers
199 W. 8th Ave., Suite 3
Eugene, OR 97401

www.wipfandstock.com

ISBN 13: 978-1-62564-842-6

Cataloging-in-Publication data:

Kauffman, Bill, 1959–.

    Poetry night at the ballpark and other scenes from an alternative America : writings 1986–2014 / Bill Kauffman.

    xvi + 426 p.; 23 cm.

    ISBN 13: 978-1-62564-842-6

    1. Conservatism—United States. 2. Populism—United States. 3. Social problems—United States. I. Title.

JC573.2 U6 K38 2015

Manufactured in the USA

For anyone who ever gave me a hand, a wink, a word of encouragement, or just cut me a break

"No person ever died that had a family."
—RAY BRADBURY

Contents

Introduction | xiii

At the Park | 1
Play Ball! | 3
Bill Kauffman Night at the Ballpark | 7
St. Dennis of the Bleachers | 9
Aw, Canada | 11
Bullish on Buffalo | 13
A Fan's Notes | 15

Writing America | 17
A Note from the Reagan Generation | 19
Frank 'n Nat | 22
From the Outhouse to the White House | 24
The John Wilkes Booth of American Poetry | 27
Jessie Fauset's Birthright | 30
Peace in River City | 35
The Beats Go Right | 37
Ray Bradbury, Regionalist | 39
Wilson's Picket | 44
J. Evetts Haley: The Texan Who Saw Through Lyndon | 46
Vonnegut's Cradle | 48
A Gem of a State | 54

CONTENTS

Don't Shoot That Mockingbird! | 56

Shelter from the Storm | 58

Elmer Kelton: The Art of Cowboying | 60

Basque in It | 66

The Patriot | 68

The Artist as a Kept Man | 73

Southern Comforts | 75

The Last Republican | 77

How I Met Eldridge Cleaver | 83

Friendly Ghosts | 85

My Pen Pal Gore Vidal | 87

I Clean My Gun and Dream of Galveston | 90

Summer Reading List | 92

American Institutions and Holidays | 95

The West Point Story | 97

The Old-Fashioned Three-Day Weekend | 134

To Hell with Earth Day; Long Live Arbor Day! | 136

Shooting Down Mother's Day | 138

The Grinch Who Moved Thanksgiving | 140

The Old College—Why? | 143

The Un-American Game | 145

TV or Not TV? | 147

And They Call it Thanksgiving | 149

In My Literary Backyard | 153

Walter Edmonds: Our Stalwart | 155

Warren Hunting Smith, the Quintessential Genevan | 168

The Oldest Living Novelist Tells All | 177

Review of *Samuel Hopkins Adams and the Business of Writing* (Syracuse University Press) | 180

CONTENTS

(John) Gardnering at Night | 183

Harriet Tubman, in a Child's Eye | 185

Ten Years After a Place in Time | 187

My Marlboro Man | 189

The Loneliness of the Long-Dissonant Reader | 191

The Utica Club | 193

The Last Picture Show | 195

At the Movies | 197

Muskets and Misfires: The Revolutionary War on Film | 199

How Not to Watch *Copperhead*: A Reply to Sidney Blumenthal | 202

Que Surratt, Surratt | 208

The Hollywood (Ten)nessean | 210

Go Home, Limey | 213

Murder, Mayhem, and Meathead | 217

Peckinpah Country | 220

Hoosiers Time | 222

Wild (Warren) Oates | 229

Thoroughly Anti-Modern Milius | 231

"Why Not Have Stories Told From Where We Are About Who We Are?" Jay Craven Films Vermont | 233

Lost History | 239

Dick & Julia | 241

Just Deseret | 244

Our (First?) Gay Vice President | 246

Mary Chesnut's View from the Plantation | 248

Poor Old Buck | 250

Unfortunate Son | 252

The Atheist Who Played in Peoria | 254

Toledo's Golden Rule | 256

CONTENTS

TR vs. the Dictionary | 258
Our First African President? | 260
The Melodious Veep | 262
O Say Can You Sing? | 264
Quaker for Peace | 266
Barry Goldwater, New Leftist | 269
The Ford Impeachment | 271
The Elector Defector | 273
Going to Mass | 275

Home, Sweet, Home | 279
The Last Gun Show? Not if Doc Spink of Attica, New York, Has Anything to Say About it | 281
Consort of the Onion Queen | 287
American Graffiti | 289
Just My Type | 291
Commencement Address, Batavia High School | 293
Thoughts for Your Penny? | 296
Clang, Clang, Go the Jail Guitar Doors | 298
Court is in Session | 300
Revolt of the Provinces | 302
Home, Boys | 305

Space | 311
Ohio's Backyard Scientist | 313
Earthling, Stay Home! | 318
Visit to a Small Planet | 320

Pols | 323
Mr. Marrou Goes to Juneau | 325
Folky-Fakey Populists | 334

Pat Buchanan: The Last American Leftist | 337

For Sick Willie, Washington is Worth a Massacre | 341

At Least He Inhaled | 344

Earl Dodge: He'd Rather Be Right than President | 347

George W. Bush, the Anti-Family President | 352

What a Country! | 355

Hey, Ralph! Why Not Another Party of the People? | 358

The Candidates from Nowhere | 361

The Republic Strikes Back | 364

Party Animus | 366

New England Patriot | 368

The America that Lost | 371

Who Needs a President? | 373

William Leggett: Manhattan's Agrarian | 375

Who Can We Shoot? | 381

Decline of the Planet of the Japes | 387

Heil to the Chief: Philip Roth versus My America | 389

The Other Eisenhowers | 395

What Was Right About the New Left?
   Or, We Haven't Had That Spirit Here Since 1968 | 397

I Love My Country. But Perhaps Not This One | 405

Bringing it All Back Home | 407

I Laughed—and I Was Ashamed | 410

Decentralism | 412

Anarchism | 417

Boulder Rocks | 421

In A Cause That Will (Or Won't) Triumph | 424

Introduction

TWENTY-SIX YEARS AGO I came home via the potholed, weed-choked road less traveled. (Don't worry: I mythicized myself in *Dispatches from the Muckdog Gazette* so you're safe here.) I fled Babylon on the Potomac for Batavia on the Tonawanda—my lorn and lonely little hometown in Western New York, land of disenchantment. I announced to my befuddled friends in DC that I was going home to become "the Hamlin Garland of the Burned-Over District," an ambition unlikely to draw competition.

We're still here. Okay, we're five miles north of Batavia in Elba, our Napoleonic hermitage. In the post-American culture of endless war and chronic detachment, immobility is the best revenge.

The essays and articles and reviews herein represent a fairly small fraction of my published work over the past quarter century. Prolificness is not next to godliness, but it'll do in a pinch.

Why these selections and not others: Caprice?

Nah. More like stubborn whimsy. Diffident pride.

I've included two items written in my mid-twenties: a *Reason* profile of Andre Marrou (who went on to run as the Libertarian Party's presidential candidate in 1992) and a Beat-inflected manifesto from Ed and Jennifer Dunbar Dorn's Black Mountain-ish *Rolling Stock*. I winced once or twice while retyping them all these years later, but as with every piece included in this volume, while today I might change a word here or there or revise a judgment, I regret nothing. This is how the world looked to me.

Throughout, I have pruned recurrent material and I have tried to excise dictional repetitions, for nothing is quite so boring as a writer playing his forty-seventh variation on a theme. Contra Jacqueline Susann and Deborah Raffin, once *is* enough. Well, maybe twice. I have restored some lines that had been removed in editing, but I've resisted the emendation temptation.

What's not here? Dozens of book reviews, mostly for the *Wall Street Journal*; political observations that would not become unstuck in time; articles I cannibalized for other books; sheaves of early writing that adumbrated

INTRODUCTION

later (and maybe, or maybe not, better) writing; op-eds and other ephemera; and the many lengthy Q&As I've conducted with a motley, sometimes voluble, elsetimes prickly, and often insightful crew ranging from Eldridge Cleaver and Shelby Foote to Joe Paterno and Charlton Heston (who, at my prompting, exclaimed his "Goddam you all to hell!" coda from *Planet of the Apes*).

What *is* here adds up to—beyond the usual mess of contradictions that is the human lot—you tell me.

Reading over the better part of a lifetime's work is an experience tristful. I am in many respects a delirious optimist, but no trip down memory lane is without its melancholy shunpikes. Brooding and wonderment are inevitable when one goes on a remembering jag. The first piece for which I was ever paid was a 1984 review of that bassetty hound of sanctimony Mario Cuomo's diaries for *Reason*. A year later, Bob Poole and Marty Zupan hired me as the magazine's assistant editor. That they took a chance on me—a twenty-five-year-old kid whose influences were a gallimaufry of the Beats, the local colorists of the nineteenth century, late '70s and early '80s punk rock, and a Loco Foco/Sons of the Wild Jackass/Huey Long–soaked populism inherited from my grandfather: tendencies quite foreign to *Reason*'s techno-libertarian gestalt—has ever been a source of amazement. The ways of *Reason*, thank God, are not always rational. I met Lucine, my wife, at *Reason*; our daughter, Gretel, is thus a sweet child of *Reason*. Landing that job—being *paid* to *write*—altered my life in the most profound ways. I don't think I've ever thanked Bob & Marty properly. I can't really, except to say: I'm grateful that you gave me a shot.

I also tip my fading Muckdogs cap to the editors of the other publications represented in this volume: Bill and Martha Treichler, Wendell Tripp, Ed Dorn, Jennifer Dunbar Dorn, Tom Fleming, Scott Richert, Karl Zinsmeister, Scott Walter, Erich Eichman, Kenneth Turan, Scott McConnell, Kara Hopkins, Dan McCarthy, Stuart Reid, Catherine Pepinster, Andrew Blechman, Bill Bradford, Jesse Walker, Jed Donahue, Matt Chominski, Jeffrey St. Clair, Ronald Hamowy, Jason Kuznicki, Jeremy Beer, and Mark Mitchell. I beam gratitude toward Jeremy, Mark, Jeff Polet, Kentucky Woman Kate Dalton Boyer, and gunner of air-balls Jason Peters, the five grains in the board of Front Porch Books, and to Jim Tedrick and Heather Carraher of Wipf and Stock. Thanks, too, to Ben Garner for technical assistance in matters far beyond my competence.

In that fugue period after I'd left the employ of Senator Moynihan and was drifting across the continent, I daydreamed about writing things that people actually read. I didn't much care how large the audience was; four

INTRODUCTION

or five kindred souls would be fine with me. What good fortune I fell into. I am a man blessed and lucky. To those who read this—to the ones who had a notion . . . thank you.

AT THE PARK

"Instead of being the head of American engineers,
he is captain of a huckleberry party."
—EMERSON ON THOREAU

Play Ball!
First Principles, 2008

"APRIL HATH COME ON," as Nathaniel P. Willis began his best poem. 'Tis the month of violets and baseball, and so I must tell you about last summer's Baseball Poetry Night, or what I like to call Shoving Culture Down Fans' Throats Night, at Batavia's venerable Dwyer Stadium. Team President Brian Paris, a veritable one-man Chautauqua of self-improvement, and I misconceived the idea; with the declamatory assistance of my daughter Gretel and Holland Land Office director Pat Weissend, Brian and I filled the between-innings air of the August 17 game between the Class A Batavia Muckdogs and the Auburn Doubledays with recitations of odes to the American Game by Charles Bukowski, Grantland Rice, the Beat poet Tom Clark, and other bards of the ballfield. It went over as disastrously as you'd expect. My Batavia, God bless her, is poetical enough in my imagination, but as for poetry appreciation . . . well, let's just say that when Brian asked the fans, "Do you want another poem or a song?" the shouts of "Song!" rivaled the New Testament crowd's cry of "Free Barabbas!"

The Muckdogs lost the game, of course, but the muse couldn't be blamed—not when your team average is a healthy man's weight and you were recently victim of the first nine-inning perfect game in the NYP since 1956.

The low minors are the heart and soul of professional baseball. Batavia is a charter member of the New York Penn League (nee PONY League), which was drawn up in 1939 over libations at Batavia's long-ago-razed Hotel Richmond, named for the railroad baron and George McClellan-backing Democratic Party boss Dean Richmond, from whom the thieving Vanderbilts stole the New York Central.

No one has stolen our team yet, though as one of the smallest cities (population 16,000) in pro ball we are not unacquainted with the abyss. The ostensible function of a minor-league team is to develop players for the majors, but the real purpose of Dwyer Stadium is to provide a gathering place for friends and neighbors across the generations to enjoy fellowship, conversation, and baseball.

I haven't followed the majors since the 1981 strike. I can reel off the starting lineup of the 1975 Kansas City Royals but I can't name a single Royal today. Besides, we in western New York have no "local" team in the bigs, the closest major league franchise being the Toronto Blue Jays, never an appealing squad, and about as Canadian as the music of Ontario's own Shania Twain.

(Is there a more pallidly cosmopolitan North American city than Toronto? If Atlanta is the city too busy to hate, as the disturbingly cold-blooded Chamber of Commerce slogan used to go, then Toronto is the city too easy for other Canadians to hate. How, I wonder, did Jane Jacobs stand it? The Canadian team I root for is the sadsack Hamilton Tiger-Cats of the Canadian Football League. Three downs are inferior to four—Canadian football could make Bill Walsh renounce the short pass—and the three-minute warning and fifty-two-yard-line are just strange, but God bless the CFL and its idiosyncrasies.)

Batavia has been pelted with epithets over the years, but *pallid* is not one of them. The Muckdogs are one of those rooted and character-packed institutions that keep the blood pumping, and we are lucky to have a superb example of what every baseball city has to have: a baseball historian.

Bill Dougherty's father founded the heating company that has borne the family surname for three generations. Bill is retired, which means he still spends five days a week running for parts and answering phones and pitching in, but when he's not hanging around the office (or even when he is) Bill is researching and writing articles on our county's early-twentieth-century town teams and ethnic nines and even traveling women's baseball teams. Just now he's in the early stages of planning a girls' baseball tournament, apt since the Burned-Over District is the cradle of the nineteenth-century movement for woman suffrage and legal equality. (Susan B. Anthony I'll keep on the bench to nag the ump, but Elizabeth Cady Stanton can bat cleanup for me anytime.)

History: "it's not made by great men!" as the best Marxist postpunk band yelped. It is, rather, an accumulation of small stories that achieve, in their interconnectedness, a solidity, a resonance. I guess we'd have to call Bill an activist historian, since his labors of love have retrieved forgotten games and people and even rewritten the major-league record book.

This story starts with Ty Cobb and the famous "suspension game." Cobb had gone into the stands in New York on May 15, 1912, to thrash a heckler who was yelling "Your sister screws niggers" and "Your mother is a whore." The heckler, Claude Lueker, had lost all but two fingers on his hands to an industrial accident, though when told he'd throttled a handless man, truculent Ty replied that he'd have beaten up Lueker even if he had been legless. Commissioner Ban Johnson suspended Cobb, his Tiger teammates struck in solidarity—even though most of them despised Cobb—and when Tiger owner Frank Navin realized that he'd be fined heavily if the Detroiters didn't take the field against the Athletics in Philadelphia, Navin and Tiger manager Hughie Jennings cobbled together a team of Philadelphia-area amateurs, semipros, and sandlot sultans which Cobb biographer Al Stump called "the most farcical lineup the majors ever had known."

As a player, Detroit manager Hughie Jennings was hit by a pitch 287 times, a major-league record that withstood the modern charge of Houston's Craig Biggio. The affable Jennings "had two ambitions in life," writes Bill James: "to become a lawyer, and to meet the pope." He did both. Even better, he met a Batavian: twent-four-year-old Vince Maney, who was working in the Iroquois Iron Works in Philadelphia and playing semipro ball. Jennings signed Maney up as shortstop for a day.

The game of May 18, 1912, was a rout. Emergency Tigers pitcher Aloysius Travers, who later became a Jesuit priest, was touched for twenty-four runs on twenty-six hits in eight innings. Who needs a bullpen? Vince Maney described the game in a letter to his brother: "I played shortstop and had more fun than you can imagine. Of course it was a big defeat for us, but they paid us fifteen dollars for a couple of hours work and I was satisfied to be able to say that I had played against the world champions. I had three putouts, three assists, one error, and no hits."

If only Bill James had been sabermetricking in 1912. For Vince also walked once and was hit by a pitch, giving him an on-base percentage of .500. Calling Billy Beane!

Maney played under an assumed name that day. He was a strikebreaker, after all—a scab of sorts, although Ty Cobb wasn't exactly Samuel Gompers. For nigh unto one hundred years the baseball record books listed Maney as Pat Meaney, forty-one, of Philadelphia. The fictive Meaney's made-up age gave him the specious distinction of being the oldest rookie ever to debut in the majors till forty-two-year-old Satchel Paige joined Cleveland in 1948.

Enter Bill Dougherty. Add countless hours at the Genesee County History Department and the Richmond Library, volumes of baseball histories, communications with the Baseball Hall of Fame in Cooperstown, and a determination to do right by a fellow Batavia Irishman. Thanks to the indefatigable Dougherty, Vince Maney has gotten his due. Open the newest edition of any standard baseball reference book or website and you'll find an entry for Vincent Maney, born and died in Batavia, NY, a Detroit Tiger of 1912.

So far as we can tell, Vince is the only Genesee County boy ever to play a game in major league baseball. A Moonlight Graham of our own. Given his due after all these years only because of the labor of another man, a Batavian who grew up enthralled with baseball and his hometown and never lost his love of either.

We are eleven weeks from the start of another season—this one a special blessing, as our good neighbors the Triple-A Rochester Red Wings rescued the Muckdogs from an off-season flirtation with extinction. Soon enough I will find myself on the Dwyer Stadium beer deck draining a beverage with historian Bill Dougherty and Steve Maxwell, whose insurance company was founded by none other than the homecoming Vince Maney many decades ago. There is a continuity still in the America that counts. Heck, the nuns at St. Joe's used to make my dad run over to Vince Maney's office for free inkblotters. We are bound, all of us, in this little place that in my imagination is bigger than the whole world.

Yeah, I know, it all leads back to a single game and an 0–2 line and an .833 fielding average, but Vince did get hit by a pitch, too, just as Batavia has been beaned as often as Hughie Jennings. There's more than one way to make it to first base. And even for those of us who never cross the plate, never score a run, there are other ways of making it home.

Bill Kauffman Night at the Ballpark
The American Conservative, 2008

WHEN IN MAY BATAVIA Muckdogs general manager Dave Wellenzohn told me that as club vice president and resident minor-league baseball litterateur I was to be honored with "Bill Kauffman Day," I replied, gamely if lamely, "Every day is Bill Kauffman Day."

To my horror, the schedule soon appeared with the September 4 game so denominated. For three months I prayed for a rainout—unavailingly. For as grateful as I was to Dave, no one with even a partially functioning nimrod detector can fail to be humiliated by such a day.

"What are you going to do on Bill Kauffman Day?" I heard all summer long. Bobbleheads were out, not because they're infra dig but rather too expensive. I knew I couldn't follow through on my threat to take the field and read from my collected works in a fake-English accent as a homonymic nod to Andy Kaufman. Throwing out the first pitch was mandatory: Friends placed wagers on whether I'd reach the plate. (Bets were off in the event of a "strong wind.")

Brian Paris, coconspirator in last year's Baseball Poetry Night, was manning the p.a. system for the last days of the season. For Bill Kauffman Day I urged an Americana diet of Townes Van Zandt, Lucinda Williams, Tom Russell, and the local Ghost Riders, the best unsigned country band in America, but Brian played Michael Buble. Oh well; he's still Mr. Irrepressible of Batavia baseball.

Serves me right, anyway. I am a chronic critic of the blaring of amplified music and sound effects during games. My friend Tom Williams and I want someday to sponsor a "Pastoral Night" in which the only sounds are ball hitting glove, bat hitting ball, umpiric declarations, and the sweet buzz of friends talking in the bleachers and grandstand.

Brian kicked off BK Day with a reprise of my disastrous oration of Bukowski's "Betting on the Muse," which begins "Jimmie Foxx died an alcoholic in a skidrow hotel room." I thought of it as a cautionary tale for the boys.

Dave called me onto the field and out I shambled, wondering, during his funny and much-appreciated encomium, if I should pitch from the stretch or full windup.

Between innings we gave away copies of my books to those who answered questions about Batavia baseball history. I feared that folks would answer the questions but then spurn the prizes. I'd find books littering the stands like dehiscent peanut shells. But neighbors act neighborly.

Gretel and her friend Megan sang the national anthem mellifluously. During the seventh-inning stretch, now unfortunately scored in so many ballparks by that empty cloud of bombast "God Bless America," the girls ignored post-9/11 protocol and instead sang my favorite, "America the Beautiful."

Gretel and Megan weren't past "Oh beautiful . . ." when a heckler started in from the beer deck: "Wrong song! Wrong song!" The girls got a huge kick out of it. How many singers have ever been jeered during "America the Beautiful"?

The Muckdogs lost, 13–4. Maybe Bukowski's derelict warning induced a dugout-wide fit of melancholia. Aptly, I suppose, the go-ahead run was allowed by our favorite Muckdog, a sidearm reliever who lists his hobbies as "reading and poetry." (The commonest avocation among the boys is "video games.") Brian wisely ignored my request to play "Knockin' on Heaven's Door" in the bottom of the ninth.

About that first pitch. After telling the crowd that my brother had promised to buy everyone in the stands a beer if I didn't throw a strike, I threw a fastball right down the pipe. I thought the radar gun clocked it in the low eighties—others estimated the mid-forties. My brother bought me a Rohrbach's, and my cousin laughed out a memory of how as kids we'd sneak into Dwyer after church and my dad would pitch us ball after ball. Almost forty years later this little stadium is still larger than all my imaginings.

St. Dennis of the Bleachers

The American Conservative, 2010

OPENING DAY FOR THE Batavia Muckdogs approaches and with it the resumption of a long, leisurely, blissful conversation in which living and dead participate.

(Alas, the dead sometimes play third base or catch for our team.)

I feel intensely the presence of those who have shared these many hundreds—maybe a thousand, by now— evenings of my life at Dwyer Stadium. Let me tell you about one such ghost.

The last time I saw Dennis Bowler was in September 2004, during one of those melancholy late-season games when the chill of summer's end is in the air, and even though I haven't darkened a classroom door for decades the thought of school lours over me like a prison sentence.

Dennis had been sick for a couple of weeks with a mystery ailment. But even at half-speed, Dennis was irrepressible.

"See ya tomorrow night," we both said as he left the third-base bleachers in the twelfth inning for the drive back to Gasport. It didn't work out that way. Dennis made it home that night and then dropped dead of a heart attack.

If ever you were minding your own business at a Western New York ballpark or high school gym and you were buttonholed by a fast-talking man telling you everything he knew about nuclear physics, British Columbia, or how to make a baseball bat, it was Dennis Bowler.

He loved to talk. He talked more than any person I have ever met, often about his ancestors or daily life in Niagara County. For a frenetic man, he was content in his place, fully at home. His stories included such local characters as the unfortunately named Israel "Izzy" Humen, for whom Dennis had an overwhelming sympathy. He hated meanness and cruelty. I suspect he had been teased and mocked more than once, and he repaid the world not in bitterness but in kindness.

Dennis loved those names and numbers that spice our lives but that we depreciate with the word "trivia." He'd ask you to name the vice president of the Confederacy (Alexander Stephens) or Hank Greenberg's lifetime home run total (331). He could recite the starting lineup of every girls' softball team in the Genesee Region League.

When Dennis turned sixty in August 2004, the Muckdogs' announcer asked him to stand up and take a bow. Dennis was so busy yakking that he never heard the chorus of "Happy Birthday."

Even then, he looked forty and acted like a coltish boy. He would race teenagers for foul balls. When he got one he'd hold it aloft, beaming like a prospector who'd just panned a gold nugget. Then he'd give it to a child.

Dennis resided in the family homestead on Ridge Road, fruitbasket of the Northeast. He lived alone and drove a rusting jalopy distinguished by its varying shades of blue. Now and then he'd stop by my parents' house to pour water down its chronically leaky radiator.

He farmed as many acres as he could and sold his produce at a roadside stand. He brought corn to the games and gave it away. He also painted houses, taught hunter-safety courses, drove a tractor for Becker Farms, and in winter he substituted at local schools. No kid who ever had Mr. Bowler as a sub forgot him.

Dennis worked hard and with an almost beatific cheerfulness, but he could not afford health insurance. He hadn't visited a doctor in many years. What if? Yeah, what if.

One abiding memory of Dennis: in his last summer, he brought a telescope to Dwyer Stadium. Not to check out the chicks; rather, Mars was at its closest approach in millennia, so he trained the scope on the Red Planet and the moon, and we took our peeks.

Dennis was so utterly without guile, so joyful, so ravenous for knowledge. He lacked entirely the internal brake that keeps most people from bringing telescopes to baseball games. And good for him.

During that game Dennis ran over to the first-base bleachers and taped a napkin to the fence. He dashed back, pointed the telescope at the napkin, and asked our then ten-year-old daughter to take a look. It read HI GRETEL.

He was such a sweet, innocent man, poor in purse but rich in spirit. Sometimes I think of Dennis keeling over in his bathroom, perhaps at three a.m., the soul's midnight, as Ray Bradbury calls it. But more often I think of him bounding up the bleacher steps two at a time, talking about Western Canada, running after foul balls, telling Gretel corny jokes, and smiling. Always smiling.

It's been almost six years now and I suspect he's still talking St. Peter's ear off.

Aw, Canada

The American Conservative, 2009

OVERCOMING MY AVERSION TO seasonally inappropriate acts—I hate leaves that turn in August or Christmas carols sung in September—some buddies and I made our annual midsummer creep over the border to cheer on the Hamilton Tiger-Cats of the Canadian Football League.

Hamilton is a steel and port city of half a million on Lake Ontario. It has history and soul and a meet resentment of Toronto, which in its endlessly advertised multicult glory is like Henry James's definition of a cosmopolite: a little bit of everything and not much of anything.

The Ti-Cats play at venerable Ivor Wynne, a circa 1930 stadium nestled into a Hamilton neighborhood that is as human as Toronto's domed Rogers Centre is hideously sterile. Not that Ivor Wynne presents a traditional tableau: the cheerleaders seem to be recruited from Hamilton's skankiest strip joints, and NFL-ish schlock-rock and TV timeouts offend the game itself.

The rules of Canadian football are familiar yet awry, like one's spouse sporting a fetchingly strange new hairstyle. The field is longer and wider (I never tire of hearing that the ball is on the fifty-three-yard line), and a single point—a rouge—is awarded to a team that kicks an unreturned ball into or out of the elongated end zone. My favorite CFL score is 1–1. Most significantly, an offense gets three downs to make ten yards. Unlike four-down American football, teams are reluctant to either waste a down with a long pass or patiently build a drive on running plays, so a premium is placed on safe short passes. Not my bottle of Upper Canada ale, but I am a foreigner so I do what all foreigners should do when visiting a country: I shut up and enjoy it and then go home.

The CFL limits imported players to twenty-two per team, but this is too lax. The league once proved a haven for quarterbacks whose race (Warren Moon) or size (Doug Flutie) ran afoul of NFL prejudices, but today the presence of American players is as irritating as seeing Europeans in the NBA and the NHL. Stay home, mercenaries.

Hamilton's adopted son George Parkin Grant, the philosopher at McMaster University, made at least one published reference to the local gridders. In *Time as History* (1969), his book on Nietzsche, he attached the word "pathetic" to "the performance of the quarterback for the Hamilton Tiger Cats this season." A hardy perennial, that remark.

Before going this year, I reread Grant's *Lament for a Nation* (1965), that rare volume written in response to a specific political episode—the eclipse of Conservative prime minister John Diefenbaker—which endures as a work of richness and imagination, a statement of Canadian nationalism that is far more than tiresome anti-Americanism.

Grant mourned Canada's reduction to "a branch-plant society of American capitalism." He honored prairie lawyer Diefenbaker and those "nationalist hayseeds" who defied JFK in trying to keep nuclear weapons off Canadian soil. The story misfits our lazy assumptions: Grant, an organic if statist conservative, was also a Christian pacifist. The Liberals who scorned Diefenbaker as a Saskatchewan hick were pro-nuke Cold Warriors who "paid allegiance to the homogenized culture of the American Empire." Grant's reactionary—and I mean that as praise—essay became a basic text of the Canadian New Left. It is as if Russell Kirk had written the most damning indictment of the Vietnam War and then become the *eminence grise* of SDS.

Grant saw as heroic Diefenbaker's last-ditch attempt to keep Canada from being absorbed into the "universal and homogeneous state" whose HQ was DC. The prime minister, operating from a mixture of "prairie populism with the private-enterprise ideology of the small town," had asserted that Canada was no mere satellite but an independent nation. For his audacity he was crushed by "the full weight of the North-American establishment."

(An aside so depressing that I have to quarantine it in parentheses: Grant's nephew, the deracinated war-craving intellectual Michael Ignatieff, is the new leader of the opposition Liberal Party. Ignatieff, who lived abroad for a quarter of a century, has said, "I do not believe in roots." George Grant, alas, would have believed all too well in Ignatieff, and in the nightmarish prospect of a self-extirpating Canada electing a prime minister who would like nothing better than to ship the eh-saying clods of provincial Ontario off to die in Iraq or Afghanistan for his globalist abstractions. No, Canada!)

Scarlett O'Hara-like, I refuse to think of Michael Ignatieff. Instead I envision George Grant in the end-zone seats at Ivor Wynne, nursing a Molson, cursing the ads for foreign corporations, and joining in a lusty chorus of Hamilton's fight song: Oskee-wee wee/ Oskee whawha/ Holy Mackinaw/ Tigers/ Eat 'em raw!

Bullish on Buffalo

The American Conservative, 2009

IF IT'S JANUARY THE Buffalo Bills must be scattered to the greens of fifty golf courses, far from the howling winds and superabundant snows of their autumnal "home." Only one Bill, backup linebacker Jon Corto, is native to the region. The remainder are about as Buffalonian as Caroline Kennedy.

The localist solution is a territorial draft, so that the Bills would be *of* Buffalo and not just mesomorphic mercenaries. Of course this would lead to an NFL based in California, Texas, and Florida, with western New York kicked into a minor league. That's okay. Majors have cash but minors have soul.

Far removed from the glory days of four consecutive Super Bowl appearances in the early 1990s, the Bills' only recent distinction came from the Sunday morning boostering of my old boss Tim Russert of South Buffalo. I remember Tim before he was a saint, when he was a hail-fellow political operative picking off Pat Moynihan's hapless Republican would-be challengers with all the zest of a giddy teenager zapping aliens in a video game. I'll bet ex-Bills QB Jack Kemp was more afraid of Russert than he ever was of Buck Buchanan.

While the Bills skidded to another sub-.500 record this season, I contented myself with Larry Felser's *The Birth of the New NFL: How the 1966 NFL/AFL Merger Transformed Pro Football* (Lyons Press). Felser was present at the creation, covering the formation of the American Football League in 1960 for the Buffalo *Courier-Express*, though I suppose his greatest distinction came in marrying Beverly, who defeated my mother in the Elba Onion Queen pageant of 1957. I don't know if mom has forgiven her yet.

Those beautiful old AFL names—Houston Antwine, Gloster Richardson, Cookie Gilchrist—evoke the dawn of my football consciousness in that antediluvian age of the tie game, the straight-ahead kicker, and the white cornerback. Felser was there and he took notes. The AFL was a spirited underdog but it was no pastoral dream: the San Diego, nee Los Angeles, Chargers were named after owner Barron Hilton's hotel chain's credit-card operation. What a loathsome derivation!

But consider Felser's take on the cartoonish villain Al Davis, owner of the Oakland Raiders. Davis, as commissioner of the AFL, hired ex-*Buffalo Evening News* sportswriter Jack Horrigan as his PR man. When Horrigan was diagnosed with leukemia, writes Felser, "Davis, a Jew, bought a votive candle in a Catholic religious supply store. Back in his office, he lit the candle as a devotion, a prayer in flame—a Catholic custom. When the office was about to close that evening, a cleaning lady informed him it was against building policy to leave a burning candle unattended. Davis took off his coat and stayed the night."

That doesn't make up for yanking the team out of Oakland for thirteen years, but Al can't be all bad.

Pro football today is nigh unwatchable due to the chronic TV timeouts which interrupt the flow of the game and remind the assembled just who is boss. After scores or changes of possession the twenty-two behemoths on the field wait meekly for a spindly TV semaphorist to give the referees the signal to resume play. What would happen if the players defied the Great God Television and just started playing? There would be consequences, I imagine.

Mauling women, popping loudmouths in bars, shooting steroids: these things the mansters of the gridiron will do, but disobey television—never.

The major-college game is just as compromised, though the exigencies of recruiting give most teams a regional accent. My football preferences are outré: I am a Catholic peacenik whose favorite teams were Brigham Young and Army before the University of Buffalo Bulls staggered into Division I in 1999. UB had the worst program in college football until Turner Gill, a devout Christian gentleman and miracle worker, came to town three years ago. Gill vitalized the team with local products James Starks of Niagara Falls and Buffalo's own Naaman Roosevelt, so that the Bulls of Buffalo are, in some sense, representative of Buffalo. This year UB played in a postseason game for the first time ever—the unfortunately named International Bowl in Toronto.

Bulls fans expected a bittersweet end: Gill would leave town at season's conclusion, lured by a fat contract from a football factory. No one—well, almost no one—would have blamed him. In America, people are expected to move for money. Loyalty is penury. Immobility is for suckers and losers.

But Turner Gill is staying. Passed over for the Auburn job—reportedly for the stupid racist reason that the coach, who is black, has a white wife—Gill is casting down his bucket where he is, at least for now.

Stay is such an underrated word.

A Fan's Notes

The American Conservative, 2013

I AM WRITING THIS on a sunny and fragrant June morning, sitting in the bleachers off the Little League field on which I played all those summers ago. My Little League coach, Larry Lee, died last week, and it is a Kauffman family habit (not an eccentricity!) to revisit places associated with the recently deceased.

I can see myself out there at shortstop for the Cubs in the National League playoff game. Bottom of the sixth, tie game, bases loaded, grounder hit my way, I field it cleanly, throw home . . . and into the dirt, skipping it past the catcher. Game over, season over, Little League career over. Shucks.

Pretty much every male relative of mine—father, brother, cousin, uncles—was all-league in baseball or football, but as for me, well, they also serve who only sit and watch from the bench. I'm a quinquagenarian now, rather to my astonishment, and I still bring out the glove to toss the ball with our daughter, who humors the old man with a game of backyard catch in the high grass.

I don't hold, however, with my Upstate landsman Frederick Exley's morose conclusion that "it was my destiny—unlike my father, whose fate it was to hear the roar of the crowd—to sit in the stands with most men and acclaim others. It was my fate, my destiny, my end, to be a fan." (Exley's books belie any such shrinking violetism.)

This is the seventy-fifth year since professional baseball came to Batavia, and we are among the last of the train-whistle towns in the low minors. I sit in these bleachers, too, with friends and apparitions, conducting decades-long conversations and hearing ghostly echoes.

Even in the bushes, alas, those ghostly echoes can get lost in the din.

Each batter has his own "walk-up music," which means that every time a home team lad strides to the plate we are treated to a ten-second snatch of his favorite song. Year in and year out, the boys' collective taste is execrable. I've yet to hear, say, X or Neil Young, though what I really long for is the sound of silence.

Conversation is the casualty in the empire of noise. I am vice president of the team but I can't get the damned decibelage turned down. John Nance Garner was right about the impuissance of VPs.

In minor-league baseball, the place, and not the players, is the thing. This place is: My old friend Donny Rock, the groundskeeper, lining the basepaths. Grande dame Catherine Roth, now ninety-two, refusing to stand for the vapid "God Bless America," which since 9/11 has afflicted our ears during the seventh-inning stretch. My mom, who has lived her entire life in our Snow Belt county, putting on her jacket when the temperature dips below eighty. Yappy Yapperton, countless sheets to the wind, yelling inanities from the beer deck. (Scratch that: Yappy is either dead or in prison today.)

The boys of summer come and go; I prefer life in the bleachers. A fair number of big leaguers have passed this way, and I follow them in the box scores. Especially Phillies' stars Ryan Howard and Chase Utley, who were, in successive years, very kind to our daughter during the Muckdogs v. Muckpuppies games. (These tilts required the boys to come to the park the Saturday morn after a Friday night game and presumed revelry. The guys who showed—Utley, Howard, and some very good-natured Latin American players—were saints.)

As for the majors: yawn.

Several years ago I had a free afternoon while visiting DC and thought I'd take in my first Nationals' game. The Metro ride to the stadium, with its passengerial cargo of black and white ball-capped fans, was a rare and heartening sight in our segregated capital city.

As I neared the ticket booth I hesitated. Did I really want to spend three hours fidgeting through interminable TV timeouts, which make between-innings breaks and coaches' trips to the mound foretastes of eternity? Nah. So attending a Nats' game remains on my list of Things to Do in DC Before I Die (along with visiting the Frederick Douglass home and the gravesites of Gore Vidal and Clover Adams at Rock Creek Cemetery).

Back in the bleachers I think of William Cullen Bryant's poetical wish that he die "in flowery June/When brooks sent up a cheerful tune." Bryant got his wish. It's the little victories that count.

WRITING AMERICA

"I do not invent my literary ancestors. If anything, they invented me."
—GORE VIDAL

A Note from the Reagan Generation
Rolling Stock, 1987

THE FORGOTTEN FRANK NORRIS, realist poet of wheat, predicted the emergence of an earthy and true muse for American novelists of the future. "Believe me," he declared, "she will lead you far from the studios and the aesthetes, the velvet jackets and the uncut hair, far from the sexless creatures who cultivate their little art of writing as the fancier cultivates his orchid.... She will lead you—if you are humble with her and honest with her—straight into a World of Working Men, crude of speech, swift of action, strong of passion, straight to the heart of a new life, on the borders of a new time."

See the borders recede and fall ignominiously over the horizon! The tyranny of the upper-crust white literati and denigration of the populist vision continues today, virulent as in brash old Norris's time. How I gag upon the "voice of a new generation" encomia that greet Ellis, Leavitt, Janowitz, McInerny, and the hive of detached young avatars, boldly sketching the generational angst, piquant in their tales of aimless youth, numbed by ludes, Alfa Romeos, and a surfeit of unfelt sex.

What is this Voice of a Generation bullshit? Did Hemingway and F. Scott and those fine old coxcombs speak for my grandfather, wiping his brow with axle grease while the Lost Generation drank from European carafes and got Parisian blowjobs? Did the Beats, sainted souls though they were, speak for my dad, surveying for the Iron Horse that Ginsberg rode first class to the Wichita love-in? Do our coke-besotted disaffected authors of Vintage paperbacks embody the dreams and aspirations of my pals, stocking shelves with Tide and chugging Twelve Horse ale to forget that it's the 220-pound wife they'll be banging tonight?

Hell no. With each cocaine contract and sale of movie rights to Judd Nelson we drift from Whitman's noble admonition to speak of the "mass of men, so fresh and free, so loving and so proud."

"Democracy is waiting for its poet," Frederick Jackson Turner confidently told his classmates a millennium ago. She waits still, patiently, though poetry has long since discarded her democratic vistas.

Where in American letters are the authentic voices of the mass of men and women, so fresh, so free, so loving, so proud, who invigorate the heartland? Our cultural ruling class damns a generation for the sins of its affluent—those noxious coastal yuppies who compose the audience for the anointed Generational Voices. We are bombarded with smug attacks on Today's Youth, delivered by paunchy old hypocrites who begrudge the children of the petty bourgeoisie the right to own a VCR.

I'm so bored with the antiyouth whining of the mildly discontented culturati: you know who you are, splitting grapefruit in bed with wifey, reading the elitist wedding page of the Sunday *Times*. Merle Haggard hit the right note: "Stop rolling downhill like a snowball that's headed for hell." And you know that if some rube dared put on a Merle record at one of your artyparties you'd laugh, derisively, do mock hillbilly sounds, then put on better haircuts like the Pet Shop Boys.

Merle was right. A Cold War and a paternalistic state have sapped our manly energy, left us a pitiful, bullying nation whose belleslettrists resemble the limp villains sketched so acidulously by Populist hero Tom Watson: "lolly-pops, vegetarians, grape-juicers, and sissy-boys." Go fist yourselves.

Partisans of Thomas Wolfe have been amply warned to hibernate these days. Wolfe, the ravenous descendant of Whitman in the American bardic tradition, instructed the aboriginal writer to "make somehow a new tradition for himself, derived from his own life and from the enormous space and energy of American life."

The presence of the frontier, the awareness of *space* and sprawling open lands, shaped the American character and instilled in us the craving for freedom, Frederick Jackson Turner argued in his definitive essay. For Wolfe, as with others in the American bardic tradition, that frontier was a double-edge sword: it offered endless opportunity for redemption, yet it attenuated the ties that ought to bind us to family, community, hometown.

At one point in *Of Time and the River* he despairs, "We are so lost, so naked and lonely in America. Immense and cruel skies bend over us, and all of us are driven on forever and we have no home. . . . For America has a thousand lights and weathers and we walk the streets, we walk the streets forever, we walk the streets of life alone." Two paragraphs later, America's naked possibilities transport him: "It is a fabulous country, the only fabulous country. . . ."

Try to imagine the pallid and weary ironists, self-conscious crucified Jesuses of my generation, Wolfe-like with thick and effusive love/hate for America. Or for anything beyond the poisonous vials and pink teenage asses their dentist/psychiatrist/arbitrager daddies spring for via the unspoken trust fund.

Gore Vidal, whose mordant Mugump historical novels impress me as beautiful expressions of elegant Americanism in the only admirable and indigenous sense of that haughty adjective—the Henry Adams tendency—says that "Wolfe was to prose what Walt Whitman was to poetry." Yes! A free Transcendentalist man of open spaces for whom unexceptional incidents of deracination unleash torrents of American longings, smack dab in the turbulent main current.

One sees, in the New Visions of our privileged oracles, no fascination with, or awareness of, the vastness and awful empty beauty of America. Gone is the enchantment with open spaces—even the freeway is a fetter. Gone is the sense of liberating freedom and terrible loneliness that our continent's amplitude inspired. The disappearance of Turner's frontier is indisputable fact for the wealthy young. The glorious Roman candle Kerouac, who sought to redefine the frontier in order to revive it, is irrelevant in Greenwich and Hollywood, and in those ivy enclaves barred forever to the Visigoths of Middle America.

One of your better hippie bands, Jefferson Airplane, requested yesterday's UMCs to "tear down the wall, motherfucker." Never mind that the group ended up tearing down the wall separating protest rock and corporate rock ("turning rebellion into money," as the sell-outs of my generation, The Clash, so presciently put it). There's nothing wrong with the destructive (and implicitly reconstructive) sentiment. And that, God willing, is exactly what we're gonna do.

Tear down the complacent, effete walls that all you goddam Lionel Trilling epigoni built. Resentment ain't unhealthy for sharpening the writer's eye—just ask Vernon Parrington, if you haven't flushed Oklahoma U's greatest football coach-English prof down the memory hole.

There are a thousand new American songs on the tips of provincial tongues, ready to resume the glorious chronicling of Norris, of Whitman, of Wolfe, of Kerouac, of Garland, of London, of our forefathers. A regeneration is at hand, a rebirth of revolutionary spirit that will take us far beyond the narrow, constricted boundaries of the neurasthenic rich and into the verdant, fertile fields of new realism.

Politics be damned, but call us the Reagan Generation if you like, our formative years spent under his rule. Or don't call us anything. I ask just one favor, dear reader: Do not call sexually confused collegiate velvet jackets the Voice of My Generation. That voice screams unheard in Fargo, in Anniston, in Batavia, and if you uncover your ears the clamor begins.

Frank 'n Nat

The American Enterprise, 2001

IN THE SUMMER OF 1821, two young men met on a stagecoach bound for Bowdoin College and struck up a fast friendship that would last throughout their lives. Fourteen-year-old Henry Wadsworth Longfellow may have impressed his classmates as Bowdoin's Most Likely to Succeed, but stagecoach passengers Franklin Pierce and Nathaniel Hawthorne did all right for themselves.

As midlife approached, Pierce was elected to the U.S. Senate from New Hampshire, while Hawthorne scratched along as a purse-poor writer of fantasies. The author had a recurring dream: "I am still at college ... and there is a sense that I have been there unconscionably long, and have quite failed to make such progress as my contemporaries have done; and I seem to meet some of them with a feeling of shame and depression that broods over me as I think of it, even when awake."

Things got better. Hawthorne's tales began to earn notice, if not royalties, and the solicitous Pierce sought a government position for his friend, finally helping Hawthorne land the post of surveyor in the Salem Custom House.

The fortunes of the Bowdoin buddies peaked in the early 1850s, when one wrote the imperishable *Scarlet Letter* and the other secured the Democratic nomination for president in 1852. After the candidate asked the now-estimable novelist to bang out a quickie campaign bio—surely an *infra dig* assignment for a genius—Hawthorne nobly acceded to his old friend's request, toiling for ten weeks to produce *The Life of Franklin Pierce*.

If the book was a dutiful production, it did evince a genuine fondness for its subject. This was no mercenary job: Hawthorne told a friend, "I have come seriously to the conclusion that [Pierce] has in him many of the chief elements of a great ruler. . . . He is deep, deep, deep. . . . Nothing can ruin him."

Such high hopes reposed in Pierce, the "Young Hickory of the Granite Hills." He defeated the Whig candidate, General Winfield Scott, whose supporters jeered that the bibulous Pierce was the "hero of many a well-fought bottle."

"No one pretends that writing the life of General Pierce is its own reward," snidely remarked one Boston journalist. The cynic! Such suspicions wounded Hawthorne, who was a conservative Democrat—his skepticism of reformers is on display in *The Blithedale Romance*—and generally disdainful of politicians. He said, charmingly, of his powerful friend, "I do not love him one whit the less for having been President."

But virtue has its rewards, too. A grateful Pierce named Hawthorne to the lucrative consulship in Liverpool; never again would the author want for money.

As a Northern man with a genuine respect for the South, Pierce might have averted the great calamity of the Civil War, but his administration was doomed from the start. In January 1853, as the Pierces prepared to move to the White House, their beloved son and only child Bennie was killed in a freak train accident. Mrs. Pierce, an extremely morbid woman on her best day, told her husband that Bennie's death was God's exaction for Franklin's ambition.

Pierce was paralyzed by fear that his wife was right. The First Lady would spend the next four years secluded in her room, writing notes to her lost boy, while the oft-drunken and guilt-wracked Pierce sleepwalked through his presidency.

The war whose coming Pierce had been powerless to stop filled both Pierce and Hawthorne with dread. As faithful New Englanders, they were Unionists, but halfheartedly so, for as Hawthorne wrote, "The States are too various and too extended to form really one country. New England is quite as large a lump of earth as my heart can really take in."

Both men were suspected of disloyalty; Pierce was eventually so execrated that Hawthorne's publisher tried to talk him out of dedicating his 1863 volume *Our Old House* to the former President. The author's reply was a classic statement of friendship. "I find that it would be a piece of poltroonery in me to withdraw" the dedication, he declared, for if Pierce "is so exceedingly unpopular that his name is enough to sink the volume, there is so much more need that an old friend should stand by him."

Hawthorne stood by him until the end. In May 1864, Pierce escorted an enfeebled Hawthorne on a carriage tour of New Hampshire's White Mountains. Death came to the author in middlenight, as Pierce slept in an adjacent room at a Plymouth, N.H. inn. In gathering the deceased's possessions, Pierce found an old pocketbook in the bottom of Hawthorne's valise. Its only content was a picture of the best Presidential friend a novelist ever had: poor desolated Franklin Pierce.

From the Outhouse to the White House
The American Enterprise, 1997

THE THINGS WRITERS DO for money.

Nathaniel Hawthorne wrote his wife, "I want nothing to do with politicians—they are not men; they cease to be men, in becoming politicians. Their hearts wither away, and die out of their bodies." But that was before Hawthorne's old Bowdoin College chum, the affable Franklin Pierce, won the 1852 Democratic presidential nomination. Hawthorne dashed off an encomiastic *Life of Franklin Pierce*, and was rewarded with a consulship at Liverpool.

Salem's Nat was mucking about in fertile soil. The campaign biography, with its often hilariously fulsome tributes, had been a staple since Andrew Jackson was lauded in a volume by Senator John Henry Eaton (whose barmaid wife had so offended Mrs. John C. Calhoun). Thirty such books were written for candidate William Henry Harrison in 1840, as the Virginia aristocrat metamorphosed into a cidery man of the people.

The astonishing thing is that so many accomplished novelists joined the deluge. William Dean Howells, not yet twenty-five, did the honors for Abraham Lincoln in 1860, and so he spent the war as a consul in Venice rather than as a blue-coated soldier. (Howells later penned a bio of his wife's cousin, Rutherford B. Hayes.) Lew Wallace (*Ben Hur*) put Benjamin Harrison aboard a chariot of his own, and Kenneth Roberts strove to animate Calvin Coolidge (though his mention of Silent Cal's Indian blood panicked the boys at the Republican National Committee).

Historian Edmund B. Sullivan laid down the rules of the genre, including:

—"Stress humble beginnings . . . a birth in a log cabin or on a farm is helpful, or in a small frame house. . . . [I]f the candidate was ever associated with New York City, gloss over that fact."

—"Play down specific religious beliefs; emphasize vaguely positive feelings toward religion."

—"Ex-generals must be basically men of peace."

—"Stress favorable nickname, if masculine sounding; invent one, if necessary." (Yet how in 1988 could "Poppy" have defeated "Duke"?)

The candidate's rise from lowly station to colossus is Algeresque; and indeed, Horatio himself wrote *From Canal Boy to President*, a life of James Garfield.

Widowed mothers were especially prized. Of Kentucky's Great Compromiser, one biographer swooned, "Much as we admire Henry Clay . . . the Statesman . . . yet do we love far more to dwell upon the 'orphan-boy' following the plough in the slashes of Hanover, and occasionally trudging his way, with a grist of corn, to a distant mill, to provide bread for a widowed mother and younger brothers and sisters."

Sophisticated moderns may laugh, but much of the corporate-media coverage of Bill Clinton belonged to this school of hagiography—though previous generations had the taste not to drag alcoholic stepfathers into the picture.

Surveying the field in 1956, James D. Hart singled out for meritorious silk-purse-making the McKinley biographer who marveled of his subject that "his shoes are always polished" and "he shaves himself . . . never cuts himself . . . and can carry on a conversation while cutting off his beard." A Thomas Dewey idolator praised the Owosso prig's height of five feet, eight inches because it was "almost precisely the same as the average of the men in the armed forces."

Hart opined that the campaign bio "still flourishes . . . as indestructible as the folk dream of the log cabin," but the old grey fare she ain't what she used to be.

They're still written, of course, but men of letters are no longer on such intimate terms with men of state. John Tyler, for instance, sent Washington Irving to Spain and John Howard Payne ("Home Sweet Home") to Tunis. Even Grover Cleveland, Uncle Jumbo, who didn't devour fiction in quite the same way he made slabs of beef disappear, counted among his confidants Harold Frederic (*The Damnation of Theron Ware*). Yet when contemporary presidents look beyond the Potomac for ambassadors and friends, they select washed-up actors or courtesans. Harold Frederic, meet Babs Streisand.

Saul Bellow toyed with the idea of a Humphrey book in 1968, but the genre today is thoroughly hack-ridden, and besides, the ghosted "autobiography" has become the volume of choice. Politicos who shamelessly read other men's words at poignant passages in their lives (Teddy Kennedy eulogizing a slain brother, Bob Dole bidding farewell to the Senate) may as well tack their own names onto the covers of campaign bios, making them autobios and gaining royalties withal.

But maybe everything that dies someday comes back. For at this very moment might some ambitious scrivener be sweating over *Plowboy From St. Albans: The Life of Albert Gore*?

The John Wilkes Booth of American Poetry
The American Enterprise, 1999

ONCE UPON A TIME, Americans bought books of poetry, and no volume was better loved than Edgar Lee Masters's *Spoon River Anthology* (1915), that erstwhile staple of high-school English class in which an Illinois town is revealed by the epitaphs on its cemetery tombstones.

Masters was a Chicago lawyer and one-time partner of Clarence Darrow, whom he disdained as a headline-hogging welsher. (He refuses to mention Darrow by name in his splenetic autobiography.) But Edgar Lee Masters came from the Land of Lincoln—Menard County—and his single most enduring poem mythicized the girl whose early death may or may not have been the emotional climacteric of Abraham Lincoln's life:

> I am Anne Rutledge who sleep beneath these weeds,
> Beloved in life of Abraham Lincoln,
> Wedded to him, not through union,
> But through separation.
> Bloom forever, O Republic,
> From the dust of my bosom!

In a span of sixteen years, Masters went from cherished prairie poet to reviled heretic. For in 1931 he published *Lincoln: The Man*, a biography of passionate bitterness and patriotic rage. Masters, you see, was a Stephen Douglas man who thought it time to even the score, given that "[t]he political history of America has been written . . . by centralists and . . . New England."

The poet was an old-fashioned states-rights Democrat with a populist bent and a burning enmity toward the Republican Party, which was "conceived in hatred and mothered in hatred." His grievance was that "every President since Lincoln has imitated Lincoln instead of Jefferson," and his intention was to bring all those statues of Honest Abe crashing to the ground, for only by smashing the Lincoln myth might America "rise out of the hypocrisy and the materialism into which it was sunk by the War."

In Masters's telling, Lincoln was "cold," "undersexed" (Mary Todd was no Anne Rutledge!), and a "Jehovah man" who may not have believed in God but fancied himself in the role, Old Testament style. Masters is relentless, scourging Lincoln for over 500 pages as intellectually lethargic, unkempt, utterly lacking the milk of human kindness, and a mediocre lawyer to boot.

The book was an act of professional suicide for Masters—himself a cold, though decidedly not undersexed, man—but one that he was born to write. His family homestead was just seven miles from Lincoln's New Salem, Illinois. Masters's grandfather had once retained lawyer Lincoln in a land dispute—which Lincoln lost. Grandfather Masters served in the Illinois legislature, where he voted against U.S. Senate candidate Abraham Lincoln "because he thought Lincoln's policies would bring on war between the states."

Hardin Wallace Masters, the poet's father, was a law partner of William Herndon, who had been Lincoln's old law partner and the author of the frankest biography by a Lincoln intimate. (Herndon was also an Anne Rutledge partisan; Mary Todd hated him.) Hardin Masters wanted to write his own Lincoln book, based on Herndon's recollections and the gossip of old-timers; he never completed it, though in a way his son did, in an act of filial piety.

Lincoln: The Man was published in February 1931, just in time for Lincoln Day, and for a few weeks the icon-smashing poet became a new John Wilkes Booth. ("Booth's bullet was the last one fired for States' Rights," wrote Masters.)

Edgar Lee Masters had grown up in Petersburg, Illinois, in a time and place where Lincoln was not yet a deity but just a man (and of course a prophet is always without honor in his hometown—leaving aside the question of whether the prophet was Lincoln or Masters). But by 1931 the sixteenth president was encased in myth even in Petersburg: angry Lincolnians threatened to erase Masters's verse from Anne Rutledge's tombstone, on which it had recently been incised. (Some regarded it as an insult to Mary Todd Lincoln anyway.)

Masters, something of a misanthrope and most emphatically not a cockeyed optimist, was not exactly shocked by the envenomed response to his book. In his own young adulthood, he confessed, "I had an admiration for Lincoln, even believing the falsehood that the War Between the States was inevitable and the result of an irrepressible conflict, though my grandfather, who knew Lincoln there in the Petersburg-New Salem country, had given me the materials for a very different judgment of Lincoln." But while the poet had his grandfather, the rest of the country made do with Carl Sandburg's hagiography.

As an old man, Masters dreamed of returning to Petersburg, the site of his Lincoln-washed youth. But he had long lost his prairie spirit; in his last years, he cocooned himself in a New York City hotel and refused even to cross the street. Only death took him home to Petersburg, where he is buried four graves down from Anne Rutledge, wedded to her not through union but through verse.

Jessie Fauset's Birthright
The American Enterprise, 1995

> For never let the thought arise
> > That we are here on sufferance bare;
>
> Outcasts, asylumed 'neath these skies,
> > And aliens without part or share.
>
> This land is ours by right of birth,
> > This land is ours by right of toil;
>
> We helped to turn its virgin earth,
> > Our sweat is in its fruitful soil.
>
> —James Weldon Johnson, from "Fifty Years 1863–1913"

The notion that African Americans are here on sufferance bare never once crossed the mind of Jessie Fauset, whose novels depicted a robust Negro middle class that was much more than George Babbitt in blackface.

Jessie Redmon Fauset was born in 1882 to a father who was a respected A.M.E. minister in Camden, New Jersey. The Fausets were on the fringe of stylish Old Philadelphia society; they were frayed gentility, polite and mannerly if occasionally behind on the grocery bill. ("There is no pride so strong, so inflexible, so complacent as the pride of the colored 'old Philadelphia,'" wrote Fauset in *Comedy: American Style.*)

Hers was a close and loving family; she was raised, she later recalled, in a "very conservative, not to say very religious, household," and she grew up with a sense of the dignity of her race. Of course when the white world impinged young Jessie met the usual slights. At the Philadelphia High School for Girls, "I happened to be the only colored girl in my classes . . . and I'll never forget the agony I endured on entrance day when the white girls with whom I had played and studied through the graded schools, refused to acknowledge my greeting."

Upon graduation from Cornell, Jessie Fauset taught French for a dozen years at Washington, D.C.'s storied Dunbar High ("The Greatest Negro High School in the World"), named after the turn-of-the-century black American poet best remembered for his exclamation, "I know why the caged bird sings!"

Fauset chose W. E. B. DuBois as her mentor. He, in turn, recognized his protégée as a distaff member of the "talented tenth" whose efforts DuBois believed would uplift the race. We must, Jessie lectured the usually unlecturable DuBois, "teach our colored men and women *race* pride, *self*-pride, self-sufficiency (the right kind) and the necessity of living our lives, as nearly as possible, *absolutely*, instead of comparing them always with white standards."

Fauset wrote stories, reviews, and poetry for *The Crisis*, the NAACP flagship, before becoming full-time literary editor in October 1919. She worked alongside the prickly DuBois for seven fruitful years, though her own experiences of the richness of segregated black middle-class life kept her from swallowing whole the white-subsidized NAACP's integrationist panacea.

Jessie Fauset disdained literary politics and petty jealousies. As a wise older brother counsels in her first novel, *There Is Confusion* (1924), "Our battle is a hard one and for a long time it will seem to be a losing one, but it will never really be that as long as we keep the power of being happy. . . . Happiness, love, contentment in our midst, make it possible for us to face those foes without. 'Happy Warriors,' that's the ideal for us."

Fauset walked it like she talked it. Her little kindnesses and generous praise encouraged the Harlem Renaissance of the 1920s. She was, arguably, the discoverer of Langston Hughes, who was forever grateful. ("I found Jessie Fauset charming—a gracious, tan-brown lady, a little plump, with a fine smile and gentle eyes. . . . From that moment on I was deceived in writers, because I thought they would all be good-looking and gracious like Miss Fauset.") Even the *rouge et noir* bad boy Claude McKay said of Fauset: "All the radicals liked her, although in her social viewpoint she was away over on the other side of the fence."

Few, it seemed, wanted to hear about Jessie's side of the fence. *There Is Confusion* was rejected by one publisher because, Fauset was told, "White readers just don't expect Negroes to be like this." Her black characters are often prosperous doctors, caterers, and modistes: the sort who have, rather than are, domestic help. There is a staidness, a steadiness about them, but they are no Oreos. They are securely colored and securely American. Or as the dancer Joanna Marshall informs a theater full of nonplussed whites: "I hardly need to tell you that there is no one in the audience more American than I am. My great-grandfather fought in the Revolution, my uncle fought in the Civil War, and my brother is 'over there' right now."

A French dance instructor in *There is Confusion* conjectures "that if there's anything that will break down prejudice it will be equality or perhaps even superiority on the part of colored people in the arts." But it has to be on colored people's terms, in one of their own vernaculars. Jessie Fauset would not beam with pleasure if she knew that seventy years hence a blanched Michael Jackson would make millions of dollars for a Japanese corporation by singing "ain't no difference if you're black or white," which she knew to be a lie.

Her four novels frequently feature tragic light-skinned African Americans who "pass" for white in a burlesque of the integrationist dream. "Emotionally, as far as race was concerned, she was a girl without a country," Fauset mourned for one such woman in her final novel, *Comedy: American Style* (1933). "Later on in life it occurred to her that she had been deprived of her racial birthright and that that was as great a cause for tears as any indignity that might befall man."

Jessie Fauset's ardent hope was that African American boys and girls be raised in the fullest knowledge of that birthright. In *There Is Confusion* Joanna comes home from school and asks plaintively, "Didn't colored people ever do anything, Daddy?" Her father then tells her "of Douglass and Vesey and Turner. There were great women too, Harriet Tubman, Phyllis Wheatley, Sojourner Truth, women who had been slaves, he explained to her, but had won their way to fame and freedom through their own efforts."

It was for the Joannas of America that Fauset and DuBois edited *The Brownies' Book*, an unprofitable monthly published from January 1920 until it folded two years later. This wholesome hodgepodge of homilies, lore, and biography was dedicated, Fauset rhymed:

> To children, who with eager look
> Scanned vainly library shelf, and nook,
> For History or Song or Story
> That told of Colored Peoples' glory.

The publication's purpose, declared the editors, was:

> To make colored children realize that being "colored" is a normal, beautiful thing.
> To make them familiar with the history and achievements of the Negro race.

To make them know that other colored children have grown into beautiful, useful, and famous persons.

To teach them delicately a code of honor and action in their relations with white children.

To turn their little hurts and resentments into emulation, ambition, and love of their homes and companions.

To point out the best amusements and joys and worthwhile things of life.

To inspire them to prepare for definite occupations and duties with a broad spirit of sacrifice.

Fauset devoted her career to acts of ancestor worship, of recovery and restoration. She translated Haitian poets. When her sister died she endowed a "Helen Lanning Corner" in the public school in which Mrs. Lanning had taught; this room was "to contain books only about colored people, especially colored children." She sponsored similar rooms in other schools. In 1932 Fauset insisted, "No part of Negro literature needs more building up than biography.... It is urgent that ambitious Negro youth be able to read of the achievements of their race.... There should be some sort of *Plutarch's Lives* of the Negro race. Someday, perhaps, I shall get around to writing it."

She didn't. A marriage—a happy, companionable union—intervened, and the illnesses of various relatives brought out the nurse in Jessie Fauset. She published no books between 1933 and her death in 1961. Unlike Zora Neale Hurston, Jessie Fauset has enjoyed no spectacular revival—nor, given the unfashionableness of her resolutely middle-class African American subjects, is she likely to.

Yet the better Afrocentric curricula are Helen Lanning Corners. The surge of interest in such distinct cultural achievements as baseball's Negro Leagues is very much in the Fauset stream. Every Ohio boy reading Langston Hughes is her son: every black girl who feels a confident, bitterless pride in her race and her country is a daughter of Jessie Fauset.

An authentic black pride (or Bayou pride or Brahmin pride or Bay City pride) needs no sugarcoating. Fauset averred, "The successful 'Negro' novel must limn Negro men and women as they really are with not only their virtues but their faults." What would she think of the cartoon Negroes manufactured by today's white-run entertainment industry?

The present obscurity of Jessie Fauset suggests that Afro-centric (or, better, Aframerican-centric) education has not gone far enough.

To say that Miss Fauset is inferior as a novelist to Jane Austen misses the point. My family's history may be less illustrious (or notorious) than that of the Rockefellers, but it means infinitely more to me; it undergirds a goodly part of who I am, and to be ignorant of one's forebears is to be forever anchorless, unmoored, "free" only in the sense that one is "freefallin," as the song goes. "Grandfather's chair may be a very humble piece of furniture," wrote the turn-of-the-century education reformer John Kennedy of good old Batavia, New York, "but it is prized beyond all price because it is grandfather's chair." This is why children in the schools of my Upstate New York should be reading Walter D. Edmonds, while young scholars in Camden should enter the fictive world of Jessie Fauset.

A localized Aframerican-centric education would find children of Philadelphia awash in Fauset and the lads at Dunbar High reciting the poetry of the school's eponym; boys and girls in Rochester would celebrate Frederick Douglass Day rather than Martin Luther King Day, and no one would graduate the Cleveland schools without a thorough grounding in Langston Hughes.

Jessie Fauset's friend, the poet Countee Cullen, memorably wrote:

> Yet I do marvel at this curious thing:
> To make a poet black, and bid him sing!

If it makes our young poets proud of their blackness, their ancestors, their heritage, and it bid them sing, then let us praise Afro-centrism!

Peace in River City
The American Conservative, 2011

OUR DAUGHTER WILL BE spending the snowy months rehearsing her role as Marian the Librarian in her high school's production of Meredith Willson's *The Music Man*, that tuneful Iowa-placed warhorse—no, parade horse—of community theater. (The flaw in community theater is that while the actors are drawn from the community, the playwrights seldom are.)

It's been an autumn of imposture, as my wife played the lead in a sharply observed one-act, "Blind Date," by the late great Horton Foote of Wharton, Texas, whom a friend calls "the last straight man in American theater," by which she does not mean that he set up punch-lines for comics. The Internet, I learned, is not wholly useless: Lucine created her accent by watching Lady Bird Johnson clips on youtube. You remember Lady Bird: the cuckquean who had the gall to scold Americans about the ugliness of highway billboards while her grotesque husband was ordering the murder of hundreds of thousands of Vietnamese and Americans in Southeast Asia. There are degrees of ugliness, Bird.

In 1966, LBJ appointed Meredith Willson to the National Council on the Humanities, but hey, everybody's imperfect. And that was the last time Mason City, Iowa, would ever have a voice in government-subsidized culture. Although Meredith had long since lit out for Southern California, the notes in his head were always Iowan. He was said to have been the largest baby (fourteen pounds, six ounces) born in Iowa, which perhaps justified that superfluous L in his surname. Meredith Willson's father, an attorney, had played baseball at Notre Dame, where he was taught to throw a curveball by the inventor of that pitch, Candy Cummings. Meredith's sister, Dixie, a literate Ziegfield Follies chorine and silent-movie screenwriter, wrote the oft-anthologized poem that begins "I like the fall/The mist and all."

So the Willsons were one of those families of talented eccentrics, some grounded and some not, who grow like beautiful weeds whenever small-town America is left alone to develop in its own way, in its own time.

Mason City also gave us Hanford MacNider, national commander of the American Legion in the 1920s and a believer in "Iowa as the Promised

Land." The Legion once was a potent lobbyist for loot, though veterans' benefits were meager recompense to those who came home legless or armless or blind or insane from the single-L Wilson's War to End All Wars. MacNider, a banker, introduced the most un-Mr. Potterish "Iowa idea," which required each Legion post to "make some unselfish contribution to its community's welfare each year or lose its charter." I'd say ninety years of sponsoring American Legion baseball teams is a pretty fair contribution.

Peace has long been an Iowa idea as well. Hanford MacNider was given to such craven and anti-American utterances as "I am ... unwilling to commit my sons or any American's sons to the policing of the rest of the world." Traitor! MacNider played football at Harvard and earned a chestful of medals in both world wars, but he had an Iowa isolationist streak that such he-men as Lindsey Graham and Rick Santorum would find suspiciously girlish.

Iowa isolationism was also embodied, in rather different bodies, by the New Left historian William Appleman Williams of Atlantic, Iowa, and by Barry Goldwater-Eugene McCarthy supporter Donna Reed of Nishnabotna, Iowa. (I'll bet Donna could have thrown a mean curveball, too; watch her fling that rock through the upper window of the old Granville house in *It's a Wonderful Life*.)

I devoted a chapter to Iowa's prewar culture—Grant Wood, Jay Sigmund, Ruth Suckow, Marvin Cone—in my book *Look Homeward, America* (2006). Its artistically fecund soil was so much richer than barren Manhattan. And it produced worthy political leaders, too, from the cantankerous Old Right skinflint H.R. Gross to the radical farm crusader Milo Reno.

Meredith Willson seems to have been fairly apolitical, though he did, mind-bogglingly, compose a march commissioned by President Ford for that phlegmatic Michigander's Whip Inflation Now (WIN) campaign. That combination is so far beyond unhip as to propel the WIN March into its own dimension of occult stodginess. Maybe the University of Michigan marching band can thump it out next time the Wolverines play the Iowa Hawkeyes?

I hear tell that there are caucuses, if not crocuses, coming up in Iowa. As far as I know, only two men in the mix—Ron Paul and Gary Johnson—come anywhere near the Iowa Idea. Not that politics is the answer. If the Mason Cities of our country are ever to reflower, they need peace and poetry and music—the mist and all.

The Beats Go Right

The American Enterprise, 1997

THE RECENT DEATHS OF poet Allen Ginsberg and novelist William S. Burroughs occasioned a round of impolite obituaries accusing the dear departed and their Beat Generation pals of being subversive perverts. Yet whatever unconventionalities went on behind closed doors, their politics were squarely American: the Beats were libertarian heretics in an age of statolatry.

Beat icon Jack Kerouac was a Robert Taft Republican throughout his life. In 1952, in the predawn of his notoriety, Kerouac supported the stolid Ohio conservative for the GOP nomination while his buddy Ginsberg, son of a "Communist beauty" mother, talked up plutocratic Cold Warrior Democrat Averell Harriman, of all people. (The Beat "Adonis of Denver," cowboy drifter Neal Cassady, said "it makes not one whit of difference who gets it.")

Kerouac's political comments read like *Chicago Tribune* editorials. In a 1948 letter, he cursed Harry Truman:

> The war scare I think is just for the sake of squeeze-playing Congress into voting Universal Military Training and the Marshall Plan. It's a dirty administration with dirty tricks-creating "emergencies" for its own political ends... I think we should arm and just dare anybody to attack, but I don't think we should be the aggressors, that wouldn't pan out.

Kerouac subscribed to and avidly read *National Review* and once appeared on William F. Buckley, Jr.'s "Firing Line," where he drunkenly uttered the immortal words, "Flat-foot Floogie with the floy floy!" He painted pictures of the Virgin Mary and Pope Paul; he disliked the Vietnam War as well as its protesters: "I'm pro-American and the radical political involvements seem to tend elsewhere.... This country gave my Canadian family a good break, and we see no reason to demean said country."

The prematurely cadaverous Burroughs was an anarchist who'd have fit very nicely into a conspiracy chat room. His favorite political writer was the hard-right polemicist Westbrook Pegler. In a typical passage, Burroughs imagined an American future of "ever-increasing governmental control over the private citizen, not on the old-style police-state models of oppression and terror, but in terms of work, credit, housing, retirement benefits, and medical-care: services that can be withheld. These services are computerized. No number, no service. However, this has not produced the brainwashed standardized human units postulated by such linear prophets as George Orwell. Instead, a large percentage of the population has been forced underground. How large, no one knows. These people are *numberless*."

To be number-less, without a number or government ID tag choking your neck, was about the best the misanthropic Burroughs could hope for. He was fond of saying, "No problem can be solved. When a situation becomes a problem, it becomes insoluble. Problems are by definition insoluble. No problem can be solved, and all solutions lead to more problems." Not exactly sloganeering for the Great Society.

The third member of the Beat triumvirate, Allen Ginsberg, was more predictable and less interesting than the others, but at least he outgrew his red diapers. He devoted his political energies to libertarian causes: the legalization of marijuana and homosexual relations, and, later, denunciations of the CIA. Despite his matrix, he never fell for the Communist con. He held Cuba and postwar Vietnam to be "police states," and he accused American Sandinista-groupies of "cowardice."

"I don't like the government where I live," Ginsberg sang, and his anarchistic bone was large enough that he'd have sung the same tune no matter where he lived.

The Beats ran deep in an American vein. They loved their country, whatever they thought of its government. In a 1959 manifesto defending baseball, the crucifix, and "the glee of America, the honesty of America," Kerouac declared, "Woe unto those who think that the Beat Generation means crime, delinquency, immorality. . . . Woe unto those who spit on the Beat Generation, the wind'll blow it back."

The spitters have outlived the Beats. But softly the wind soughs.

Ray Bradbury, Regionalist
First Principles, 2008

Byzantium, I come not from,
But from another time and place
Whose race was simple, tried and true;
As a boy
I dropped me forth in Illinois.
A name with neither love nor grace
Was Waukegan, there I came from
And not, good friends, Byzantium.

—RAY BRADBURY

EVERY SUMMER SOLSTICE MY daughter Gretel and I sit on the front porch and read the opening chapters of Ray Bradbury's *Dandelion Wine* (1957), the finest evocation of a boyhood summer I have read. If ever a science fiction writer has deserved the honorable tag of "regionalist," it is Ray Bradbury of Waukegan, Illinois.

Critic Wayne L. Johnson once described Bradbury as having "one foot amid the tree-lined streets of Green Town, Illinois in the 1920s and '30s, and the other foot planted on the red sands of Mars in the not-too-distant future." He is a pastoral moralist who jokes that he eats metaphor for breakfast, lunch, and dinner; his line of descent has little to do with Jules Verne or Robert Heinlein and instead can be traced to the Nathaniel Hawthorne of "Rappaccini's Daughter" and "Young Goodman Brown." Like Hawthorne, he has Salem connections: in 1692, Mary Bradbury was convicted of witchcraft, though she escaped hanging. I'll wager that her descendant hopes she really was a witch.

Bradbury's people were among his hometown's earliest settlers. A great-grandfather was mayor of Waukegan in the 1880s, and the author's creative memory was carved by the ravines of his native city, as Sam Weller emphasizes in his fine biography *The Bradbury Chronicles* (2005).

He left Waukegan at age thirteen, when his family followed the sun westward, and though the starstruck boy loved Los Angeles (W.C. Fields once signed Bradbury's autograph book and told him, "There you are, you little son of a bitch!") he would forever recall, and transmute into myth, twilit summer evenings on the Bradbury family's front porch. Not a day went by, said Bradbury, "when I didn't stroll myself across a recollection of my grandparents' northern Illinois grass, hoping to come across some old half-burnt firecracker, a rusted toy, or a fragment of letter written to myself in some young year hoping to contact the older person I became to remind him of his past, his life, his people, his joys, and his drenching sorrows." (He really did write such a letter: As a forty-something-year-old man, Bradbury returned to Waukegan, walked the ravine of his childhood, and located the oak tree in which he had, decades earlier, deposited a note to his older self. He poked around in a squirrel hole of the tree until he found the message from boy to man. It read: "I remember you.")

Like H.L. Mencken, Gore Vidal, Ernest Hemingway, and other original Americans, Bradbury "had the advantage," wrote Russell Kirk, "of never attending college," which "constricts people," in Bradbury's words. He was an autodidact, a library rat, who also cherished old people—not the self-pitying valetudinarians (though they, too, are made in the image of God, albeit a kvetching deity) but wise wizened elders. "I was a boy who did indeed love his parents and grandparents and his brother, even when that brother 'ditched' him," he writes. The grandfather in *Dandelion Wine* is vintner of this "common flower, a weed that no one sees . . . but for us, a noble thing." Grandfather Spaulding disparages the maintenance-free turf that a young newspaperman threatens to bring to Green Town (the fictive Waukegan), instructing the fellow in the joys of grass and its mowing, for "it's the little savors and little things that count more than big ones. A walk on a spring morning is better than an eighty-mile ride in a hopped-up car, you know why? Because it's full of flavors, full of a lot of things growing. You've time to seek and find."

(From the what-might-have-been file: the songwriter Jimmy Webb worked on a musical of *Dandelion Wine* that, alas, seems never to have flowered. Imagine the craftsman who wrote "Wichita Lineman," which *Creem* justly called "one of the most perfect pop records ever made," and "Galveston," among the most effective of all antiwar songs, scoring Green Town. Oh, the things that never were!)

I cannot think of another writer whose work is so redolent of a season and a month. Not June and summer, contra *Dandelion Wine*, for Ray

Bradbury is October's storyteller; in his epigraph to the collection *The October Country* (1955), he describes his land as " . . . the country where it is always turning late in the year. That country where the hills are fog and the rivers are mist; where noons go quickly, and midnights stay. That country composed in the main of cellars, subcellars, coal-bins, closets, attics, and pantries faced away from the sun. That country whose people are autumn people, thinking only autumn thoughts. Whose people passing at night on the empty walks sound like rain . . . "

This is where he sets the second novel of his Green Town trilogy, the "dark carnival" fable *Something Wicked This Way Comes* (1962), the story of an Illinois town of the 1920s visited one October by a mysterious circus whose owner and ringmaster promises maturity to callow boys, eternal life to worn-out men, youth and beauty to gnarled old maids. "Unconnected folks, that's the harvest the carnival comes smiling after with its threshing machine," says Charles Halloway, the wistful and exhausted library janitor who finds, in his son, the means to resist the tempter and accept mortality, limits, and the homely pleasures of life in Green Town, Illinois. (Bradbury scripted an underrated film of this novel, released in 1983.)

The final piece of the Green Town triptych is the long-awaited *Farewell Summer* (2006), set in the summerlike October of 1928, the year of *Dandelion Wine*. Though not as bad as its pans would indicate, *Farewell Summer* was the *Godfather III* in the trilogy. It is no *Dandelion Wine*, but nor does it detract from that work, which Bradbury, in his characteristically lyrical (my view) or overwritten (the view of his critics) style, has described as "the boy-hid-in-the-man playing in the fields of the Lord on the green grass of other Augusts in the midst of starting to grow up, grow old, and sense darkness waiting under the trees to seed the blood." The characters and character of Green Town feed each other, grow strong and individuated in their commingling; *Dandelion Wine* is, I think, his most beautifully realized book.

The Green Town novels established Bradbury as a Midwestern pastoralist of tremendous skill and one of the best novelists of American boyhood. His reputation as a science fiction master rests on two novels, *Fahrenheit 451* (1953) and *The Martian Chronicles* (1950), and a passel of stories.

The prophetic quality of *Fahrenheit 451* resides not so much in the image of burning books. Who today would even bother to incinerate the works of Sean Hannity or Al Franken? They probably read better in ash anyway. Rather, it is in the way that technology and bureaucracy vitiate the family, deprive it of essential functions. Fire Captain Beatty explains to the late-blooming rebel Montag: "Heredity and environment are funny things. You can't rid yourselves of all the odd ducks in just a few years. The home environment can undo a lot you try to do at school. That's why we've lowered the kindergarten age year after year until now we're almost snatching them from the cradle." (Not that the well-meaning advocates of mandatory preschool have *any such thing in mind* ...)

As the foregoing quote suggests, Bradbury has a libertarian streak, which flared especially in his work in the 1950s. As he explained at that time, "Science fiction is a wonderful hammer; I intend to use it when and if necessary, to bark a few shins or knock a few heads, in order to make people leave people alone."

Since his earliest stories Ray Bradbury has warned of the potential of technology to replace its makers, to substitute the artificial and the efficient for the clumsy and human. (See his masterpiece "The Veldt," a story, in Kirk's description, "of children abandoned by modern parents to the desolation of the Screen.") The forlorn Professor Faber tells Montag in *Fahrenheit 451*, "It's not books you need, it's some of the things that once were in books. The same things *could* be in the 'parlor families' today. The same infinite detail and awareness could be projected through the radios and televisors, but they are not. No, no, it's not books at all you're looking for! Take it where you can find it, in old phonograph records, old motion pictures, and in old friends; look for it in nature and look for it in yourself."

As this passage indicates, Bradbury is not a technophobe. He rather likes gadgetry, in the manner of a bright Green Town boy reading *Popular Mechanics* and fussing with radio tubes. Though sometimes disparaged by science-fiction hardware buffs as a Luddite, he is an effervescent optimist, confident that we needn't choose (as he put it in one poem) "Einstein or Christ" but can have "*both*."

Thus in *The Martin Chronicles,* as American expansion plays out on our planetary neighbor, Bradbury's poetic appreciation of the frontier virtues vies with his melancholic awareness of the omnipresence of cupidity and the lust to dominate. He later explained to an interviewer, "You don't have to give in to the wilderness, and you don't have to kill it. You can work with it." Well, maybe.

Ray Bradbury has never given in to cheap despair or the illusion that air conditioning and moondoggles signal the inexorable march of Progress and Light. He is Waukegan in its Golden Age, between the wars, the Waukegan of grandfathers sitting on porches with grandsons, telling family legends and transmitting winemaking secrets, and while those grandsons may grow up to design rocketships and even fly to Mars, they will, in the world and wishes of Ray Bradbury, bring Waukegan with them. Of course Waukegan/Green Town is dirt and earth, not just memories, and it can never be transplanted. Something is lost and something is gained in such moves, and Ray Bradbury—more than any other American writer—has taken the measure.

Waukegan, Bradbury knows, is as mythopoeic as any place on earth or in time, if its sons and daughters will just remember. He remembers. In a lovely passage from a 1974 introduction to *Dandelion Wine*, Bradbury writes that:

> [O]ne of the last memories I have of my grandfather is the last hour of a Fourth of July night forty-eight years ago when Grandpa and I walked out on the lawn and lit a small fire and filled the pear-shaped red-white-and-blue-striped paper balloon with hot air, and held the flickering bright-angel presence in our hands a final moment in front of a porch lined with uncles and aunts and cousins and mothers and fathers, and then, very softly, let the thing that was life and light and mystery go out of our fingers up on the summer air and away over the beginning-to-sleep houses, among the stars, as fragile, as wondrous, as vulnerable, as lovely as life itself.
>
> I see my grandfather there looking up at that strange drifting light, thinking his own still thoughts. I see me, eyes filled with tears, because it was all over, the night was done, I knew there would never be another night like this.
>
> No one said anything. We all just looked up at the sky and we breathed out and in and we all thought the same things, but nobody said. Someone finally had to say, though, didn't they? And that one is me.
>
> The wine still waits in the cellars below.
>
> My beloved family still sits on the porch in the dark.
>
> The fire balloon still drifts and burns in the night sky of an as yet unburied summer.
>
> Why and how?
>
> Because I say it is so.

That, my friends, is the voice of a beautiful soul.

Wilson's Picket

The American Conservative, 2011

EDMUND WILSON WAS so securely American that he didn't bother with vapid assertions that he lived in a "free country." Instead, he acted as if he lived in such a place and as if the proper course for an independent insubordinate American writer was to walk his own path, no matter how poorly marked or overgrown, and then write up his journey. That is why this exemplary American man of letters spent his final years as an exile at home.

In 1962, a year into the observance of the Civil War centennial, Wilson published his magnum opus, *Patriotic Gore*, a massive study of the literature and litterateurs of what Gore Vidal has called the "the great single tragic event that continues to give resonance to our republic." Wilson's title, taken from "Maryland, My Maryland"—"The despot's heel is on thy shore. . . . Avenge the patriotic gore that flecked the streets of Baltimore"—promised something other than Bruce Catton.

Patriotic Gore is best known for two things: Wilson's witticism that "the cruelest thing that has happened to Lincoln since he was shot has been to fall into the hands of Carl Sandburg" and the book's twenty-four-page introduction, a bracingly (and brazenly) dyspeptic essay that compares national governments to "sea slugs" in their mindless aggression—though unlike the slugs, nations have publicists who weave elaborate moral defenses of their violence and voracity. Wilson assesses every American war since James K. Polk's Mexican adventure and tallies the cumulative cost: "staggering taxes," the "persecution of non-conformist political opinion," an "extensive secret police," and "huge government bureaucracies."

Wilson groups Lincoln with Bismarck and Lenin as "uncompromising dictator[s]" who "established a strong central government over hitherto loosely coordinated peoples." Yet Wilson, who recognizes Lincoln's "magnanimity" and acute intelligence, is no Confederate apologist. As a good Yorker from the cradle of abolitionism, he understands that "what [the South] fought for was really slavery" and that too many Southern Democrats were expansionists who would have annexed half the Western Hemisphere if given the chance.

His favorite Confederate is Vice President Alexander Stephens, the indomitable invalid Georgian whose opposition to conscription and defense of habeas corpus vexed the centralizers of the CSA.

Wilson explained to his friend and admirer Robert Penn Warren that the introduction was his attempt to "remove [the war] from the old melodramatic plane and consider it from the point of view of an anti-war morality." But "anti-war morality" had been driven into a Mennonite-radical Catholic ghetto in the age of Robert McNamara.

Wilson's introduction is one of the great libertarian statements in American letters, which is why the minie balls flew upon publication. The editors of the ironically named *Life* denounced Wilson for his "crotchety hogwash." *American Heritage* refused to run a favorable notice by Daniel Aaron. No wonder, for the introduction expressed "the disillusion of a populist radical . . . the scorn of a Tory anarchist and aristocrat of the mind for the rainbow slogans of American foreign policy," in George Steiner's estimation.

Arthur Schlesinger tried to talk Wilson into junking the introduction, which he attributed to Wilson's "inbred, robust isolationism." (How robust? Asked why he disliked the British, Wilson replied, "Because of the American Revolution." Forget, hell.)

"The disaffection of [Upstate] New York toward the Civil War . . . is behind my own attitude," explained Wilson. He was a proprietary patriot. The country belonged to him—he was an American, dammit, and he would not be bullied by hall monitors or lectured by jingoes.

Wilson followed *Patriotic Gore* with the saturnine polemic *The Cold War and the Income Tax*. (He was against both.) These books, along with *Apologies to the Iroquois* and *Upstate*, mark the magnificent roar of a patriot of the old republic protesting the ruin of his beloved country. Thematically, they are of a piece. For instance, he compares Secretary of State Seward to the satanic Robert Moses, enemy of the Iroquois, who repellently boasted, "I can take your house away from you and arrest you for trespassing if you try to go back to it." Sick simpering tyrants indeed.

Edmund Wilson ended *The Cold War and the Income Tax* with a plangent confession: "I have finally come to feel that this country, whether or not I continue to live in it, is no longer any place for me." The nation's most distinguished literary critic was a stranger at home because, as a good American, he detested militarism and cant.

"Whenever we engage in a war or move in on some other country, it is always to liberate somebody," wrote Edmund Wilson fifty years ago. He could have written it yesterday.

J. Evetts Haley: The Texan Who Saw Through Lyndon

The American Enterprise, 2000

J. EVETTS HALEY WAS raised in Midland, Texas, and worked his family's ranch along the Pecos River, punching cows instead of a time clock. As a young man he had an epiphany: "History was right here at home"; so he would spend his lifetime recording the story of his Texas Plains. He also composed one of the best-selling—if now wholly forgotten—political biographies ever written.

After graduating from West Texas State, Haley roamed the plains, amassing a vast collection of cattle-related Texana. His *Charles Goodnight: Cowman and Plainsman* (1936), which has been called the finest biography of a frontiersman, tells us how to skirmish with Comanches, treat rattlesnake bites, and pull an arrow out of a man's neck. Through a "flow of tobacco juice and profanity," Goodnight, who was born three days after Texas declared independence, explained the code of the panhandle to his bookish young landsman, and for the rest of his life Haley would live by that code in an often uncomprehending world.

Haley was fired from the University of Texas in 1936 when he denounced President Roosevelt and assumed leadership of the "Jeffersonian Democrats of Texas." The obstreperous Haley remarked after taking his stand, "it's going to mean I'll get fired, but my folks never started for San Jacinto and then turned back." He added, "I will welcome being fired and go back to my old job of punching steers—those that escaped Henry Wallace's cow killers."

The poetical rancher would write the lives of cowboys and oilmen, store-keepers and outlaws, bank robbers and patrolmen, but his most notorious work (and the book for which he was virtually crucified) was an act of atonement "for the shameful part Texas has played in foisting" on Americans an "evil genius": Lyndon Baines Johnson.

A Texan Looks at Lyndon: A Study in Illegitimate Power (1964) is one of the great stories in self-publishing. Even small houses shied from a book that followed, with Texas Ranger doggedness, the trail of theft, defalcation, and vulgarity left by the President of the United States. As Bill Modisett relates in his biography of Haley, when a publisher asked the author if his lawyer had vetted the book for libel, Haley replied, "Hell, he says there's libel on every page, that's what he says. But I'm a historian. . . . [M]y obligation is to tell the truth. . . . When it comes to lawyers, I'll talk to them about a matter of policy. But when it comes to history, I don't ask them, I tell them!"

So Haley published the book himself, with the proceeds from a cattle sale. In *samizdat* fashion, Americans unsatisfied with the sonorous officialisms of Walter Cronkite and Hugh Sidey bought an astonishing five and a half million paperback copies.

Reading the book today, one is struck by the eerie parallels to a later tactile southern Democratic President and maudlin cracker with the hots for every woman not his wife. The habitual lying, the craving of power for its own sake, the blistering of subordinates too cowardly to tell the Great Man to take a flying leap: LBJ comes off as a slightly less unctuous Bill Clinton.

Haley depicts Lady Bird Johnson as a "Lady Macbeth," cold and calculating, caring "more about her husband's career than her husband"—although Lady Bird had the grace to disappear into Texas once their time was up.

In one sense, the book has aged poorly: The reader cringes when the segregationist Haley huffs and puffs over LBJ dancing with the wives of African American congressmen. But his essential thesis—that Johnson was a power-mad liar and crook of Texas-sized proportions—has been validated by the first two volumes of Robert Caro's definitive biography.

Haley was "fully aware of the terrible recriminations of illegitimate power that may, with certainty, be expected to follow" the book's publication; the IRS, FBI, and even postal inspectors paid their disrespects to the Plains' Tom Paine. The lapdog press was sicced on Haley; overnight, the distinguished historian was diagnosed as being "a case of unhospitalized paranoia." Imagine: He claimed that Johnson had stolen the 1948 Senate election and had become a millionaire many times over by virtue of talents other than shrewd market calculations!

J. Evetts Haley lived ninety-four years, though his cow-punching days ended at age eighty-two, when he was thrown from his mount while helping during spring branding. He left us a priceless record of his Texas Plains—and an example of how anchorage in a regional culture can sustain a man who tells Truth to Power, fully aware that Power may reply with both barrels.

Vonnegut's Cradle

First Principles, 2009

Kurt Vonnegut, *Armageddon in Retrospect*, with an introduction by Mark Vonnegut (New York, NY: Putnam, 2008), 232 pp.

> All my jokes are Indianapolis. All my attitudes are Indianapolis. My adenoids are Indianapolis. If I ever severed myself from Indianapolis, I would be out of business. What people like about me is Indianapolis.
>
> —Kurt Vonnegut, 1986

IN THE RECENT "REGIONALISM" special issue of the *University Bookman*, Jeremy Beer, Hoosier boy, ranked Kurt Vonnegut second (behind Booth Tarkington but ahead of Ross Lockridge Jr. and Theodore Dreiser) in Beer's Genuinely Objective Rankings of Indiana Authors, Twentieth Century Division.

Seeing the silver medal hanging 'round Vonnegut's neck gave me a bit of a start. Not that I disagree with Beer's assessment—though I'd transpose Vonnegut with Lockridge, the most tragic of America's one-book novelists, who two months after publication of his Whitmanesque *Raintree County* (1948) sucked carbon monoxide in his garage till he was dead. (An unfounded rumor that I wish were true had it that he died listening to the Indiana high-school basketball tournament on the car radio.)

But Kurt Vonnegut's inclusion seemed strange because he wore the scarlet letters SF, and other than Ray Bradbury of Waukegan, Illinois, we seldom think of science-fiction writers as tied to any particular place, at least any place smaller than a planet. Billy Pilgrim, the wanderer in Vonnegut's best novel, *Slaughterhouse-Five* (1969), became "unstuck in time," and the science-fiction shelves in any library would be a lot thinner if the authors and characters thereon had not also become unstuck in place.

Armageddon in Retrospect, a posthumous collection of previously unpublished writings on war and peace, confirms Jeremy Beer's judgment: Kurt Vonnegut, whatever else he was, was Indianan, not Tralfamadorian. As this product of James Whitcomb Riley School once said, "I trust my writing most and others seem to trust it most when I sound most like a person from Indianapolis, which is what I am."

He sure was. Kurt Vonnegut Jr. was born into a wealthy family, certainly by Indianapolis standards—a magnificent Amberson, of a sort, though the sources of that soon-to-dissipate wealth were buildings on his paternal side and beer on his mother's.

Vonnegut wrote about his lineage in *Palm Sunday* (1981), noting with pleasure that in his genealogical digging "I find no war lovers of any kind." In between one-liners he also discussed his bloodline in his final speech, which he wrote for the Year of Vonnegut, a joint undertaking of various community organizations in his hometown. Vonnegut died two weeks before he was to have given the talk, which was then delivered on April 27, 2007, by his son Mark at Clowes Hall at Butler University and which is reprinted herein.

From the grave, as it were, Vonnegut spoke with pride of his forebears and their accomplishments: the Vonnegut Hardware Company of Clemens Vonnegut Sr.; the architecture of Kurt Vonnegut Sr. and Bernard Vonnegut, the novelist's grandfather, whose works included a locally famous department store clock. Their descendant, or his shadow, told the gathering that "my grandfather, the architect Bernard Vonnegut, designed, among other things, The Athenaeum, which before the First World War was called 'Das Deutsche Haus.' I can't imagine why they would have changed the name to 'The Athenaeum,' unless it was to kiss the ass of a bunch of Greek-Americans."

Actually, he knew all too well the reason. The name change and the many other manifestations of anti-German hysteria during the War to End All Wars disgusted Vonnegut, as did his parents' willingness "to make me ignorant and rootless as proof of their patriotism." But there were to be more egregious crimes committed later against his family's handiwork. Referring to his hometown's disastrous episodes in urban renewal, Vonnegut once said: "'Renew' is the wrong term, of course. What the city does is architecturally destroy itself. It cannibalizes the types of graceful and delicate architecture that made it a thing of beauty. So I guess there was something harrowing for my father: existing in a city, a provincial capital like Indianapolis, witnessing the systematic replacement of works of art, many of which he helped create, with a bunch of amorphous cinder blocks."

Vonnegut was conscious of his link to an earlier generation of Hoosier writers. "With the passage of time," he wrote in his Butler speech,

> [N]obody will know or care who [Booth] Tarkington was. I mean, who nowadays gives a rat's ass who Butler was? This is Clowes Hall, and I actually knew some real Clowses. Nice people.
>
> But let me tell you: I would not be standing before you tonight if it hadn't been for the example of the life and works of Booth Tarkington, a native of this city. During his time, 1869 to 1946, which overlapped my own time for twenty-four years, Booth Tarkington became a beautifully successful and respected writer of plays, novels, and short stories. His nickname in the literary world, one I would give anything to have, was 'The Gentleman from Indiana.'
>
> When I was a kid, I wanted to be like him.
>
> We never met. I wouldn't have known what to say. I would have been gaga with hero worship.
>
> Yes, and by the unlimited powers vested in me by Mayor Peterson for the entire year, I demand that somebody here mount a production in Indianapolis of Booth Tarkington's play *Alice Adams*.

A nice gesture, that. Tarkington was a great American novelist whose Growth trilogy, the centerpiece of which is his masterpiece *The Magnificent Ambersons* (1918), is as out of fashion as the pince-nez and the Tenth Amendment. His rediscovery, if only—especially—in his native ground, would be a blessing. But Vonnegut's conjuration of his literary landsman raises a prickly point.

To wit: In his last interview, with the leftist magazine *In These Times*, Vonnegut said, "[E]veryone needs an extended family. The great American disease is loneliness. We no longer have extended family. But I had one. . . . I was surrounded by relatives all of the time. You know, cousins, uncles and aunts. It was heaven. And that has since been dispersed."

The passive voice here carries the hint of self-exculpation. Vonnegut *chose* to spend his adulthood in Cape Cod and then on the Upper East Side of Manhattan, a celebrity in precincts quite alien to his native ground. His hero Tarkington, by contrast, had stayed in Indianapolis. One wonders—at least I wonder—if the marked inferiority of Vonnegut's later work was due, in part, to his immurement in that gilt sepulcher of American fiction, that anti-Indianapolis, Manhattan.

Though uprooted, Vonnegut at his best charted his course using the lodestars of his boyhood. Indianapolis-bred Gregory Sumner, who is writing a Vonnegut biography, quotes his subject:

[E]verything I believe I was taught in junior civics during the Great Depression—at School 43 in Indianapolis, with full approval of the school board. . . . America was an idealistic, pacifistic nation at that time. I was taught in the sixth grade to be proud that we had a standing Army of just over a hundred thousand men and that the generals had nothing to say about what was done in Washington. I was taught to be proud of that and to pity Europe for having more than a million men and tanks. I simply never unlearned junior civics. I still believe in it. I got a very good grade.

That ingrained antimilitarism perfuses *Armageddon in Retrospect*, whose first piece is a May 29, 1945, letter from the author to his family, explaining that "I've been a prisoner of war since December 19th, 1944." For once there are no jokes, only a terse narrative of his boxcar trip to the POW camp: "The Germans herded us through scalding delousing showers. Many men died from shock in the showers after ten days of starvation, thirst and exposure. But I didn't."

Prisoner Vonnegut endured the trip only to witness the February 1945 destruction of Dresden by Allied bombs, an experience on which he would draw to write *Slaughterhouse-Five* and other fiction, including pieces in this book. In Dresden, writes Vonnegut, "were the symbols of the good life; pleasant, honest, intelligent. In the Swastika's shadow those symbols of the dignity and hope of mankind stood waiting, monuments to truth. The accumulated treasure of hundreds of years, Dresden spoke eloquently of those things excellent in European civilization wherein our debt lies deep. I was a prisoner, hungry, dirty, and full of hate for our captors, but I loved that city and saw the blessed wonder of her past and the rich promise of her future."

Private Vonnegut survived the bombing in a slaughterhouse meat locker. In its aftermath, he and his fellow captives were ordered to wade ankle deep in "an unsavory broth" of viscera searching out the dead, whom they found in charred pieces. "Civilians cursed us and threw rocks as we carried bodies to huge funeral pyres in the city," he writes, until the impossibility of transporting that many corpses and limbs became apparent and the job was turned over to men with flamethrowers who "cremated them where they lay."

This didn't square with those civics lessons learned in the public schools of Indianapolis. Without ever losing sight of the evil of the Nazi regime, Vonnegut declares, "The killing of children—'Jerry' children or 'Jap' children, or whatever enemies the future may hold for us—can never be justified."

(Not included in this volume is a prewar editorial from the *Cornell Daily Sun* in which Vonnegut, true to his Midwestern pacifist roots, defended the most controversial isolationist of the day: "Charles A. Lindbergh is one helluva swell egg, and we're willing to fight for him in our own quaint way.... The mud-slingers are good. They'd have to be to get people hating a loyal and sincere patriot. On second thought, Lindbergh is no patriot—to hell with the word, it lost it's [sic] meaning after the Revolutionary War.... The United States is a democracy, that's what they say we'll be fighting for. What a prize monument to that ideal is a cry to smother Lindy.")

Several of the stories in *Armageddon in Retrospect* concern American POWs in 1945 Germany: Vonnegut territory. Typical is the character who is so hungry that "if Betty Grable had showed up and said she was all mine, I would have told her to make me a peanut butter and jelly sandwich." These are, for the most part, decent men, believers in the verities, who find themselves in a topsy-turvy world in which collaborators and snitches are the top rails. What's an Indiana Boy Scout to do? Refuse. Resist. Laugh. Vonnegut said that his afflatus—the reason "stuff came gushing out" of him—was "disgust with civilization." But he was not a misanthrope, just a man who never lost his capacity for righteous outrage. Wars, he believed till the end of his life, are hell and the negation of all that Jesus taught. The draft-dodgers and chickenhawks who lie and drag us into them should be boiled in that viscera broth.

About Jesus. Descended of a long line of freethinkers, Vonnegut, a self-described "Christ-worshipping agnostic," was a nonbeliever who respected, even praised, varieties of religious belief. He knew that sniping at religion can become tiresome. You need village atheists—you just don't want atheist villages. Vonnegut's doodles and doggerel decorate the book; among them is this apothegm, above a skull and crossbones: "Darwin gave the cachet of science to war and genocide."

Vonnegut sometimes called himself a socialist. My late friend Barber B. Conable Jr., long-time ranking member of the House Ways and Means Committee, told me that every now and then his old Cornell classmate lobbied him for better tax-law treatment of authors. Even socialists resent the IRS, I guess.

On that note, the collection includes an amusing anarchist fable ("The Unicorn Trap") about an honest serf and his harpy wife arguing over the husband's potential elevation to tax collector for Robert the Horrible. Their exchange:

"If a body gets stuck in the ruling classes through no fault of their own," she said, "they got to rule or have folks just lose all respect for government." She scratched herself daintily.

"To their sorrow," said Elmer.

"Folks got to be protected," said Ivy, "and armor and castles don't come cheap."

They still don't, Ivy.

****

Vonnegut once asked his son Mark, "Does anyone out of high school still read me?"

I hadn't in many years. As a teenager I played the usual *Slaughterhouse-Five* to *Breakfast of Champions* to *Player Piano*/*Cat's Cradle* combination, after which the enthusiasm fizzles. *Happy Birthday, Wanda June? Slapstick?* I cringe to recall. Vonnegut wrote some bad books, but he wrote some very good ones, too. In our age of an America perpetually at war, he is, perhaps, more necessary than ever.

The U.S. invasion of Iraq, writes Mark, "broke his heart not because he gave a damn about Iraq but because he loved America." His crest fell; didn't anyone else believe those civics lessons? "It wasn't until the Iraq War and the end of his life that he became sincerely gloomy."

The last piece of advice Kurt Vonnegut ever offered was this: "We should be unusually kind to one another, certainly. But we should also stop being so serious. Jokes help a lot. And get a dog, if you don't already have one."

You got a better idea?

A Gem of a State

The American Conservative, 2010

I AM POLYBIBLIOUS—NOT, I hope, polybilious—in that I often read two books over the same period, alternating as the mood strikes. Seldom are they counterpoints or complements; they are merely the cheerfully incongruous products of happenstance. During a recent week of travel, I paired Vardis Fisher, Idaho's gift to local color and regional history, with a whole lotta pages (*When Giants Walked the Earth*) on Led Zeppelin, a headachingly boring band I have never liked, not for a single godforsaken beat. (I did learn that Led Zeppelin's most interesting, if sinister, member, Aleister Crowley disciple Jimmy Page, votes Tory.)

Yesterday I broke up Willa Cather with a 1952 hockey novel for boys (*Scrubs on Skates*) written by Scott Young. I'd long wanted to read one of Young's YA novels. He is the father of Neil "There is a town in North Ontario" Young, provincial Canada's gift to American music. Scott's edifying tale is set in Winnipeg and references streets also mentioned in Randy Bachman's melancholic anthem of Manitoba (and its betrayal by talented sons), "Prairie Town."

You will note that the only obscure figure cited above is the one who stayed home: Vardis Fisher, who is known today, if at all, as the author of *Mountain Man*, source of one of Robert Redford's best films, *Jeremiah Johnson* (1972), scripted by the anarchist surfer John Milius.

Vardis didn't surf, but the apostate Mormon did play football (150-pound starting center for the University of Utah), tutor Wallace Stegner, novelize his place and his frontier forebears, and compile a WPA guide to Idaho in the publication series that is the New Deal's best legacy. He also drove away most of his modest readership by producing a bizarre twelve-book history of mankind called the *Testament of Man*. That's the thing about cranks: they can't help themselves.

Like so many American writers, Vardis Fisher hated FDR, despised the regimenting state, and proclaimed "a distaste for American graves in foreign fields, no matter how thick the poppies might be." (Project for a young

Idahoan: track down and write up the political columns Fisher penned for the Idaho *Daily Statesman*, which sound like 180-proof Old Right.)

Fisher seems to have been almost a parody of the cantankerous libertarian/village atheist. He was "temperamental, obstinate, rude, ill-tempered, [and] tactless," his biographer Tim Woodward concedes. But he was a true son of Idaho, crotchety and strange yet pertinaciously loyal, and can you blame him for resenting that part-time resident Ernest Hemingway was feted as the Gem State's author?

Woodward quotes Fisher lamenting his neglect: "[I]f I had stayed in Manhattan and gone on teaching, and if I had learned to scratch some backs in New York and had cottoned up to some of those important people in the literary world—it would have been easy enough to do—and if I had slipped the word to them that I was saying good-bye to Idaho as Glenway Wescott said good-bye to Wisconsin, and had agreed that it was a desolate land out there not only in regard to rainfall but also in regard to culture and everything else, and that it was very good to get back to the complex of culture in New York—with all that, my sales record and my review record would have improved. And I don't think that's rationalizing."

Maybe. But if you walk away from (or never join in the first place) the daisy chain, you can't complain when they forget your name. Home, however, is a different matter: healthy places remember. Tim Woodward tells me, "Our state falls all over itself to honor [Ezra] Pound, who left as an infant and never returned, and Hemingway, who came here primarily on vacations. Fisher, meanwhile, is pretty much ignored."

I am not much of a Fisher man, but then I have no private Idaho. If I did, I would beg this of my neighbors: Pull for Boise State football, but know that homegrown Idahoans make up just 20 percent of the Broncos' roster. Read Hemingway, but admit that flighty Mariel and model-suicide Margaux are the Idahoans, not their grandfather. Thank Senators William Borah and Frank Church for fighting in their own ways to preserve the Republic, but deplore that not a single member of your congressional delegation—including Larry Craig, the Mr. Goodbar of the airport stall, just another of the numberless D.C. Republican closet cases—has the guts to vote against these damned wars.

What I am trying to say, Idaho, is shield your eyes against the coastal glare and look homeward, for there are rare and wild flowers pushing up from your untended graves.

Don't Shoot That Mockingbird!
The American Conservative, 2010

COLLIN WILCOX DIED LAST October, just as I was about to settle in for an annual viewing of *To Kill a Mockingbird*. Wilcox was the North Carolina actress whose surly white-trash ejaculation Gregory Peckwards—"A chiffarobe!"—is one of several lines from the movie that have entered our family lexicon. (It's just ahead of "He's gone and drownded his dinner in sirrup" and behind "You wrong, man—you *dade* wrong.")

I don't think any American is permitted to exit teenagerhood without visiting the "tired old town" of Maycomb. My daughter's tenth-grade class has gotten around to Harper Lee's novel, though she and I read it together a couple of years ago, for in my own high-school days I dodged the Mockingbird draft, lighting out instead for the era's Kurt Vonnegut-Richard Brautigan territory.

An uprooted Southerner once told me that *TKAM* was the Southern novel for people who hate the South, but I don't think so. The racial injustice done Tom Robinson disfigures Maycomb, but it doesn't define Lee's town. Besides, the harshest criticisms of any place come from those who truly love and belong to it. For American examples, see Gore Vidal, Edmund Wilson, William Appleman Williams, Sinclair Lewis, and Edward Abbey.

Harper Lee, who turned eighty-four on April 28, still resides in her hometown of Monroeville, Alabama, an act that says everything that needs to be said about her loyalty to her place. A mutual friend tells me that she is a witty lady with a generous streak and a fondness for Christian charities.

What struck me about the novel was young Scout's love of her father, the noble lawyer Atticus, and that father's love of his town. In one of the book's loveliest lines—not uttered in the film, alas—Atticus asks Scout to "remember this, no matter how bitter things get, they're still our friends and this is still our home." There is a world of meaning in that sentence.

Lee told the story of Atticus Finch and Tom Robinson and the recluse Boo Radley not to damn her people but to commemorate them. She confessed her desire to "chronicle something that seems to be very quickly going down the drain. This is small-town middle-class southern life as opposed to the Gothic, as opposed to *Tobacco Road*, as opposed to plantation life."

"As you know," said Lee in the early 1960s, "the South is still made up of thousands of tiny towns. There is a very definite social pattern in these towns that fascinates me. I think it is a rich social pattern. I would simply like to put down all I know about this because I believe that there is something universal in this little world, something decent to be said for it, and something to lament in its passing."

Late as we are in the American derangement—or are we early in its salutary realignment?—this cherishing of the small-town South, even while acknowledging historic cruelties, is all to the good.

I must have seen the movie twenty times, and spare me your sneering about arrested middlebrowism. Was there ever a more startling film debut than Robert Duvall's turn as Boo Radley? Has there been a better children's ensemble than Alabama actors Philip Alford and Mary Badham and Connie Stevens's half-brother(!) John Megna as Dill, little Truman Capote? (Megna went on to chant "bonk bonk on the head" in a famous "Star Trek" episode.) Ever hear the word "chiffarobe" used in another film?

The occasional cringe-inducing moments of liberal fantasy—as when the black citizenry, packing the segregated courtroom balcony, stands as one when Atticus passes by—I chalk up, perhaps unfairly, to the vanity of Gregory Peck, who, as Charles J. Shields revealed in his 2006 Harper Lee biography *Mockingbird*, complained at diva-ish length that his character didn't have enough screen time. Peck's sanctimony works very well in the film, however; it infuses, rather than embalms, Atticus Finch. Thank the casting gods that Universal's first choice—Rock Hudson—didn't get the part.

I don't suppose I'll ever read the book again, but many elements of the movie repay repeated exposure, from Elmer Bernstein's superb score to Horton Foote's screenplay, a model of concision and concinnity from which extraneous characters in the novel (such as annoying Aunt Alexandra) are wisely excised. And the supporting performances are magnificent. James Anderson, who played the malevolent Bob Ewell, was a drunken Alabama-born method actor so lost inside his part that he came to hate Gregory Peck.

For all this we can thank the tomboy who worshipped her father and aspired to be "the Jane Austen of south Alabama." Happy birthday, Nelle Harper Lee.

Shelter from the Storm
The American Conservative, 2010

THE WEEK THAT WISCONSIN voters threw out Russ Feingold, the only stepgrandson Fighting Bob La Follette had left in the U.S. Senate, I went to hear an Upper Midwesterner of similar pedigree, Bob Dylan of Hibbing, Minnesota.

I actually saw some heads without hoarfrost, a pleasing contrast to the last time I paid a column's wages to sit in a hockey arena and listen to music. When my brother and I attended a Bruce Springsteen concert a couple of years ago, we surveyed the crowd and figured we must have wandered into a tour stop by the Ray Conniff Singers.

Lord knows I loved Bruce back in the *Darkness on the Edge of Town/Nebraska* days, after he had shed his early Dylan mimicry and set out to be the John Steinbeck of Freehold, New Jersey. My buddy Chuck and I would snake around town in his old jeep yowling, "If she wants to see me/You can tell her that I'm easily found. . . ." Unfortunately, while we were easily found, she sure didn't want to see us.

Politically, Bruce was nowhere near as interesting as the early punks or even that Mormon-Jewish hybrid Warren Zevon. (From Crystal Zevon's warts-aplenty 2007 portrait of her ex-husband, *I'll Sleep When I'm Dead*, comes this account of the Zevons' child-custody dispute: "Warren got on the phone; he was obviously drunk. . . . He said, 'I'm to the right of your father and Ronald Reagan and if you think I'm going to let my daughter be raised by some fucking Communist hippie, you're sadly mistaken.'" But really, who can resist a songwriter who begins a lyric, "I went home with the waitress/The way I always do/How was I to know/She was with the Russians, too?")

Dylan, on several other hands, has been a Goldwater admirer, born-again Christian, and proponent of agrarianism as the "authentic alternative lifestyle." He was formed in Minnesota before he ever saw Greenwich Village. In his memoir *Chronicles*, the singer, mindful of his roots in that frozen ground, writes of Charles Lindbergh, F. Scott Fitzgerald, Eddie Cochran, Sinclair Lewis, and Roger Maris as men he "felt akin to," freethinking sons of the North Country who "followed their own vision, didn't care what the pictures showed them."

Lindbergh's congressman father, whom the *New York Times* tagged the "Gopher Bolshevik," was a fierce critic of Wall Street, Woodrow Wilson, and the war machine. Charles Lindbergh Sr. was a progenitor of a vigorous Minnesota antiwar tradition that found expression in men such as Senators Henrik Shipstead and Eugene McCarthy before degenerating into the boring Cold War social democracy of Hubert Humphrey and Walter Mondale or the Republican polenta of Pawlenty.

Bob Dylan is very much in the Lindbergh-McCarthy tradition, as Norwegian academic Tor Egil Forland explained in a 1992 *Journal of American Studies* paper titled "Bringing It All Back Home *or* Another Side of Bob Dylan: Midwestern Isolationist." But then Dylan is sixty-nine, and old enough to remember when the people of his place looked askance at empire. There were giants in the earth in those days.

When the Masters of War ("even Jesus would never forgive what you do") requested the presence of American sons at the blood orgies of 1917, 1941, 1950, and 1964, it was the Upper Midwest, with its Non-Partisan Leagues and retro-Progressives and Sons of the Wild Jackass, that brayed "No!" Where are their offspring? I don't mean to be impertinent or importunate, Dakotas and Minnesota and Wisconsin, but we look to you for La Follettes and Nyes and McGoverns and you give us Al Franken and Ron Johnson?

Turn off the goddam television, would you please, and turn on Wisconsin!

Feingold had his flaws but he was the only member of the Senate with the guts to vote against the Patriot Act; as Jesse Walker of *Reason* writes, he also "voted against TARP, was decent on the Second Amendment, and was one of the rare liberals to reach out to the Tea Parties instead of demonizing them." He was neither red nor blue—each a scoundrel hue.

Senator Feingold quoted Dylan in his concession speech: "My heart is not weary/It's light and it's free/I have nothing but affection for those who have sailed with me." Dylan closed our concert with "Ballad of a Thin Man," rasping, "Something is happening here/But you don't know what it is/Do you, Mr. Jones?"

I'm no more perceptive than Mr. Jones, but one thing is all too clear: the Upper Midwest, historic home of the American peace movement, has come down with an awfully bad case of laryngitis. And it's gettin' dark—too dark to see.

Elmer Kelton: The Art of Cowboying
The American Enterprise, 2006

ELMER KELTON WAS VOTED "Great Western Writer of All Time" by the Western Writers of America, a daunting title to work under, though he bears it modestly. There is, after all, that modifying adjective: Western.

Kelton, who turned eighty in April, has his academic champions, but he acknowledges that "the Western field is a literary ghetto. Critics don't read a Western unless the book is contemptuous of its subject matter. If you write out of love for your subject matter they'll dismiss you."

Elmer Kelton loves his subject matter. He was born to it, after all. And if the Western is a ghetto, it is a remarkably rich ghetto populated by the likes of Edward Abbey (*The Brave Cowboy*), Jack Schaefer (*Shane*), Larry McMurtry (*Lonesome Dove*), and other novelists whose mortal sin, it seems, is setting their tales in open spaces rather than in the confines of the faculty lounge or city tenement. Elmer Kelton has an utter mastery of his subject; a distinctive, even arresting, point of view; and a narrative talent honed by writing for the Western pulps. His best work, *The Time It Never Rained* (1973), can be read as character study, regional literature, and philosophical novel: find me a navel-gazing *New Yorker* writer of the last thirty years who has squeezed out a single book as rich, layered, and unsettling.

Following a lunch of—what else?—thick steaks, I spoke with Elmer Kelton in his study in the home he and his wife built half a century ago in the ranching town of San Angelo, Texas. His library overspills with books on Texas, cattle, and the West; his musical tastes run to Bob Wills, Roy Acuff, Willie Nelson, and Bill Monroe. He reels off the original lineup of the Sons of the Pioneers.

His father, a ranch foreman named Buck Kelton, came from a line of cowboys; his mother, Bea, was a schoolteacher whose male relatives worked as roustabouts in the oil fields. "In an oil-patch town like Crane," where he attended school, recalls Kelton, "a boy who excelled in English and won spelling bees was automatically suspect."

I ask about his youthful cowboying skills. "Pretty inept," Kelton says with a smile. "My three younger brothers were all better cowboys than I was.

I got lost a lot—turns out I was nearsighted. We'd go out to gather cattle and if they were 100 yards away I'd miss 'em. Dad told me pretty early I'd better find some other way to make a living."

Being a novelist was not exactly what Dad had in mind. When Elmer, as a senior in high school, told Buck Kelton that he wanted to write, the old cowboy replied, "That's the way it is with you kids nowadays—you all want to make a living without having to work for it."

Buck relented. Elmer went on to the University of Texas and a career as a journalist and novelist. He made his first story sale in 1947 to the pulp magazine *Ranch Romances*; fifty-nine years later, his corpus has grown to forty-five novels. Although Elmer never knew if his father read any of his books, Buck did "help me with details" on matters from windmill-raising to the proper way to castrate a colt. ("I'd held a rope but never did use the knife.")

Like most writers, young Elmer was a listener, not a talker. "Cowboys, especially in the days before television, were pretty good storytellers. As a kid I loved to sit around and listen to them talk. I soaked it up like a sponge."

Kelton is no typewriter cowboy rhapsodizing over the purple sage in purple prose; he knows whereof he writes. He spent fifteen years on the farm-and-livestock beat for the *San Angelo Standard-Times*, followed by stints as an editor at *Sheep and Goat Raiser Magazine* and *Livestock Weekly*, "the Bible of the ranch business." As TCU director of ranch management John Merrill has said, "In terms of birth, upbringing, and everyday involvement, he is the real thing and has been all his life."

Kelton's West is not Hollywood's West: his cowboys are as distant from John Wayne as they are from *Brokeback Mountain*. He writes from inside the life of a ranch, with a brand of realism redolent of cedar brush and live oak, prickly pear and jackrabbits. He had a ravenous appetite for Westerns as a child, absorbing everything from Zane Grey to Roy Rogers, but "I knew the difference between fantasy and the reality I saw around me all the time. The reality was muddy and bloody and hot and cold. I wanted to write about cowboy life as I saw it to be."

Kelton's is a generous spirit; his cowboys, Mexicans, ranchers, Indians, and frontiersmen are depicted sympathetically, humanely, without ideological blinkers or idealization. His work contains moments of beauty and depth that remove it from the fetters of genre, as when the Pat Garrett-like shootist in *The Day the Cowboys Quit* (1971) helps to build a fence to protect the grave of a man he has lynched.

With *The Day the Cowboys Quit*, Kelton, in the words of his academic exegete Judy Alter, began to "use the western setting as a vehicle for studying mankind, rather than as an end in itself," in novels that "are characterized thematically by the moral complexities wrought in men's lives by change and stylistically by a narrative voice that speaks clearly of West Texas."

This gunfire-free novel is about a strike, of all un-Texan things, and is based on an 1883 incident in which cowboys in the Lone Star state's Canadian River country rode off their jobs. You might expect a morality play featuring sinister avaricious ranchers versus brave-hearted ranch hands, but that's not Kelton's way. His characters are not galloping cliches. The most bullying rancher makes a compelling defense of his position. And given that Kelton dedicates the book to, among others, the famously right-wing Texas historian J. Evetts Haley (author of the classic anti-LBJ volume *A Texan Looks at Lyndon*), *The Day the Cowboys Quit* is a poor fit for an AFL-CIO syllabus.

Rather, as in so many of Kelton's novels, the reader catches the sough of "The Times They are a Changin'." Independent cattlemen are giving way to "syndicates, Yankee bankers, English money, and all that." The best of the cowboys live by a democratic, egalitarian code in which independence and honesty are valued more than any numbers that can be indited on a ledger, but their ranks also include chiselers, thieves, and the usual run of cowards, including one wretch who utters what, to Kelton, is that most self-damning of all statements: "There ought to be a law."

The strike fails. The cowboys lost, as one supporter explains, because "we cheapened what we stood for when all we could agree to ask for was higher wages. We should have talked about dignity and freedom; those things count for more than money. Money's soon spent, and when it's gone it leaves no mark. But when a man loses dignity, that leaves a mark on him that stays."

The camp cook, unwilling to leave his post, tells the reluctant leader of the strike, "We're comin' into a time when the individual don't count for much, Hitch. You'd just as well get used to the idea." To which Hitch responds, "Stand back and take it like a sheep? No, Trump, even if we lose, we need to fight and kick all the way to the slaughterhouse."

But they do lose. Consistently, throughout Kelton's major novels, the principled men who embody the classic American virtues kick all the way to the slaughterhouse. Kelton's work has an elegiac quality, but he is not merely a mourner of things lost. "People think ranch life has been an island of stability in a sea of change," he tells me. "It's not that way. Without innovation it wouldn't have lasted. The big trail drives that started after the Civil War were an innovation. Fences were an innovation. We have a far better marketing system than we used to have: driving cattle to Kansas is a pretty hard way to get to market. Nowadays we have country auctions scattered around small towns. A fellow has got a local market. On the other hand, there's a lot more regulation than there used to be. We're getting to be smaller and smaller cogs in bigger and bigger wheels."

Kelton resists the temptation to write happy endings for men who do not accommodate themselves to the times. He is too honest, too much his father's son, for that. "My dad told me the history of a lot of the ranches and ranch operators in the Midland-Odessa country," says Kelton. "He knew most of them and cowboyed for a lot of them in his youth. No matter how funny Dad's story was, it usually tended to end on a sad note. Invariably the rancher seemed to have gone broke eventually and lost it all."

Ranching, he says, "isn't always a good living, but it's a good way of life."

Another of Kelton's memorably stubborn Texans is Wes Hendrix of *The Man Who Rode Midnight* (1987), with its rare contemporary setting. Wes is a wizened seventy-seven-year-old rancher who looks "more like Gabby Hayes than John Wayne." Developers have Wes's ranch in their sights, for it stands between them and their vision of a man-made lake that will flood the town with "recreational tourism" dollars. Even in those pre-*Kelo* days there is an inevitability to Wes's failure; no matter how fiercely Kelton's cowboys resist, they are "old men brittle like the dried-out stalks of last year's corn, no longer able to bend, standing futilely against the winds of time that one day soon must break them."

"My primary theme has always been change and how people adapt to it or don't adapt," says Kelton. Seldom in American history has the capacity for adaptation been tested as severely as it was during the desolating (and desiccating) drought that parched West Texas in the 1950s—the event that inspired *The Time It Never Rained*. "I could never have written it without my experience as a reporter," says Kelton. "That drought was my daily running story as an agricultural writer for seven years." He describes those who persevered through the long dry spell as "tough, resilient, and almost militantly independent."

The Time It Never Rained is a great novel, and I do not limit that appraisal with the constricting adjective "Western." Literature is as at home on the range as it is on the quad, and a Texas novelist doesn't have to be surnamed McMurtry to commit it.

The book's subject is a Jonah-like rancher named Charlie Flagg, a "broad-shouldered man who still toted his own feed sacks, dug his own postholes, flanked his own calves" on middling-sized acreage. Flagg lives by a simple credo: "I'm not sayin' any man is wrong because he doesn't pattern himself after me; what anybody else wants to do is his business, not mine. I just want to live by my own light and be left the hell alone."

But as a band of militantly independent longhairs once sang, sometimes they just won't let you be. As the drought stretches from months into years, Charlie's neighbors beg, lobby, and eagerly accept feed, checks, and hay from Washington. Charlie resists, telling the almsmen, "That ain't the way I was brought up, or you either. . . . We was taught to believe in a man rustlin' for himself as long as he's able. If you get to dependin' on the government, the day'll come when the damn *federales* will dictate everything you do. Some desk clerk in Washington will decide where you live and where you work and what color toilet paper you wipe yourself with. And you'll be scared to say anything because they might cut you off the tit."

His contumacy is not rewarded. The other ranchers resent him for acting "like our own consciences talkin' to us, tellin' us how far we've strayed from what we believe in. Nobody likes his conscience naggin' at him." His son reproaches him as a relic, and a selfish one at that. Everything he has worked for turns to dust and blows away. Arid year follows arid year, yet still Charlie hangs on, selling off his cattle and buying lowly goats, cutting loose the Mexican family with which he has a complex and evolving relationship, and always rebuffing offers of government aid.

"I have heard Charlie described as a mythical character representing old-fashioned ideals of rugged individualism and free enterprise," Kelton has said. "To me, there was nothing mythical about him. He was real." ("My mother was convinced that Charlie was my father," says Kelton.)

Kelton is no didact; he shuns the easy political point. *The Time It Never Rained* is not an Ayn Rand fantasy of a superman vanquishing his inferiors. Charlie is a man out of time, a ghost of an earlier America whose survival is uncertain in the brave new world aborning. He is an anachronism whose adherence to a vanishing code both dooms and ennobles him. He is, we may be sure, a Democrat of the Grover Cleveland stripe as displayed in Cleveland's message upon vetoing a $10,000 appropriation for seed grain to Texas during the drought of 1887: "Federal aid in such cases encourages the expectation of paternal care on the part of the Government and weakens the sturdiness of our national character."

Kelton has described his own politics as "very independent," which he translates to "very conservative though liberal in the racial area." The legendary 10th Cavalry of black "Buffalo soldiers" was stationed at San Angelo's Fort Concho, and Kelton has written of racial conflict and the beginnings of understanding. Yet he never ascribes modern attitudes to 1880s cowboys.

In *Wagontongue* (1972), Isaac Jeffords, a black cowboy in post–Civil War West Texas, is part of a ranching crew but apart from it as well, taking his meals on the wagontongue, aware of the unbridgeable gap between himself and the white men he rides with. Isaac and Pete Runyan, a skilled white cowhand who resents blacks, make a perilous journey together. They do not, as they would do if this were a movie of the week, become wisecracking ebony and ivory partners, Will Smith and Tommy Lee Jones, but they do come to realize that each is a man, capable, possessing a certain dignity. The last thing Pete says to Isaac is, "I ought to've killed you a long time ago. You got a head as hard as a rock; you won't listen to a damn thing a man tells you. You're uppity, and you got a mean streak in you a yard wide. But I'll give you one thing: you ain't nobody's pet. If there was any way you could bleach that black hide...."

To which Isaac responds, "Damn little chance of that, and damn little chance that you'll ever change either. Looks like we just got to take each other the way we are." Which is, just maybe, the first step on the winding path that leads to brotherhood.

Saturating Kelton's work is his love of West Texas. Kelton is no flowery panegyrist of the tumbleweed; growing up amongst men who regard poetical expression as effeminate will stifle one's urge to write odes to cacti. But he loves his land just the same. As he writes in *The Day the Cowboys Quit*, "Some people would never understand the hold this land could take on a man if he stayed rooted long enough in one spot to develop a communion with the grass-blanketed earth, to begin to feel and fall in with the rhythms of the changing seasons. There was a pulse in this land, like the pulse in a man, though most people never paused long enough to sense it."

Buck Kelton, Elmer's father, "never was totally convinced that I was making an honest living because there wasn't a whole lot of sweat involved. That's how he measured work—by whether you sweated or not."

Writing forty-five novels extracts its own measure of sweat. So, for that matter, does tracking down *The Time It Never Rained*. "The Western shelf is in the back of the store," says Kelton. "You gotta hunt for it."

Hunt for it. You'll be glad you did. Elmer Kelton is a great American novelist—no "Western" modifier necessary.

Basque in It

The American Conservative, 2009

I HAVE NEVER REALLY given a damn about my own mongrel ethnicity—I care about place, not race—and besides, there are many mysteries to which I don't particularly want to know the answer. I heed Dr. Zaius's advice to Charlton Heston in *Planet of the Apes*: "Don't look for it, Taylor. You may not like what you find."

But when a genetically tested family member on my wife's side learned, quite to his surprise, that torrents of Basque blood course through his veins, I figured that I'd help my wife and daughter fit into their good shepherd heritage.

The first thing I did was order a bumpersticker featuring a menacing-looking Basque nationalist. Hey, Spain—hands off *Euskal Herria*!

Second thing I did was look up famous Basque-Americans. The bookends are Ted Williams and "American Idol" runner-up David Archuletta. The Armenians claim William Saroyan and Cher, so we'll call that a draw.

Third and wisest act on my Basque list was a return to the novels of Robert Laxalt, whose literary acquaintance I had made shortly before he died with his hydrophobic novella *Time of the Rabies* (2000).

Robert Laxalt (1923–2001) grew up in a Carson City hotel run by his mother while his father was off in the mountains herding sheep. As a young Nevada newspaperman, Robert refused offers to helm United Press bureaus in Los Angeles and Mexico City, for as he explained, "I was a Nevadan to the core."

In 1957, Robert published *Sweet Promised Land*, a widely praised account of his father's return to the Basque village of his youth. The book's success set him up for a literary celebrity that fleeted. For Laxalt's people have never been Minority of the Month; his state's image as a desert mottled by slot machines is crass and arid. So Robert Laxalt turned his back on the Manhattan publishing world, founded the University of Nevada Press, and wrote histories of Nevada, novels of ranch life, family portraits, and clear-eyed affectionate depictions of his neighbors, from Basque sheepherders to the lost souls of Las Vegas.

One Laxalt son stayed west, but another flew east: Robert's brother Paul, who after serving as governor of Nevada did two terms in the U.S. Senate.

Robert fictionalized his brother's rise in *The Governor's Mansion* (1994), in which Leon Indart, the honest but canny son of a Basque family very much resembling the Laxalts, is elected governor of Nevada. (Typically, Leon, after having lunch with a mob hitman named "Icepick Willie," pronounces him "the nicest man" who "wants to help.") Leon tolerates organized crime in Las Vegas because "these are our people and gambling is what keeps the state alive." *The Governor's Mansion* is one of the very few political novels in which a conservative Republican is presented sympathetically, if unheroically.

A Carson City mintmark is a rarity to be desired, but the real Leon Indart must have mistranslated it as Crystal City. For upon retiring from the Senate, Paul Laxalt did not return home to Nevada, but instead traded on his name as a Washington lobbyist. Prostitution is legal in Nevada but mandatory in D.C.

I have no scunner against Paul Laxalt, Reagan confidant and a well-liked senator, but I measure such men against the standard of my late friend and landsman Barber Conable, who for two decades represented us in the House with an integrity and placefulness that almost makes me believe that Madison's design once had a chance of succeeding. Upon his retirement, Mr. Conable was offered the usual thirty (million) pieces of silver to betray his homefolks and stay on as a D.C. lobbyist, but as he once told me, "There's nothing deader than a dead politician. I recall my friends Wilbur Mills and Al Ullman coming to lobby me after they had gone to their rewards one way or another, and I would duck into doorways to avoid them because they would be asking for things that I knew they didn't believe in. They were pure mercenaries." So Conable came home. Most don't. Whoring out is far more lucrative.

Robert Laxalt wrote of a recurring dream in which his fictive counterpart returns to Carson City and searches, vainly, for the house in which he grew up. "No house of that name was ever here," an old man tells him. "No one by that name ever lived here."

I don't suppose lobbyists are troubled by such dreams.

One Laxalt brother's name decorates public buildings in the Nevada he long ago abandoned, but it is the other brother, the one who stayed home, whose name is written in the desert sands and aspen groves of the Silver State. Wanna wager whose Nevada lasts longer?

The Patriot

Chronicles, 2003

Dreaming War: Blood for Oil and the Cheney-Bush Junta by Gore Vidal (New York: Nation Books), 197 pages, $11.95

EDWARD ABBEY USED TO say that he took great pride in getting more radical as he got older—no easy task for the anarchist son of a communist father, but an impeccably American maturation just the same. As the American Empire staggers into senseless senescence, what patriot, whether populist, reactionary, or just cantankerously American, isn't being radicalized by a Cheney-Bush state that bids to make FDR's reign look like an edenic age of flower-power pacifism and carefree liberty?

Our greatest living man of letters, seventy-eight-year-old Gore Vidal, has grown into our greatest living dissident. If his latest work, *Dreaming War*, does not pass muster with the literary critics of the Department of Homeland Security, so much the better. For patriotic Gore Vidal is fighting a last valiant battle to preserve—no, to reclaim—the American republic that once was.

Vidal as pamphleteering elder is in the mold of his forebear Edmund Wilson, who contributed the corrosive classic *The Cold War and the Income Tax* (1963), in which the absent-minded Sage of Talcottville explained his guileless failure to pay the publicans from 1946–55. Wilson concluded in this strange and prophetic little book that the United States had become "self-intoxicated, homicidal and menacing"—this before LBJ had fulfilled his promise to bring the Great Society to Vietnam, at a cost of only a million-plus Vietnamese and 58,000 American boys dead, and a few sleepless nights for Robert McNamara.

In his radical old age, Edmund Wilson protested with equal vigor the depredations of the unspeakable Robert Moses, who was stealing land from the Tuscarora Indians on which to build a power plant, and the state highway department's destruction of the elm tree in front of his house in order to widen one of the highways that were so sacred to the Greatest Generation. A patriot of the America that had produced Bronson Alcott and

Johnny Appleseed, Henry Thoreau and James Fenimore Cooper, Frederick Douglass and Eugene V. Debs, Wilson despaired that "our country has become today a huge blundering power unit controlled more and more by bureaucracies whose rule is making it more and more difficult to carry on the tradition of American individualism; and since I can accept neither this power unit's aims nor the methods it employs to finance them, I have finally come to feel that this country, whether or not I continue to live in it, is no longer any place for me."

And so off Wilson went, hopping down the Bunny Trail, burrowing ever further into his ancestral home of Talcottville, New York. Mary McCarthy called him an "unreconstructed isolationist," which brings us to Gore Vidal.

Gore Vidal, then a mere stripling in his thirties, was almost alone in praising Wilson's alternately exasperated and despondent polemic. Now it is his turn to play the Ghost of America Past. The most brilliant essayist of his age, Vidal, like Wilson, has taken up the pamphleteer's pen in his two most recent works, *Dreaming War* and *Perpetual War for Perpetual Peace: How We Got To Be So Hated*.

"How Gore Vidal Got To Be So Hated" would make for an interesting essay in itself, but I get the feeling we've been down that path before. (See the March 1989 issue of *Chronicles* and the resultant "Stop Payment" orders on foundation checks.)

So what are the policy prescriptions of this dangerous radical? Eliminate the income tax and devolve the taxing power to states and municipalities. Call off the ruinous drug war. Decentralize political power along the lines of the Swiss cantonal system. Bring home our troops. Slash the "atrocious taxes that subsidize this permanent war machine." Decimate the budget of the War Department (coyly renamed the "Department of Defense" by the amusingly surnamed President True-Man). Fine ideas all, and within the Jeffersonian tradition. Gore Vidal ought to be a revered elder of the libertarian side of the American right. Alas, said side has simply vanished. As far as I can tell, there is no place for old-fashioned Americans in the party of Limbaugh and Rumsfeld. Hell, I voted straight Green last November and even that didn't seem nearly radical enough.

The essays in *Dreaming War* comprise a witty and erudite isolationist critique of U.S. foreign policy since Pearl Harbor. You must remember that Vidal was a teenaged populist who was catechized in Bryanite truths by his Roosevelt-hating grandfather Thomas P. Gore, the blind Senator from Oklahoma whose pet cause was submitting any congressional declaration of war to a popular vote. ("Congressional declaration of war": an archaism today on the order of "the cat's pajamas.")

Young Vidal grew up "at the heart of an isolationist family"; he was a leader of the America First Committee at Exeter before enlisting in the Navy. Even in the bleakest hours of WWII, General Robert E. Wood, chairman of that noble Middle American committee, kept a tally of the isolationists in uniform and the warhawks on the homefront. Or as Vidal writes, "in our politics the sissies are always cheerleading the real guys to go on to give their lives." That pipping squeak you hear behind the clanking of the tanks is George W. Bush, yell leader at Andover.

Vidal was raised on plausible tales of Rooseveltian perfidy, of disregarded warnings of the Japanese attack on Pearl Harbor, and he asks, quite naturally, if 9/11 might not have been "a replay of the 'day of infamy' in the Pacific sixty years earlier?"

As a populist whose bloodlines run through Oklahoma, South Dakota, and Mississippi, he wonders what on earth U.S. soldiers are doing 8,000 miles from their homes. He understands that an isolationist America is a peaceful America; had we minded our own business, bin Laden and his deranged murderers would be as indifferent to our land as George W. Bush is to the works of Nathaniel Hawthorne.

Dreaming War features Vidal in full populist voice, and anyone who would criticize him as "anti-American" simply doesn't know what a real American sounds like. Let him speak for himself:

—"Our people tend to isolationism and it always takes a lot of corporate manipulation, as well as imperial presidential mischief, to get them into foreign wars."

—"[O]ur more and more unaccountable government is pursuing all sorts of games around the world that we the spear carriers (formerly the people) will never learn of."

—"Since George Washington, the isolationist has always had the best arguments. But since corporate money is forever on the side of foreign adventure, money has kept us on the move."

Vidal is a proprietary patriot. The country is his, his ancestors built it, and he has been an exemplary citizen-writer of the sort once found in antebellum America. His sense of belonging to America enables him to perform acts of lese majesty with glee and impunity. For instance, Vidal has a healthy disrespect for Harry Truman, the near-sighted Godzilla who taught the mothers and children of Nagasaki a thing or two about weapons of mass destruction. Truman, in committing us to an apparently eternal involvement in the broils of Europe—precisely the mistake against which Washington and Jefferson warned—"replac[ed] the republic for which we had fought with a secret National Security State" whose subjects we are. A draft, loyalty oaths, the uprooting of millions of American boys in the service of militarism, "the highest personal income taxes in American history": such were the rotten fruits of a Cold War that waged war on republican government, local culture, and good old American individualism with an effectiveness the grim commies must have admired from afar.

The Constitution is a dead letter; since Truman, we have lived under the poisonous assumption, writes Vidal, that "the United States is the master of the earth and anyone who defies us will be napalmed or blockaded or covertly overthrown. We are beyond law, which is not unusual for an empire; unfortunately, we are also beyond common sense."

Vidal's politics are really quite simple. As he once told an interviewer, "I hate the American Empire, and I love the old republic."

To what extent the Bush whacking of Iraq was motivated by oil, Israel, or—my choice—simply the mad logic of empire, I have no idea. I only know that committing the young men and the treasure of the United States to the semi-permanent policing of the other side of the world is not in the American interest, and is especially not in the interest of the small places, the havens of particularity, the villages and neighborhoods that produce what is healthy about American culture. Gore Vidal is right: the petulant rich kid in the White House and his retinue of war-dreamers are the enemies of this country. They dream war; we dream America. Welcome to their nightmare.

"Today, we are not so much at the brink as fallen over it," remarks Vidal. Not that he, too, isn't an American Dreamer, given to fits of optimism. In his giddier moments, he dreams of "the coming impeachment trial of George W. Bush." Sweet dreams—and maybe constitutional government—are made of these.

Vidal concludes an essay on Guatemala, scene of his underrated early novel *Dark Green, Bright Red* (1950), with this exchange:

> I was at school with Nathaniel Davis, who was our ambassador in Chile at the time of Allende's overthrow. A couple of years later Davis was ambassador to Switzerland and we had lunch at the Berne embassy. I expressed outrage at our country's role in the matter of Chile. Davis "explained" his role. Then he asked, "Do you take the line that the United States should never intervene in the affairs of another country?" I said that unless an invasion was being mounted against us in Mexico, no, we should never intervene. Davis, a thoughtful man, thought; then he said, "Well, it would be nice in diplomacy, or in life, if one could ever start from a point of innocence." To which I suppose the only answer is to say—Go!

POETRY NIGHT AT THE BALLPARK

How about it, patriots? If it's long past morning (if not mourning) in America, the chimes of midnight have yet to ring. Go!

The Artist as a Kept Man
The American Conservative, 2009

QUINCY JONES, NOT CONTENT with having inflicted "We are the World" upon we of the world and withdrawing Peggy Lipton from circulation, has inspired a petition campaign begging President Obama to hatch a Secretary of the Arts, presumably to oversee a U.S. Department of Culture.

The quick answer to this was provided by the painter John Sloan in 1944: "Sure, it would be fine to have a Ministry of the Fine Arts in this country. Then we'd know where the enemy is."

We are in for at least four years of earnest middlebrow culture-vultures sucking up to the new president, whose reported tastes run from the exemplary (Marvin Gaye, Bob Dylan) to the execrable (Toni Morrison, Philip Roth) and include, as far as I can tell, not a single writer or musician from his native Hawaii. For shame, oh rootless one!

"A good writer," said Ernest Hemingway, "will never like any government he lives under. His hand should be against it and its hand will always be against him." That hand should not be extended stateward reaching for alms. The Armenian-American writer and pacifist William Saroyan, who refused to shake FDR's hand at a reception, had the right idea. So did William Faulkner, who turned down a gala at which President Kennedy was honoring Nobel Prize winners, explaining that the White House was "too far to go for dinner."

It still is.

I wrote a good deal about government subsidy of the arts back in the early '90s, when the National Endowment for the Arts was marinating in Andres Serrano's urine. I did enjoy debating the subject: on my side were Faulkner, Hemingway, Lawrence Ferlinghetti, Edward Hopper, Ed Abbey, and Charles Bukowski; for the NEA were the listless ghosts of Archibald MacLeish, Lyndon B. Johnson, and Kitty Carlisle, who, to tell the truth, was the last lass to feel the lash of Thomas E. Dewey's 'stache.

The dirty little secret of the NEA—and the reason I fully expect the neoconservatives to embrace a Department of Culture and fill it with moles—is that it was sold as a Cold War propaganda agency. Endowment godfather Frank Thompson, the New Jersey congressman later imprisoned for his role in the Abscam sting, called it "a program of selling our culture to the uncommitted people of the world," while President Kennedy lauded music as "part of our arsenal in the Cold War." (Not that Kennedy went overboard for artsy stuff. After enduring the Bolshoi Ballet, he told an aide, "I don't want my picture taken shaking hands with all those Russian fairies.")

By some strike of lightning—probably conducted via the book-reader Laura—George W. Bush appointed one of our best poets, Dana Gioia, to chair the NEA. About halfway through his run I was asked to serve on an NEA grants panel. What the hell. I did it, though to shut up the anarchist in my conscience muttering "You gotta be kidding!" I donated the very modest stipend to local civic groups.

Maybe I should have taken as my model the great Gore Vidal, whom JFK appointed to the President's Advisory Council on the Arts. Vidal "made it a point never to attend a meeting" because "I didn't believe that government—particularly one as philistine and corrupt as ours—should involve itself in the arts in any way. I am Darwinian in such matters: What cannot adapt dies out."

The NEA staff impressed me. So did the other panelists. I liked them, and if we disagreed over the principle and practice of state subsidy of the arts, well . . . life is short.

I requested a recorded vote on the panel's recommendation and cast my negative on very lonely localist and libertarian grounds. Eight of the fifteen agencies that made the final cut were based in either New York or California, confirming the enduring truth of Edward Banfield's observation that "the real reason for the passage" of the NEA act "was, and is, to benefit . . . the culture industry of New York City."

New York Senator Herbert Lehman, in arguing for art subsidies in the 1950s, looked out over the land of Chuck Berry, Thomas Hart Benton, and Eudora Welty and saw "an aesthetic dust bowl" whose aridity contrasted with Manhattan's vibrant culture of Tin Pan Alley, *Time* magazine, and Ethel Merman. Impose MOMA on Oklahoma! After all, we are the world.

Thanks but no thanks, Quincy. A Secretary of the Arts would be to the arts as John Ashcroft, Alberto Gonzales, and Eric Holder are to justice. I'll stick with Ralph Waldo Emerson: "Beauty will come not at the call of the legislature. . . . It will come, as always, unannounced, and spring up between the feet of brave and earnest men." Or as the punks used to say, DIY. Do it Yourself.

Southern Comforts
The American Conservative, 2011

THE SOUTH, REPATRIATED EX-SLAVE Ned Douglass lectured his Louisiana neighbors in Ernest J. Gaines's novel *The Autobiography of Miss Jane Pittman*, is "yours because your people's bones lays in it; it's yours because their sweat and their blood done drenched this earth."

The latest U.S. census confirms that the grandchildren of the Southern diaspora are going home: American blacks are returning to their ancestral region. The revenants include novelist Gaines, seventy-eight, who now makes his home on the plantation on which his people have lived and died since the days of slavery. As a boy, he picked cotton on that land. He also wrote letters for his mostly illiterate elders, a training in dialect and dialogue worth a dozen MFAs.

Despite years in San Francisco exile, Gaines has placed all his fiction in rural Louisiana, never venturing even as far as New Orleans. "I picked my own back yard—and there's nothing wrong with that," he says. "After all, Yoknapatawpha County was good enough for Faulkner," with whose volumes Gaines's masterwork, *A Lesson Before Dying*, deserves kinship.

"My folks have lived in the same place for over a hundred years in Pointe Coupee Parish in South Central Louisiana. I can't imagine writing about any other place," Ernest Gaines says. "Everything comes back to Louisiana."

Including its native sons.

Gaines is said to have pictures of Faulkner and Booker T. Washington on his walls. His characters sometimes kick against what they view as Washington's conciliatory, even acquiescent, advice, but they live the classic Washingtonian injunction to "cast down your buckets where you are."

Booker T.'s harshest black critics were condescending graduates of elite colleges who were embarrassed by their Southern brothers and sisters in the sticks. In contrast, Washington, writes Robert J. Norrell in his rich *Up From History: The Life of Booker T. Washington*, "had an emotional connection to the unlettered freed people of the rural South and a deep appreciation of their speech, music, humor, and religiosity." Washington's annual Tuskegee

Negro Conferences brought together black farmers and teachers, for he insisted that the "uneducated" men and women of the countryside possessed wisdom and talents that no book could impart.

Ernest Gaines had his own model of rural endurance: Miss Augusteen Jefferson, his crippled great aunt. "Until I was fifteen years old, a lady raised me who never walked a day in her life," he says. "She crawled over the floor as a six month old child might do." Miss Augusteen cooked, washed, sewed, gardened, and whipped miscreants, without benefit of ambulation. "My aunt never felt sorry for herself," Gaines says, and one doubts that with the memory of that fortitudinous woman, the adult Gaines spent much time on the usual writerly whining about being blocked or broke.

Gaines, who says he talks to God "between rows of sugarcane," has restored the tumbledown church of his youth. He and his wife also care for the cemetery in which sleep his people, his community—those who make up his past and his imagination. His colleagues Marcia Gaudet and Reggie Young describe an annual rite at the Mount Zion River Lake Cemetery in Cherie Quarters, Oscar, Louisiana: "[I]n late October of each year, when pecans cover the cemetery grounds, shortly before All Saints' Day, [Mr. and Mrs. Gaines] lead a gathering of family members and friends . . . in a special beautification ceremony dedicated to honoring the dead by cleaning their final resting places and offering them a gift of communion from the living."

The recovery of abandoned cemeteries and neglected graves is a noble act of African American cultural patriotism evident today in, for instance, the Negro Leagues Grave Marker Project. Among the grandest such efforts was the 1973 journey of Alice Walker to a weed-choked cemetery in Fort Pierce, Florida, burial ground of the great novelist and folklorist (and Taft Republican) Zora Neale Hurston, whom Ernest Gaines says is "the only Black writer who has influenced my work." (Hurston, who called FDR "the Anti-Christ" and Truman "the butcher of Asia," had spirit and she had genius, which is why no one still knows quite what to make of her.)

"I was born in the South, I have lived and labored in the South, and I expect to be buried in the South," said Booker T. Washington.

He was. So was the resplendent Zora, and so was Miss Augusteen Jefferson, whose unmarked grave is in the cemetery her great-nephew tends. Mr. Gaines is receiving the Cleanth Brooks Award for Lifetime Achievement from the Fellowship of Southern Writers this spring—for his novels, to be sure, but his homecoming and ancestral piety merit awards all their own.

The Last Republican
The American Conservative, 2008

The Selected Essays of Gore Vidal, edited by Jay Parini (New York: Doubleday), 458 pages, $27.50

"Gore Vidal is America's premier man of letters," says Jay Parini in his introduction to *The Selected Essays of Gore Vidal*, and if after reading Vidal on William Dean Howells, Tennessee Williams, various dead Kennedys, and "American sissy" Theodore Roosevelt the reader denies it—well, hie on back to the MFA prison.

The *Selected Essays* were written over the course of a half-century (1953–2004), or almost one-quarter of the lifespan of the republic that is Vidal's primary subject—though it might more accurately be said that Vidal has been a contumacious patriot of the Old Republic for nigh the entirety of the post-republic era. As such he is a man out of time in the United States of Amnesia, as he calls his native and beloved land.

What a pleasure these essays are. One imagines Gore Vidal at his writing desk, hint of a smile creasing his mouth as he mints Saint-Gaudens gold piece-quality-witticisms with Lincoln penny-like frequency. Here he is on Ohio's greatest novelist: "For a writer, Howells himself was more than usually a dedicated hypochondriac whose adolescence was shadowed by the certainty that he had contracted rabies which would surface in time to kill him at sixteen. Like most serious hypochondriacs, he enjoyed full rude health until he was eighty."

"It should be noted that Vidal is conservative in many respects," writes Parini. "He stands behind individual choice, the limitation of executive power, and preservation of the environment. Like his grandfather, he dislikes the empire . . . He would return us, if possible, to the pure republicanism of early America."

That grandfather, the blind Senator Thomas P. Gore (D-OK), was a first-rate populist foe of war and FDR. He was a peace Democrat, which is why no one has ever heard of him. Vidal's education owed more to home than academy, as he read aloud to the senator, from whom he inherited an isolationist opposition to foreign wars, a populist suspicion of concentrated capital, a freethinker's hatred of cant, and a patriot's detestation of empire.

Like Mencken, Ray Bradbury, Hemingway, and other original Americans, Vidal escaped a college sentence. He is the scourge of sciolism, of credentialed arrogance. As he writes of his friend's mistreatment while speaking to snotty drama students at Yale: "Any student who has read Sophocles in translation is, demonstrably, superior to Tennessee Williams in the unruly flesh."

The foaming and thoroughly ideologized haters of Vidal are simply incapable of writing prose anywhere near as tautly conversational, as confidently but never pedantically erudite, as amaranthine as the master. Vidal commits an unforgivable sin in our age of the national Hall Monitor: humor. Is it any wonder they hate him? Vidal inevitably gets the best of the carpers in any exchange, because he is funny and they are not. Or in his words, "I responded to my critics with characteristic sweetness, turning the other fist as is my wont."

His best essays are often sympathetic readings of such forgotten or undervalued American writers as the Ohio (Ohio again!)-bred satirist Dawn Powell (who "always knows how much salt a wound requires"); *Tarzan* creator Edgar Rice Burroughs (a talented action writer who was "innocent of literature" but as a drifter, cowboy, gold miner, and railroad cop was, like Vidal, "perfectly in the old-American grain"); and Tennessee Williams, "the Glorious Bird," whose work Vidal assesses with affectionately critical eye. The personal anecdote he deploys expertly. Of a dinner with Williams and his magnificently termagant mother:

> Tennessee clears his throat again. "Mother, eat your shrimp."
> "Why," counters Miss Edwina, "do you keep making that funny sound in your throat?"
> "Because, Mother, when you destroy someone's life you must expect certain nervous disabilities."

One of my favorite Vidal essays is his appreciation of William Dean Howells, who brought Ohio into the *Atlantic Monthly* and championed the new realists and regionalists of the late Gilded Age. He is a man after Vidal's own heart: "Since Howells had left school at fifteen he had been able to become very learned indeed."

Howells was barely of shaving age when he wrote a campaign biography of Lincoln. Precocious, "an ambitious but not insane poet," he obtained a consulate in Venice thanks to his connection with Salmon P. Chase, the Free Soil Buckeye and constitutionalist who as Lincoln's Secretary of the Treasury and later Chief Justice of the Supreme Court is one of those men, like Robert A. Taft and Bob La Follette, who really ought to have been president.

Howells later wrote another campaign biography, this time of Ratherfraud Hayes, for whom the 1876 election was stolen from Samuel Tilden, the pornography connoisseur known in real-estate circles as "The Great Forecloser," but Howells's legacy was one of the truly great American novels, *The Rise of Silas Lapham* (1885). Again, the subject is vivified through a close reading of the novels and perfectly placed anecdotes.

There is, I suppose, a sense in which a eulogist often is singing a song of himself. We laud in others what we perceive, or hope for, in ourselves. Vidal says of Howells that he "wrote a half-dozen of the Republic's best novels. He was learned, witty, and generous." Just so with the eulogist.

Likewise, Vidal is fond of his kindred spirit Edmund Wilson, also a proprietary patriot. The country was founded by such as Vidal and Wilson, their people shaped it, and they will not let it go without a fight, which is why in its collapse they turned withering fire upon its enemies. Wilson and Vidal were brave, though it was really a sense of patriotic duty, I think, that impelled their lonely stands against the empire that was erasing their ancestral republic.

Wilson ("the most interesting and the most important" critic of midcentury) was a polymathic old American autodidact (Princeton years excluded) of the Vidal school: "When he died, at seventy-seven, he was busy stuffing his head with irregular Hungarian verbs." Vidal appreciates Wilson in his late autumn, when he really hit his stride with *Patriotic Gore* (whose introduction, comparing Lincoln to Lenin and Bismarck, got the energetic Bunny expelled from the warren), *The Cold War and the Income Tax*, *Upstate*, and *Apologies to the Iroquois*.

Also like Wilson, Vidal regards federal taxes as confiscatory and the fuel by which an anti-American war machine is run. "Why," he asks in his 1972 essay "Homage to Daniel Shays," "do we allow our governors to take so much of our money and spend it in ways that not only fail to benefit us but do great damage to others as we prosecute undeclared wars—which even our brainwashed majority has come to see are a bad proposition because of the cost of maintaining a vast military machine, not to mention a permanent draft of young men (an Un-American activity if there ever was one) in what is supposed to be peacetime? Whether he knows it or not, the middle-income American is taxed as though he were living in a socialist society." In 1951, most self-described "conservatives" would have nodded their heads in agreement with this observation. But that was before the "conservative movement" sacrificed hearth, home, peace, liberty, and tenderness on the block to wars without end and tanks with 501(c)(3) tread.

Vidal dislikes Wilson's clinical diaristic record of his sexual irruptions. "In literature, sexual revelation is a matter of tact and occasion," writes Vidal, who, contrary to the idiotic canard that he is a "gay writer," has written about his own sex life sparingly. He is impatient with those modern writers who, once they "could put sex into the novel, proceeded to leave out almost everything else." He is what he calls a same-sexer, though where sex intercrops with politics he is libertarian, demanding only that the state leave adults alone to pursue whatever consensual conjugations they please.

He disdains the hatchet, though no one levels the critical boom quite as crushingly, in a single sentence, as Gore Vidal. Of John Updike's memoir *Self-Consciousness* (1989): "Dental problems occupy many fascinating pages." Of Herman Wouk's *The Caine Mutiny* (1951): "from Queequeg to Queeg, or the decline of American narrative." Reviewing Donald Barthelme's *Guilty Pleasures* (1974): "This writer cannot stop making sentences. I have stopped reading a lot of them." (This is in the midst of a hilarious essay based on voluntary exposure to the academy-bound American metafictionists, who provide "the sense of suffocation one experiences reading so much bad writing.")

The inevitable Arthur Schlesinger, ineligible receiver in those Kennedy touch football games, is noticed and dismissed: "*A Thousand Days* is the best political novel since *Coningsby*." Unlike "Professor Pendulum," who fretted over the imperial presidency only when Richard Nixon darkened the White House, Vidal, as a good Anti-Federalist, views the president, whether Democrat or Republican, as "a dictator who can only be replaced either in the quadrennial election by a clone or through his own incompetency." Executive orders, executive agreements, executive privileges: he would scrap them all. He admires the Swiss cantonal system and would borrow from it to revive our torpid federalism. He favors national referenda, a pet cause of his grandfather, one of the first proponents of the war referendum that later took shape as the Ludlow Amendment. He would "stop all military aid to the Middle East," repeal "every prohibition against the sale and use of drugs," and "withdraw from NATO."

He is very much in the American libertarian vein, though his conviction that "monotheism is the greatest disaster ever to befall the human race" is unlikely to appeal to many conservative readers. He is a Bill of Rights stalwart, however, who takes the now wildly unfashionable view that kooks and outcasts have liberties, too. These include the Branch Davidians, who "were living peaceably in their own compound at Waco, Texas, until an FBI SWAT team . . . killed eighty-two of them." As early as 1953 he spoke of "these last days before the sure if temporary victory of that authoritarian society which, thanks to science, now has every weapon with which to make even the most inspired lover of freedom conform to the official madness."

He patriotically detests the National Security State, which hijacked the country circa 1950 and has not given up the controls yet. In the late 1980s Vidal called for a "neo-Clayite" candidate to campaign on internal improvements and avoidance of foreign quarrels. I wish he had run the race himself. But by 1992, three such men were running: Ross Perot, Jerry Brown, and Pat Buchanan, in the most interesting political year of the post-republic era. Each, in his particular way, appealed to heirs and offshoots of the old Thomas P. Gore/Bob LaFollette/America First populist tradition. Vidal sensed a "potentially major constituency—those who now believe that it was a mistake to have wasted, since 1950, most of the government's revenues on war." He scorned Buchanan's Catholic understanding of sexuality but conceded that "he is a reactionary in the good sense—reacting against the empire in favor of the old Republic, which he mistakenly thinks was Christian."

Every now and again the reader is reminded that Vidal's bloodlines run south. He chides G. William Domhoff, who is "given to easy liberal epithets like 'Godforsaken Mississippi'" even though "except on the subject of race, the proud folk down there are populist to the core." So is Vidal. He is with Shays, with Bryan, with the America Firsters. He envisages an alliance of the "not-so-poor" and the poor and predicts that the "politician who can forge that alliance will find himself, at best, the maker of a new society; at worst, in a hole at Arlington."

While his subject has been America and the push-pull debate over its empire, Vidal rejects novels "which attempt to change statutes or moral attitudes" as "not literature at all" but arid propaganda. Thus he is capable of the greatest fictive rendering of Abraham Lincoln in all of American literature—the novel *Lincoln* (1984)—despite being largely out of sympathy with Lincoln's politics. For Vidal desires the president to be cut down to constitutional size, and Lincoln, he writes, "levied taxes and made war; took unappropriated money from the Treasury; suspended habeas corpus."

Yet Lincoln, that most confounding of presidents, was also thoughtful, wise, and an erstwhile critic of expansion. His old law partner Billy Herndon claimed that Abe never read a book straight through, but at least he did not make fun of book-writers. The contrast with the current warmaker in the White House reflects well on the nineteenth century, or poorly on us.

And so I must end with a lovely and poignant passage from Vidal's Howells essay. It is the kind of vignette that would appeal only to a man with a country:

For some years I have been haunted by a story of Howells and that most civilized of all our presidents, James A. Garfield. In the early 1870s Howells and his father paid a call on Garfield. As they sat on Garfield's veranda, young Howells began to talk about poetry and about the poets that he had met in Boston and New York. Suddenly, Garfield told him to stop. Then Garfield went to the edge of the veranda and shouted to his Ohio neighbors, "Come over here! He's telling about Holmes, and Longfellow, and Lowell, and Whittier!" So the neighbors gathered around in the dusk; then Garfield said to Howells, "Now go on."

Today we take it for granted that no living president will ever have heard the name of any living poet. This is not, necessarily, an unbearable loss. But it is unbearable to have lost those Ohio neighbors who actually read books of poetry and wanted to know about the poets.

Thus speaks Gore Vidal, America patriot.

How I Met Eldridge Cleaver
The American Conservative, 2012

WHEN I WAS BARELY forty I wrote a memoir of sorts (*Dispatches from the Muckdog Gazette*). I was rather young for that, but one man's chutzpah is another man's megalomania. The book cut awfully close to the bone, though to my everlasting gratitude my hometown chose to fete rather than lynch me. I remain astonished.

In writing about the living—maybe the dead, too?—the ideal is bracing honesty tempered by solicitude for the subject's (or his survivors') feelings. This ideal is impossible to achieve, so one errs on the side of honesty or human decency—take your pick. Ruth or ruthlessness?

The question came up while reading William Dean Howells's recollection "My Mark Twain." The native Ohioan Howells, author of a great American novel (*The Rise of Silas Lapham*), served as editor of *The Atlantic Monthly* and dean of post-Civil War American letters, but his posthumous reputation went into an eclipse whose totality occurred when Sinclair Lewis gibed in his Nobel Prize acceptance speech that Howells had "the code of a pious old maid whose greatest delight was to have tea at the vicarage."

I thought of Lewis's crack as I read that Howells agonized over whether or not to relate the shocking fact that Mr. Clemens had once been drunk. Howells chose circumspection on the grounds that "to say a man has been drunk is to say a thing from which the reader instinctively recoils." (Less reticent, Twain remarked of Howells's chatterbox wife Elinor that when she entered a room "dialogue ceased and monologue inherited its assets and continued the business at the old stand.")

I don't want to pick on Howells, whom I read with respect, if not ardency. (Gore Vidal's appreciation "William Dean Howells" is superb.) Howells lived for a time under the Buckeye Sun in Columbus, as did Phil Ochs, who wrote: "I've been all over the country/But I don't believe I've had more fun/Than when I was a boy in Ohio." (Howells preferred Boston, but to each his idyll.)

William Dean Howells was a friend of Twain's and others he profiled; for the most part, I have been not friend but interlocutor of the almost famous, which carries a less burdensome set of obligations. I've been lucky to have conducted lengthy Q&A's with several dozen writers and politicians and historians and even football coaches (Joe Paterno: I liked him, so no Sandusky jokes) over the last quarter century.

The only person I've ever interrogated while he was in his cups was my old boss Pat Moynihan, during a memorably bibulous lunch shortly before his death. Among my favorite interviewees was novelist and Civil War epicist Shelby Foote. I showed up at his stockbroker-Tudor home in Memphis about noon. Foote, long-haired, wearing ratty pajamas, answered the door and drawled, "Ah wuz jes' fixin' ta go ta thuh whiskey stoah." He had more cool in one grey hair than every Southern expatriate writer in Manhattan combined.

My first interview was back in 1985, when Lynn Scarlett, an engaging New Leftist who wound up in G.W. Bush's subcabinet, and I traveled to Berkeley to spend the day chatting with Black Panther Eldridge Cleaver for *Reason*. When Eldridge—a loquacious and fascinating guy—got up to take a whizz, we glanced at his files. The two I remember were devoted to "Sperm" and whether Jim Morrison was extant or extinct.

I also interviewed a one-time Panther sympathizer, Clarence Thomas, who impressed me as friendly and intellectually curious. I liked the Booker T. Washington-Marcus Garvey-Malcolm X self-help streak in Thomas, then EEOC chairman.

Ted Kennedy later used that interview in the Thomas hearings to paint the nominee as a radical libertarian. If only! (In fairness, Senator Kennedy was kind to me when as a callow legislative assistant I had to explain to him some long-forgotten—and surely profligate—amendment. The two most polarizing members of the 1980s Senate—Ted Kennedy and Jesse Helms—were so much more genial than abrasive "moderate" jerks such as Lowell Weicker, Joe Biden, and Arlen Specter.)

My single-day round trip record was to and fro San Angelo, Texas, where I had lunch with Elmer Kelton, whose *The Time it Never Rained* is among the finest Western novels. We went to a steakhouse, San Angelo being cattle country. I have very few eccentricities—ask my wife!—but I disdain forks. For an instant I considered whether to eat that steak with knife and spoon, but I took one for the tine.

I have many more interview memories, but nothing as scandalous as Samuel Clemens getting tipsy. I suppose I should hustle over to the vicarage. Maybe via the whiskey stoah.

Friendly Ghosts

The American Conservative, 2009

OURS IS AN OCTOBER house, shrouded by spreading maples. Its creaky floorboards of pine and chestnut were hewn in the 1830s, as Upstate New York was ablaze with the religious and reform manias through which we earned the appellation of the "Burned-Over District." Ancient spiderwebs lattice the basement. (I really should knock them down, but then where would the ancient spiders live?) The previous owner, a willowy eccentric, assured us that "pixies and fairies frolic in the garden," but aside from a few house guests, I've yet to see that. Nor have I seen a ghost, even though for nigh unto a century our county's leading spiritualists called this their earthly home.

When we moved in seventeen autumns ago, my wife and I read aloud *Dracula*. The only other auditor was our lab-mutt puppy, who, thus forewarned, never did become a biter. (When our infant daughter came home from the hospital two winters later, I walked her to sleep to Cormac McCarthy's *All the Pretty Horses*. Okay, so it's not *Goodnight, Moon*, but at least it ain't *Blood Meridian*.)

My parents order the same breakfasts at the same diners on the same days every single week, and I suppose I have inherited this orderliness in my seasonal reading habits. Come October, I take the same old friends off the bookshelf. I could no more grow tired of them than I could be bored by the resplendent reds and oranges of an Upstate fall.

First up is always Stephen Vincent Benet's *The Devil and Daniel Webster*, in which the Godlike Dan'l defends a New Hampshireman who has sold his soul to Scratch. (No, it wasn't David Souter.) As my daughter and I read it this year, I thought about Webster, re-elected to Congress in 1814 on the "American Peace Ticket"—a name reeking of treason in our twenty-first-century America of perpetual war. William Dieterle made a superb film of Benet's story, but why has no movie ever been made of Webster's gargantuan life?

We read Poe, of course, and after the House of Usher collapses into the tarn, I eye the fissure in our foundation with a certain foreboding. Irving's

"The Legend of Sleepy Hollow," with its sumptuous description of a Dutch repast, confirms my taste for oly koeks (whatever they are) over Little Debbies. Next up is Nathaniel Hawthorne's allegory "Young Goodman Brown," in which a Salem Puritan finds—or does he?—that "There is no good on earth; and sin is but a name. Come, devil; for to thee is this world given." The Cheney family motto, I'll bet.

Why has no American novelist written about the strange yet fortifying friendship of Hawthorne and President Franklin Pierce? We've such a fantastically rich history, yet men drain away their days watching the living dead wrestle animated corpses on MSNBC and Fox.

I had approached Russell Kirk's ghost stories with dread, fearing that on the scare-meter they'd register even lower than the supernatural tales (*Turn of the Screw* aside) of Henry James, in which, at most, a spinster's petticoats are rustled by a draft. Yet Kirk's ghostly tales, collected in *Ancestral Shadows*, cast a spell. I annually read "Saviourgate," in which a harried man has a restorative whiskey and chat at a small hotel on the borderland between this world and the next; and "An Encounter by Mortstone Pond," wherein a used-up man meets and emboldens his younger sorrowful self. There is, in Kirk's diction and pace, a fustiness which in other writers might seem an affectation, but hey, who am I to complain about stylistic idiosyncrasies?

Here's another book that ought to be: *Ghost Stories by Reactionaries*. To the finest of Kirk and James add tales (from *Black Spirits and White*) by the architect Ralph Adams Cram, who designed that most Octoberish of campuses, the Hudson River Gothic West Point. And throw in H.P. Lovecraft, upon whose headstone is incised one of my favorite epitaphs: "I AM PROVIDENCE." Forget the Old Ones. The horrors of Cthulhu pale before this Lovecraft observation:

> A man belongs where he has roots—where the landscape and milieu have some relation to his thoughts and feelings, by virtue of having formed them. A real civilization recognizes this fact—and the circumstance that America is beginning to forget it, does far more than does the mere matter of commonplace thought and bourgeois inhibitions to convince me that the general American fabric is becoming less and less a true civilization and more and more a vast, mechanical, and emotionally immature barbarism de luxe.

Now *that* is terrifying.

My Pen Pal Gore Vidal
The American Conservative, 2012

Now he belongs to the Ages....

Well, why not? Edwin Stanton's grandiloquent sendoff for the martyred Lincoln applies to Gore Vidal, author of the best fictive treatment our sixteenth president is ever likely to get. Plus it would have appealed to Gore's fair vanity.

Gore Vidal's favorite subject was his country. From Aaron Burr and Daniel Shays to Eugene V. Debs, America and its protagonists were his. This land was made for you and me? Of course it was.

So many healthy springs once fed our politics: they were rural, populist, patrician, pacifist, libertarian, anti-monopolist, prairie socialist, Main Street isolationist. Gore Vidal was explicator, dramatist, and even avatar of these American currents—which have no place in the dreary humorless social-democratic textbook history which bores our children and suffocates our discourse.

On a Sunday afternoon of torrential rains and crashing thunder (sound effects supplied by the Almighty in winking tribute to the anti-theist Vidal) I sat down and read through the sheaf of letters constituting our long epistolary friendship.

Each missive arrived in a pale blue envelope bearing the return address "La Rondinaia/Ravello (Salerno)/Italy." His tone was often light self-mockery, unless the subject was, say, Arthur Schlesinger Jr. (Amused by Schlesinger's surprisingly evenhanded review of one of my books, Vidal wrote, "As no bandwagon is complete without 'there is this pendulum' clinging to its buckboard, you seem to have launched a juggernaut out of Batavia." Not exactly.)

Gore's "favorite US pol (in my lifetime, that is)" was Huey Long, who had promised to make General Smedley "War is a Racket" Butler his Secretary of (Anti?) War. Cue the assassin's bullet.

Vidal was an aristocratic populist. It was as if Henry Adams had fallen for William Jennings Bryan.

"As always, the unconsulted people are cowardly isolationists," mused Gore as yet another of our endless wars began. Left-right rumblings against the empire heartened him: "They are terrified that anti-imperials will get together and revive America First, no bad rallying cry."

I tried to get him to run in the 1992 Democratic presidential primaries, but he demurred: "If I had the energy, I'd make Huey Long seem like Robt Alphonso Taft—But too much sand's slipped through the hourglass."

While he saw the value of devolving power from the capital to the provinces, Vidal maintained an independent liberal's skepticism of my decentralism, asserting that "if a state, exercising its rights, should wish to execute all spinsters over forty (my father's dream!), then a Power Higher"—presumably a Bill of Rights-enforcing federal government—"must protect the minority from the majority."

He enjoyed the sound of my hometown, and so his letters are filled with exhortations to "Preserve Batavia" and "Hail Batavia." A decade ago he told me he was preparing to write a "counter-book" to my *Dispatches from the Muckdog Gazette*, but when one hits one's octage, energy flags.

Vidal's sense of place encompassed not only Ravello but his native Hudson Valley, especially his place of birth, West Point, of which he wrote: "what I find intolerable is the presence of women. Boys don't like girls around when they do boy things. Fortunately, we'll never again win or, perhaps, fight a war based on the bonded squad. Girls with lasers in outer space will prevail."

He rather liked the current laser-pointing schoolmarm, Hillary Clinton. When she visited him in Italy, he found her "unexpectedly droll and (expectedly) quick." Curiously, the late Carl Oglesby, who headed SDS when it was healthily rebellious (before the Weathermen blew it apart), also insisted to me that Hillary, who had admired Carl in her Goldwater Girl goes Left phase, was sharp. In public, at least, she hides her little light well.

Another name from the '90s, Newt Gingrich, has praised Vidal's *Lincoln*, and Vidal had a soft spot for Newt, too. In early 1995 he predicted that "Newt will self-destruct but he's the blueprint for the 1st (post-Lincoln) dictator—New Age, spacey, Fun." Beats Dick Cheney.

Gore's last line in his last letter to me, after predicting that "the approaching economic collapse" will "stop the wars," was "I'm always an optimist!"

Maybe not, but he was always a patriot. With slashing wit and Adamsian erudition, Gore Vidal, in his essays and historical novels, lit roads not taken, the America we might have had. Not a bloated bullying arrogant superpower but a modest republic whose citizens—not subjects—cultivate their own gardens.

That's what Gore Vidal wanted. That's why the empire-lovers hated him. Yet a century hence, Americans will still read, with pleasure and profit, for laughs and for edification, *Burr* and *Lincoln* and *Screening History* and those magisterial essays.

So long, Gore. I'll be reading you in all the old familiar places.

I Clean My Gun and Dream of Galveston
The American Conservative, 2012

Is THERE A BETTER antiwar pop song than "Galveston," which Jimmy Webb wrote and Glen Campbell sang in the Vietnam-hued year of 1969? Therein, a young soldier daydreams of his Texas home by the Gulf and the girl he left behind. He describes the things he misses—"seawaves crashing," "seabirds flying in the sun"—and confesses that "I am so afraid of dying" without seeing girl or Galveston again.

There is not a single note of preachiness or abstraction in the song. Yet in elevating home over foreign crusades, "Galveston" borders on sedition. It really ought to be banned under the Patriot Act.

I had hoped that Glen Campbell would sing "Galveston" when I saw him in concert at the University of Buffalo in the waning days of his morbidly (and accurately) titled "Goodbye Tour." He did not disappoint—though he did forget the name of the composer, turning to his banjo-playing daughter (who looks like a young Laura Dern) and asking, "Who wrote this?"

Such are the spontaneities when live performance intersects with Alzheimer's disease.

There's been a load of compromisin' on the road to Glen's horizon. It's a long, long trail a-winding from Delight, Arkansas, to the Malibu Country Club. Aside from his signature song, the John Hartford-penned "Gentle on My Mind," and those achingly lonesome Webb-Campbell collaborations—"Wichita Lineman," "By the Time I Get to Phoenix," "Galveston"; Jimmy Webb understood location, location, location—Glen Campbell churned out his share of schlock. He also made the worst acting debut in the history of cinema in the John Wayne version of his fellow Arkansan Charles Portis's *True Grit*. (Portis, Campbell, Johnny Cash, Levon Helm, Senator Fulbright—Arkansas gave America a lot more than America ever gave Arkansas. A priapic president excepted, of course.)

In his daily life, by all accounts, Glen Campbell could be ungentle and mindless. But hey, "Wichita Lineman" is, as *Creem* declared, "one of the most perfect pop records ever made," and Campbell cut a beautiful Christmas album which my mom played throughout all my childhood Decembers. That's worth something; it's worth more than something.

The mood of the milling preconcert crowd was somber, even funereal. The world is fading out of focus for Glen Campbell, a little more each day, and there was a hint of voyeurism about the whole enterprise. Dementia is seldom a hot ticket. Surely this show would fall somewhere between heartwarming and wince-inducing.

Campbell was never as cool as, say, Johnny Cash or John Doe or John Fogerty, but nor was he a lounge lizard or muzak-maker. I had assumed that the audience would be a mix of hipsters and the elderly, but hipsters were vastly outnumbered by hip replacements.

(Speaking of which, the title song of Campbell's haunting valedictory album "Ghost on the Canvas" was written by Paul Westerberg of the late great Minneapolis punk band The Replacements. October turned out to be Replacements month in our family. Two weeks earlier, while on a tour of the nineteenth-century Hudson River School painter Frederic Church's Persian-style redoubt Olana, I had noticed—how could I not?—that one member of our group was clad in leather and chains. He was strolling the grounds with his wife and his parents. His mom proudly wore a hoodie bearing his name and image: it was Tommy Stinson, another Replacement. When an old lady asked Mrs. Stinson about the silhouette on her sweatshirt, she beamed. "That's my son. He's a musician." Aren't proud moms great?)

Glen's voice was rough, and despite a stage ringed with monitors he fumbled lyrics. But his fingers remembered the chords, and the filial cast of his band, which included two sons and a daughter (all from his fourth wife), seemed a real comfort to a man who in his most lucid moments must see premonitions of blackness and blankness. When his daughter good-naturedly interrupted Campbell as he started to play a song he'd finished playing a minute earlier, he grinned and said, "That's why I brought my kids up good."

After barely more than an hour, Campbell closed the concert with "A Better Place," a simple and lovely song he wrote for his final album. Backed by his children, he sang:

> Some days I'm so confused, Lord
> My past gets in my way
> I need the ones I love, Lord
> More and more each day

Glen Campbell ended his last song with a promise that "A better place awaits/You'll see." Then his daughter took him by the hand and led him from the stage, into the darkness.

Summer Reading List
Counterpunch, 2003

Burr and *Lincoln* by Gore Vidal—America, by a true patriot and our greatest living man of letters.

The Brave Cowboy by Edward Abbey—An anarchist Western. In the film version (*Lonely are the Brave*, starring Kirk Douglas's jaw), screenwriter Dalton Trumbo shamefully changed the hero's crime from rescuing a draft-resister to harboring a family of adorable illegal immigrants. Abbey: Brave. Trumbo: Coward!

The Octopus by Frank Norris, *Giants in the Earth* by Ole Rølvaag, and *The Grapes of Wrath* by John Steinbeck—The great American novel: take your pick.

Babbitt by Sinclair Lewis—A regionalist dystopia by a Minnesota Firster. George Babbitt is a fool not because he is provincial but because he has bought into the lie of mass culture. If you drink at Starbucks and watch *Sex and the City*, you're Babbitt.

The Magnificent Ambersons by Booth Tarkington—You've seen Welles's butchered movie; now read the superior novel.

Jayber Crow by Wendell Berry—The finest book ever written about a barber. Berry is the exemplary American agrarian.

Dandelion Wine by Ray Bradbury—Just lovely. My daughter and I read the opening pages (about the first day of summer) every summer solstice. Yeah, I know, dandelions yellow the yard in May, not June, but maybe things were different in Ray's Waukegan.

Look Homeward, Angel by Thomas Wolfe and *On the Road* by Jack Kerouac—I loved these books when I was twenty-three, and *I apologize for nothing*!

The Adventures of Wesley Jackson by William Saroyan—An Armenian-American pacifist confronts The Good War and loses his career. Saroyan was a soldier when he wrote this charming story of a nineteen-year-old draftee who discovers that "our own army was the enemy." Office of War Information commissar Herbert Agar—a turncoat bastard who had been a Kentucky distributist before going proto-Ashcroft—threatened him with a court martial and tried to kill the book. Saroyan nailed the chickenhawks but good: "when everybody else got shipped overseas they were still writing scenarios for films encouraging everybody else to face death like a scenario writer."

The Killer Inside Me by Jim Thompson—Inspired an aptly bleak album by one of my all-time favorite bands, Green on Red.

Raintree County by Ross Lockridge, Jr.—Indiana golden boy writes 1,000-page Whitmanesque novel, then kills self. No one has read this book for fifty years, but I love it.

Crazy Legs McBain by Joe Archibald—Hey, it's my list. Every fall I read this 1961 boys book about an unlikely college football star, a gawky kid who runs punts back ninety yards, makes one-handed catches, and piledrives the pretty boy-rich kid quarterback's face into the turf. Go Bobcats!

AMERICAN INSTITUTIONS AND HOLIDAYS

"When a nation's Holy-days are treated with indifference and neglect, it should be considered a sign of national degeneracy and decay."
—WALT WHITMAN

The West Point Story
The American Enterprise, 1999

"THIS IS A VERY sentimental place," says Colonel Charles F. Brower IV (Class of 1969), professor and head of the Behavioral Sciences and Leadership Department at West Point. "It's hard to figure that out, but things have profound meaning when they're built upon so much experience and tradition."

Over six months I asked dozens of West Pointers, "What is your favorite spot?" on these 16,000 acres, and no one who answered "the cemetery" did so without a halt, a swallow, a dab at moistening eyes. No matter if our chat had been starchy or informal, acronym-clotted or fluid: mere mention of the West Point Cemetery carried an emotional charge like a bolt off nearby (and ominously named) Storm King Mountain.

The dead (7,000) outnumber the cadets (4,000) at West Point. Pennies and pebbles rest on the grave markers: tokens of remembrance, many left by strangers, for the families of the departed are often far away. As if sent by central casting, deer lope past the white headstones at dusk. Some of the inhumed died in war (George Armstrong Custer, tourist favorite), others in peace (Army coach Red Blaik, whose football-shaped stone bears the legend, "On Brave Old Army Team"), one on the launching pad (Ed White, who was incinerated aboard Apollo 1). But in the end, their loyalties lie with West Point, as they lie under West Point.

What is it about the U.S. Military Academy that inspires fealty unto the grave? Its business, after all, is death. It can be "a place of bleak emotions, a great orphanage, chill in its appearance, rigid in its demands. There was occasional kindness but little love," as writer James Salter (1945) recalls. Yet he adds, "In its place was comradeship and a standard that seemed as high as anyone could know. It included self-reliance and death if need be. West Point did not make character, it extolled it. It taught one to believe in difficulty, the hard way, and to sleep, as it were, on bare ground."

I came to West Point not with starry eyes but with a suspicious mind, as the song goes. I expected a grey, unrelievedly martial world. That is not what I found. (Indeed, at my first stop, the West Point Club restaurant, I was serenaded in the men's room by the piped-in sounds not of Wagner or Sousa but of Michael Bolton and James Taylor—which made me, at least, want to kill kill kill.)

There is, inevitably, a Potemkin-village quality to any tour of what is, after all, a military installation and government operation. The Public Affairs Office was exceptionally cooperative over the many months of this story's gestation, but even our heroically indefatigable guide, Deb DeGraw, could not comply with a request to meet with "disgruntled cadets." We saw, for the most part, the best West Point has to offer—and one need not be a worshiper at the Church of the Pentagon to appreciate the Academy's virtues, notably an honor code that demands truthfulness in our age of Big Lies.

Philosophy professor Louis Pojman is, at first glance, an unlikely defender of West Point. He is no Sergeant Stryker or military wannabe who gets weak-kneed at the sight of a man in a uniform. "You might say I've been a convert to West Point," he says. Pojman has led the peripatetic life typical of an academic (or a soldier) and has found amidst the Gothic Gray "a kind of idealistic commitment that reminds me of Notre Dame. I've seen so much debauchery and decadence at American colleges; this is really an oasis. There are few academic settings where character and moral values are taken so seriously, where discipline and integrity are valued as highly, where young people are learning to accept stress in their youth. If our nation is to survive its shallow hedonism, it will be because of training like that of West Point." (This, mind you, from the greenish author of the standard text *Environmental Ethics*, and a man who notes proudly that "almost my whole class became vegetarians" after one semester's course. He is dedicating his next book to his cadets—"who will give new significance to the green uniforms." The implication—that West Point is training tomorrow's officers for a military of pollution-fighters—explains why most of the Academy's critics today are firing from the right flank at what they see as a feminized casualty of the sensitivity wars.)

****

For its first century of existence, the U.S. Military Academy at West Point was an institution both revered and reviled. It produced Robert E. Lee, who never collected a single demerit and went on to serve as its superintendent, and Ulysses S. Grant, who said the happiest day of his life was "the day I left West Point." The Academy is credited with preserving the Union and with destroying the Founders' ideal of a citizen-army. Abolition of the Academy was a live issue in Congress until the twentieth century, whose wars made heroes and celebrities of West Pointers like Douglas MacArthur (1903), Dwight Eisenhower ('15), and Omar Bradley ('15).

Gradually, West Point became enveloped in a romantic haze: It was a place of dashing cadets, of smart parades across the Plain, of Saturday football games along a resplendent Hudson River. Young boys devoured Red Reeder's novels of cadet life; reverential movies were made, from *The Long Gray Line* to the ineffable *West Point Story* (1950), in which James Cagney and Virginia Mayo dance and wisecrack their way into the hearts of some really swell cadets.

Then came Vietnam. Linebacker-halfback Sam Bartholomew ('66) remembers the war's first obvious impact on the Academy as comical: "The football team had the 'Chinese bandits'—defensive specialists. Whenever the bandits would go in the cadets would put on coolie hats"—until the Secretaries of the Army and Defense banished the coolies and their commie imagery.

But as the war expanded, West Point grew grimmer. Graduates were coming home as corpses. Thirty of Bartholomew's classmates died in Southeast Asia; more than 100 were wounded.

The cadet buzz-cut became the symbol of a myrmidon who was willing to kill and die for Robert McNamara and Lyndon Johnson. Current Commandant John Abizaid ('73) bitterly recalls going to Boston College for a football game and "being saluted with 'Sieg Heil.'" West Point lost its allure; the once-choosy Academy had to admit every single qualified applicant to fill the entering class in 1968.

The Academy has recovered nicely. Once more it is among the nation's best math and engineering schools. The cadets are top-notch, their leaders are impressive men, hazing is verboten, no one ever skips class, and the cadets call you "sir" whether they mean it or not. Yet in some respects, this is not the West Point of MacArthur and Eisenhower, let alone Lee. Although all graduates receive a B.S., English majors roam the grounds. Women parade across the Plain—and live in the co-ed barracks. (Don't you dare call them dorms!) For $300 million a year, West Point graduates 900 second lieutenants every May, and as the USMA approaches its bicentennial in 2002, we ought to ask again the most fundamental questions: What is West Point? And *why* is West Point?

"SOMETHING LARGER THAN MYSELF"

"Of the river scenery of America, the Hudson, at West Point, is doubtless the boldest and most beautiful," said nineteenth-century poet Nathaniel

Parker Willis. The British coveted this strategically vital bend in the Hudson; had they captured the batteries at West Point they could have severed the link between New York City and the interior of the country—a severance that might have pleased later Americans, but that would have disrupted communications and supplies and perhaps proved fatal to the Revolutionary cause.

In April 1778, a 500-yard-long iron chain was stretched across the Hudson at West Point; the English could not pass, although their wily treachery is recalled in the Old Cadet Chapel, built in 1837, which borders the cemetery. The chapel's walls are studded with black marble tablets memorializing the generals of the Revolution. The most eloquent, for its stark omission, gives only rank and birthdate—the name, Benedict Arnold, has been left off. Arnold took command at West Point in August 1780; perfidiously, he had planned to betray the patriot cause by turning the post over to the king's men.

As early as 1776 the Continental Congress debated the creation of a "Military Academy for the Army," so that we would not have to rely on foreign engineers in the unlikely event of future wars. In 1782 a "Corps of Invalids"—surely a name to frighten off potential aggressors!—was established at West Point whereby lame veterans would teach mathematics to younger officers.

Henry Knox and Alexander Hamilton convinced George Washington of the necessity for a national military academy; two days before his death at Mount Vernon, the ex-President took quill in hand and endorsed "a Military Academy" as being "of primary importance to this country."

Hamilton's arch-foe, Thomas Jefferson, had opposed such an academy on the grounds that it was "unauthorized by the Constitution." As was so often the case, President Jefferson disagreed with citizen Jefferson, and in March 1802, he signed into law the legislation creating the United States Military Academy. The USMA was a ramshackle affair for fifteen years. In 1812, the corps consisted of a single cadet, for Jeffersonians led by Secretary of War William Eustis stinted the Academy on grounds of parsimony in government and a belief in the citizen militia as opposed to the dreaded standing army.

A humorless New England martinet named Sylvanus Thayer, the thirty-third cadet to be graduated from West Point, saved the Academy when he was appointed Superintendent in 1817. Thayer instituted summer encampments, which persist to this day, as well as daily grading, the ranking of cadets, and rules so strict as to invite disbelief, if not open rebellion: Cadets were not permitted to read novels, play musical instruments, possess cooking utensils, or send unauthorized letters to loved ones. Thayer also turned West Point into the best engineering and science school in the country—and, in ways not much acknowledged anymore, fundamentally altered the Academy's mission.

For as Stephen Ambrose wrote in *Duty, Honor, Country: A History of West Point*, "Graduates of the Academy would not even be expected to remain in the Army, where there probably would be no room for them in any case, but they were expected upon their return to civil life to join the local militia company and direct its training and, in war, its fighting." Thus the Academy was intended to reinforce the militia system and not become the heart and mind of that entity the Founders feared above all others: the standing army. Yet by 1838 Congress had imposed an obligation of four years' service on graduating cadets, and it has fluctuated thereabouts ever since.

There was an engaging casualness to West Point in its infancy. Twelve-year-old boys were appointed cadets, as were married men who left the grounds at night on conjugal visits. Suffused with the spirit of '76, men took no guff from officers if they believed them to be scoundrels or bullies. Sylvanus Thayer insisted that "Gentlemen must learn it is only their province to listen and obey," but typical was the cheeky cadet who cut off a Thayer adjuration with the remark, "Major Thayer, when I want your advice I'll ask you for it!"

Abolition of the Academy was a live issue in the 1830s and 1840s. (Congressman Davy Crockett called it "not only aristocratic, but a downright invasion of the rights of the citizen, and a violation of the civil compact called 'the Constitution.'") But the Mexican War saved its bacon, as several graduates performed with distinction.

Although three-quarters of the West Point grads who fought in the Civil War wore the Union blue, Confederate President Jefferson Davis was of the class of 1828, and the Confederate generalship was dominated by products of this school for soldiers. Senate Republicans took up where Crockett had left off: Senator Zachariah Chandler of Michigan demanded abolition of this viper's nest that had produced more traitors "within the last fifty years than all the institutions of learning and education that have existed since Judas Iscariot's time." Moreover, Northern West Point generals like George McClellan (1846) seemed shy of carnage; one Republican politician charged that the Union army was riddled with "scores of luke warm, half secession [West Point] officers in command who cannot bear to strike a vigorous blow lest it hurt their rebel friends or jeopardize the precious protectors of slavery." (Bloodthirsty politicos chastising military men for their caution is not uncommon; recall Secretary of State Madeleine Albright's immortal—immoral?—question to General Colin Powell: "What's the point of having this superb military you're always talking about if we can't use it?")

The bitterness of Union veterans over their treatment by haughty West Pointers made the Academy's very existence an issue until the last of the vets had died off. ("What's the meanest kind of dog?" went a joke told by Civil War soliders. "A Pointer." "What's the meanest kind of Pointer?" "A West Pointer.") Illinois Senator John Logan, Republican candidate for vice president in 1884, wrote *The Volunteer Soldier of America*, a defense of "citizen-soldiers" against the "hostility of West Point," which exists "to crush . . . the volunteer and his aspirations for recognition." (Try to imagine a major political figure today calling for the abolition of West Point. This sacred cow took about a century to raise.)

William Faulkner famously said that in the South, the past not only isn't forgotten—it isn't even past. At no American school is the past so present as at West Point. (Faulkner's visit to the Academy in 1962 was one of his last public appearances. "I had the layman's notion that this was a stiff, regimented place where robots move to numbers," he said, "and I've found it's a little different.") Cadets are made to understand that they are part of the Long Gray Line, which stretches back into a misty past and ahead to an unknowable future: from the halls of Sylvanus Thayer to the shores of West Africa. "Much of the history we teach was made by people we taught," is a point of pride at the Academy; West Pointers commanded both sides in fifty-five of the sixty major battles of the Civil War and supplied 89 of 155 U.S. ground commanders during the Second World War.

It would be a dull cadet indeed who could walk these grounds for four days, let alone four years, and not get the message: We Produce Great Men. West Point's baseball team plays at Doubleday Field, named for Abner Doubleday (1842), who in legend if not fact invented baseball. The grounds are dotted with cannon, festooned with regimental flags, decorated with statuary reminders of wars past. George S. Patton faces the library—an in-joke, for legend has it that the "turnback" (i.e., flunked) Patton scarcely visited the place during his five years as a cadet. ("Pa I am stupid there is no use talking I am stupid," he wrote his father, signing his letters "your goaty son.")

Most of the buildings were constructed at the dawn of the twentieth century; they are gray and forbidding, neo-Gothic monuments with a gargoyle here and there, perhaps as homage to the Hudson's venerable reputation as host of goblins and headless Hessians. Though the design has been called "grimly purposeful," there is a spooky, eldritch quality, and it is no surprise that Ralph Adams Cram, whose architecture firm was responsible for most of the structures, was a master of the ghost story.

Ritual and tradition animate (critics say "deaden") every aspect of West Point, from R-Day, when parents transfer more than 1,100 sons and daughters to the USMA and watch them parade at sunset, to graduation day, when the 900 or so survivors will toss their white hats into the sky at Michie Stadium, and hundreds of children scramble after the prizes (cadets often hide pictures, dollar bills, and charms inside). The sight of a cadet pushing a child in a wheelchair in pursuit of a hat—and the child's delight at its possession—could make H. L. Mencken bawl. Proud parents beam, yet there is a hint of sadness in the air, for their children are gone now for five more years, scattered around the globe, in their new family, the U.S. Army, and "home" will be a series of temporary bases. (Lest we drown in the bathos, the hard fact remains: "War was the reason West Point existed," as Lucian Truscott IV wrote in *Dress Gray*. "Everything else was filler.")

It is ceremony, just as much as the shared tribulations that grow harsher with each retelling at alumni gatherings, that imbues cadets with a lifelong attachment to a place of gray walls and bitter Februaries. The Saturday morning parades in the fall, three hours before kickoff time, stir the hearts of visitors and annoy the sleep-deprived cadets, who respond by cracking jokes in the ranks and passing along the coordinates of comely spectators. But the stiff dignity of a march serves a purpose. Novelist Ed Ruggero (1980) told me, "I was in the fourth regiment, the last to leave the parade field. . . . By the time we passed in front of the Superintendent's reviewing stand the band was playing, 'The Army Song.' Looking through the files of bayonets and rifles ahead of me, I could see the Supe's house, the dark trees in the garden, the hills beyond. It was always on that stretch that I felt most distinctly that I was part of something larger than myself, something worth belonging to."

A note on West Point argot and hierarchy is in order. Freshmen are plebes, sophomores are yearlings, juniors are cows, and seniors are firsties. The Superintendent, or Supe (currently Lieutenant General Daniel W. Christman) runs the place; the Commandant of Cadets (Brigadier General John P. Abizaid) is in charge of the student-soldiers, particularly their military training. The Dean of the Academic Board (Brigadier General Fletcher M. Lamkin Jr.) rules the academic roost. The corps of cadets is divided into four regiments, twelve battalions, and thirty-six companies; a tactical officer, or "tac," usually a West Point graduate, supervises each company. Every two years the companies are scrambled, to mimic the transient nature of the real army.

Superintendent Christman, who graduated first in the class of 1965, lives in the 1820 federal-style home of Sylvanus Thayer, a football's throw from the cadet barracks. ("It's like living in a two-room apartment attached to a museum," he says, with the papers and furniture and bric-a-brac of former Supes Thayer and Robert E. Lee and Douglas MacArthur.) Superintendent has become a "career job"—next stop, Retirement Village—for three-star generals who serve here for five years, on the theory that this positioning elevates them above petty service politics.

Superintendent Christman is popular with the cadets; despite expanding military training, he is regarded as something of a liberalizer, though nowhere near as thoroughgoing as the greatest liberalizer in the Academy's history, Douglas MacArthur, who, with memories of the merciless hazing he took in his plebe year, became Superintendent in 1919 and proceeded to broaden course offerings, bring in civilian professors, codify the honor system, greatly expand the sports program, and break down the utter isolation of the cadets, who were permitted more leaves and more mail.

The Superintendent's office is lined with portraits of his predecessors, including MacArthur, who delivered his "Duty, Honor, Country" valediction in May 1962 to a mess hall assemblage that included a plebe from Ohio named Daniel Christman. ("Today marks my final roll call with you," MacArthur told the hushed cadets. "But I want you to know that when I cross the river, my last conscious thoughts will be of the corps, and the corps, and the corps." MacArthur's wife, almost alone among auditors, was unmoved, but as she explained, "I'm afraid I didn't find it particularly exciting. This is the twenty-ninth time I've heard it.")

"West Point enjoys two centuries of tradition untouched by progress," as one gag goes, but that's a lie. The Academy is sensitive to changes in U.S. foreign policy. MacArthur told the cadets, "Your mission remains fixed, determined, inviolable—it is to win our wars." But Christman explains, "We define wars much more broadly than MacArthur ever envisioned. Our mission is to win at any operation: restoring power in Dade County, Florida, if we're asked to do that, or killing Iraq's Republican Guard, if necessary." The curriculum has mutated in response to Iraq, Somalia, Serbia, et al. "We've moved away from an emphasis on Western European Judeo-Christian history," says the Superintendent. "We're teaching a lot more about Islamic history, Arabic and Chinese, understanding Africa and South Asia." For one never knows where next the armed forces of peacekeeping will alight.

No one better personifies the changes at West Point than Lucian Truscott IV, *enfant terrible* of the Class of 1969. His first novel, *Dress Gray*, in which a maverick cadet, Ry Slaight, takes on a villainous commandant in trying to discover the murderer of a gay cadet, was banned at West Point; 20 years later, he does book signings here.

Truscott is the son of a West Pointer, grandson of the man who commanded the Allied landing at Anzio, and a descendant of Thomas Jefferson.

(He'll be buried with his family at Monticello.) He was a refractory cadet who accumulated demerits the way kids collect baseball cards. His writing career began as a sophomore, with a letter to the *Village Voice* that read, "Abbie Hoffman's an idiot." He graduated 658th in his class and was drummed out of the Army after one year.

In *Dress Gray*, a character tells Ry Slaight, "Someday, this place is going to change. It won't happen while you and I are here, but we'll see it in our lifetime. You can count on that."

Well, change did come, and it is reflected in Truscott's sequel, *Full Dress Gray* (1998). Ry Slaight, who quit the Academy at the end of *Dress Gray*, is back—as Superintendent of a multicultural West Point at which he is "charged with defending that which he had once challenged with such vehemence." The novel succeeds as a page-turner, despite its cartoon villains: the two bad guys are scions of a "tobacco-farming family" and "the Nassau County Republican machine." Eek! Cigarettes! Al D'Amato! But what is fascinating about *Full Dress Gray* is the extent to which Truscott has now fully embraced an institution at which he was about as *persona non grata* as you can get.

Dress Gray reads as if written by a radical democrat of the early nineteenth century: a Davy Crockett who questions the very need for West Point. *Full Dress Gray*, despite the sinister machinations of an evil commandant and his cadet henchmen, is a virtual valentine to the Long Gray Line. "My attitude hasn't changed," says Truscott, who can sound gruff even through a bad cold. "One of the great ironies of my life is that . . . I end up being a defender of the administration." I ask what he would reform about West Point. He replies, "I wouldn't do anything different than what Superintendent Christman is doing right now."

Truscott—once barely more presentable than the Major General whose name is absent from the Old Chapel plaque—returned last summer to a welcome fit for a prodigal son, supping on the fatted calf at the Supe's house. General Christman says, "I devoured *Full Dress Gray*. And having read his cybertraffic on the West Point Forum, I found myself agreeing an awful lot with what he said."

Truscott had drinks with Dean Lamkin, who says, "In his heart of hearts he's a patriot and believes in this institution." As, indeed, he does. Even in his pariah years, Truscott drove a car with a West Point license plate. ("It's useful with cops.") And he doubts he'd have graduated from any other school: "If I'd gone to Berkeley I'd have flunked out in six months for chasing hippie chicks. West Point probably is the only place I could have graduated from, because it *made* you have discipline—and in those days I was rather lacking in the discipline category."

POETRY NIGHT AT THE BALLPARK

"YOU BROUGHT NOTHING INSIDE EXCEPT YOURSELF"

Before a contumacious teenager can be turned into a disciplined, tradition-minded cadet, he or she must be admitted to West Point, which since 1843 has operated an official quota system, through which appointments to the Academy are primarily allotted by states and congressional districts. About three-fourths of the new cadets each year have been nominated by a member of the House or Senate; the other places are reserved for soldiers from the regular Army, sons and daughters of career soldiers, and other military-connected candidates. "Most people think your mom or dad has to make a contribution to your member of Congress, and that's absolutely not true," assures Director of Admissions Colonel Michael L. Jones (1970).

The cadet profile is a guidance counselor's dream. For the class of 2001, the mean SAT scores are 620 verbal and 644 math; 90 percent earned varsity letters, and almost two-thirds were team captains. Ed Ruggero writes, "While West Point attracted some of the brightest students in America, they were not the same kids who would have gone to Harvard or MIT. They were the kind of students who did well at Penn State and the University of Texas."

A knack for trigonometry is not enough. The admissions department rank orders candidates by a "whole candidate score," which also takes into account "leadership skills" and performance on a physical aptitude exam, which includes pull-ups, a standing long jump, a basketball throw, and other feats beyond the ability of your typical MIT geek. Physical standards are lower for female applicants.

In May 1998, the Washington, D.C.-based Center for Equal Opportunity released a study claiming to show "a substantial academic qualifications gap between black and white applicants who have been accepted for future enrollment" at West Point. Using data from the incoming plebe class in the fall of 1995, the CEO found that white admittees outscored black admittees by an average of forty points on verbal SATs and sixty points on math SATs.

Academy officials replied with the usual boilerplate about "diversity" and the ever-useful "problems with methodology," but they need not have been defensive: After all, West Point is based on a quota system, albeit one with a geographical base.

Whatever leg up affirmative action gives blacks today at West Point is dwarfed by the preferences granted to southern and western whites in antebellum days, when young men from the interior of the country simply did not have access to the kind of education enjoyed by the sons of prosperous East Coast families. Throughout the nineteenth century, Superintendents begged Congress to tighten admission standards, to no avail, for the ingenious congressional appointment system was a rich source of patronage.

Besides, some of the unlettered turned out rather well: For instance, a Virginia country boy named Thomas J. Jackson, dressed in homespun, gained admission despite making it painfully clear that "he could add up a column of figures, but as to vulgar or decimal fractions, it is doubtful if he had ever heard of them," as a classmate said. The examining board admitted him, in an obvious case of affirmative action for hard-working crackers, and his diligence and native smarts soon made him one of the class of 1846's better students. (In the war that followed Thomas J. Jackson picked up the nickname "Stonewall," and now you know the rest of the story.)

The first black graduate of West Point, Henry Ossian Flipper (1877), declared, "If my manhood cannot stand without a governmental prop, then let it fall. If I am to stand on any other ground than the one white cadets stand upon, then I don't want the cadetship." Today, says Louis Pojman, the green-ish philosophy professor, "there's a little bit of affirmative action and the cadets hate it. When they see someone get pushed up because of her gender or because they need a black person, they talk. That's a demoralizer, but it doesn't happen much."

If nineteenth-century West Point had an aristocratic tincture, the current corps of cadets is largely middle class. "In this century our nobles have not encouraged their sons to go to West Point," notes Gore Vidal, who was born in the cadet hospital, son of West Point's star quarterback Gene Vidal (1918). The almost comically genteel nature of the haughty nineteenth-century cadet is illustrated by a story told of the painter James McNeill Whistler, who arrived in 1851 and left two years later, done in by his "unfortunate opinion that silicon was a gas." An instructor once reproved Whistler: "What! You do not know the date of the battle of Buena Vista? Suppose you were to go out to dinner and the company began to talk of the Mexican War, and you, a West Point man, were asked the date of the battle. What would you do?"

"Do?" replied Whistler coolly. "Why, I should refuse to associate with people who could talk of such things at dinner!"

The Academy acts as a leveller. As a general explains in John P. Marquand's novel *Melville Goodwin, USA*, "Rich boys had a harder time than poor boys at the Point. You threw away your past the minute you started walking up the hill from the railroad station, and everyone was like everybody else once the crowd was all checked in. It would not be such a bad idea to have an arch at the entrance to the Point on which would be written some statement to the effect that you brought nothing inside there with you except yourself. Pocket money, family and chauffeurs did not matter at the Point."

In his critical *Ivory Fortress: A Psychiatrist Looks at West Point* (1974), former West Point shrink Richard U'Ren wrote of a gathering of cadets and parents: "One cadet's father, from Virginia, came dressed in a Brooks Brothers suit, while another's, from Louisiana, wore a blue bowling shirt: yet it was impossible to determine which cadet belonged to which father." Whether this is a refreshing obliteration of class distinctions or an appalling triumph of enforced sameness and dull uniformity is for each reader to decide.

****

West Point solicits candidates as any school does, and it soon may make use of an old friend: television.

Fans of TV's "golden age"—those gilded nights when living rooms across the land were invaded by Topo Gigi and Efrem Zimbalist Jr.—may recall *The West Point Story*. Whatever the artistic shortcomings of the series, it served as a valuable recruiting tool, and it is a measure of the Academy's determination to sell itself to American teendom that Hollywood producer Beth Sullivan gained the full cooperation of everyone from the Superintendent on down when she filmed a pilot episode last summer for a proposed new series to be titled *West Point, U.S.M.A.*

Sullivan committed the treacly CBS drama *Dr. Quinn, Medicine Woman*, in which Jane Seymour battled prejudice, sexism, and degrading environmental practices on the frontier; word is—surprise!—that the villain of *West Point, U.S.M.A.* is a cranky old grad who can't accept the presence of women at his alma mater. Commandant Abizaid says, "My fear is that it will turn into *West Point 10996*," a soap opera on the Hudson, in which models will embody duty, honor, country, pulchritude. Superintendent Christman, by contrast, insists that *West Point U.S.M.A.* will be "a value-laden show" in which, ideally, he will be personated by Clint Eastwood and General Abizaid by Danny DeVito.

At all events, Sullivan is still peddling her pilot. General Christman actually accompanied her to a meeting in California with CBS brass. At press time, the show had not been picked up.

THE BURDEN OF BEAST

New cadets arrive in late June, and if they are not feted at frat mixers and juice-bar receptions, they don't expect to be. "When I first came here, I had this idea that upperclassmen were going to be hitting me," laughs firstie Thurman McKenzie, a varsity track athlete.

They don't hit you anymore; instead, the teenaged newcomers are thrown into "Beast Barracks," the decidedly feral nickname for Cadet Basic Training, or CBT. (I promise to go light on the acronyms, lest the reader be overcome by the urge to drop to the floor and start squat-thrusting.)

Brigadier General John Abizaid is the Commandant of Cadets, or commanding officer of the corps. (Since 1812, every supe and commandant has been a West Point grad.) Sturdily built and witty, Abizaid is a "soldier's soldier," says an admiring subaltern. "It's really funny to watch these guys come in here with their hats on backwards, and next thing you know we turn them into soldiers," Abizaid says as he shows me a video of Beast Barracks. (West Point is big on promotional videos set to incongruous rock music. In this one, new cadets are soldierized to the tune of "Takin' Care of Business," that classic '70s ode to idleness. Another video shows West Pointers peacekeeping in Somalia to the strains of U2's "Where the Streets Have No Name." A subversive comment on Pax Americana? Nah.)

For six weeks, more than a thousand eighteen-year-olds will wake at 5:20 a.m. and spend their days running, rappelling, shining shoes, and studying their M-16s as though they were geometric theorems. When addressed by an upperclassman, they can say one of four things: Yes, sir; No, sir; Sir, I do not understand; or No excuse, sir. (Cadet Mattox of Los Angeles says that after plebe year, "I even began my prayers, 'Sir.'") New cadets are permitted one ten-minute call home each week. Televisions are not permitted, and exceptions will not be made for *West Point, U.S.M.A.* Between 4 and 9 percent will quit during Beast Barracks, and it's a long ride home, especially for dropouts from small towns, who typically have been given a hero's sendoff.

Beast Barracks is to some extent cadet-run. New arrivals are divided into squads of ten; upperclassmen act as squad leaders in what is seen as a manufactory of leadership. Some are bullies, others want to be everybody's pal; some inspire, others berate. But the grant of responsibility usually does its job: junior Bryce Bowman of suburban Buffalo, New York, says that being a squad leader was the experience that made him feel finally, fully, part of the Long Gray Line.

The new cadets do almost everything, right down to shoeshining, as a team. "Cooperate and graduate" goes one adage, for as former English professor Pat C. Hoy says, "Few believe they can make it alone. Those who try usually fail. A lone rifleman does not wage war and win." (Hoy, who went on to teach at Harvard, lamented, "at Harvard, where I see so few signs of restraint, I'm yearning for the gifts of community. At West Point I had yearned for freedom and solitude.")

Those who have endured Beast Barracks describe it best. "It's an initiation far harder than Army basic training," according to General Norman Schwarzkopf (1956), "designed to drive out those plebes who can't handle physical and psychological stress, and teach the survivors the discipline and basic skills they need to get along at West Point."

Separated from family, friends, and hometown, the fledgling passes through this summer crucible and emerges a West Point cadet. Something has been gained—and lost, as well. Critic U'Ren writes, "Since cooperation and discipline are esteemed so highly in the military, individualism and self-reliance—the old civilian virtues—must be ruthlessly expunged." Colonel Kerry Pierce, director of the Office of Policy Planning and Analysis, stresses that cadets must learn that "the group is more important than the individual," and as this is at odds with the dominant American ethos, it belies the hackneyed claim that West Point is "quintessentially American." It is not—for better and/or for worse.

An eager plebe named Timothy Leary, who would leave West Point for greener (and yellower and bluer) pastures as Harvard's LSD guru, thrilled to his Beast, which he called "a total assault on the nervous system. Familiar homegrown habits of dress, grooming, posture, gait, and language were drilled out and military bearing was drilled in. Far from regretting my loss of individuality I was delighted at being admitted to this masculine elite." (He would soon despair that "we cadets were not being groomed for battlefield strategies, not for innovative thinking, nor scientific logic but to fit, unquestioningly, into an enormous gray bureaucracy.")

Beast Barracks is prominent in West Point lore not only for the ingenuity of the hazing—forcing the newcomers to drink Tabasco sauce and toothpaste, stand at attention on their heads, warm toilet seats for upperclassmen, and other wholesome hijinks now largely banished—but for its "West Pointicization": Memorizing old football scores, Academy facts, and, most colorfully, bizarre definitions. "How's the cow?" upperclassmen ask the lowly plebe, to which he responds, "Sir, she walks, she talks, she's full of chalk, the lacteal fluid extracted from the female of the bovine species is highly prolific to the nth degree."

Irreverence is not among the qualities contributing to an applicant's whole candidate score, but it ought to be. A long-standing joke (updated every few years for inflation) has it that West Point is a "$250,000 education, shoved up your ass a nickel at a time." Upperclassmen are nigh unanimous in proclaiming a sense of humor as the *sine qua non* of a successful plebe year. The healthiest way to deal with a picayune regulation—besides quitting—is to obey and have a good laugh later. "I remember making it back to my room, closing the door, and laughing so hard" at the absurdity of it all, says one junior. Then he fell asleep, woke up before sunrise the next morning, and did it all over again.

(Colonel Rick Kerin, professor of English and '72 grad, recalls, "The great irony is [Lucian Truscott] was the biggest hazer there was. He used to torment the plebes." To which Truscott pleads guilty: "There's a tendency, when you're eighteen years old, in a new environment, and people are yelling at you, to just want to give up. My experience was you didn't get guys to not give up by being nice to them. They learn they can endure pretty much anything—that's why they don't give up.")

The cruder forms of hazing have largely vanished—one of the Academy's ubiquitous "mission statements" declares that instilling "sensitivity to the needs and feelings of others" is a purpose of Beast Barracks—but today's regimen is perhaps more demanding than in Tabasco-guzzling days. That old spoilsport Commandant Abizaid has de-emphasized fraternity froth and rededicated Beast Barracks to "rifle marksmanship, road marches, tactical training," and other military skills, for as he says bluntly—his manner of speech is so forthright, so unadorned, that he probably speaks to his mother bluntly—"West Point is not going to school to be a physics major; it's learning to drive a tank."

"I know the definition of leather ['the fresh skin of an animal, cleaned and divested of all hair, fat, and . . . '—oh, never mind] but this summer the things we were asked to memorize were much more military: the soldiers' creed and everything about our assault rifle and grenades," says plebe Andrew Scott, a descendant of General Winfield Scott, old Fuss 'n' Feathers of Mexican War fame, whose remains repose in the West Point Cemetery. Andy's sister, Katherine, is a firstie, a battalion commander: She lives in Scott Hall, named after her preening ancestor. Sibling relations are strange, though not necessarily strained, at West Point. "We can talk to each other," says Kate. "No plebes can interact with upperclassmen, that's fraternization. But it's my brother, so I'm allowed to recognize him. If I was walking across the area and saw him, he wouldn't just come up and say, 'Hey, Kate.' He would stand at attention. But he can come over to my room. I can give him advice, but I try to stay away from giving him unfair advantages. That's not what a brother or sister is for; we can be there for moral support."

The generals who run West Point today are products of the Vietnam years: the Academy's nadir. In 1970, the Superintendent, Samuel W. Koster, resigned under pressure for his role in covering up the My Lai massacre. A poll of firsties in 1971 found that more than half regretted coming to West Point. (It wasn't all bleakness, though. The highlight of Vietnam-era protest along the Hudson came on Moratorium Day 1969, when 200 Vassar girls presented flowers to the cadets, who greeted them with wry cordiality. One football player, offered a daffodil, promptly ate it; another cadet announced that he had to leave, as he was late for "poison-gas class.")

In the aftermath of the war, a West Point captain said, "the Vietnam War has taught us something about leadership. You can't be out of touch with the people you are going to lead. In Vietnam, if you gave an order that the troops didn't understand, they might say, 'Fuck you, Jack. I'm not going. See you around.' Someone who comes out of this place has to know how to deal with that kind of thing."

Thus the emphasis by Christman & Co. on "ridding this institution of vestiges of sophomoric behavior." The Supe concedes, "There was for far too long a feeling that we could hector and berate a plebe and that was okay, that somehow he'd go out into the Army and not be affected by that. Well, I saw too many junior officers deal with their platoon or company the way an upperclassman dealt with a plebe—and you don't do that."

"SIR, THE DESSERT TODAY IS OREOS"

Much as Commandant Abizaid may be loath to admit it, West Point is a school; each cadet's room contains a personal computer but not a gun. (The computer's cost is deducted from their pay, which totals about $7,000 a year.) Typically, a cadet rises at 6:00 and spends the bulk of the day in class, until mandatory athletics in late afternoon. Leisure time—or study time, as it were—is reserved for evenings. Taps is played over the barracks intercom at 11:30; lights must be out by midnight, except for firsties (a recent liberalization). Televisions are not permitted for a cadet's first two years; plebes may have stereos after their first Christmas, but the noise mustn't travel down the hall. Drinking and drug use are verboten—a marijuana haze does not envelop the barracks—although a small amount goes on, sub rosa, as it always has. (Cadet George Cushing wrote in an 1854 letter, "Tobacco is prohibited, but I never saw so much used before.")

In some respects these are typical college kids—Gary Conway, director of cadet radio station WKDT, tells me that the corps prefers alternative rock and country to John Philip Sousa—but in other ways . . . well, as Bryce Bowman asks, "In how many colleges do you wake up and say to your roommate, 'How do we clean our room today?'" Nor are there many schools in which fatigued students who start to nod off in class are encouraged to stand in order to stay awake. Unnerving to the instructor, one might think, but they seem not to mind.

In his retirement at Gettysburg, where he could walk around Cemetery Ridge and Little Round Top and all those other lyrically named bloodbaths he had studied half a century before, Dwight Eisenhower wrote, "The pleasures of a cadet's life were the same in my day as they were in Grant's and probably are today—the forbidden food tidbits smuggled in from the outside and enjoyed in barracks after taps, the long winter evenings spent in unauthorized meetings discussing graduation prospects, the practical jokes on each other or on the lowly plebe." We all play tricks on our memories—Ike fails to mention his seduction of the West Point dentist's wife, an act that won him corps-wide admiration—but the homely pleasures of cadet life remain constant. They are bonded through common trials; these friendships, which will last past a lifetime, give their lives shape and ballast.

"This is not a monastery," insists Supe Christman, despite the T-shirt that reads, "Sex Kills . . . Go to West Point and Live Forever." Whereas once the plebe was forbidden to go home from R-Day until the next summer—an obvious attempt to sever him from family and home—today he gets two weekend passes before his first Christmas, and in subsequent years "weekend opportunities grow exponentially," says Christman.

Ed Ruggero worries about this. "West Pointers are often criticized for being socially immature, probably as a result of being locked up for four years. They get out to their first assignments and many of them act like high school sophomores (I was one of those). In recent years cadets have been given more privileges—leaves, passes, etc.—with the idea that they'll know how to act. I don't think this will make them soft, but I am concerned that it will dilute those bonds that come from shared experiences. I believe this is one of the problems the Naval Academy faces; midshipmen are a lot closer to being college students than are West Point cadets. They also have many of the same problems other college students have (cheating, drugs, sex scandals)."

Ruggero may be playing the part of Old Grad—each class is convinced, says Christman, that theirs was the "last time when Beast Barracks was still Beast Barracks"—but he is asking the question that West Point has asked—and answered differently every few years—since 1802: What is the proper balance between regimentation and liberty? A restive cadet in the 1970s asserted, "The central, ironic paradox of Academy life is that the institution attempts to build leaders by denying them room for individual choice, thought, and initiative." Or as a critic of the academies puts it, "Compare . . . this to the lifestyle of an ROTC . . . cadet who attends a civilian university. These cadets, generally, hold jobs to help pay for their education and some even have families to support. They must decide on their own whether or not to stay up late, go to class, stay in shape, etc. It is incumbent upon them to discipline themselves," whereas "Academy cadets have most of their decisions made for them. . . . The Academy may produce a more regimented officer, but not necessarily a more self-disciplined one."

****

At 12:05 p.m., the 4,000 members of the corps of cadets eat lunch in cavernous Washington Hall, underneath an assortment of early American and state flags.

I am guided to the table of Company C-4 by Joanna Pietrantonio, a firstie from Southern New Jersey, a platoon leader who looks as though she could be cast as the pretty and wholesome cadet—the anti-Heather Locklear—in *West Point, U.S.M.A.* She is an English major who likes T. S. Eliot, Emily Dickinson, Ezra Pound, and opera. There are ten of us, including three plebes who sit, ramrod straight, at the end of the table opposite "Table Commandant" Iker, a friendly firstie from Oklahoma. The table commandant sets the tone for the table, which is conversational but not raucous. Among those at our repast is Ben Celver, a wrestler from Auburn, Washington, who took last year off and did volunteer work in Nepal, Bangladesh, and India to "escape the concrete, materialist society I'm in here sometimes." Celver is an engaging fellow: a real self-improver, the sort who "if I'm reading a book and I don't understand a word I look it up." Imagine Jack Kerouac at West Point—athlete, Christian, a boy with wanderlust whose post-Army dream is "to go to a little high school, teach English lit., and coach wrestling, just like my father."

Lunch today is sloppy joes and scalloped potatoes (dietician Dawn Roper tells me that the cadets prefer "pizza and wings, like all teenagers"); the entire corps is served simultaneously in a herculean feat of scullery. In twenty minutes, our plates will be cleaned.

One of the plebes reports, "Sir, the dessert today is Oreo cookies." This news is digested, and I reflect on the self-discipline it takes to announce, without smiling and with a sense of gravity, the presence of black and white cookies. We eat and chat, all but the plebes, who are quiet. They are permitted to eat unmolested, however, unlike in days of yore. (Sam Bartholomew recalls, "I'll never forget July 4, 1962. I had a big steak, strawberry shortcake, and french fries dumped in the trash because an upperclassman thought I had mixed up the first and last names of the actress in *Godzilla vs. Frankenstein*.")

AMERICAN INSTITUTIONS AND HOLIDAYS

A plebe still may not speak to an upperclassman unless spoken to. I ask the trio of plebes, "Do you dread being in the presence of these guys, the upperclassmen?"

"Yes, sir," they reply in unison.

Lunch has been wolfed down, and a plebe stands to report, "Sir, there are two and a butt end stalks of broccoli left." (I found this sober-faced accounting of the table's scraps very funny, and was reassured of the cadets' basic normality when, later, Ben Celver told me that he and his classmates also find it hard not to crack smiles.) At meal's end, the command is given to all cadets, "Brigade rise," and the plebes of C-4 stand and shout, "Go Cowboys, fire it up, C-4, yee-hah, you know it." Cadet Pietrantonio tells me that C-4 is the only company that makes its plebes yell its motto. It's "loud and obnoxious," she says with a smile, but "our company is really close," unlike her company of her first two years, which "was not cohesive" and had "a lot of arguing and resentment toward the chain of command."

****

Ardent West Pointers speak of the corps as Christians speak of the body of believers. West Point is no longer an Episcopalian redoubt—is any place this side of the Connecticut suburbs?—but the hillside Cadet Chapel remains a looming (and booming—its 20,000-pipe organ is the largest in the world) Gothic hillside presence. Catholic and Jewish chapels also grace the grounds; there are no plans—yet—for a mosque.

Mandatory chapel attendance was struck down by the Supreme Court in 1973—a good thing, says staff chaplain Scott McChrystal, for it "served the purpose of inoculation: you take something so you don't get it later." The chaplain is an ordained minister with the Assemblies of God—you can't get much farther from West Point's historic Episcopalianism—and has an unusual resume: He was a platoon leader in Vietnam and a tactical officer at The Citadel before he heard The Word. He estimates that about half the cadets participate in some form of worship—many in such parachurch groups as Officers Christian Fellowship or Navigators—although he curses the enemy Time. "There are ample opportunities to integrate your faith with what we do. But if you don't grab ahold and make time, that will get squeezed out by seemingly more urgent requirements. My son [a plebe] is pressed to find even 10 minutes for devotion in a day."

There is probably less racial segregation at West Point than at other institutions of higher learning. There are no "black tables" or "ethnic dorms" of the sort found elsewhere. (Cadets do note that Asian students tend to hang together; the "Asian Connection," they call it.)

As for politics, the corps is more Republican than most student bodies this side of Hillsdale College. Cadets are careful not to denigrate the Commander in Chief in front of outsiders with pads and pencils, but seldom is heard a venerating word about President Clinton. Gore Vidal, who has written about his birthplace with both affection and mordant wit, captured the irony of a military academy full of "conservatives" with his observation that "the ideals of socialism are anathema to them even though, paradoxically, the West Pointer is entirely cared for by the state from his birth in an Army hospital (if he is born into a military family) to taps at government expense in a federal bone-yard."

For all the humanizing—or weakening, critics say—reforms of recent years, West Point can be stern, forbidding, mirthless. Most cadets do time in the slough of despond. In *The Circle in the Spiral*, the 1998 arts and literature annual of the corps, cadet Gerald Brennan wrote of a classmate's suicide:

> Oftentimes it seems difficult to contemplate any existence apart from these gray walls; though they drain the spirit and leave little in return, they become familiar after a time and sometimes they seem almost comfortable in spite of their coldness. But then I go home on leave, or away to the city with my friends, and I remember that it is the people, not the walls, that make a place home. I see, too, that there is a far livelier world outside this place, a world that isn't nearly so dark and confusing as it appears to be at night from Trophy Point.

SOMETIMES A STUDENT . . .

The B.S. is the only degree granted at West Point, although cadets may major in nineteen fields, including such unscientific frivolities as History or Philosophy and Literature. But every cadet takes the same thirty-one-course core: sixteen are in the "humanities and social sciences," fifteen are "math, science, & engineering," a balance disturbing to those who fear the Academy is becoming just another college. (Albeit one that requires students to study "Terrain Analysis" and offers courses in "Low-intensity Conflict.") "People say we've turned into Penn State," sighs Commandant Abizaid, but "there are no civilians walking around in beads and sandals. We are not training people to be doctors and lawyers and candlestick-makers—we're training them to be soldiers."

The catalogues contain the usual guff about the twenty-first century, our allegedly shrinking world, and "performing global duties in a multicultural environment," but there are no cakewalk courses of the sort that keep the Ohio State football team eligible. West Point offers "not a single course in AIDS awareness, or music appreciation, or bowling, or physics for poets and lovers," says Dean Lamkin.

"The heart of this academy must forever be the junior rotating faculty," insists Superintendent Christman. These are captains and majors with master's degrees, often West Point grads, who teach for three years and then march back into the Army. They compose 62 percent of the faculty; another 22 percent are civilians with doctorates, and the remainder are Academy Professors, military men with Ph.D.s who lead the departments and stay until retirement.

"Scholarship is not as important as teaching," says Lamkin. Unlike other deans, he weighs an applicant's skill in the martial arts. "Would you hire a brilliant mathematician who was a so-so soldier?" I ask. "Absolutely not," he replies. "I cannot be putting up an example that bifurcates the academic and military development of cadets."

The preponderance of military men among West Point's faculty is often excoriated by outsiders. Early in this century Harvard's president Charles W. Eliot offered the classic criticism: "No school or college should have its teaching done almost exclusively by recent graduates of the same school or college who are not teachers and who serve short terms. West Point, so far as its teachers are concerned, breeds ... a very bad practice for any educational institution."

Does West Point's professoriate stack up against a top civilian faculty? "No," says Professor Pojman, a civilian Ph.D. with academic tours of duty at Oxford, Berkeley, and NYU, among others, "but it doesn't have to. Almost 90 percent of the courses here are core courses: You need people who know that course, you don't need world-wide scholars. For most teaching at universities, you don't need a Ph.D. That's a myth." Moreover, "these officers are there for them," putting in office hours that would make a State U. prof's head spin. (The civilian professors are often similarly dedicated. Says Dean Lamkin, "I interview each of them personally and I ask, 'Do you believe in duty, honor, country?'" Hint to prospective interviewees: Answer Yes.)

Norman Schwarzkopf, who taught engineering mechanics, declares, "West Point taught the military ethos in the most effective way imaginable: It gave us war heroes for teachers." Instructor Schwarzkopf would often "put aside the textbook, sit on the edge of the desk, and talk about what it means to be an officer, about values and morality and honor. I felt that was my responsibility far more than teaching the principles of friction and why wheels roll down hills. Sure, I wanted the cadets to understand mechanics—but only so they'd graduate and become good Army officers."

Then there is the chronic time squeeze. A faculty member in the 1970s asserted, "although there are potentially great students at the Academy, very few of them ever attain that status." Professor Pojman concurs, noting that "the biggest difference between [cadets] and good students elsewhere is that they don't have the time to develop into scholars."

Classes at West Point are much like those in a typical selective university, except they're not. For one thing, no one struggles in. "They don't consider cutting class," says Colonel Rick Kerin. "They don't consider being late. It's just ingrained." Cadets stand at attention as class begins; the "section marcher" announces their presence. Responses begin, invariably, with "sir" or "ma'am." Class size is almost always below eighteen. Humanities classes are seldom lectures; they take the form of extended dialogues, as in Professor Kerin's drama class, whose twelve members discussed Ibsen's *A Doll's House*. Its feminist themes were chewed over, but sacrifice, chivalry, and honor also worked their way into the hour. (Don't suppose that classroom discussion at West Point pits troglodytes against Neanderthals. As at most schools today, the theme of the freshman composition course is "diversity and multiculturalism," by which is not meant the experience of Swedish Americans and Welsh Americans.)

I also sat in on Major Kellie Simon's "Discrete Dynamical Systems and Introduction to Calculus," a required course for plebes. Major Simon is a rotating instructor with a no-nonsense class demeanor. After the morning salute, she sends her plebes immediately to the blackboards, in teams of two. They scrawl their names in the upper corner of each pane and spend the next fifty-five minutes "working problems" that were absolutely incomprehensible to your innumerate fly on the wall. After much conferring, head-scratching, and trial and error, one cadet team comes up with the right answer and is invited by Major Simon to enlighten the others. Cadets who don't get it are invited—nay, strongly encouraged—to come by for extra instruction, for at no college in America are teachers as available for tutoring. (Nor is one likely to overhear a calculus student at any other school of higher learning ask, "Did you have boxing today?")

Every plebe takes a freshman literature course that consists largely of poetry: contemporary poetry, not Kipling and "In Flanders Fields." While some of the military instructors view it as sissy-ish, Terry Freeman, the founder of West Point's visiting poets program, argues, "No one familiar with the ugliness of the simplistic, heavy-handed, impersonal rhetoric that sometimes infests military discourse can doubt that sensitizing cadets to the beauty and power of poetic language will ennoble and enrich their leadership in a profession that must involve saving lives more than it does taking them." (Jefferson Davis would have approved. As Secretary of War, he wrote President Buchanan, "It has long been the subject of remark that the graduates of the Military Academy whilst occupying the first rank of scholars in the exact sciences were below mediocrity in polite literature. Their official reports frequently exhibited poverty of style.")

Freeman and his successor, Colonel Kerin, have brought such poets as Mark Strand, Robert Pinsky, and Charles Wright to give readings—which the poets do with great enthusiasm, for as Kerin says, "we buy 1,000 books or so of theirs as course texts," which often quadruples the poet's sales. The visiting poets are pleasantly surprised. As one, Jorie Graham, remarked, "What moved me deeply was the way [the cadets] searched through the literature, from Shakespeare to contemporary poetry, in order to determine a right moral choice in a situation where, increasingly, that is impossible."

SOMETIMES A SOLDIER...

So what are they: college students receiving military training or soldiers talking college-level courses? "We are all confused," chime in several top-rank firsties to whom I posed the question.

Commandant Abizaid is not confused. "Cadets are future officers of the United States military," he says forcefully. "They are not college students. They take college courses in the process of becoming officers in the Army." There is no hand-wringing among the military instructors over the dearth of meditation time at the Academy. "We understand that the cadet lifestyle denies the possibility of contemplation," one faculty member has said, "but then who wants a platoon leader who contemplates the order to take the hill?"

Upon graduation a cadet becomes a second lieutenant in the U.S. Army and is obliged to serve at least five years. The highest-ranked grads choose their branch—infantry for the gung-ho, Corps of Engineers for the calculating—while the "goats" (lowest-ranked cadets) get the leftovers. There are special programs that can get you out in two years, as football players with NFL dreams have discovered.

A cadet may drop out without incurring any further military obligation until his cow year. "Walking into class the first day of third year is like breaking a mirror," goes one old joke. "Both bring seven years of bad luck." Quit thereafter—or be separated for bad grades or misbehavior—and you're in the Army now, as a lowly enlisted man.

This past summer, on the Sunday before classes began, Commandant Abizaid instituted an Affirmation Ceremony at which the incoming cows were presented with second lieutenant's bars to carry until graduation. He has also—to the discomfort of some upperclassmen—required cadets to address each other by their shadow ranks: plebes are privates, yearlings are corporals, cows are sergeants, and firsties are lieutenants.

A large majority of those retaking the oath arrived at West Point with aspirations that went beyond soldier. (The "South Hudson Institute of Technology" is one mocking nickname for the Academy.) "I came desiring Sparta," says Lieutenant Colonel Michael Chura ('80), deputy director of the Department of Military Instruction; "I was in a minority."

Colonel Pierce, director of policy planning, says that only 20 percent of male cadets (and 14 percent of females) in the classes of 1998–2002 came to West Point primarily out of a "desire to be an Army officer." (These figures are obtained from surveys of cadets during the first three days of Beast Barracks; "How are you enjoying it so far?" is not among the questions.)

So why do they come? They want a challenge; a good education—a *free* education if you don't count the five-year obligation as payment in full. But then again most people join the military for reasons other than the smell of gunfire. The armed forces are the nation's largest government jobs program, and the recruitment ads on TV sell the military as a kind of Job Corps with tanks and helicopters. Michael Chura spent two and a half years as a recruiter; he found that people join the regular Army for job security and as a means to get money for college, "so why should West Point be any different?"

Those who expect their post-Beast education to be math and engineering with a few marches thrown in are soon disabused. Summers are devoted to military training: after plebe year, they train at nearby Camp Buckner, learning to fire the M-16 and survive in the woods and taking ever-popular demolitions training; they also spend a week at Fort Knox, where tank-driving is among the skills acquired. The next summer cadets act as squad leaders at Camp Buckner or Beast Barracks or sojourn in actual Army units around the country. Finally, the summer before becoming a firstie, half the class leads training at Camp Buckner or Beast, while the other half is posted at bases around the world.

The downside of placing cadets in charge at Camp Buckner, according to one cow, is that "it's their first time making decisions, and their mistakes cost 1,000 people their time and make them hate it." The upside is, well, that it's their first time making decisions, and mistakes cost time, not lives. West Point takes upon itself the burden of being a "leadership laboratory."

As Superintendent Maxwell Taylor stated in 1946, "West Point is essentially a school for leaders."

There is also leadership by the book: juniors must study Military Leadership, which includes classes on "Vertical Dyad Linkage Theory." Old-fashioned West Point-haters would have a field day with this; as the Academy's one-time scourge, *Harper's Weekly*, scoffed, "war being an art, not a science, a man can no more be made a first-class painter, or a great poet, by professors and textbooks; he must be born with the genius of war in his breast."

(The classic pedant, and perhaps the most famous instructor in the Academy's history, was Dennis Hart Mahan, who taught engineering from 1830–1871. "Most of the men who would lead the major units in the Civil War learned the art of war from Mahan," Stephen Ambrose has written. Mahan, who always carried an umbrella, was a great pedagogue, if an easy target for sport. He taught "Engineering and the Science of War," although he never saw a moment's combat in his life. The story is told of the graybeard Mahan asking a cadet—a veteran of the War Between the States—how to perform a particular duty. "No, sir! That is all wrong!" thundered Mahan. The cadet explained, "But, professor, that is just as I have performed that duty practically as a soldier many times during my battle service." To which Mahan responded, "I don't care what you did or what you saw during the Civil War, you stick to the text!")

Robert Shaw, a North Carolinian, son of a disabled Vietnam vet, is First Captain of the class of 1999. The first captain is a sort of valedictorian-plus: selected on the basis of his academic and military records, he is responsible for the entire corps. ("We old first captains must never flinch," said one—"Black Jack" Pershing—to another—Douglas MacArthur.)

Shaw is a rarity: a First Captain who is a product of the U.S. Military Academy Prep School, located in northern New Jersey, which over ten months prepares enlisted men and high-school grads for the Academy. Each year about 150 prep schoolers enter West Point; they rise to the top quickly, for as Shaw says, "The prepsters are the ones who already know everything as far as wearing a military uniform, shoeshine, room appearance." Yet a stigma also attaches itself to USMAPS grads, for an inordinate number are jocks who lacked the grades to make West Point on their first go-around. (More than a third of black West Point cadets started at USMAPS, as compared to 11 percent of whites. Yet USMAPS alumni graduate from West Point at a rate slightly above average.)

"I went to college," says Shaw. "First semester I did so well they asked me not to return, so I enlisted in the infantry and spent just short of three years in the 82nd Airborne Division." His platoon leader was a West Pointer who pushed, pulled, and lobbied Shaw into USMAPS.

Shaw is a true believer. He speaks reverently of his hero, General James Gavin, the 82nd Airborne assistant commander on D-Day. (And a West Point critic: "the Academy," said Gavin, "tends to stultify curiosity.") Shaw says that "the most rewarding" thing he has done at West Point is mentor two plebes: a sophomore task that provides genuine leadership training.

"There's worse ways to go," says Shaw, when I ask if he ever thinks about dying in battle. He is not vainglorious about it; his father's disability is more real to him than John Wayne movies. At an 1880 West Point reunion of the Grand Army of the Republic, General William T. Sherman (1840) said, "There is many a boy here today who looks on war as all glory, but boys, it is all hell." Despite the CNN interventions of the 1990s—"There's nothing more moving than having an infantryman or soldier help a young child across the street or help stabilize a region without having to resort to violence," says Major Peter Bechtel, a political science instructor—one suspects that many of these cadets will someday find hells that make Somalia look like Eden.

WHERE THE GIRLS ARE

The nineteenth-century poet Charles Fenno Hoffman asked of West Point, "Where dost thou find a fitter place on earth /To nurse young love?" Alas for these young hearts, the point is moot.

Cadets may date each other, but the Academy takes parietals to new heights. Hand-holding, let alone kissing, is PDA—public display of affection—and thus forbidden in view of others. Male and female cadets may visit each other, but the door must remain open, and they are not allowed to sit on the same piece of furniture. (What cadets do with each other off the post is their own business, though an off-post romp between a plebe and upperclassman would be fraternization, and thus illicit.)

"Sometimes the two sexes don't look at each other in a favorable way here," says Joanna Pietrantonio. "When a guy dates a girl cadet, he usually gets some flack from his classmates." She has been dating Joe Benson, starting tight end on the Army football team, for over two years, and concedes, "it's hard to maintain a relationship because we only get to see each other at night."

Private displays of affection are not unknown. One graduate of the Class of 1998 impregnated his cadet girlfriend, secretly married her, then had the marriage annulled and deposited the baby with family for safekeeping. Given that regulations state, "Any cadet who is married prior to graduation, or who has custody of a child or incurs a legal obligation to support a child prior to graduation shall be separated from the military academy," one might have assumed that the lovebirds would be headed for points non-West. But these are litigious times, and since the annulment erased, Kennedy-like, the cadets' marriage, they remained part of the Long Gray Line. (Pregnant cadets may take a one-year leave of absence and return, sans baby.)

Which brings us to the broader question, one that Academy officials insist has been answered once and for all: Should women—who compose 15 percent of the class of 2002—be at West Point?

In 1975, Congress ordered the academies to admit women the next year. (Delaware Republican Congressman Pete du Pont was the prime sponsor of integration.) Former Superintendent William Westmoreland protested, "Maybe you could find one woman in ten thousand who could lead in combat, but she would be a freak, and we're not running the Military Academy for freaks," but old General Body Count had thrown away his credibility in Vietnam. The women came.

Finding a West Point official today who will criticize the sexual integration of the Academy is like stumbling across a Honus Wagner baseball card. Lieutenant Colonel Rick McPeak, a professor of popularity-fading Russian ("We miss our Empire!" he jokes) and member of the last all-male class at West Point (1980), recalls that former Dean General Gerald Galloway once began a lecture to the faculty, "If you don't think women should be at West Point, please leave by the door behind you." The exodus did not commence. McPeak explains, "When the Army adopts a policy, many looking from the outside say, 'You just salute; you have your views and you go on.'" Well, no. "When the Army adopts a policy, there is an expectation that you will internalize the values associated with that policy." What West Pointers regard as praiseworthy loyalty can seem to a civilian like Winston Smith learning to love Big Brother.

Not all men in the early '80s classes behaved chivalrously. "When a woman comes up to a cadet and says, 'Good morning, sir,' and the response is, 'Good morning, bitch,' we have a real problem," says McPeak. "Those things were going on twenty years ago. Either I'm naïve or that's ancient history now."

Lucian Truscott suggests that the old atmosphere instilled a kind of gynophobia in cadets. "When I was a plebe if you dropped out of a run or couldn't do your pushups, some upperclassman stood over you and said, 'You're a pussy.' After you get out of West Point, 99 percent of those guys are going to marry someone who's got a pussy, and it wasn't healthy to go off into the world and think that to have characteristics like a girl is bad."

The sharpest critics of letting girls in continue to be old grads. Karl Day ('57) of the Family Research Council says that "mixing and mingling of young females and young testosterone-laden males who are warriors is disruptive of unit cohesion, morale, and discipline. Feminization has degraded the Academy and required a broadening of academics to accommodate women who are not particularly engineering-focused." He explains the attitude gap between old and new grads: "There's a remarkable difference between those who have seen serious warfare and those who have experienced made-for-TV wars, where you put Marines on the beach and there are cameras already there. There's going to be a big change in this country when the body bags start coming back in size 34B."

The party line is that things are going swimmingly and that only a few mossbacks still gripe about women. Dean Lamkin sounds fed up, as if he's sick of hearing for the 500th time that females ruined the Point and how today's kids couldn't shine the Goat of 1947's shoes. "I don't need to respond to the class of 1951," he says. "I don't need to respond to anyone but the people of the United States. We've got the greatest student body in the world, and for somebody in an older class to question the morals, the ethics, the intelligence, the dedication of these cadets is totally out of line. That means they haven't been back here in thirty years. They don't know what they're talking about."

So have women changed West Point? Does West Point change women?

Kate Scott, the descendant of Old Fuss 'n' Feathers, fiancée of a fellow cadet, a woman whose bloodlines on both sides run West Point gray, says, "There are times when it's clear that there's a difference between me, a female cadet, and a regular cadet. A regular cadet!" she catches herself. "When we have a big dance and all the male cadets bring their dates in dresses, it's pretty obvious that you're a female cadet, wearing a uniform. But usually it's not a big deal." (Women are allowed to wear earrings after plebe-year Christmas.)

Major Peter Bechtel, whose sister is also a West Point graduate, insists that the presence of women has changed little. "I've seen the same camaraderie [at Camp Buckner], the same discussion. If there's profanity or jokes in a bus, they're said without regard to who's around. It's not the case that they're trying to protect the girls."

"Is it harder to discipline women?" I ask First Captain Robert Shaw. "Not at all," he replies, which is the right answer, though it's hard to see such a polite young man screaming in an eighteen-year-old plebe girl's face. Reverse roles and complications multiply. Professor McPeak recalls a female platoon leader who had a nightmare: "I give an order and everybody ignores me." McPeak remarks, "I would never in all my life" have such a concern.

(On the other hand, Bryce Bowman suggests that "women are better at military bearing" because they aren't forever scratching themselves.)

Among the most trenchant critics of sexual integration is James Webb, a Naval Academy graduate and former Secretary of the Navy, whose essay "Women Can't Fight" remains the classic exposition of the theme. "There is a place for women in our military, but not in combat," wrote Webb. "And their presence at institutions dedicated to the preparation of men for combat command is poisoning that preparation." (One cadet suggests that "it's kind of a waste" to put women through summer infantry exercises, in light of the prohibition on women in combat.)

Given that West Point is training its cadets to serve in an army whose mission is, more and more, the occupation of various Third World countries for purposes of nation-building, infrastructure creation, and "peacekeeping," Webb's conclusion retains its relevance: "[I]f it is the consensus of Congress that the service academies no longer perform their historic function of preparing men to lead in combat . . . it would be logical and cost-effective to close them down. . . . If the taxpayers . . . want simply to buy a brain with military training, they can purchase that combination through an expanded ROTC program at a fraction of the cost." (Academy officials deny that ROTC is "a fraction of the cost" of an Academy education, pointing out that since the Cold War, most colleges and universities have battened on federal subsidies.)

Both Lucian Truscott's *Full Dress Gray* and Ed Ruggero's *The Academy* feature conservative members of Congress seeking to defund West Point, for as the senator in Truscott's book charges, "we have an Army today that is being feminized, and much of the responsibility for this trend lies with West Point." Yet Truscott dismisses the prospect of real live conservative opposition to West Point. "There's no percentage in it for 'em. They all appoint kids up there, they go to the Army-Navy game, West Pointers inhabit all the military-industrial complex companies." Davy Crockett ain't in Congress anymore.

HONOR THY MATER

"A cadet will not lie, cheat, or steal, nor tolerate those who do."

That is the West Point honor code, the thirteen words that are "the reason this academy is here," says Cadet Honor Captain Richard Gorini.

The honor code was not formalized until 1922; prior to that, cadets were sometimes expelled for cheating, sometimes not. "In the early days an officer's spoken or written word was his bond," says West Point historian

Steve Grove. "Cheating went on when Thayer was here, and he called the boys in and said, 'You mustn't do that kind of thing,' but it wasn't looked at as an honor violation."

The code is the property of the cadets. They administer it, though the Superintendent can reverse a verdict of "found," or guilty, a matter of frustration to some cadets.

This is the way it works, at least on paper: a cadet who has reason to believe that another has lied, cheated, or stolen must report this violation (after confronting the cadet, if he so chooses) to the Cadet Honor Committee within twenty-four hours. This sets in motion a series of investigations by Honor Committee members, which may culminate in a hearing—a trial, really, for the accused has certain rights, including to legal counsel—before a panel of four Honor Committee members and five randomly selected cadets. If six of the nine find that the cadet under suspicion intentionally violated the code, he is "found" and will be expelled, unless the Superintendent intervenes. (The Superintendent cannot, however, reverse a "not found" verdict.)

In recent years, according to Colonel Anthony Hartle, a professor of philosophy and chairman of the Honor Review Committee, "we have around 100 investigations a year, about fifty go to an honor hearing, and about twenty-five are found. About eight or nine are separated"; the rest receive lesser punishments.

Although a disproportionate number of cases involve plebes, upperclassmen who violate the code are dealt with more harshly. Honor Officer Christopher Eastburg says, "If I was found for having committed an honor violation, I would suffer much harder sanctions than if I was a freshman, because the longer you're here, the more you're supposed to internalize integrity." (Those who run afoul of West Point regulations—say, by leaving one's room after taps to meet a girl or grab a drink—will be punished if caught, but unless these offenses involve lying, cheating, or stealing, they are not infractions of the honor code.)

Until 1973, a cadet who was "found" by his peers and refused to resign was silenced; that is, subjected to as complete an ostracism as possible. He was not spoken to; if he dared bring a girl onto the dance floor, everyone else walked off. Among those silenced was cadet Timothy Leary, who was "found" by his peers for lying about the possession of booze. The administration reversed the verdict, but Leary went "days without talking to a single person," except for Superintendent Robert Eichelberger, who "felt the silencing was wrong" and invited the shunned cadet to make a weekly trip (non-hallucinogenic) to his office for a chat. Leary left in 1941, concluding that "Nothing good for America could come from those gray gothic piles."

The "toleration" clause, added in 1970, is the hardest for cadets to swallow. Ultimately, a cadet must be prepared to turn in a roommate or buddy for an honor violation. "It would be really, really difficult to turn in a friend," says one first-class cadet. "I would never do it." Nor, he guesses, would most of his classmates. (Twenty-five years ago a cadet told Richard U'Ren, "Most of us know where our loyalties are, and we ignore the toleration clause. I don't like to squeal on my brothers.")

Those who seem over-zealous in reporting fellow cadets are derided as "Honor Nazis." In George S. Patton's day they were called "quilloids," and the friendless Patton was among the most disliked quilloids. Not that Patton cared: He endured pitiless hazing for asserting that VMI was tougher than West Point.

Defenders of the toleration clause deny that it encourages "squealing." Karl Day explains the stakes: "I don't want my son going into combat with a platoon leader who will go out on patrol about 200 yards, sit down for three hours, and come back and render a false report. The place we teach them not to do that is the Academy."

Is it possible to *teach* honor? Cadets receive forty-four hours of honor education, primarily cadet-led bull sessions about "ethical dilemmas" ranging from U.S. Army massacres (My Lai) to illicit leg-shaving (Tailhook). Colonel Rick Kerin suggests that teaching honor has become a necessity: "When I came to West Point, I didn't encounter much in the way of values, particularly with respect to honesty and integrity, that was at all different from what I'd been taught at home. I'm not sure I can say that now of the cadets who come here."

Nevertheless, the Academy is not the sort of place where one needs a bike lock or car alarm. "I leave my office unlocked," says one civilian professor. "People leave their valuables in hallways, and they invariably remain there—even if left for a week or so. I've never felt more secure."

West Pointers take with them a code of honor that acts as lodestar in the wider world. As Bryce Bowman says, "When I'm home, I'll be in a situation and say, 'What would I do at West Point?'"

MY ARMY, MY WIFE

When I asked my long-time former congressman for names of West Point grads in our area (rural Western New York), he smiled. "Once I appoint 'em to the academies, they're gone for good." Standing armies are uprooting forces: soldiers are scattered to the corners of the globe, and few ever make their way back home for anything more than a visit. Colonel Hartle, whose tone bespeaks his native Cunningham, Kansas, says, "It sounds cold-hearted, but I never thought a whole lot about Kansas. Your roots simply change: The focus is on the organization."

The West Point ring is worn on the same finger as the wedding ring; sometimes they are fused, but as volumes of evidence have shown us, the military and the family are not a good fit. Numerous are the pathologies associated with "military brats," or children of career soldiers who grow up homeless, always moving, never stable. Cadets are not unmindful of the price they will pay. Rare indeed is the grad who weds his or her high-school sweetheart. Those who hold onto the girl or boy back home are known as members of the "2 Percent Club." Joanna Pietrantonio has dated Joe Benson for more than two years, but "we're not engaged," she says. "We've talked about it, but unfortunately there's a high divorce rate for people who get married right out of West Point so we're going to wait."

In Ed Ruggero's novel *The Academy*, the protagonist discovers that his own imperfect family has been supplanted by the corps of cadets, for "he had more in common with these people than he had, perhaps, with his own father." But it is an inadequate substitute family indeed that permits some members to remain anonymous. Congress swelled the corps from 2,500 to 4,400 in 1974, and though it has since been trimmed to 4,000, might this still be too large?

Colonel Hartle does not advocate a smaller corps, but his explanation of why silencing would be ineffective today is revealing: "If you said a cadet was silenced you'd have a quarter of [the corps], half of them, who would have no idea who the person was. It's a slight exaggeration but I think I knew the face of every person in my class. When my son graduated in 1989, it would not have occurred to him that he should know" his classmates' faces.

Historically, the most incisive criticism of West Point, the one leveled by Andrew Jackson and Davy Crockett, is that it created an elite military caste that was estranged from the broader society and contemptuous of the citizens, who, after all, keep them in their dress grays. As the authors of one sharply critical book, *West Point: America's Power Fraternity* (1973), asked, "Should Americans trust an institution that produces men who don't trust them?"

In 1962, education researcher David Boroff noted that cadets "have a lofty disapproval of young people" as "soft, selfish, egocentric." Today, Professor Pojman says, "These kids go home and see friends from high school: They're smoking, drinking, even on drugs. They feel a mild estrangement. Remarks about 'fat Americans' have come up a few times in my classes." (Those obese countrymen, it should be remembered, are footing the bill for the fit and trim corps.)

I spoke with one cadet, an outstanding student and athlete, who had not been home in two years. Another pitied his old friends, who are "still in this little town, they don't know about the larger world, they don't know about Iraq." This disparagement of the local, of the little, is a commonplace among displaced people, as though it is more important to know about Iraq than to know one's neighbor. Part of this estrangement, of course, is simply accelerated maturation. Cadet Eastburg recalls, "You grow up in the first six months. When I went home at Christmas freshman year everybody else was still playing video games, and I was like, 'Wow, I've really changed a lot.'"

ON BRAVE OLD ARMY TEAM

Superintendent Douglas MacArthur, who played left field in West Point's first-ever baseball game against the Naval Academy, instructed that these words be incised upon the gymnasium and in the mind of every cadet:

> Upon the fields of friendly strife
> Are sown the seeds
> That, upon other fields, on other days
> Will bear the fruits of victory.

No American school takes athletics more seriously than West Point. Sylvanus Thayer instituted exercise as a part of the curriculum in 1817, although gymnastics was dropped in 1861, when West Pointers were engaged in tasks rather more pressing than dismounting the parallel bars.

The head of physical training at West Point bears the Dungeons and Dragons-ish title "Master of the Sword." She is currently Maureen LeBoeuf, a lithe and serious Olean, New York native who admits, "It's a disappointment when I walk in. 'Master of the Sword'—people expect to see Xena the Warrior Princess." (She does keep a toy *Hercules* sword behind her desk.)

"While most universities and colleges are eliminating their physical requirement, here we have 168 hours over four years," says Colonel LeBoeuf. Male plebes must take boxing; females take self-defense. Other requirements include gymnastics, swimming, and a battery of fitness tests culminating in the "famous indoor obstacle course, which cadets love to hate." Climbing, vaulting, swinging, rolling, shimmying up ropes, and carrying medicine balls: it is every non-athlete's recurring gym-class nightmare. The obstacle course is run during cow year in "an old typical gymnasium—we tell them it's the same dust Eisenhower sucked," smiles Colonel LeBoeuf. Standards are lower for women, though administrators are quick to tell Old

Grads that the average female cadet does more pushups and situps than did the average male cadet of thirty or forty years ago.

Consistent with MacArthur's dictum "every cadet an athlete," intramural sports are mandatory for all four years, and one's performance in what is elsewhere known as phys-ed makes up 15 percent of a cadet's overall grade. Varsity athletes usually get automatic As, which brings us to the most glamorous aspect of West Point: Army football, and in particular the Army-Navy game, the emotional centerpiece of the cadet year. (Among the first bits of plebe knowledge memorized during Beast is "What do plebes rank?" The answer: "Sir, the Superintendent's dog, the Commandant's cat, the waiters in the mess hall . . . and all the Admirals in the whole damn Navy.")

The first Army-Navy football game was played at West Point on November 29, 1890, after a challenge from a group of midshipmen. The cadets were relative strangers to the game of the oblate spheroid—only two had ever played before—but a challenge is a challenge, and led by Dennis Mahan Michie, son of legendary professor Peter Smith Michie, Army took the field and was routed 24–0. Those were, indeed, different days. At one point, Navy faked a punt and ran the ball for a touchdown, a bit of razzle-dazzle that drew cries of outrage from the West Point side, for as the affronted cadets explained, gentlemen *do not* fake punts. (Among the early football skeptics was James McNeill Whistler, who protested that "to dispute . . . for a ball kicked round the field . . . is beneath the dignity of officers of the United States"—a fairly presumptuous remark by a dropout, though a sentiment common among artsier collegians.)

Even today, Army-Navy is "without question, it's not even close" the greatest rivalry in football, says Coach Bob Sutton. It's like "when you play a brother or a real close friend. You want to beat them because you're really playing against yourself." ("I've never heard any trash talking" in the Army-Navy game, says fullback Ty Amey.)

The game traditionally is the final regular season contest of the college year. "Most of the seniors, this is their last football game ever, and that leads to an unbelievable commitment by those players to pour everything out," says Sutton. Unlike most games, which ebb and flow depending on the score, "Army-Navy just elevates every quarter, and it has nothing to do with what's on the scoreboard." The cadets and midshipmen stand throughout the game; when Army digs in for a goal-line stand, the cadets chant, charmingly, "Fix bayonets!"

Army-Navy is usually played in Philadelphia, but there may be no more spectacular place to watch a college football game than at West Point's Michie Stadium, dedicated in 1924 to Army's first football hero, who was killed in 1898 in the Spanish-American War. On October Saturdays, the trees are ablaze with a splendor to still any Hudson Valley poet's heart; three cannon on the shore of Lusk Reservoir boom whenever Army scores. The assembled 40,000 fans go light on the home team, even when it falls behind by several touchdowns, because, after all, they, unlike many of the gridders on the other side of the ball, went to class yesterday, and will go again on Monday.

West Point and the other academies are the only Division I football programs to pay their players over the table, although $600 or so a month probably couldn't pay a University of Miami linebacker's monthly cellphone bill. The squad is much larger than other teams—180-plus—and while Army might never beat Tennessee, a randomly selected team of eleven West Point cadets would destroy a randomly selected team from Tennessee or any other civilian school.

The problems Coach Sutton faces are not those that bedevil his Division I counterparts. For instance, the typical plebe loses fifteen to twenty pounds during Beast summer, which pretty much rules out freshmen starting on the offensive line. (Plebes do not, however, call their teammates "sir" in the huddle.)

A former Air Force assistant coach has observed that "At every other school in America, the hardest part of any football player's day is football practice. At the military academies, the easiest part of a football player's day is football practice." Still, some cadets call the players "get-overs": a variant of "shirker." They are excused from most of the parades; they get bigger portions at mealtime; they avoid certain scut tasks. To which former tight end Bryce Bowman replies, "Okay, we'll switch: you go out and get your head knocked around for three hours by 300-pounders, and I'll deliver laundry."

I ask Coach Sutton if football is like war, expecting the "it's-just-a-game" reverse, but he takes the hand-off and plunges in with a qualified yes. "All the elements that are involved in battle are present here on a smaller level. They need to function as a unit under stress. You've got to be trained, to have great poise, and maintain your composure in chaos. Nothing goes as planned, because you don't have control over your opponent." (George Marshall, a VMI man, once said—perhaps apocryphally—"I have a secret and dangerous mission. Send me a West Point football player.")

Army's record (3–8 last fall) lags behind the won-loss record of the U.S. military, but then again there are no Grenadas on the schedule. While Army competes in the Patriot League in most other sports, the football team is a new member of the motley Conference USA, a collection of mostly Southern schools (Tulane, Cincinnati, Memphis, Louisville, Houston, Southern Mississippi, and East Carolina) which are about as rivalrous with Army as Colorado School of Mines is with Bowdoin. But times have changed. "Conference affiliation is mandatory for a Division I school that is serious about competing at that level," says Superintendent Christman. The league has a TV deal with Fox Sports Net and tie-ins with the Liberty Bowl and the oddly named Humanitarian Bowl, which presumably frowns on personal fouls. Army football can rake in close to $12 million, supplying the lion's share of the Academy's $15 million athletic budget.

(The basketball team, overshadowed by Army football, is best known for producing a tough Polish point guard named Mike Krzyzewski, class of '69, who played for a mercurial locker-kicking, chair-throwing wildman named Bobby Knight. Krzyzewski coached Army to NIT appearances in 1977 and '78 before building a perennial powerhouse at Duke. Although the height restriction on cadets has been removed, seven footers with soft touches—hell, seven footers who can tie their shoes—aren't clamoring to get in.)

AND WHEN I DIE...

When I asked Director of Admissions Colonel Michael L. Jones his favorite spot at West Point, he replied softly, "My roommate's grave. Randy Carlson. He was killed in Lebanon." Haltingly, he continued, "Randy went to The Citadel for a year before he came here, and he is the reason I graduated. He dragged me through math for two years; without him, I never would have made it. During the really hard times plebe year we would go to the cemetery because it was a really quiet place where no upperclassmen were around. We could do our homework, we could read Scripture, we could talk. We had a favorite tree.

"Randy and I were later stationed here when he was in the French Department and I was in admissions. He left in May of '82. The last night before he left we had him over for supper; he never married so he was like a second father for our kids. Then he and I walked down to the cemetery and Randy told me that night that if anything ever happened to him he showed me where he wanted to be buried. Three months later I had to bury him there. So when I need to get away from life, that's where I go: I go to talk to Randy and just sit there."

Every cadet is required to learn "The Corps," an anthem written a century ago by West Point chaplain Bishop Herbert Simpson.

> The long gray line of us stretches
>   Through the years of a century told,
> And the last man feels to his marrow

> The grip of your far-off hold.
> Grip hands with us now, though we see not,
> > Grip hands with us, strengthen our hearts
> As the long line stiffens and straightens
> > With the thrill that your presence imparts.
> Grip hands—though it be from the shadows—
> > While we swear, as you did of yore,
> Or living, or dying, to honor
> > The Corps, and the Corps, and the Corps!

Old men cry at the singing of "The Corps." Someday, tears will course down the cheeks of graying women, too. They will recall marches across the Plain, surviving "Discrete Dynamical Systems," beating Navy, tossing hats in the air after a mind-numbing speech by a cabinet official or Vice President. And they will think of the white crosses in the cemetery, of classmates returned to dust well before their allotted three score and ten years, dying in Serbia or Africa or some other place on the map that can never mean to a member of The Corps what this gray gothic redoubt in the Hudson Highlands means.

The Old-Fashioned Three-Day Weekend

The American Enterprise, 1997

WHEN TRADITION FACES OFF against the almighty buck, smart gamblers put their money on the money. Consider one of the overlooked revolutions of 1968, when Congress decided that George Washington's face on the dollar bill trumped George Washington's Birthday. The Uniform Holiday Act of 1968 provided that beginning in 1971, Memorial Day, Columbus Day, Veterans Day, and Washington's Birthday (later demoted to the beloved "Presidents' Day") were to fall only on Mondays.

For years, Florida Senator George A. Smathers, best known as JFK's sidekick in the pursuit of venereal happiness, had been the Braveheart of the three-day weekend. Smathers even wanted to junk Thanksgiving Thursday and bid bye-bye to the Fourth of July six years out of seven.

The Monday holiday bill found its weightiest ally in the U.S. Chamber of Commerce. The chamber's arguments for uprooting the old holidays were no more elevated than the bottom line:

- It would reduce absenteeism—no more calling in sick on Friday after getting smashed on a Memorial Day Thursday.
- Production would not experience midweek disruptions.
- Travel-dependent industries would prosper.

When the bill came to the House floor in May 1968, shrewd supporters had tacked on a provision establishing Columbus Day as a national holiday. This ensured the measure's passage, despite the futile effort of Rep. Edward Derwinski (R-IL) to rename Columbus Day "Discoverers of America Day" as a way to honor Polish explorer Jan z Kolna and "put an end to the Polish jokes which have swept the country." (Lech Walesa eventually did that.)

The Daughters of the American Revolution "vigorously protest[ed] this downgrading of our national heroes," but the white-haired bluebloods were no match for Chamber of Commerce greenbacks. Neither was the ramshackle Lord's Day Alliance, whose director complained, "Most ministers like long holidays about as much as they do the devil. The choir, ushers, Sunday school teachers, and the whole congregation join the mass exodus."

Congressman Robert McClory (R-IL), who co-managed the bill on the floor, gamely conjectured that families would spend the long weekends visiting Arlington National Cemetery, Gettysburg, and other "famed battlegrounds and monuments," including, presumably, the Tomb of the Unknown Shopper.

New York Democrat Samuel Stratton, self-proclaimed "father of Monday-holiday legislation" (but no friend to the Father of our Country), declared that three-day weekends would "refresh and restore the spirits and the energies" of federal employees.

The bill's cantakerous opponents were not impressed. Michigan Republican Edward Hutchinson called it "a rejection of our historic past"; North Carolina Democrat Basil Whitener grumbled that "a few business organizations would make more profit on Mondays" at the expense of "the tradition and background of our Nation. . . . Let us not peg everything to the dollar."

Rep. Joe Waggonner (D-LA) thundered, "Holidays and commemorative events were not created for the purpose of trade or commerce. . . . You have helped to destroy history for future generations." The intrepid Waggonner, whose district must have had mighty few Knights of Columbus, even took aim at Mr. 1492: "I think it needs to be said since we seem to be so proud of Columbus, that when he left for this country he did not know where he was going, and when he got here, he did not know where he was, and when he got back, he did not know where he had been."

The traditionalists had a monopoly on wit. Fletcher Thompson (R-GA) offered an amendment to rename our holidays "Uniform Holiday No. 1, Uniform Holiday No. 2," etc. The immortal skinflint H.R. Gross (R-IA), who had opposed spending government money to keep lit the eternal flame over JFK's grave, proposed to move Christmas and New Year's Day to Monday. The Mondaynes were not amused.

The Uniform Holiday Act of 1968 passed the House, 212–83, and the Senate by voice vote, without debate. "This is the greatest thing that has happened to the travel industry since the invention of the automobile," rejoiced the president of the National Association of Travel Organizations.

Rep. Dan Kuykendall (R-TN) saw it differently: "If we do this, 10 years from now our schoolchildren will not know what February 22 means. They will not know or care when George Washington was born. They will know that in the middle of February they will have a three-day weekend for some reason. This will come."

This has come.

To Hell with Earth Day; Long Live Arbor Day!

The American Enterprise, 2000

ONCE UPON A TIME in America, schoolchildren celebrated a lovely little holiday called Arbor Day. The children would sing songs about Johnny Appleseed, recite Joyce Kilmer into the ground, learn the difference between an oak and a maple, and bundle up against the spring chill to go plant an actual tree. The planting, like Arbor Day itself, was both symbolic and practical, and a nice lesson in the ways in which conservation and renewal begin at home. Fittingly, Iowa painter Grant Wood made Arbor Day the subject of one of his iconic paintings.

But that was then, and this is now. Beyond its hometown of Nebraska City, Nebraska, Arbor Day has faded into virtual obscurity; its historic date, April 22, will be given over this year to that dreary drizzle of agit-prop known as Earth Day. The difference between Arbor Day and Earth Day is the difference between planting a tree in your backyard and e-mailing a machine-written plea for a global warming treaty to your UN representative.

The date of Arbor Day has always varied from state to state, usually depending on the planting season: its very lack of fixity was part of its human-scale charm. California observes it on March 7, Luther Burbank's birthday, but before its recent transplantation to the last Friday in April, most states declared it to be April 22, the birthdate of J. Sterling Morton of Nebraska City, the father of Arbor Day.

Morton was a newspaper editor and member of the Nebraska Board of Agriculture. Desirous of windbreaks, shade, lumber, and the simple aesthetic pleasure of that woody wonder that only God can make, Morton proposed a statewide tree-planting festival. He got his wish: On April 10, 1872, more than one million trees were planted in Nebraska, and over the next sixteen years 350 million new trees brought a sylvan touch to the prairie state. Other states picked up on the idea, and by 1882, schoolchildren around the country celebrated Arbor Day with parades, ceremonial plantings to honor the dead, and the introduction of seeds to ground, which begins the miracle.

But perhaps in its reliance on the public school system Arbor Day contained the seeds of its own destruction. States, and later the federal government, could not resist tweaking Arbor Day. It became Arbor and Bird Day in some places, which was harmless enough, but before long it was hijacked by the highwaymen of the Good Roads movement—the apostles of progress who would go on to pave America with your ancestors' tax dollars.

By the teens, the U.S. Bureau of Education was flooding the nation's schools with bulletins promoting the bizarre hybrid "Good Roads Arbor Day." You see, "If a people have no roads, they are savages," as bureau propaganda put it. Properly instructed on Good Roads Arbor Day, the young scholars might grow up "to relieve our country of this stigma of having the worst roads of all civilized nations." Which they did: Who says public education doesn't work?

(Piling yet another progressive cause atop the faltering branch of Arbor Day, the organizers of the West Virginia Arbor and Bird Day cheeped, "We can have a good system of consolidated schools only where we have good roads.")

Nevertheless, Arbor Day survived, frequently observed in hamlets and parks and neighborhood schools—until it was clear-cut by Earth Day.

Earth Day was not of ignoble birth. It was the brainchild of Wisconsin Senator Gaylord Nelson, a thoughtful liberal, who envisioned it as a national teach-in on the environment. The first Earth Day, April 22, 1970, was a hectoring mix of street theater, corporate P. R., and speeches by such paragons of self-restraint as Senators Ted Kennedy and Bob Packwood. (The most prominent public opponents of the first Earth Day were the often ridiculed but usually dead-on ladies of the Daughters of the American Revolution.)

In the three decades since, Earth Day has become a pagan holiday for pallid urbanites and technology-enslaved yuppies whose field trips to the outdoors often end in paralyzing fears of Lyme disease. Earth Day is about as green as a $100 bill.

So on April 22 of this year, when the networks and the schools and the politicians are droning on about the oppressive bore that is Earth Day, commit a simple act of resistance and patriotism: Observe Arbor Day. Plant a tree.

Shooting Down Mother's Day
The American Enterprise, 2002

IN THE ANNALS OF easy votes, one might expect to find a prominent place for the congressional resolution to establish Mother's Day. Yet the first Mother's Day legislation was hooted down in the U.S. Senate.

Mother's Day was the brainchild of Anna Jarvis, a Philadelphia woman stricken with grief over the death of her saintly mother in May 1905. Two years later, Miss Jarvis organized memorial services for her mother in Philadelphia and her hometown of Grafton, West Virginia. Then, in one of those mad boundless leaps taken only by the most irrepressible holiday entrepreneurs, Anna Jarvis went national. She decided that henceforth, on the anniversary of her mother's death, *all* Americans ought to honor the women who gave them birth.

In May 1908, freshman Senator Elmer Burkett (R-NE) put Miss Jarvis's proposal before his colleagues. It was not a Hallmark moment.

The senator explained that Mother's Day legislation was a special request of the Young Men's Christian Association, which, he noted, was doing valiant work in the "gathering together of the boys for social intercourse." (A theme later elaborated upon by the Village People in their timeless disco tribute.) Mother's Day, said Senator Burkett, would remind "boys from the country who are in the cities and among strangers" to think of "the old homes they left behind and the mothers who gave them birth."

Senator Burkett's mawkish but sincere discourse was met by a hail of mockery. The neophyte legislator was astonished by the ridicule heaped upon his innocent proposal. "I did not expect that a single objection would be offered," he averred; he was offended to hear "light made of it" by his gray colleagues.

Senator John Kean (R-NJ) immediately moved to amend Burkett's measure by striking everything after "Resolved" and substituting the Fifth Commandment: "Honor thy father and thy mother."

Senator Henry Moore Teller (D-CO) scorned the resolution as "puerile," "absolutely absurd," and "trifling." He announced, "Every day with me is a mother's day."

Senator Jacob Gallinger (R-NH) judged the very idea of Mother's Day to be an insult, as though his memory of his late mother "could only be kept green by some outward demonstration on Sunday, May 10."

"There are some thoughts that are so great and so sacred that they are belittled by movements of this character," lectured Senator Charles Fulton (R-OR), who went on to suggest the consecration of "Mother-in-Law Day."

Besides—and this objection may strike modern ears as especially bizarre—whether or not young men honored their mothers was *none of the federal government's business.*

"It is not a proper subject for legislation," declared Weldon Heyburn (R-ID). "[T]he sentiment that exists between the parent and the child" is "too sacred to be made the subject of bandying words" and symbolic and unconstitutional legislative resolutions.

By a margin of 33-14, the Senate contemptuously returned this first Mother's Day resolution to committee. But a few Constitutionalist pettifoggers were not going to stop Anna Jarvis. She enlisted the potent support of the World's Sunday School Association. By 1914, members of Congress were falling all over each other in praise of a federally sanctioned day of maternal homage. Mother's Day, celebrated on the second Sunday of May, was here to stay. (The logical companion to Mother's Day, Father's Day, took decades to catch on, despite assiduous propagandizing by the necktie industry.)

But a funny thing happened on the way to the florist. Anna Jarvis, the mother of Mother's Day, became its harshest critic.

Jarvis denounced the florists and greeting-card manufacturers who battened on her day. In vain, she urged sons and daughters to buy buttons instead of flowers for mom; she called greeting cards "a poor excuse for the letter you are too lazy to write." The embittered Jarvis concluded that "charlatans, bandits, pirates, racketeers, kidnappers and other termites" had corrupted "with their greed one of the finest, noblest, truest Movements and celebrations known."

The spinster Jarvis, who never had children, died alone in a Pennsylvania nursing home. She had come to agree with those early Senate critics who derided the establishment of a national Mother's Day. Clergymen sympathetic to Jarvis urged that Americans shun the commercial interests and honor their mothers with a hand-picked dandelion and either a hug or a hand-written letter. Sons and daughters are still free to take their advice.

The Grinch Who Moved Thanksgiving
The American Enterprise, 2000

As you prepare to dig into the turkey and stuffing this November 23, *stop!* You've got the wrong day!

George Washington issued the first National Thanksgiving Proclamation on November 26, 1789, but the early Presidents, disproportionately Virginian and of a states' rights disposition, regarded such commemorations as excessively Yankee and Federalist. Even John Quincy Adams, the ultimate codfish President, was reluctant to be seen as "introducing New England manners" nationwide by a public acknowledgement of Thanksgiving.

The antebellum New England novelist and editor Sarah Josepha Hale is to Thanksgiving what Stevie Wonder is to Martin Luther King Day. The indefatigable Hale propagandized ceaselessly for the glory of late November Thursdays, pumpkin pie, roasted turkey, "savory stuffing"—everything but the Detroit Lions. It took thirty-five years and a civil war, but Mrs. Hale's efforts paid off when President Lincoln declared the last Thursday in November a national day of Thanksgiving and a legal holiday.

Andrew Johnson, ever the contrarian, designated his first Thanksgiving Day in December, but his successor, Ulysses Grant, began a seventy-year practice by resetting the date to the last Thursday in November. Still, the states were free to go their own ways, and Southern governors often opted for idiosyncratic observances or none at all. As Thanksgiving historian Diana Karter Appelbaum notes, Texas Governor Oran Milo Roberts refused to declare Thanksgiving in the Lone Star State, remarking, "It's a damned Yankee institution anyway." But the South, too, eventually succumbed to this succulent and sacred day.

Then along came Franklin D. Roosevelt.

It seems that Thanksgiving was to fall on November 30 in 1939, a matter of consternation to the big merchants of the National Retail Dry Goods Association (NRDGA). The presidents of Gimbel Brothers, Lord & Taylor, and other unsentimental vendors petitioned President Roosevelt to move Thanksgiving to the previous Thursday, November 23, thus creating an additional week of Christmas shopping—and to the astonishment of those

Americans without dollar signs in their eyes, the President did so. (Not all merchants favored the shift. One Kokomo shopkeeper hung a sign in his window reading, "Do your shopping now. Who knows, tomorrow may be Christmas.")

Opinion polls revealed that more than 60 percent of Americans opposed the Rooseveltian ukase; dissent was especially vigorous in New England. The selectmen of Plymouth, Massachusetts, informed the President, "It is a religious holiday and [you] have no right to change it for commercial interests." Thanksgiving is a day to give thanks to the Almighty, harrumphed Governor Leverett Salstonstall of Massachusetts, "and not for the inauguration of Christmas shopping."

Although the states customarily followed the federal government's lead on Thanksgiving, they retained the right to set their own date for the holiday, so forty-eight battles erupted. As usual, New Deal foes had a monopoly on wit, if not votes. A New Hampshire senator urged the President to abolish winter; the Oregon attorney general versified:

> Thirty days hath September,
> April, June, and November;
> All the rest have thirty-one.
> Until we hear from Washington.

Twenty-three states celebrated Thanksgiving on November 23, and another twenty-three stood fast with November 30. Two states, Colorado and Texas, shrugged their shoulders and celebrated both days—Texas did so to avoid having to move the Texas/Texas A&M football game.

This New Deal experiment in Gimbelism lasted two more years, until finally the NRDGA admitted that there was little difference in retail sales figures between the states that celebrated Thanksgiving early and those that clung to the traditional holiday. Without fanfare, President Roosevelt returned Thanksgiving 1942 to the last Thursday in November. Mark Sullivan noted that this was the only New Deal experiment FDR ever renounced.

Just as Roosevelt's refusal to observe the two-term tradition set by George Washington necessitated the Twenty-Second Amendment, so did his flouting of Thanksgiving precedent require corrective legislation. In a compromise of sorts, FDR signed into law a bill fixing Thanksgiving as the *fourth* Thursday—not the last Thursday—in November. Never again would Thanksgiving fall on November 29th or 30th. The states followed suit, although Texas held out until 1956.

This year, as it happens, Thanksgiving falls on a Roosevelt day: November 23. So as you fight the traffic on November 30—the real

Thanksgiving—give a thought to Sarah Josepha Hale, and thank FDR for that extra week of Christmas shopping.

The Old College—Why?
The American Enterprise, 1996

ONE OF THE MOST annoying lines in contemporary pop music is from Rod Stewart's "Maggie May," in which the wrinkled Scot sings, "It's late September and I really should be back at school." To those who loathe college life, Stewart's sentence, with its casual and arrogant assumption of privilege, conjures images of shaggy-haired rich kids tossing Frisbees on the quad as marijuana smoke wafts through an air that is thick with hostility toward the outlying "townies."

For the vast majority of Americans, the superior lyric would be, "It's late September and I really should be playing football/harvesting pumpkins/reading Hawthorne." There are a handful of supple fellows who can live in both worlds: Vernon Parrington, our greatest literary historian, taught English and coached football at the University of Oklahoma, but Parrington only proves that the better the Sooner.

It may be unthinkable now—like a day without television—but in days long gone, America's ephebi had attractive alternatives to the college track. Though we've not had a college-less president since Harry Truman and are unlikely ever to have such again, the oldest callings—parenthood, farming, carpentry, storytelling—still require no parchment, at least not yet. To take one example, many of the most distinctive and iconoclastic American writers of our century fall into two categories: those who hated college, and those who never bothered to go.

The latter group is vast and various: it ranges from H.L. Mencken to Ernest Hemingway to Gore Vidal to Ray Bradbury to William Saroyan. They were joyful participants in what Vidal calls "the worst perversion of all, autodidacticism."

American writers used to be able to serve their apprenticeships on newspapers, rather than in Masters of Fine Arts programs in soulless multiversities. "If you would learn to write," instructed Ralph Waldo Emerson, "'tis in the street you must learn it.... The people, and not the college, is the writer's home."

The irrepressible Henry L. Mencken recalled, "At a time when the respectable bourgeois youngsters of my generation were college freshmen, oppressed by simian sophomores and affronted with balderdash daily and hourly by chalky pedagogues, I was at large in a wicked seaport of half a million people, with a front seat at every public show . . . and getting earfuls and eyefuls of instruction in a hundred giddy arcana, none of them taught in schools."

Mencken as grad student is no more plausible than Bill Clinton as Benedictine. Thomas Wolfe (the first one) found graduate students an "intellectual peasantry—dull, cold, suspicious of any idea they had not been told to approve," and it was the genius of Mencken (and most autodidacts) to think *outside* the prescribed boundaries. (Rarely will you meet a thoughtful non-college-educated person whose political views conform to the contours of the "liberal" or "conservative" procrustean beds.)

Who would say that Mencken's education, in his and his family's Baltimore, was inferior to the one he'd have received if his old man had shipped him off to Princeton? Could he have majored in "Baltimore" at Princeton? More to the point, can one major in "Baltimore" at Johns Hopkins?

A recent critic of institutional schooling, the Kentucky poet-farmer Wendell Berry, charged that "the child is not educated to return home and be of use to the place and community; he or she is educated to leave home and earn money in a provisional future that has nothing to do with place or community."

And so Jennifer College ends up on K Street. Or Wall Street. Or anywhere beyond Baltimore or Kentucky.

Golden ages turn sere; that was then, and this is now. An H.L. Mencken of 1996, whose only credential was a coruscant prose style, could pound the pavement from dawn to dusk, 365 days a year, and after all that leather his resumes would sit in Gannett and Knight-Ridder wastebaskets from Miami to Puget Sound. "Frankly, Henry," the gatekeeper of the newspaper chain would tell him, "you're not a bad writer—I could see you eventually working your way up to our Style section—but in all candor, corporate policy prohibits me from hiring you without that degree. I can recommend a few good journalism schools. . . ."

So, undergraduates, September has arrived, and everyone says you really should be back at school. You might give a thought to Henry Adams, who recalled his Harvard days none too wistfully: "The chief wonder of education is that it does not ruin everybody connected in it, teachers and taught." If you have a subversive soul, then read books that aren't on any reading lists, and give special study to your own Baltimore, wherever that may be.

The Un-American Game
The American Enterprise, 1998

AMERICANS DO NOT SPEAK Esperanto or measure in meters, but a third insidious agent of homogenization—soccer—is making alarming headway among our youth. Patriots, arm thyselves with baseball bats.

Teams of savages have kicked balls (or enemies' skulls) toward goals since time began, but the English codified soccer in the mid-nineteenth century. The game then was spread throughout the world by British tradesmen, soldiers, missionaries, and imperialists. In India, Egypt, Korea, South Africa, and elsewhere, soccer was taken up by local elites eager to mimic the Brits. Indigenous games fell before the sinister black-and-white ball. Soccer, as sports historian Bill Murray writes, was the British Empire's "most enduring export." The fabled "sport of the dispossessed," as P.C. apologists call it for its popularity in the Third World, is in fact a legacy of British imperialism.

In the Middle East, the game was introduced by British oil workers. The Shah of Iran pushed it as a tool of westernization. The Boer War established the game in South Africa, where, some years earlier, hundreds of Zulus had quite sensibly ripped a soccer ball to shreds after watching British sailors play a game.

Yet the virus never infected Americans. Soccer was played in a few immigrant-heavy New England textile towns in the nineteenth century, but the sons of these immigrants learned to play wholesome American sports such as baseball and real football. In 1924, Thomas Cahill, secretary of the U.S. Football Association, predicted that his European game soon would "rank only second to baseball as the leading pro game," but Americans remained so indifferent that Cahill's association eventually gave up its preferred name and accepted the demeaning term "soccer."

Why did soccer fail in our land? Setting aside the obvious fact that it is an excruciating bore, the usual explanation is its foreignness. Local clubs of the 1930s and '40s had such unlovely monikers as the Chicago Croatians and the San Pedro Yugoslavians. Not exactly the Yankees. Even today, prominent "American" players are often foreign mercenaries or the ponytailed sons of college professors.

In 1943, *Time* asserted that the "U.S. lack of interest [in soccer] is due mainly to U.S. distaste for sitting outdoors in wintry winds and sleet," which does not explain why Green Bay's Lambeau Field and Buffalo's Rich Stadium are packed on December Sundays.

In 1952, the secretary of the National Federation of Secondary Schools ventured, "It's hard to interest American kids in a sport in which they can't use their hands." Why Americans should be more attached to their hands than other people he did not explain.

Two U.S. professional leagues were launched in 1967. Fewer than one percent of the players in the larger of the two leagues were American; teams sent their players and coaches to Berlitz classes to learn English, but their efforts were for naught. CBS actually broadcast several games, but the handful of fans were aghast when it was revealed that players had been instructed to feign injuries in order to make time for commercials.

The North American Soccer League prospered for a mayfly's life in the 1970s, thanks largely to the aptly named Cosmos team of New York City (actually New Jersey), which featured the legendary Brazilian Pele. The likes of Elton John and Henry Kissinger promoted the NASL, but provincials snubbed the cosmopolitan sport. As one Tulsa cabbie told a reporter when asked why he didn't follow the NASL'S Tulsa Roughnecks: soccer is for guys "in short pants, a Communist game, too slow and boring."

World Cup 94, the first soccer championship played on American soil, was a colossal flop, despite the corporate subsidies lavished by Coca-Cola, Mastercard, and the usual suspects. The title game, a thrilling 0–0 tie in regulation between Brazil and Italy, did not win millions of new fans.

Today, Washington, D.C. consultants imagine that American roadways are filled with sport utility vehicles driven by harried lawyer-moms carting the kids to soccer practice. Not where I live. Admittedly—and distressingly—more and more kids are playing organized soccer. But on the gloriously disorganized playgrounds, baseball, basketball, and real football still reign—for now.

Still, it can't be denied that soccer has gained a toehold in this country that was the first to expel the Brits. So now is the time for all good sports to come to the aid of their country: Blissfully ignore World Cup 98, and reintroduce your children to the distinctly hands-on American game of baseball.

TV or Not TV?

The American Conservative, 2010

IN MY HOMEBOY NOVELIST John Gardner's *October Light*, the cranky Vermont patriot James Page, annoyed by television's "endless, simpering advertising . . . blasphemy and high treason," lifts his twelve-gauge and blasts his sister's set "to hell, right back where it came from." Elvis did likewise with his pistol when Robert Goulet filled the screen, though last I heard it was perfectly legal to shoot ham.

Haughty dismissals of TV can be tiresome, if not as tiresome as the idiot box itself. I had the same Marcia Brady reveries as every other fourteen-year-old boy, and I am none—well, not much, anyway—the worse for the wear.

Sometime over the last decade or two—at my advanced age the years pour out as sand through the hourglass—we simply stopped watching television. Or very nearly so, as I masochistically kept an eye on the Buffalo Bills, and my wife and daughter chose a favorite show each season (most recently, "The Office").

Until last spring, that is, when from every mountaintop rang the message to convert, ye analog heathens, and worship the digital god. I am afraid that instead of falling to my knees I wallowed in techno-nescience. Since I had never bothered to learn what an analog broadcast was, I sure wasn't going to brush up on digital. Ignorance, if not bliss, at least saves me from "The View."

So we let expire the food-stamp-like coupon for a converter box the government had sent. Our negligence felt like a minor act of sedition. Other than the Bills' latest autumnal collapse, we haven't missed a thing.

With Christmas approaching, a much-loved relative generously offered to buy our daughter a TV for her room. We said no thanks. She asked again, rather more insistently. Our refusal was—well, my family is used to my quirks, but our stubbornness in this matter seemed so . . . Amish.

I was going to present, in my defense, the abundant evidence that children with televisions in their rooms score lower on standardized tests, but since I despise those tests my hypocrisy meter buzzed. Besides, why should I have to defend myself for barring the door to Bill O'Reilly, Ellen DeGeneres, Katie Couric, and "Two and a Half Men"?

Russell Kirk famously threw a TV out of a second-story window of his home in Mecosta, Michigan, but the damned things are like zombies: they keep coming on, no matter how furiously one fights them off. My friend Kara Beer tells me that one of Kirk's daughters had friends audiotape episodes of "Charlie's Angels," to which she would listen intently at recess. (I love that image: *listening* to "Charlie's Angels.")

Like most Americans under sixty, I grew up with the living room television as an essential appliance. I can still sing a lusty chorus of the theme songs to "The Brady Bunch" and "The Partridge Family." At odd moments I wonder where Susan Dey is.

But the omnipresence of the box has become oppressive. The idea that at this very moment a teenager in Butte, a down-and-outer in El Paso, and a grandmother in the Great Smoky Mountains are absorbing the same televised soma fills me with dull dread. Television has done more to erase local culture and color than any other noxious device in our place-effacing empire. To welcome it into one's home is like inviting in a vampire, a selective service agent, or a highwayman bearing an eminent domain check.

A new pestilence, the political talk show, has infected discussion in diners and coffee shops and other free-speech nooks in the land of the discreet. When I was a stripling, politically interested folks who hadn't been broken to the liberal/conservative bit often had eclectic views, offering refreshingly human alternatives to the cramped prisons of Americans for Democratic Action and the American Conservative Union.

Today, a distressing number of such folks, having spent too much time being drained of vital fluids in cable's morgue, parrot the inanities of the Hannitys. Go Team Red! Go Team Blue! Those are people who died dyed.

My friend Carolyn Chute has it right. In October she organized a "TV Shoot" so that her friends in Maine could bag a glassy rectangle or two.

Does this now verge on thought-crime? When I worked in the U.S. Senate long ago, a lobbyist from the City of New York informed me that citizens possess a "right to cable TV." Tucked away, one presumes, beyond life and liberty but within the pursuit of horniness. Yet is shooting a TV felonious assault or felicitous assault?

"We're caught in a trap/I can't walk out," sang Elvis, but if the off switch doesn't work, James Page's twelve-gauge ought to do the trick.

And They Call it Thanksgiving
The Independent, 2001

THERE ARE FEW THINGS sadder than a Thanksgiving table surrounded by empty chairs. Wartime brings such heart-wrenching tableaux: the missing soldier, the absent daughter, the stranded son. And now the missing include a strange new category: the father who was incinerated while sitting at a desk or frantically whispering his goodbyes to loved ones over a cellphone as terrorists crashed a plane into a building. His widow and children, desolate and bereft, are unlikely to overflow with thanks on this funereal Thursday.

Thanksgiving has evolved over the years into a celebration of the family, and those Americans not blinded by Second World War nostalgia understand that war and militarism are the family's most ferocious enemies. The common fear as Americans sit down to Thanksgiving dinner 2001, and the country's troops are deployed in Afghanistan, is that the chairs might not all be filled come Thanksgiving 2002.

So the grace that is said before the turkey is carved will be a little less perfunctory this year. "God is great, God is good, let us thank Him for our food," may be a weak rhyme, but it will be said with a new vigor.

Thanksgiving is usually our loveliest secular holiday, a cornucopia of pumpkin pie, stuffing, football and, of course, the emblematic and savory turkey. The enduring image of Thanksgiving is of the English Pilgrims, newly arrived on these shores, sitting down to a three-day harvest feast in 1621 with ninety Wampanoag Indians, as native and immigrant enjoy cooked squash and fellowship and pan-racial harmony. It's really quite a beautiful dream, and has sometimes come true.

President George Washington issued a National Thanksgiving Proclamation on November 26, 1789, but his successors dropped the practice on the grounds that Thanksgiving was a holiday peculiar to New England. Sarah Josepha Hale, author of the nursery rhyme "Mary Had a Little Lamb," made the cause her own, preaching poetically of the need for an American day of gratitude, but it took the horrible, fratricidal American Civil War to nationalize Thanksgiving. In 1863, President Abraham Lincoln declared the last Thursday in November a national day of Thanksgiving and a legal holiday on which Americans were to thank "Almighty God" for "the blessings of fruitful fields and healthful skies."

He also commended to God's "tender care all those who have become widows, orphans, mourners or sufferers" during wartime—a request that takes on special meaning this Thanksgiving for 3,000-plus families in New York City and its environs, afflicted first by the destruction of the World Trade Centre and then by last week's plane crash in Queens.

Today, Thanksgiving gatherings reflect two Americas. The mobile, prosperous partakers of the global economy, who scatter to the winds in search of money and position, reconstitute themselves in extended families only at Thanksgiving, or perhaps Christmas. These reunions, however bathed in love they may be, are marred by the knowledge of their transience. The hugs and laughter and exclamations of "my-how-the-children-have-grown!" are pregnant with loss. For these get-togethers are sorrowfully brief, and the inwardly weeping grandparents and adult children are aware that on the morrow the family will again splinter for another year. This year the partings will be especially hard, for our next year may be filled with carnage and bloodletting.

Family life must be continuous to have meaning: without proximity, kinship fades. And such proximity is mostly found in the other America, the community of materially poorer rural and working people. They ain't got money, or visibility, but they do have each other, and this blessed stability is worth more than a garageful of 4x4s. (Film-makers and middle-class novelists depict Thanksgiving as an uneasy assemblage of quibbling neurotics, an image that rooted Americans find foreign and unfunny.)

This year, the two Americas are joined in mourning, as well as perplexity. Most Americans of whatever station really don't understand why Arab Muslims don't like us. Whatever our government's sins, we the people are overwhelmingly non-imperialist and wholly uninterested in Middle Eastern affairs. "Why don't they just leave us alone?" we wonder, the mind's eye returning to the sight of two jets smashing into the World Trade Centre, and the question is repeated by those innocents on the other side of the globe whose families have the misfortune of being "collateral damage." For a day, at least, the American uneasiness will be calmed—a bit.

The significance of the celebration for Americans was made plain this past week when President Bush hailed the release of the missionaries held hostage in Afghanistan. "The good news is they'll be coming home for Thanksgiving," he said. But plenty of others won't be. The widespread fear of flying will keep many of the far-flung from going home this year, giving Thanksgiving a certain forlorn quality, as the uprooted professionals of the successful class spend the day alone, or with other deracinated pilgrims of mobile America, connected to their extended families only by the flimsy tether of a telephone cord—or, even more pathetically, via email.

But the depression lifts on the day after. Few non-retail employers are Scrooge enough to demand work on the Friday following Thanksgiving, which is now hallowed as the opening day of the Christmas shopping season. For the lonely, a day of gift-buying can chase away the melancholy; for those of us enbosomed in family, Friday is leftover day, with its menu of turkey soup, turkey sandwiches, and everything short of turkey ice-cream.

These are parlous and jittery days in America. Our fields remain as fruitful as in Lincoln's time, but our skies are far from healthful. We shall thank God for our families and communities, and pray for those at war, or those with war in their hearts. We might even remember that the first European Americans saw this land as a haven for dissenters, an isolated Eden at ocean's remove from the quarrels of the Old World. If such an ideal America seems impossibly distant in these dark days, well, at least we have the dream of peaceful Pilgrims and Indians.

IN MY LITERARY BACKYARD

"If only I had one predecessor in French history! But no, none..."
—ARTHUR RIMBAUD

Walter Edmonds: Our Stalwart
New York History, 1992

IN DECEMBER 1991, I drove along Governor Dewey's dubious legacy, the New York State Thruway, to visit Upstate's biographer, novelist Walter D. Edmonds. Mr. Edmonds lives in Concord, Massachusetts, Valhalla of American writers. His circa 1870 home and garden stand along the banks of Thoreau's river and not far from the hillock in Sleepy Hollow Cemetery in which repose the families of Emerson, Thoreau, Hawthorne, and Edmonds's ancestors, the Alcotts. This is a curious place for Edmonds. He has roots in ghostly Concord, but the plain folk of his novels are far removed from fey Transcendentalists and earnest reformers. One shudders to imagine Chad Hanna running into Bronson Alcott.

Mr. Edmonds is courtly and eighty-eight (at the time of our meeting); his accent, fittingly, is a hybrid of high Brahmin and Oneida County hick. He has wrapped an old flannel shirt around his button-down and tie; his cat, Poupette, ambles over couch and table and tape recorder and guest with feline insouciance.

Walter Dumaux Edmonds was born in 1903 to the central New York aristocracy. His father practiced law in New York City, so the boy early on understood that New York is two—at least two—different states. ("Upstate is a country," as Carl Carmer, the Oak Orchard-bred folklorist, used to say.) He speaks with obvious pride of his birth—on the farm in Boonville rather than in Babylon on the Hudson—and he says that Edmund Wilson envied him his local nativity. One of the news clips he is proudest of is from the *Boonville Herald*: "Boonville Boy Writes Book."

(What is it about Utica? Although it is upstate New York's eighth largest city, its environs nurtured three of our finest literary men: Edmonds, Harold Frederic, and Edmund Wilson. Not to mention the two greatest political personages of their day—Horatio Seymour and Roscoe Conkling.)

From the first, Edmonds was enchanted by life in the Black River country. "I was much closer to the farm life than I was to the family life, and much more at home in the farmhouses," he says. The Black River Canal, a feeder to the Erie, was "right within view of our back porch. You couldn't see the boats, but you could see the steersmen and the mules or horses. It was about three-fourths of a mile, and I regret to say that we used to throw tomatoes at them. They'd done nothing to us—it was sheer vandalism—but we knew they couldn't pursue us for any length of time."

This son of an aestivating laird was filled with curiosity about the lives of the local people. He recalls one eventful stay in Boonville: "I spent a winter on the farm. Father thought it would be good for my health and he made me promise to be outside every day for at least three hours. Most of the time I would snowshoe up and down the river. I had a good many friends up and down the river and I'd spend time with them. Most of the material [for *Rome Haul*] came out of things they told me. Also, in the farmhouse that winter I found two scrapbooks my grandfather in Utica had kept from before father's birth in 1850. A lot of them had to do with happenings on the canal. That's where I got the reference to the canal agency for bachelor boaters. Supplying girls—I don't know what that would be today!"

At Harvard, young Edmonds began writing about life along the canal. An early story, "The End of the Tow-Path," caught the eye of Professor Charles Townsend Copeland, who helped him sell it to *Scribner's*. "It was the only story I wrote in longhand," remembers Edmonds. "[Copeland] said, 'You take it back and get it typed and I'll send it down to Max Perkins at *Scribner's*.' That was the opening of my junior year but they didn't publish it till I graduated. I was very cross about that."

Rome Haul appeared shortly thereafter, in 1929, and for the next two decades Walter Edmonds established himself as the most significant Upstate novelist since Harold Frederic. His early novels sold well and received friendly notices; his short stories, some of which were collected in *Mostly Canallers* (1934), appeared in such magazines as the *Atlantic Monthly* and the *Saturday Evening Post*. *Drums Along the Mohawk* (1936) was kept from a lengthy stay atop the best-seller lists only by the contemporaneous issue of Margaret Mitchell's *Gone With The Wind*. (Edmonds's original title, *The Starving Wilderness*, was scrapped because "in the Depression that wasn't a happy title at all.")

Edmonds recalls the writing of *Drums*: "I read [Harold Frederic's] *In The Valley* and that was an influence. I was thinking about it as I wrote *Drums Along The Mohawk*. I had a terrible time getting *Drums Along The Mohawk* started. I worked at it for over a year and I had 800–900 pages of manuscript stacked up ... [It] became a children's book called *Wilderness Clearing*. But then I finally hit on the beginning that I have. It's not a terribly good beginning: it's serviceable ... I [started] in July of 1935 ... and I finished it on New Year's Eve."

Frederic was an influence, but Upstate's other eminent American novelist was not. "I thought [James Fenimore Cooper] was perfectly ridiculous," chuckles Edmonds. "I remember mother reading all of Fenimore Cooper and I was fascinated but I said this is nonsense. Nobody could see a nail at 400 yards: even if he could hit it, he just wouldn't see it! I know just what happened. He came back from England to his father's planned development in Cooperstown and he threw his weight around as the squire and then he got around, asking about things in the woods, and I can just see the old-timers telling him ridiculous things and he swallowed the whole works and they came out in his book."

Hollywood filmed *Drums Along The Mohawk*, as well as *Chad Hanna* and *Rome Haul* (twice), which had been adapted by Marc Connelly and Frank B. Elser as *The Farmer Takes A Wife*. "I didn't like it very much," says Edmonds of *Drums*, one of director John Ford's few botches. The pampered French poodle Claudette Colbert was badly miscast as a frontier wife, although Henry Fonda made a fine Gil Martin. (Fonda, whose family name graces a town in Montgomery County, appeared in film versions of all three Edmonds novels. His first big break came on stage in *The Farmer Takes A Wife*. *Drums Along the Mohawk*, sandwiched between the extraordinary Ford-Fonda collaborations *Young Mr. Lincoln* and *The Grapes of Wrath*, secured Fonda's burgeoning reputation as the apotheosis of the "good old American type.")

Beginning in the 1940s, Walter Edmonds wrote a series of books for young adults. But his muse was deserting him. A year's research on Anti-Masonry failed to fructify; a planned Civil War novel petered out after just one installment in the *Saturday Evening Post*. The well was dry. His friend Bernard DeVoto later told him that early success is the worst thing that can happen to a writer—Edmonds agrees.

Edmonds came back nicely with the National Book Award-winning *Bert Breen's Barn* (1975), a novel for young adults. He is now at work, "haphazardly," on a series of vignettes about his early life with father.

Mr. Edmonds is a solitary man, not given to schmoozing with the literati or chumming it up at Writers Conferences. Although he spearheaded the second great efflorescence of Yorker prose, he barely knew his comrades-in-arms Carl Carmer and Samuel Hopkins Adams, and knew Henry W. Clune not at all. There was, he says (and Mr. Clune concurs), no Upstate literary mafia as existed among, say, the Southern Agrarians. Certainly clannishness has its drawbacks, but we could have used our own *I'll Take My Stand* in the 1930s.

Mr. Edmonds tells a funny story about the first time he met Mr. Adams: "Samuel Hopkins Adams came up a couple of times to Northlands, our place [in Boonville]. He went all around the house on his first visit, saying what furniture was worth having and what was bogus . . . He was a very forceful old boy. Most of the furniture there had been in my grandfather's house in Utica, so unless they were making spurious Victorian furniture in Utica . . . [He was] without any animosity or scorn, he was just interested in it. My wife was trying to suppress a giggle and I felt much the same way."

Walter Edmonds was born five years too late to serve in the First World War; his work bears no trace of Lost Generation cynicism or world-weariness. Nor was he affected by the debunking stepchildren of the local colorists: he never even read Sherwood Anderson's *Winesburg, Ohio* or Edgar Lee Masters's *Spoon River Anthology*, and not until our Main Streets had been knocked down or boarded up did he acquaint himself with Sinclair Lewis.

"I'm not an intellectual," Mr. Edmonds insists. "I've always tried to make my characters real through their behavior, which I think is as good a way to judge a person as any. I don't try to practice psychiatry in their minds."

Among contemporary writers, he admires Eudora Welty above all. (In *One Writer's Beginnings*, Miss Welty writes that her father offered her mother a choice between living in Jackson, Mississippi, or the Thousand Islands. Of what literary riches were we deprived when Mrs. Welty made the wrong choice?)

Edmonds claims not to have had an overarching plan, but his oeuvre suggests otherwise. *Drums Along The Mohawk* shows us the settlement of the Mohawk Valley and the price of Independence; *Rome Haul* and *Erie Water* (1933) describe the canal, the first great stimulus to development; *Young Ames* (1942) and *Chad Hanna* (1940) give us Jacksonian America in all its enterprising, democratic exuberance; *The Big Barn* (1930) depicts agrarian New York at its pinnacle; and *The Boyds of Black River* (1953) traces the decline of the rural gentry. Edmonds had little interest in what came after: upon reaching the twentieth century, he turned his cart around and went back to the beginning, writing *The Musket and the Cross* (1968), a voluminous history of the struggle between the French and English for colonial America. Appropriately, Tom Dolan, the boy hero of *Bert Breen's Barn*, one of Edmonds's only excursions into our century, spends his time spelunking about an old barn, looking for a hidden nineteenth-century fortune.

The hallmarks of Edmonds's novels are a robust frontier humor and a respect for the pioneering virtues. His characters are plain people—Dan Harrows, Gil Martins—who by dint of hard work and native sense create a life and community in a big country.

A note of elegy plays through Edmonds's works. The agrarian, Jeffersonian New York that Edmonds sees as the Revolution's happy result is altered, in ways subtle and obvious, by the first great internal improvement of young America, the Erie Canal. When *Chad Hanna*'s Mrs. Huguenine says, referring to the spirit of '76, "I wish I'd been born in that time. I'd have liked it," we are sure that she speaks for the author.

In *Rome Haul*, the appositely named Dan Harrow leaves his Tug Hill farm to make his fortune on the canal. He finds adventure, and a facsimile of love, but after a season or two he returns to the plow. At the outset of his journey, Harrow is befriended by a grizzled peddler, who hails the canal as "the bowels of the nation! It's the whole shebang of life!" The whore with whom he takes up warns Dan that "people live by different notions" on the canal, but Harrow plows ahead, mindful of the peddler's maxim that "canawlers keep a-moving." Tired of moving, deserted by his Molly, Dan leaves the canal to take a job superintending a dairy farm north of Boonville—where we find him ten years later in *The Big Barn*.

Dan Harrow is torn between the canal and the farm: he wants to be a yeoman, yet he also yearns for the footloose, independent life of a canaller. The vast farm that Harrow oversees in *The Big Barn* seems, as rootedness sometimes does, like a prison. How much more exciting—and, Edmonds suggests, ultimately meaningless—is the brawling, boozing, wenching life on the canal.

The Big Barn is an elemental tale of strong-willed tyrant Ralph Wilder, autocrat of 100,000 acres of the Black River Country. Ralph determines to build an immense barn that will be "bigger than the Ark," marvels one loafer at the general store. Ralph is pure action: "He'd own slaves down south, but he almost manages that up here anyway," observes his son Henry, a frail aesthete who has returned from Massachusetts with his wife, Rose Lane. (I had assumed the "Rose Lane Wilder" was a nominative nod to the woman who persuaded her mother to write the *Little House on the Prairie* books; not so. "I've never read them," says Edmonds.)

Ralph Wilder's obsession with the barn is concomitant with a growing awareness of his mortality: "That barn will stand a while . . . Maybe people will say who built it. That's something." Personal tragedies rob Ralph of his reason to believe: Henry is reported missing in the War Between the States, and his other son, Bascom, is killed by a cuckolded husband. The burden of the farm falls on Rose's shoulders; her life, suddenly, is informed by purpose. "The rhythm of daily labor had made its claim; she began to feel that she had always lived this daily round, that she would always live it. When Ralph was gone, she could see herself following it to the end, and her body growing older in the shadow of the barn." Rose may be Edmonds's fullest female character; Ralph is his most tragic.

For a man somewhat patronizingly known as a "canal writer," Edmonds can seem surprisingly ambivalent about Clinton's ditch. His third novel, *Erie Water*, is full of those minor characters that he drew so well—itinerants, preachers, snake-oil salesmen. They prophesy in dire tones about how the canal will destroy the old, and presumably honorable, way of life, and usher in a new world of bills and credit and debt and impersonality.

Erie Water follows a stout lad from Uniontown, Jerry Fowler, up and down the towpath. Fowler is enterprising and hard-working; in Edmonds's world, such qualities guarantee success. ("I'm a Horatio Alger type," admits Edmonds.) Jerry Fowler signs on to build locks, and labors so single-mindedly that his wife lights out, moving in with a farm family, the Hallecks, who remind one of prosperous Joads.

Erie Water is Edmonds's weakest novel; Jerry and his wife Mary are curiously lifeless, more ciceroni than characters. But the book nicely illustrates Edmonds's ambivalence about the canal, whose ardent fan he is said to be. Edmonds is nigh-reverent toward the sweat and toil off Irish and African brows that built the canal, and the seat-of-the-pants engineering and solid craftsmanship that undergirt it. Nevertheless, the canal "is changing this whole land," the eldritch Merwin Gandy tells Jerry.

Gandy is a stock figure in the Edmonds repertory: one of those eccentrics, often a backwoodsman or itinerant preacher, who is part sage, part holy fool. *Erie Water* features a passel of rascals and their view of the creeping ditch is far from roseate. A salty farmer early on bemoans, "This canal ain't going to do me no good. . . . It's too far off. All they're going to do is tax me for it. Don't I pay high enough anyway? Here's my wife needing a new wheel and we're trying to get round to hire a schoolmaster now." Crack carpenter Self Rogers observes, "Afore this damned canal a man just said he'd work. Now he signs a paper. A man is captured and held legal." Snake-oil salesman cum Shaker Isachaar Bennet complains to Jerry of the declining sense of community now that progress has come: "It seems these people want to get to being gentrified. Learning is a splendid thing if you can take it just for knowledge. But to them it means money, setting up above your neighbors. One year a man will go to help his neighbor, Joe, nine miles off. Next year that same man's in a town, incorporated under statute, and he says, 'That Joe must be a backward man. He's still living under logs.'"

Finally even Jerry, monomaniacal canal builder Jerry, the classic ambitious poor boy on the make, has his doubts. Aboard a canal boat, pompous ass Vanderbilt Blue is bloviating about the progressive "vision" the canal represents. "I should think the diggers had the hardest job," Jerry offers.

Blue scoffs, and points at a barn in the distance. "You don't want to look at that farm, nice as it is," he lectures. "That's not the wonder. The wonder is the canal that made this farm prosper." Edmonds concludes the scene: "But Jerry saw the barn."

The canal may be in some respects a baneful thing, an engine of unwanted progress, but it's also a monument to the toilers, to the workaday "Paddy on the Canal." Edmonds writes:

> Roberts wanted to see [the water pour into the canal] because of the shape it would have, the form for the picture he had seen in his mind's eye; the rodsmen and the axemen because it meant the end of their stay in this piece of wilderness; the cooks because it meant that they would no longer have to wash the plates of Irishmen and negroes. To the contractors it would mean profit or loss. To the farmers in Ohio it would mean a decent price for wheat. To the merchants in the east it would mean cheap transportation. Even in New York City it would mean money in the hope chest of Tammany Hall.
>
> His face lengthened.
>
> But to himself and to these wild Irishers, who had chopped at stumps, who had shoveled where half of each shovelful ran back at their toes, who had wheeled barrows, who had had the sun on their backs, the frost in their feet, the cold wet against their bellies, the ague and fever in their lungs, who had had stumps to pull, and piles to drive in quicksand, limestone to blast, and rock to devil which no force but their own could loosen, this water meant the sweat they had dropped in labor; it meant the blood of life in their veins; it meant the end of the job.

This marvelous feat of engineering and bullwork was the *ne plus ultra* of American Whiggery—never mind that the American System was a mere glint in Henry Clay's eye when the first shovel broke ground. The canal was what the Jeffersonians liked to call an "infernal improvement," a subsidy to the merchants who were gradually supplanting independent farmers as the backbone of the republic. The farm that transfixed Jerry Fowler is gone now. So is the prosperity that the canal brought. The bleakest vaticinations of Self Rogers and Merwin Gandy may not have been realized, but their decentralized agrarian republic lies amouldering. (Actually, these cussed old men foresaw an Upstate very much like that depicted in Kurt Vonnegut's 1952 dystopian *Player Piano*. Set in Walter Edmonds territory, *Player Piano* presents an America in which craftsmanship and independence have vanished. The young men of Upper York—those not lucky enough to become mandarins in huge government-run corporations—are forced into the army or onto public-works crews performing make-work. The Jerry Fowlers of Vonnegut's Central New York are sots or insurrectionists; the Erie Water is spookily stagnant.)

In *The Boyds of Black River*, Edmonds's only post-Civil War novel for adults, a family dynasty is breathing its last. As the twentieth century impends, the Boyds, a once great horse-racing family, are short of cash and thoroughbreds, reduced to "shabby gentility." They are revived by the arrival of the hoydenish Kathy O'Chelrie, a New York City actress who marries the final Boyd and brings life back to the old house and its inhabitants.

The Boyds of Black River tiptoes to the fin de siecle—there is talk of McKinley and that mad agrarian Bryan, and a newfangled motorcar is sighted, only to be outpaced by a horse—but Edmonds leaves us at the century's doorstep. The Boyds are set aright, treasury and stable enriched, but the author will take us no further. The twentieth century, with all its gadgetry and ideology, holds no allure for Walter Edmonds. He is rather like the Boyds' Uncle Ledyard, whose first encounter with the automobile is somewhat chary: "Uncle Ledyard got in and closed the door and said, 'Good morning,' to the chauffeur like a man saying good morning to Charon."

Still, life in the Black River country retains its charms. In one of the few instances in Edmonds's fiction in which the regions meet, New York City stage star Candida Brown visits the Boyd estate. She gushes: "You who've lived here all your lives have no idea how exciting it all is. It has a tang. It makes me think—do you know?—exactly of the first time I tasted caviar."

"You won't find any caviar in this house, my girl," [Admiral Porter] told her dryly. "But Ledyard's got some whiskey that is damned good."

Edmonds's most exuberant character is the eponymous Chad Hanna, a "do-nothing, no-account" who is closer to a Yorker Huck Finn than a diligent Dan Harrow. Loafing around Canastota, Chad stumbles upon the Underground Railroad, saves a slave, and joins a two-bit circus as it traverses the state from Albany to Albion.

The year is 1836: Jackson is preparing to pass the wand to Van Buren, a depression is around the corner, and sectional rancor is swelling. Chad, we feel certain, will choose the Union a quarter-century later, with the same reluctance with which he saves the runaway. "I'm not no abolitionist," he avers—no pinch-cheeked Miss Grundy reproving drunks and caning hellions—but "the business [of emancipation] might have some fun in it." With the same lack of high-mindedness, rural New Yorkers marched off to war not long after.

Chad Hanna showcases Edmonds the story-teller. We get somersaults, horse stealing, a dog-toothed boy, and a lion revived with mineral water.

Chad is a rounded, full-bodied character, unlike, say, Jerry Fowler of *Erie Water*.

The supporting cast in *Chad Hanna* is boisterous fun. An Edmonds stock character, the wry oldster, is here in the form of Revolutionary pensioner/idler Elias Proops, who tells lovelorn Chad, "The way I've always looked at marriage, it's all right except you've got to live with a woman." Of an inept Italian juggler and his new assistant, someone says, "She makes a good partner for Fiero. I always said there wasn't no sense to a man tossing balls all alone. He's crazy about her. He wants to throw knives at her too, now."

And yet the old Edmonds ambivalence about progress pops up here and there. Circus agent Mr. Bisbee muses, "I remember how we used to cuss the mud and wish for solid roads. Well, we're getting the roads, and look what they're doing to us. They've turned us into a little show, and a thing has to be expensive now before it can be a genuine wonder."

Mrs. Huguenine, the wife of the circus's impresario, tells the roustabout after he's fallen in love with the daughter of a slave-catcher: "A man oughtn't really to get married unless he's saved up fifty dollars. In the old times, you didn't need cash money. You got a cow off your parents and you took up free land with an axe and a rifle. . . . But nowadays it's difficult. Folks are trading in stores for their food and they spend money on their clothes."

Only once—apart from his novels for young adults, notably *Cadmus Henry* (1949), the tale of a green Confederate balloonist—has Edmonds ventured outside his native ground: the result was *Young Ames*, a critically panned work that Edmonds says he wrote "just to make money when the college bills were due."

John Ames is an ambitious, orphaned boy from Troy bent on making his fortune in New York City. He is taken on as an errand-runner at a trading house; through pluck, adolescent sagacity, and a dash of unscrupulous rascality he succeeds in business and love. This is Horatio Alger, with a Yorker twist, and if one accepts the implausibilities it is an amusing read.

"It was great fun writing it," recalls Edmonds. "I know nothing about business; I have no sense of finance. I had a book called *Merchants of Old New York* and I got a lot of stuff out of that. It was perfectly ridiculous, but everyone took it seriously."

Young Ames is not one of Edmonds's stronger efforts, but it hardly deserves execration. The figure of Andrew Jackson is always hovering in the background. Young Ames's boss, the Federalist Mr. Chevalier, despises Jackson; Ames himself exemplifies the energetic spirit of Jacksonian America. (Indeed, the boy impersonated Old Hickory's nephew at one point on a Southern sojourn.) Historians have long recognized the protean face of

Jacksonianism: its style was frontier, egalitarian, demotic, but through their laissez faire economic policies the Jacksonians liberated a new entrepreneurial class. They were capitalists of a sort; bitterly opposed to Nicholas Biddle's National Bank but eager to make the economic clime conducive to success for ambitious young men of few means like Young John Ames.

In a scene that Edmonds carries off with admirable facility, John meets Old Hickory on a trip to Washington. The boy is undaunted and bold, much to the president's pleasure; Jackson expounds upon American principles and even tosses in some lagniappe advice on how to propose to a girl. Ames's "ambition," writes Edmonds, "was the same instinct . . . that raised a man like Andrew Jackson out of obscure beginnings."

Edmonds himself is a Jefferson-Jackson man whose name shall ever be tied to the Whiggish canal. But for the most part, his characters are resolutely apolitical. (Or anti-political.) When a taproom Whig firebrand demands of Chad Hanna, "How do you stand on Masonry?" he replies coolly, "I don't stand on anything but my own feet."

The utopian and reform fires that burned over our district in the first half of the nineteenth century do not so much as singe the Edmonds corpus. Joseph Smith makes a cameo appearance in *Erie Water*: he is said to have "shifty eyes" and he makes Jerry Fowler "queasy." Jemima Wilkinson, John Humphrey Noyes, the ladies of Seneca Falls: they are absent from Walter Edmonds's Upstate of plain people. Chad Hanna enlists, on a whim, in the cause of abolition, but only because the slave-freeing business "might have some fun in it." A pity that Edmonds never got a handle on his Anti-Masonry novel: What would his earthy pragmatists have made of the millenarian fanatics and shrewd operators who rode the Blessed Spirit to Congress and the state legislature in the 1830s?

The Civil War looms throughout in the background of *The Big Barn* (and *Cadmus Henry*, which takes place in Virginia). Ralph Wilder and the boys are gung-ho warhawks, as is Edmonds, for a familial reason: "One of my ancestors, Samuel Joseph May, a Unitarian minister in Syracuse, was a leading abolitionist and a great friend of Gerritt Smith and Frederick Douglass. He kept what I am told was the fastest buggy in Syracuse, and all the time he didn't allow his wife more than a candle to sew by. She went blind, but he kept his horseflesh up to standards because he ran the main underground station in Syracuse. At night he would take one or two slaves in his buggy and run north."

There was significant Copperhead sentiment in these parts, so it's meet that Edmonds's predecessor, Harold Frederic, depicted antiwar Democratic farmers sympathetically in works such as *The Copperhead*. Frederic was an admirer of his fellow Utican, Governor Horatio Seymour, a principled opponent of the federal government's suspension of habeas corpus and other circumventions of the Constitution.

Edmonds disclaims any didactic intent in his novels, although in the introduction to *Drums Along the Mohawk* he wrote: "To those who may feel that here is a great to-do about a bygone life, I have one last word to say. It does not seem to me a bygone life at all. The parallel is too close to our own. The people of the valley were confronted by a reckless Congress and ebullient finance, with their inevitable repercussions of poverty and practical starvation.... They suffered the paralysis of abject dependence on a central government totally unfitted to comprehend a local problem. And finally, though they had lost two thirds of their fighting strength, these people took hold of their courage and struck out for themselves."

He wrote that, he says, as an Upstate Republican worried over the centralizing trends of the New Deal. He was never much on politicos, although Thomas E. Dewey once asked him to write his campaign biography. "I was rather incensed," remembers Edmonds. "I'd sort of believed in Dewey [and his] statements to the press that he wouldn't betray the people of New York by running for president." It is a measure of Walter Edmonds's gentlemanliness that he was genuinely surprised when a politician reneged on a promise.

Walter Edmond's accomplishment is enormous and underknown. He has fictionalized the history of Upstate New York from the Revolution till the dawn of our industrial century. An Edmonds anthology referred to his books as "stalwarts," reliable draft horses, but his prose was touched with felicity too. No naive singer of bucolic charms, he nevertheless gloried in "the shape of the land with its even trim, the little curves and hollows that the eye would never trace in grass; and in itself it showed the sweeps of the sower's hand, sweeps like the curve of the scythe blade where the seed had fallen, taken root, made milk and grain, been reaped—a cycle for the eye to grasp in a single glimpse."

His pioneers are practical, earthy men and women. They are giants in the earth, embodying what Lionel D. Wyld, in *Walter D. Edmonds, Storyteller* (1982), called the "Yorker-based philosophy of individual worth and dignity, of commonsense approaches to the problems of living, and of simple pleasures which sometimes show how very close sadness is to laughter, tragedy to comedy."

Edmonds's generation—his coevals include Edmund Wilson, Rochester novelist Henry W. Clune, and *Saturday Evening Post* short-story writer George Brooks of Pearl Creek—had a self-confidence, a sureness that their home was a region of worth and dignity, a self-governing bulwark of the American republic. Edmonds, Clune, and Wilson were no strangers to elegy: none was overly taken with the modernized Upstate struggling to be born. Their dirges sound ever more plaintive today. When Henry Clune wondered in 1930 whether "the old spirit of neighborliness that gave such a distinct character to the average residential street before the advent of the motor car, the movie and other institutions of the present era that tend to take people out of and away from their homes, anywhere exists," he was rephrasing the fears of Self Rogers and other cussed independents in the Edmonds ensemble.

When Edmund Wilson, the cranky sage of Talcottville who envied Edmonds the acceptance of the locals, mourned, "I have come to feel that this country, whether or not I live in it, is no longer any place for me," he could've been Isaachar Bennet watching the canal cut its swath through the virgin forest.

(Wilson told Edmonds to his face that he found his books "terribly dull" but thought him unequalled in writing about animals. He fiddled with a piece for *The New Yorker* along these lines, but nothing, apparently, ever came of it. Alas.)

"It's been going downhill so fast," says Mr. Edmonds of his country. "I am appalled at the widening between poverty and extreme wealth [and] the corrupting of the American Dream, which never was getting a lot of money. It was getting independence, the ability to lead your life as you wanted to lead it, do your business the way you wanted to do it. But it didn't mean getting money, money, money all the time." (Edmonds's distaste for the latter part of our bloody century has concrete roots. His childhood home in New York City—"the old Federal house on 11th Street"—was blown up on March 6, 1970, by the infamous Weatherman homemade pipe-bomb explosion.)

What a contrast Edmonds, Clune and company make with the youngest generation of New York writers—we who were bequeathed a Thruwayed, Rockefellered, Atticaed, television-blinded Upstate. Mistah Hanna, he dead. You can find him in an unmarked mass grave, buried with Natty Bumppo and David Harum and Theron Ware.

We drove back along Governor Dewey's Erie Canal, the New York State Thruway, which has inspired no fiction, no romance, no Walter Edmonds. As the canal destroyed the Upstate of Self Rogers, the Thruway killed the York of small shopkeepers and self-contained towns along that old Indian trail, Routes 5 and 20. I rolled down the window and listened for a lonesome drum, but all I heard was the whoosh of rushing cars, and all I saw was a sky of grey.

But gloom passes. I recalled the opening scene of *Rome Haul*: Dan Harrow and the old peddler arrive in Boonville and behold the welcoming brick of The Hurlburt House. Decades later, Frederick Exley, in his toper chronicle *Pages From a Cold Island* (1975), fantasizes about owning none other than that selfsame Hurlburt House. Perhaps the novels of Walter Edmonds offer us a roadmap. In the words of T. S. Eliot: "And the end of all our exploring/Will be to arrive where we started/And know the place for the first time."

Warren Hunting Smith, the Quintessential Genevan

Crooked Lake Review, 1993

"TO BE MERELY QUEER is no achievement, but to be brilliantly individualistic is a fine art which Geneva brought to perfection." So declares Warren Hunting Smith in *The Misses Elliot of Geneva*, a delightful novel first published in 1940 and now reintroduced to Upstaters in the *Crooked Lake Review*.

I chatted with Mr. Smith recently in the summer house behind the grand brick Victorian in which he was raised on the family property on Castle Street in Geneva. Next door is the house in which his father was born; down Castle Street a ways is the observatory his granduncle constructed for William R. "Sky" Brooks, the Phelps village photographer who became the most prolific comet discoverer (he found twenty-seven) in astronomical history.

Mr. Smith led a professional double life: he was both an editor of the Yale Edition of the Horace Walpole correspondence and a chronicler of old Geneva. Half his time was spent in Georgian England, the other half in the genteel Geneva of the prewar era. Never the twain shall meet? Not quite. The Pulteneys, who laid out Geneva, were denounced by Walpole.

Mr. Smith is the only man I've ever met whose favorite contemporary American novelist is Louis Auchincloss—"the one who deals with the world I'm familiar with." That world is running down with the century; the WASP ascendency has passed. For better or worse, there are now more practicing Muslims in these United States than practicing Episcopalians.

To those of us who do not remember the America of the WASPs, Warren Hunting Smith has vouchsafed two wonderful books, one a history of his hometown, the other an affectionate satirical novel resurrecting the old Episcopal Geneva of impecunious razor-tongued lady aristocrats.

The history is *An Elegant but Salubrious Village*, a title borrowed from the early-nineteenth-century travel writer Elkanah Watson's verdict on Geneva. A local house, W. F. Humphrey, published the book in 1934, when

Smith was but twenty-eight years of age. It is saucy and impudent, very much a young man's work, and a thoroughgoing delight. With nonchalant superciliousness, young Smith honors his own tribe, particularly the established families of South Main Street—"a citadel of culture in a commercial nation, a haven of leisure in a bustling world, an oasis of Southerners in a land of Yankees"—while dismissing "the uglier parts of Geneva"—for instance, the Methodist church.

Smith acknowledges his callowness in the preface to *An Elegant but Salubrious Village*: "A book of this sort should preferably be written by some mellow old gentleman, full of those memories which younger people can acquire only with painful research. Unfortunately, no such old gentleman has shown any literary interest in Geneva, so I have ventured to usurp the vacant place.... In fifty years more, perhaps, I shall be able to write a really thorough account of Geneva."

More thorough, perhaps, but surely not more entertaining. Mr. Smith writes as a witty young snob: "The very name 'Geneva, New York' is a sort of protective coloring, suggesting provincialism of the worst sort. We feel, when we hear it, as we do when we hear of someone named George Washington Schwartz or Michelangelo Snooks; it is as much a surprise to find real charm in this town with the pretentious foreign name as it would be to discover that Mr. Schwartz is really descended from the Washington family, or that Mr. Snooks is actually one of the Buonarroti."

Smith is properly proud of his hometown, which is "no cramped and provincial assembly of village lawyers and doctors." He doffs his hat westward to Canandaigua, the seat of Ontario County, only to give it the back of his hand. "Geneva," he writes, "unlike Canandaigua, never became a hotbed of lawyers. Indeed the distinctive Geneva profession, if any, has been that of doing nothing at all."

Well, not exactly nothing. True, the "old Geneva families . . . soiled their hands very little with business," but they had an enviable surety about them. The city's apotheosis is the gray-haired lady stepping down Main Street, head held high despite her threadbare clothes: "There is no fluttering hesitation in her manner, no false pretenses, no striving to keep up appearances. She knows that her family rank, her breeding, and her sharp tongue entitle her to a position from which she can look down on mere millionaires with disdain. She greets her friends cheerfully; puts incompetent shop-girls in their places ('I can see no excuse for stupidity!') and as she goes on her way, we realize that we have seen one of Geneva's choicest institutions—the Indigent Gentlewoman."

Indeed, the Indigent Gentlewoman rivalled Horace Walpole as the steady flame in Smith's professional life. Born into a city overrun with piquant old ladies, he has ever been under their spell. In the preface to his doctoral dissertation, *Architecture in English Fiction* (Yale University Press, 1934), Smith thanked "those dear sentimental ladies of eighteenth-century fiction, with whom I have 'kept company' for three pleasant years."

He soon found suitable replacements closer to home. For while at New Haven, Smith began work on what was to be his only published novel, *The Misses Elliot of Geneva*.

The Misses Elliot are "Primrose and Candida, names which had a somewhat virginal sound, appropriate to the one hundred and sixty-five years of celibacy which their two lives represented." They live near South Main Street, and from their cottage they hurl thunderbolts at "foreigners, Democrats, High Churchmen, and companies that didn't pay dividends." (And, as with all old ladies of whatever station, the "little bandits" whose doting aunts they most certainly are not.)

"There was something Olympian about their wrath," Smith writes; "they didn't scowl and sputter like cross old women, nor did they raise their voices to a cackle; they merely stood in majesty, filling the air with crackling sparks of invective." And woe unto those who cross Primrose's and Candida's path. The sisters possess adamantine wills: they are given to walking out of Trinity Episcopalian church when they detect papist heresies. Stricken with scarlet fever, they ignore the quarantine and make their daily rounds, sending horrified friends scattering to safehouses.

Although Mr. Smith spent vacations and spare moments at the Castle Street house, he was domiciled in New Haven. A friend in that city read *The Misses Elliot* and passed the manuscript to an editor at Farrar & Rinehart, which purchased it on the recommendation of poet Stephen Vincent Benet, who wrote, "This is a genre piece but with a certain universal application. It hasn't any particular plot—it's just the story of two old-maid sisters and through them of a certain kind of individualistic American small-city society, independent, crotchety, brisk and always speaking its mind. It's slight, but I found it delightful."

Farrar & Rinehart brought the book out—in two printings—in 1940. Reviews were kind. In the *New York Times* Louise Maunsell Field called *The Misses Elliot* "very entertaining" and "gently humorous."

Yet because many of the characters—including the eponyms—had obvious real-life models, "it distressed some of the older inhabitants," Mr. Smith recalls.

"My family were not very enthusiastic. My father thought that it was a rather unkind book. They were preparing for a certain amount of flack. One old friend of the family said, 'I wonder why when somebody has written a very good book about Geneva he should turn around and write one that is most objectionable."

"I had one indignant letter from a nephew of the original Misses Elliot who said I held his aunts up to ridicule. Whereas one of his cousins told him, 'I don't think you have any right to write that. Cousin Virginia was just a hellion. She deserved everything she got.'" Mr. Smith—calling him "Warren," even on the homeliest page, seems an impertinence—laughs heartily.

"They were to some extent composites," the author says of his tart heroines, "but I didn't have to exaggerate their prejudices, which were very intense and very vocal. I merely sharpened their utterances."

The indignant Genevans were wrong, and Mr. Benet was right; this charming book is, in its irreverent way, deeply respectful of the sisters Elliot and their hometown. It's also chockablock with *bons mots*, e.g., "every old lady had to have either an old beau in the cemetery or a new one in the parlor, and preferably several of each."

Though the tone is light throughout, we know we are witnessing the last magnificent specimens of a dying breed. "They felt that the United States of America was, in a spiritual sense, almost their own property, just as they felt that Geneva almost belonged to them."

Edmund Wilson wrote of much the same feeling in his autumn elegies *Upstate* and *The Cold War and the Income Tax*. The country really did, once, belong to those old WASPs, but it does no more, and all the former owners have left is their sting.

I have ancestors who chauffeured a couple of the great and not-so-great Upstate families, and from this end of the stick Mr. Smith's grand dames can look like withered cheapskates who put on ridiculous airs. Still, it's hard not to be a bit elegiac. Primrose is dead and Wal-Mart sits athwart Geneva, and who is to say that progress is always benign?

Mr. Smith tried the novel again. He speaks warmly of one tale of a lady who believed that "the way to make a nursing home special was to have a centenarian as one of the inmates. The one she finally ended up with was an elderly black cook who had worked for one of the local families. I had a lot of fun with that but it didn't go over with the publisher, so I did nothing more about it."

****

Popular historian Carl Carmer pronounced Geneva "the most distinctive of upstate cities." Located above Seneca Lake, it was once known as the Charleston of the North. It had a southern feel, dotted by porticoed Greek

Revival mansions built by the city's early aristocratic families, transplants from Maryland and Virginia.

The vigilance of local citizens, Mr. Smith among them, kept Geneva from the ruinous fate of so many small Upstate cities. The idiotic "slum clearance" program, which destroyed historic townhouses and brick tenements teeming with life and transferred slum dwellers to impersonal public housing concentration camps, swung the wrecker's ball in Geneva, but most of the city's notable commercial buildings and residences were saved.

My Batavia's midcentury decline can in some ways be traced to the sons and daughters of the established families, who fled for greener pastures and took with them a bedrock of civic responsibility. The same was true, to some extent, of Geneva, but the old ladies stayed (because they had nowhere else to go?) and it is due largely to stubborn pride that Geneva is still . . . Geneva.

"Poverty is a blessing to old Geneva ladies, though they themselves don't seem to think so," Smith wrote in *The Misses Elliot*. "It keeps them rooted to their native soil when other people are losing their local flavor abroad. It makes them keep the old-fashioned clothes and antique ornaments which seem almost a part of them. It gives them the chance to perform the little acts of grace which only poor old ladies know that other poor old ladies need."

Smith devoutly hoped in 1931 that "Geneva, with her unusual residential attractions, will never be transformed into that hideous monster, an American industrial center," and it wasn't, but his country's involvement in the Second World War just one decade later almost claimed Geneva as a municipal casualty. The Sampson naval training station, twelve miles to the city's south, loosed 45,000 young men on the old maids' paradise. The result was hardly edenic: Geneva went honky-tonk. Which would have been fine, if all it gave Geneva was a spicy fillip. Alas, the government remodelled many of the fine old homes into makeshift barracks, and the city took on ramshackle airs. Rochester newspaperman Arch Merrill, returning after an absence of twenty-six years, wrote, "I hardly recognized the old town. It was like seeing your dignified maiden aunt toss aside her prayer book and pince nez and swing into a strip tease."

Perhaps it is best that Primrose and Candida never lived to see that.

****

Mr. Smith is a kindly man and a gracious employer, say his nurses. And he is—as we all are—very much a product of his upbringing. I ask him if he shares the Elliots' prejudices. "Having grown up in that atmosphere, to some extent I can't help sharing it, but I'm much more open-minded than I think my parents were. I remember my father being quite distressed to hear that I was taking out in New Haven a girl with some foreign name." I love the way he says foreign; like John Houseman hissing "they ehn it" in those classic Smith Barney commercials.

I ask him if the old families still dominate Geneva politics. No, he says, the current officials "are not the well-known people at all; they are apt to be shopkeepers and dealers and people like that."

He smilingly recalls Mr. Chew, the leading banker of bygone years. "He said, 'Geneva is a city of homes and a few stores and that's enough. We don't want factories, they bring foreigners, and we don't like that.' The Chamber of Commerce would disapprove of him heartily." Mr. Smith chuckles, in a tone that suggests he's not paid his Chamber dues in many a year.

Mr. Smith wrote in *The Misses Elliot* of old Genevans: "They didn't have much money, but in Geneva that doesn't matter." Indeed, the novel and *An Elegant but Salubrious Village* drip with disdain for parvenus. But while the social wall between the old families and the new money still exists, the barrier is crumbling. "I remember there were people who moved down to Main Street who owned a sauerkraut factory and were very much looked down upon by the families around them. But I think nowadays anybody with a good deal of money, if, shall we say, civic-minded, would be accepted."

Did he ever dabble in politics? He is aghast. "Oh no, I never had anything to do with politics. Somebody suggested once that since I had independent means I ought to go into politics because I would be above the more ambitious average politicians, but of course a retiring scholar like me would be the worst person to try anything like that!"

****

While working on the Walpole edition Mr. Smith published *Hobart and William Smith: The History of Two Colleges* (Hobart and William Smith, 1972). His connection to the latter, a girls' school, is familial: granduncle William Smith, one of three brothers who founded a prosperous tree nursery in 1846, endowed the college that bears his name with a gift of half a million dollars in 1908. (I was taken aback when I found not a single Horace Walpole reference in *Hobart and William Smith*.)

William Smith comes off as a vivid eccentric in his grandnephew's account. He was a bachelor, a spiritualist, and a man sometimes called a misogynist who nevertheless was befriended by the daughter of fervid abolitionist Gerrit Smith (he who bought John Brown's guns) and was encouraged by her to found a college for women.

William was no dabbler in spiritualism; he was a true believer. He visited the colony at Lily Dale, where no one ever dies, and his descendant still possesses a notebook of William's "filled with letters beginning 'Dear Mr. Smith,' and signed by such names as Socrates, Julius Caesar, and 'your loving aunt, Sally Coleman.'" He toyed with establishing a spiritualist school before settling on William Smith College.

"Oh yes, I remember Uncle William," says Mr. Smith. "I'm probably the last person who can remember him since he didn't circulate in Geneva society and wasn't interested in children."

"One reason Uncle William never put up a gravestone to his mother was that since he was corresponding with her through the spirit world, he wasn't particularly interested in her mortal remains." (Mr. Smith, no spiritualist, put up a tombstone in the old Washington Street Cemetery a couple of years ago.)

Warren Hunting Smith retains a tie with Hobart and William Smith; the new library bears his name. The school itself, however, while the city's largest employer, is less and less a part of the life of Geneva. "The people of the college have little interest in civic affairs," concedes Mr. Smith.

(Besides Warren Hunting Smith, two other estimable New York writers have Hobart connections: Phelps's Bellamy Partridge of *Country Lawyer* fame and the late Frederick Exley, author of *A Fan's Notes*, who fled the cold for the University of Southern California, only to return to drink himself to death amidst his beloved Thousand Islands.)

I launch into one of my favorite routines, about how Mr. Smith's was the last generation of Upstate men of letters. I read the roll call: Walter D. Edmonds, Henry W. Clune, Carl Carmer, Samuel Hopkins Adams. Do you feel any kinship with them, I burble.

"No, none whatever I should say."

Well, did you ever read them?

"No, I never read them."

This is not unexpected: Smith is a Genevan through and through, less so an Upstater. As a regional writer he is best classed with William Kennedy, whose Albany, like Geneva, contrasts starkly with its purlieus.

I ask him what I always ask eminent old writers: do you ever go back and read your stuff?

"No, I seldom read them. Sometimes favorite passages. I'm sometimes delighted to find that I wrote as well as I did." He does not say this immodestly, just as a matter of fact.

He may not communicate with the dead, but Mr. Smith is given to an admirable filiopietism. He edited the letters of his cousin Adele Mali (Geneva Historical Society, 1979) on the centennial of her birth, and he seems the sort who always knows what the nieces and nephews are up to.

The homestead is now more a museum than a home, filled as it is with the furniture and artwork and gewgaws of a century and a half of Smiths. The family divested itself of the nursery business in the 1950s. Mr. Smith wrapped up the Walpole edition in 1982 with a five-volume index—"without a computer," he notes with pride.

Warren Hunting Smith turned eighty-seven in October. He admits to "excellent" general health, though a series of ailments has confined him largely to chair and bed. "My walking is pretty shaky, and it takes two people to hoist me to my feet," he says, but he still perambulates about the flowery family grounds.

And he paints. His most recent book, *Gentle Enthusiasts in Art* (Geneva Historical Society, 1986), honored the Sunday painters and amateur artists and sketching parties of his youth. In the Misses Elliots' day Geneva had been "a town where nearly everyone could at least sketch," and Mr. Smith, for one, does to this day.

He also still attends, when he can, Trinity Church, worshiphouse of the Elliots, towering Gothic redoubt of old Episcopal Geneva. When all is ashes and embers, Trinity Church will no doubt be left standing.

Only one close relative, a nephew, lives in Geneva. (There are cousins.) Most of the old ladies have fulfilled the prophecies of the actuaries. The Misses Elliots' "many-gabled cottage" was torn down long ago. "The site is an access area now to a college property," says Mr. Smith; "it has a walk across it and some ornamental planting." Better than a parking lot.

In a series of sketches titled *Originals Abroad* (Yale University Press, 1952), Smith wrote that his subjects "were not important people, to their contemporaries or to us; their lives were not exemplary. They were not the builders of the British Empire but merely citizens who went forth as witnesses to the infinite variety of the national individuality and character; Britain's reputation for vigor and originality came from the careers of just such spirited (if wayward) characters as these."

So, too, for Geneva. Whatever her current fortunes—and this bosky lakeside city of residences looks pretty damn good to a child of Upstate's Dresden—Geneva, at its acme, its brilliantly individualistic golden age, is preserved for us in the works of Warren Hunting Smith.

In a region in which "she's different" is the supreme put-down, Mr. Smith is our witty champion of idiosyncrasy. "Even the obscurest Genevans are somehow distinguished, and know how to live like individuals and not like a flock of sheep," he wrote six decades ago. In word and deed, Warren Hunting Smith is the quintessential Genevan.

The Oldest Living Novelist Tells All
Los Angeles Times Book Review, 1990

HENRY CLUNE, WHO WILL turn 101 years of age in February, has been chatting for two hours about old friends like Jack Johnson, Babe Ruth and Gypsy Rose Lee when talk turns to sales of his new book, *Souvenir and Other Stories* (James Brunner: $20; 218 pp.).

"It's lost all its momentum," he grouses. The first edition sold out of Rochester's largest store after a book-signing "that pretty near killed me," and a second printing is weeks away. "Very discouraging," he grumbles, and for a moment America's oldest working writer sounds like any neophyte novelist cursing his publisher.

For the better part of a century—from 1913 to 1969—Henry Clune wrote a popular column for his hometown paper, the Rochester *Democrat & Chronicle*. In his spare and slack time he wrote six novels and seven books on regional subjects. "I am a provincial by instinct, by design and by practice," he boasts, and he stands on what he stands for: Clune has lived in Rochester and the neighboring village of Scottsville for all but a few wanderlust years.

Clune is in remarkable shape for . . . well, for a man his age. "My hearing is defective—like everything else," he says, but his left ear isn't bad, and he can read, just barely, with an array of magnifying glasses. He enjoys an occasional martini and he still writes, mostly letters but now and then an essay or short story. He walks unaided; until his ninetieth year, he ran forty-yard wind sprints barefoot across his lawn every morning.

"I indulged the illusion that I was moving with speed and grace," he chuckles. "Years ago, the village doctor came up and told my wife I shouldn't do that anymore. The doctor died twenty years ago." (Clune's wife, the 1920 U.S. Olympic swimmer Charlotte Boyle, had died the week previous at the age of ninety-one. He remains alert and curious, but wonders "if I'll ever get over the death of my wife.")

Henry Clune was born in 1890, on the cusp of the Lost Generation. He came *before* Fitzgerald, Dos Passos, Hemingway, and Wolfe. Expatriatism never tempted him; although he did report, for a time, from the killing fields of Europe, the magnet of home was too strong. He was capable of saying, deadpan, "I liked London . . . but it wasn't Rochester."

At home, Clune presided over Rochester's literary solstice. He edited a short-lived journal that launched the careers of playwright George S. Brooks and a young Marjorie Kinnan Rawlings, who covered boxing and burlesque under the Clune-supplied pen name Lady Alicia Thwaite.

Clune's early novels grazed the bottom of the best-seller list, but luck deserted him at a couple of critical junctures. "I had a lot of near misses," he sighs. "I'd be wearing diamonds if I had all the stuff they told me I'd have."

His first novel, *The Good Die Poor* (1937), a picaresque newspaper tale, was purchased by Warner Brothers as a Bette Davis-Edward G. Robinson vehicle. The movie never was made. His next novel, the prescient political satire *Monkey on a Stick* (1940), was an amusing exercise, praised by Dawn Powell but otherwise forgotten.

Then came Clune's magnum opus. For years he had worked on a massive novel about a ruthless, steel-willed industrialist whose genius enriches a city and destroys its fusty Victorian social hierarchy. Clune called the novel, which was loosely based on the life of Rochester's George Eastman, *The Stars Have Monstrous Eyes*. His editor, Cecil Scott, renamed it *By His Own Hand*, an awful title better hung on some ponderous paperback with lumpish prose and an embossed cover.

"When I signed the contract at the Grosvenor Hotel," he recalls, "George Brett, the president of Macmillan, said, 'Mr. Clune, if you'll sign this contract we believe we've got the most popular success since *Gone With the Wind*.'"

Clune readied himself for a fame that never came. Orville Prescott of the *New York Times* ridiculed the book as "vulgar petty gossip," and though it went on to win qualified praise and sell 55,000 copies, it fell far short of Brett's promise.

In best auctorial fashion, Clune still bears Prescott a grudge. "It was a hatchet job," Clune says, and he thinks he knows the reason why: "One minor character says she was bored with boys telling her about a Psi U house party at Williams. Mr. Prescott was a Psi U at Williams."

Fortune also frowned upon Clune's fourth novel, *The Big Fella* (1956), which charts the rise and fall of a rapscallion political boss in a Northeastern city. When editor Scott was invalided with an eye infection, the book's publication was delayed three months. In the interim, Edwin O'Connor's *The Last Hurrah* appeared, and *The Big Fella*, one of the finer novels written about American politics, disappeared in O'Connor's shadow.

Clune's last two novels, *Six O'Clock Casual* (1960) and *O'Shaughnessy's Cafe* (1969), went virtually unnoticed. A Vietnam novel—sympathetic to the anti-war side, as befits this old America First isolationist—never found a publisher.

Back in print at 100, Henry Clune hasn't any grand illusions about *Souvenir* outselling *Gone With the Wind*. "I don't care" about the public's inattention, he avers. "I have no interest in that. I like two or three of the stories and I'm pleased to see them in print."

The best of *Souvenir*'s seven stories are portraits of people adrift in a world no longer theirs. The dowager queen of Rochester presides over an emptying salon; an octogenarian makes an eye-opening visit to a porno theater; an ex-con discovers that his daughter is irretrievably lost to him. Clune writes of the dowager: "It was the past in which she lived; the future had no meaning for her." Nor, for most of his characters, does the present.

When he tires of talking about his new book, Clune grabs a volume of Thomas Macaulay's essays from a table loaded high with Swift, Gilbert White, and Hemingway. He asks a visitor to read a favorite essay ("Mirabeau") aloud. Clune huddles close, his good left ear cocked.

"Isn't that beautiful?" he marvels at one limpid sentence. "Old as I am, I try to learn to write from Macaulay."

We discuss cherished authors for a while, and when John P. Marquand's name comes up, Clune, a trifle embarrassed, makes a confession. "In recent times I reread Marquand's *H. M. Pulham, Esquire*, and I dipped into *By His Own Hand* to see if it has anything comparable." He halts, grins. "Maybe there was."

Clune was never much good at literary politicking. He doubts that *Souvenir* will lead to a reassessment of his oeuvre, and he is loath to trade on the novelty value of his Methuselahan age. When local admirers suggested a public tribute for his 100th birthday, Clune scotched the idea. "They want you on display like the bearded woman in the Ringling show or the two-headed calf on the carnival lot."

Silent-screen hedonist Louise Brooks, a sometime friend of the novelist, used to call Clune "a goddamn bourgeois." He does not demur; indeed, his work ethic is a source of pride.

"I never had any great gifts," he says, overly modest, "but I could work. I try. If I had ten years more, I might do pretty well."

Review of *Samuel Hopkins Adams and the Business of Writing* (Syracuse University Press)

New York History, 2000

SAMUEL HOPKINS ADAMS—MUCKRAKER, HAMILTONIAN, chronic novelist, curmudgeonly regionalist—is covered by a "shroud of obscurity," according to his biographer Samuel V. Kennedy III. This neglect has deepened over the years despite (or perhaps because of) Adams's Stakhanovite output: the late sage of Owasco Lake makes his sister Upstater Joyce Carol Oates look as though she suffers from a protracted case of writer's block. Over the better part of a century, Adams published more than fifty novels and numberless magazine articles adding up to more than 10 million words. The contours of his career suggest that he was a particularly diligent hack—Kennedy commends his "readable prose," which is not quite extravagant praise—but Mr. Adams's regional works are of lasting value, and he lived with gusto and an admirable Auburn flair.

Samuel Hopkins Adams was born in Dunkirk in 1871 to a liberal Congregationalist minister and his evocatively named wife Hester, descendant of the Declaration-signing Stephen Hopkins. From his father Adams may have inherited a penchant for the easy cause favored by all Right-Thinking People: Sam Adams would spend a distressingly large portion of his career shooting at such barrel-filling fish as quack-medicine peddlers, fraudulent advertisers, and the Harding administration. But his grandfathers Adams and Hopkins fired the boy's imagination. The former, a Rochesterian, told tales of the Erie Canal, on which he once worked and in which Sam (nicknamed "Huck") and his cousins swam.

Grandfather Hopkins, of Auburn, though lacking the cachet of the canaller, introduced Sam and the cousinage to his friend Harriet Tubman, who sang "Go Down Moses" to the chillun and attended a matinee of *Uncle Tom's Cabin* with Sam's grandmother. Adams's recollection of Tubman, "A Slave in the Family," was later collected in *Grandfather Stories* (1955). As

Kennedy reveals, in 1945 *Reader's Digest* rejected this little gem for the department that ought to have been known as the "Most Unforgettable White Character I Have Met."

Adams attended Hamilton, where he raised hell and played on the college's first football team. ("Well do I remember Sam Adams," said *New York World* sports editor George Daley, a former Union halfback. "When he made a tackle, bones rattled and the arnica bottle was needed.") Upon graduation he left for the *New York Sun*, a Hamilton haven, and within a decade he was raking muck for *McClure's* and *Collier's*, taking on the beef trust, tuberculosis (which lacked for eloquent defenders), and, as a good Democrat, President Theodore Roosevelt, who snarled of Adams, "I do not regard him as a truthful man."

In 1905, Adams made his mark on American journalism with a six-part series in *Collier's* titled "The Great American Fraud." His exposure of the patent medicine industry, with its absurd claims for inedible syrups and alcohol-soaked panaceas, spurred the passage of the Pure Food and Drug Act.

The duality that runs throughout Upstate political history—earnest reformism on one hand, and demotic plainspokenness on the other—was embodied in Mr. Adams. He participated in the most ridiculous excesses of World War One propaganda, signing up as a "Four Minute Man" for George Creel's Committee on Public Information and slandering any pacifist, German-American, or socialist who had the temerity to question Mr. Wilson's war—and then in 1940 he joined the America First Committee, convinced that another world war would mean an end to American liberties. He supported prohibition—but once demon rum had been banished from freedom's land by constitutional amendment, he became a latitudinarian who told the *Cleveland Press* that his favorite hobby was "[w]atching my friends violate the Volstead Act."

Adams began writing fiction, confident that "there are only two basic plots: that for the adventure story of which mystery is an offshoot, and that for the love story." His torrential output earned middling reviews and occasionally brisk sales; under the pen name Warner Fabian he wrote the *succes de scandale Flaming Youth* (1923). At least twenty movies, silents and talkies, were made from Mr. Adams's stories and novels, and if most were dogs, Frank Capra did turn "Night Bus" into the smash *It Happened One Night*. (Star Claudette Colbert wrote a friend after shooting wrapped up, "I've just finished the worst picture in the world!")

After the Second World War, Mr. Adams turned largely to regional and juvenile fiction; *Canal Town* (1944), his enjoyable novel of Palmyra in the 1820s, can be found on most any used bookstore shelf in Upstate. He collected the stories of his forebears, particularly Grandfather Adams, into the charming *Grandfather Stories*, which may well be his most enduring work, and the book that keeps Adams in our hearts and minds for many years to come.

Adams and his second wife, the peppery Jane, who called her beloved "the little bastard" and "the old prune," made Wide Waters, their home beside Owasco Lake, the literary and martini-consuming capital of Central New York. Mr. Adams's ashes were spread over the lake upon his death in 1959, and though he has been forgotten by our often-amnesiac region, he is fortunate that Samuel V. Kennedy III, a neighbor boy from across the lake who attended Adams's memorial service forty-plus years ago, has produced a solid biography of our prolific native son.

Kennedy's subtitle is no mere afterthought: his book contains more details of Mr. Adams's advances, sales, royalties, and the usual writerly requests for loans than most non-accountant readers will care to know. But Kennedy has done well by Adams; he has atoned for ignoring the old man's advice to choose Hamilton over Cornell those many years ago. Let us hope that Kennedy's is the first flowering in a great efflorescence of Upstate biograpy: we have so many twentieth-century cultural and political figures (Henry W. Clune, Josephine Young Case, Carl Carmer, Barber B. Conable, Jr., Kenneth Keating, John Gardner) whose life stories have yet to be told. May Mr. Kennedy's book lead the way.

Vernon Parrington wrote of William Cullen Bryant, "He may not have been a great poet, but he was a great American." Whatever the verdict on the literary worth of Samuel Hopkins Adams, he was a great Upstater.

(John) Gardnering at Night
The American Conservative, 2008

How many of us share a hometown with our favorite writer? Anaïs Nin and Ayn Rand did, but I'm not talking about self-love. Since I wasn't born in West Point or Sauk Center or Baltimore or Henry County, I'm outta luck. But we play the hand we're dealt, which is why on a Saturday evening for the last dozen Octobers about twenty of us have gathered to read from the works of Batavia's John Gardner, the once prominent novelist whose audacious ambition was to reinfuse American literature with a moral purpose.

Gardner, one of the last American writers to grow up on a farm, was a hippie Republican anarchist who explained his politics to the *Atlantic*: "I am, on the one hand, a kind of New York State Republican, conservative. On the other hand, I am a kind of bohemian type. I really don't obey the laws. I mean to, but if I am in a hurry and there is no parking here, I park."

His best-known novel—the only one still read, as far as I can tell—is *Grendel* (1971), told from the Beowolfian monster's point of view. He set *The Resurrection* (1966) and *The Sunlight Dialogues* (1972) in our town, to which he dreamed of returning and finally did in a coffin, killed in a 1982 motorcycle accident. Here he is buried and remembered, even as English departments shoot him from the canon.

Our literary-culinary venue is the Pokadot, Gardner's favorite diner, the unselfconsciously funky eatery at the epicenter of the Italian-Polish southside. (Gardner, a Welsh Presbyterian, frequently teased his people for their anti-Italian-Catholic prejudices while sharing them: a neat way to have your *torta* and eat it too.) A middling speller, Gardner wrote his mother—a former English teacher—just before *The Sunlight Dialogues* came out boasting that in the book he had set a scene in the diner and spelled "Polkadot" correctly. Alas, in a nod, perhaps, to simplified spelling, the diner dispenses with that silent "l."

Pokadot readers have included Gardner's family and friends and people mentioned in his books, but most of us—teachers, a dairy salesman, our independent bookseller, and my wife, daughter, and I—know him only through the stories he wrote and the stories that are told about him still. (My dad, a few years behind him in school, said that Gardner was "weird.")

A few regulars sit at the counter and sip coffee, bemused by the proceedings—maybe even edified, I like to kid myself.

I read this year from Gardner's *Poems* (1978), which he prefaced by saying that "relatively little of this present assembly . . . is worth the life of a buttonwood tree." Not exactly an advertisement for himself.

He was a man of overwhelming regrets, as you would expect of someone who as an eleven-year-old boy dragged a cultipacker, hitched to the tractor he was driving, over his six-year-old brother's skull. What man wouldn't spend the rest of his life seeking nepenthe? (Gardner's best short story, "Redemption," is a barely fictionalized account of the accident and its aftermath.)

I closed with "Persimmons," in which he writes of being

> suddenly grieved over things long forgotten—
> the farm where I grew up, in New York State,
> where I paid no attention to all my father taught,
> so that now I cannot tell for sure a Baldwin
> from a Jonathan or some other breed of apple.

Learn your apples and listen to your fathers, I sententiously instructed the teenagers in the audience.

At evening's end, Leonard, a southside character, invited us all to step outside and drink with him from a bottle of Polka Dot Riesling, which he noted was $9.99 (minus a two-dollar rebate) at the liquor store. Why not? Gardner was a boozehound. Leonard poured the wine into coffee mugs and we helped him drink it.

Ellicott Street, home of the Pokadot, is undergoing reconstruction, and we of the anarchic (no officers, no dues, no rules, but somehow we survive) John Gardner Society have offered to install a polkadot bench blazoned with the word LOVE, the graffito that sets in motion *The Sunlight Dialogues*. The polkadot Batavia LOVE bench—bet no one does that for Updike or Bellow.

You know what? Gardner is not even among my hundred favorite American novelists. But he is ours. That is enough.

In "The Death of the Hired Man," Robert Frost wrote, "Home is the place where, when you have to go there, They have to take you in."

The literati against whom John Gardner railed have formed a circle to keep him out. That's okay. We are his home, and we take him in. Hell, we'll even read him, if it comes to that.

Harriet Tubman, in a Child's Eye
The American Enterprise, 2006

ARAMINTA ROSS, LATER KNOWN as Harriet Tubman and best remembered as Moses, the preternaturally wise conductor who never lost a passenger on the Underground Railroad, is perhaps the historical personage most familiar to the latest generation of American schoolchildren. The bare facts of her life—escape from slavery, daring raids to rescue other bondsmen from servitude, untimely fits of narcolepsy, service as a Union spy in South Carolina—are extraordinary, but most textbooks are too rigid and unimaginative to convey any sense of what Harriet Tubman was really like. If only a good novelist had known her, the reader murmurs. Well it just so happens . . .

Tubman made her home in Auburn, New York, on property that had belonged to Lincoln's Secretary of State and her ardent admirer, William Seward. And it was in Auburn, a generation removed from the War, that Harriet met a boy named Samuel Hopkins Adams, the fortunate son of a notably cultured Upstate family.

Young Adams had inherited an ample sense of self-worth from his grandsires, who were the subject of Adams's best book, *Grandfather Stories* (1955). As Adams told the tale, a "visiting New England lady" once accosted his paternal grandfather:

> "Adams? Adams? Do you claim kinship with the Boston Adamses?"
> "There is a Boston branch, I believe," he answered cautiously.
> "I refer to the Presidential Adamses," the lady said haughtily.
> "Ah! I was personally acquainted with the Honorable John Quincy Adams. A very respectable gentleman. He may well have been a connection of our line, though, being no brag-hard, he would naturally not press the claim."

The New York Sam Adams, too, would grow into a crusty character. When the forceful old boy was a forceful young boy, his days were not infrequently occupied by visits from "Aunt Harriet" Tubman. Sam's great-aunt,

Sarah Hopkins Bradford, had written a pair of books about Tubman, and it was because of Aunt Harriet that young Sam and his friends played slaves and overseers rather than cowboys and Indians.

Harriet Tubman would walk the two miles to Adams's maternal grandfather's house. Grandfather Hopkins would ask, "Harriet Tubman, will you sing for my grandchildren?" and after a modest demurral Harriet "would clap her stringy hands upon her bony knees, rock her powerful frame, snap her eyes," and sing "Go Down, Moses" in the same great baritone in which she once sang her song of deliverance to escaping slaves following the North Star.

The children, being children, would ask impertinent questions ("Show us your mark, Aunt Harriet") and she would reveal the scars left by the whip.

Harriet Beecher Stowe's dramatics left Harriet Tubman unimpressed: "When our grandmother once took her to a matinee of *Uncle Tom's Cabin*," Adams recalled, "she expressed approval of the theme but was critical of Eliza's escape across the ice, declaring the affair ill-managed and intimating that she could have handled it better."

"'Bloodhoun's!' she said disdainfully, eyeing the two disconsolate mastiffs who appeared in the role. 'I nevah made no min' of bloodhoun's.'" (Adams transcribed Tubman's remarks in her rich dialect, and while it may strike our ears as awkwardly anachronistic he also captures her in a way that later writers, hamstrung by p.c. etiquette, do not.)

Although her date of birth remains a mystery, Harriet Tubman lived close to if not beyond ninety years. She was a fixture about town, and often was seen sweeping clean the front yard of the Harriet Tubman Home, which her respectful neighbors in Auburn had endowed as a residence for indigent African Americans.

Tubman, one of the great heroines of our history, deserves better than mummification in dry textbooks. We are lucky that Samuel Hopkins Adams, the young novelist-to-be, never forgot her sly wit and superabundant humanity. When Sam and his cousins asked her, "Did you kill lots of people?" Aunt Harriet disappointed them by answering no.

"Why not?" they wondered.

"Whuffoh I want to kill folks?" replied Harriet Tubman. "Nobody nevah kill me."

Ten Years After a Place in Time
The American Conservative, 2013

THOMAS WOLFE, THE ADJECTIVAL Tar Heel, not the dandified Virginia expositor of *The Right Stuff*, philosophized in his execrably titled *You Can't Go Home Again* that "A man learns a great deal about life from writing and publishing a book."

He can say that again . . . and again. (I'll always love Wolfe, who meant a great deal to me when I was younger, but one of my favorite stories about the logorrheic author is that he prefaced the manuscript that became *Look Homeward, Angel* with an assurance that "I do not believe the writing to be wordy, prolix, or redundant.")

March 2013 marks the tenth anniversary of the simultaneous launching of the Iraq War and my memoirish tale of going home again (and what I found there), *Dispatches from the Muckdog Gazette*.

I guess there just wasn't enough space in the American attention span to accommodate both these events, so despite the best efforts of the good folks at Henry Holt, shock and awe hogged all the headlines. Those bastards Bush and Cheney—what infernal timing they have!

I did, however, learn a bit about life from that experience.

Honesty is not just the best but the only policy for a writer. As Thoreau counseled, "Say what you have to say, not what you ought. Any truth is better than make-believe." Given that this book's subject was my hometown of Batavia, New York, there was no way to be honest without bruising feelings. To have been cautious or solicitous would have caused severe anemia and crashing boredom.

A month or so before publication I came down with the usual auctorial premonitions of disaster. There was a good deal of anticipation around town surrounding publication, to which my reaction was "Holy Crow—people here are actually going to *read* this." What, I wondered, was the modern equivalent of being run out of town on a rail?

For in *Dispatches*, I treated with wit (half-wit, if you don't like it) and gleeful scatter-sprayed invective the ethno-religious conflicts that once rived—and, in a way, fortified—my town. As a typical American mongrel, with mixed bloodlines and a shambling sympathy for all sides of the American divide, I claimed an exemption from oppressive sensitivity codes. I wrote about the faded WASP ruling class from the point of view of the once-déclassé Italian and Irish Catholics, and I wrote about the latter from the p.o.v. of the former. After all, I'm dago, mick, limey, kraut, papist, Prot . . . that's a pretty wide free-fire zone.

Wolfe described "with bitter chagrin" the reception of *Look Homeward, Angel* (1929) by his hometown of Asheville, North Carolina. The vitriol fell like acid rain. But then Wolfe had fled North Carolina for exile in the Vampire City.

He wrote of a tormentor:

"One venerable old lady, whom I had known all my life, wrote me that although she had never believed in lynch law, she would do nothing to prevent a mob from dragging my 'big overgroan karkus' across the public square."

I heard through the grapevine of—mercifully few—people who were offended by my Italian jokes. (My Stella lineage provided insufficient protection—but then my grandmother always said we were "northern Italian, almost Swiss.") From the other side, I was taken to task by the octogenarian grande dame of our city, who had grown up in pre-sprawl Long Island and still sounded like it.

She confronted me after a concert at St. James Episcopal Church. "I'm baaah-lee speaking to you," she announced.

Wolfe-like, I had known my venerable critic since I was a boy. I threw my hands up in mock surrender.

"Sorry . . . sorry," I stammered, certain that I knew the source of her displeasure: my raillery about upper-crust Protestants.

"How *could* you say that I have an ox-cent?" she asked in her inimitable accent.

I laughed. "Is that all?"

"Yes. And why must you use so much profanity?"

I acknowledged my literary Tourette's. Within the month she was speaking to me again. As I write this she is ninety-two and we're still pals.

Various outlets sold upwards of 800 copies of the book in Batavia—an extraordinary number for a rural working-class burg of 15,000 souls. As for sales in the rest of the good old USA . . . I blame Bush.

I had used as an epigraph this line from Sinclair Lewis's *Cass Timberlane*: "To its fugitive children, Grand Republic will forgive almost anything, if they will but come back home."

You *can* go home again. And if they'll forgive me, they'll forgive anyone.

My Marlboro Man
The American Conservative, 2011

I RECENTLY HAD LUNCH with my favorite model. Nah, not Cheryl Tiegs, pin-up girl of many a 1970s lad, but Bill Clune, the fittest-looking eighty-five-year old since—well, since his dad, who lived to a hale 105.

Bill rode the whirlwind for a decade, 1955–65, as perhaps the highest-paid male model in America. He worked with the chichi photographers of the day: Irving Penn, Richard Avedon, Mark Shaw, Frank Scavullo (whom success renamed Francesco). Bill was television's first Marlboro Man, though he struck his cowboy pose sitting atop a split-rail fence in the Elliot Unger Elliot Studio on West 54th Street, five thousand martinis east of the lonesome prairie.

Bill had pedigree. His father, Henry W. Clune, was the star of Frank Gannett's Rochester newspaper and a novelist praised by the likes of Dawn Powell. His mother, Charlotte, daughter of adventurer Joe "King of the Klondike" Boyle, swam the 100-meter freestyle for the 1920 U.S. Olympic team at Antwerp.

Their son, however, was floundering. He'd been fired from his weekend Rochester DJ job—spinning "Clune's Tunes"—after a mike caught him uttering mild profanities during a Mutual Network religious program. That was probably the last time Lady Luck rejected Bill Clune.

At loose ends in 1953, he climbed into his 1941 Ford and with $100 in his pocket drove to New York City. Reversing that tired Frank Sinatra song, Bill figured that if he couldn't make it in Rochester, he may as well take Manhattan.

A friend introduced him to John W. Harkrider, who had directed the 1929 Flo Ziegfield extravaganza *Glorifying the American Girl*. Harkrider, whom Bill remembers as a "nut box," got him a job posing as a rapist for Howell Conant in *True Detective*. Bottom's barrel was being scraped, but Bill was on his way. (So was Conant, who would be Grace Kelly's palace photographer.)

Soon, Clune's long-nosed handsome mug was all over the place: *Harper's Bazaar, Mademoiselle, Esquire, Vogue, Life, The Saturday Evening*

Post. He had the outdoor look prized by Marlboro, which had been a lady's cigarette—its motto was "Mild as May"—until undergoing phalloplasty on Madison Avenue. (Bill was a stranger to the demon weed, so he spent the weekend preceding the Marlboro shoot gagging his way through a self-taught smoking tutorial.)

Hearst columnist Dorothy Kilgallen gushed, "Flicker scouts are excited about the male model of the moment—Bill Clune. He's the son of a Rochester newspaperman, and the experts think he may be another John Wayne." Patrick Wayne was closer to the mark, though you can glimpse Bill as the coalmine owner in Martin Ritt's cave-in *The Molly Maguires*.

Bill surveys his career with a charmingly wide-eyed wonder. Did he dislike anyone? "Dorian Leigh," he spits out, suggesting that the author of the autobiography *The Girl Who Had Everything* didn't. He also cites Millie Perkins, the New Jersey model who played the mysterious woman in Monte Hellman's 1967 cult western *The Shooting*: "God she was nasty."

Bill bought the farm in 1958: a Greek Revival farmhouse and eighty acres in Livingston County, New York, where he raised ducks and pigs and cattle and chickens. On Saturdays, he and his wife would "hop in the car and go driving looking for real people because the rest of the week I was living in an unreal world."

Look magazine ran a four-page profile titled "The Double Life of a Farmer" in which Bill was depicted riding a tractor, oiling a hay cutter, sitting in a hayloft, and otherwise modeling the agrarian life. His wife was pictured aiming a .22 at something—maybe a woodchuck, but quite possibly at Bill, who was a chronically unfaithful husband. He lost the farm when he lost his wife.

Bill's friend Colin Fox, the British sailor who donned an eye-patch as the Hathaway Shirt man, once was asked how people respond when they find out he's a male model. "Contempt," Fox replied. "This is usually followed by envy. They're thinking: 'Look at that conceited imbecile, making all that money just for smirking into a camera.'"

Yet Bill muses that his experience flip-flopped the stereotypes. Life on the farm is thought to be all honest toil and the world of high fashion a pit of glamorous decadence. But he greatly admired the work ethic of the best models and photographers, and he was puzzled to receive checks from Uncle Sam paying him for not growing corn or wheat. Sometimes the focus is hard to find.

Bill works still, his plummy voice much in demand for voice-overs. He's also peddling a memoir: the story of how Boy Scout virtues—be punctual, helpful, friendly—and a prodigious heterosexual appetite kept him plenty busy in the *Mad Men* age.

The Loneliness of the Long-Dissonant Reader

The American Conservative, 2010

In *A Tragic Honesty*, his biography of Richard Yates, Blake Bailey describes a scene sure to send a there-but-for-the-grace-of-God shiver down the spine of any writer who has ever approached a podium, book in hand, straining to hear the sound of one hand clapping:

> That winter he was invited to give a reading at the University of Massachusetts (Boston), but not a single person showed up. He sat in the silent lecture hall while his two sponsors gazed at their watches; finally Yates suggested they adjourn to a bar. He didn't seem particularly surprised.

Poor Yates. But then that's what he gets for agreeing to do a reading. Authors with functioning a-hole detectors—admittedly, most need new batteries—understand that humiliation is a lurking presence at any public appearance, and when Kate Winslet finally wants to meet you, it's long after you're dead.

My Batavia homeboy John Gardner, no slouch himself in the adjourning to the bar department, told an interviewer, "In those days I would wear a crushed velvet robe—I'm shameless, right!—with a huge silver chain. I felt that every time I did a reading I was cheating the people because they came hoping for something very exciting. I wanted them to think that their five dollars or seven dollars or whatever was worthwhile. So I wore this robe, so that when they went home, at least they could say, 'I went to the most boring reading in history, but, boy, did that guy dress funny!'"

As luck would have it, my crushed velvet robe doesn't fit me anymore, so I have no such sartorial fallback when I do a reading. If I'm desperate enough I wear the tie that helped me earn second place in a Marcello Mastroianni lookalike contest. (You can imagine what the other guys must have looked like.)

POETRY NIGHT AT THE BALLPARK

John Gardner had an ample hambone; like Allen Ginsberg omming and howling his way through an evening's verse, he probably was incapable of boring an assembly, even one of Yatesian sparseness.

I've never quite addressed a vacant room—usually a few stragglers happen by, or if it's a local talk at least my family fills in a row of seats—but I once was the only pair of ears at a reading by a fine poet. He was embarrassed, I was embarrassed, but he read a couple of poems with a winningly defiant abashment and then we had a good long chat that solidified a friendship. One sympathetic reader (or auditor) is all you really need.

Colleges and universities can guarantee any writer an audience, as long as a professor dangles the carrot of "extra credit" in front of enough grade-grubbing students. Other venues are dicier. Before I spoke at a political rally an incredulous member of the crowd, scanning the roster of speakers, asked the organizer, "You mean this guy's gonna stand there and read a book?"

Well, uh, yeah, the organizer replied.

"You gotta be fuckin' kidding!"

Not even the crushed velvet robe could have saved me then.

There is a going-down-with-the-ship nobility in playing to an empty house, or lecturing to a listener-less lyceum. In the summer of 1979 I saw Gang of Four play in a Buffalo bar to an audience of eight people, one of whom kept drunkenly yelling "REO Speedwagon." Talk about driving home the lyric "At home he feels like a tourist"! Yet the band thrashed about as if their lives were at stake that night. I don't give a damn if Gang of Four were art-school Maoists; they exhibited the spirit of Joe DiMaggio's explanation of why he hustled in what seemed to be a meaningless game: "There is always some kid who may be seeing me for the first or last time. I owe him my best."

And so here is where I offhandedly mention that I'm giving a mercifully brief talk—I won't call it a "reading," lest I invite the curse of Yates—on Thursday, July 29, at seven p.m. at Lift Bridge Books in Brockport, New York, a great indie store located a stone's throw from that first and most romantic infernal improvement, the Erie Canal. The subject is my latest, *Bye Bye, Miss American Empire* (how's that for a wishful thinking title?), which is bound for glory or the remainder bin, you guess which. In deference to Gang of Four, I won't fill your head with culture, and I won't give myself an ulcer.

The Utica Club
The American Conservative, 2013

SHORTLY AFTER ENTERING WEDDED bliss a quarter-century ago, my wife, a Los Angelena, told me that she wanted to see two cities: Utica and Cleveland.

I, as is my wont, made her dreams come true.

This fall I had the good luck to revisit the literary capital of the Mohawk Valley twice in a matter of weeks. First I spoke at Utica College, under the aegis of the school's Ethnic Heritage Studies Center and the Alexander Hamilton Institute, in a celebration of Utica and her faithful literary son, Eugene Paul Nassar. Upstate New York literature maven Frank Bergmann and Hamilton College history professor Bob Paquette arranged the event, which afforded me the great pleasure of meeting Gene Nassar. (As a biographer of the Anti-Federalist Luther Martin, who despised the nationalist Hamilton and defended his murderer Aaron Burr, I got a real kick out of the Alexander Hamilton imprimatur.)

My other Utica venture was to pay homage at the Forest Hill Cemetery to Harold Frederic, novelist and bigamist, whose story "The Copperhead" I adapted for a film to be released this spring. Details—and Oscars, surely—to follow.

Every small American city deserves a Gene Nassar. Mr. Nassar grew up among the Lebanese Christians of East Utica. As an adult, he established himself as a noted scholar of such poets as Wallace Stevens and Ezra Pound while remaining rooted in the old neighborhood as a professor at Utica College and historian of his city, which he loves, sins and blemishes too, with the ardor of a native son.

Utica was once a baseball rival of Batavia's in the New York-Penn League, and I like to think that the minor-league qualities of such cities—their intimate scale, the blending of the homely and the idiosyncratic, their unexpected tolerance of eccentricity—are the true soul of America. And of baseball. The majors are built on home runs and TV timeouts and twenty-dollar parking fees. To hell with 'em. To hell with the Empire, too.

The glory and richness of America come not from its weaponry or wars, which debase us as much if not more than the relentlessly vulgar and witless products rolling off the entertainment industry's assembly line. Rather, our numen is found in our regions, our little places, the unseen America beyond the ken of our placeless rulers.

A national culture exists only if fed by a thousand and one local, particularistic streams. American culture without Utica and her sister cities is ... what? Ke$ha? Katie Couric? *Entertainment Tonight?*

William T. Coggeshall, state librarian of Ohio (and later a Lincoln bodyguard), explained three years before the War came that "It is not enough ... that a national literature exists. It is required of a nation, which combines wide differences of characteristics, that each shall have its own representation. A Republic of letters may be a confederacy of individualities, [just as] a Republic in politics may be a confederacy of States."

Before any potent or meaningful decentralist political movement develops in this country, we're going to have to rediscover the places in which we live. We have to remember *why* we love our country—and the reason isn't that "We're Number One!" or that we can sprawl out on the couch chanting "USA! USA!" as the bombs drop and the televised chickenhawks cackle.

That isn't patriotism. It isn't even a parody of patriotism. It's an allegiance to ... nothing.

America, the myth goes, is a land of perpetual motion, of restless pioneers striking out for the West, or in our time, of restive television addicts lighting out for Las Vegas, with the mini-set in the SUV playing "Two and a Half Men" DVDs so that unlike the Joads, members of this fambly don't have to talk to one another. We are, supposedly, always moving, never stopping, consumed by what William Cullen Bryant called "the vain low strife that makes men mad."

And yet the best American writers—even those who follow their characters on rafts down the Mississippi, even those who write books titled *On the Road* or *You Can't Go Home Again*—are almost always attached to a *place*. Not a home page, but a real, individuated place that is different from any other place on earth: Sarah Orne Jewett in South Berwick, Maine. Sinclair Lewis in Minnesota. Wendell Berry in Henry County, Kentucky. Thoreau in Concord.

The regionalist impulse in American letters is greater now than at any time since the mid-1930s. Backwoods New England. Romantic North Dakota. East Utica. Writers are looking homeward. Standing on what they stand for, as Edward Abbey used to say. Only good can come of this. The Little America ain't dead yet.

The Last Picture Show
The American Conservative, 2011

ANOTHER SUMMER HAS SLIPPED away, he said in melancholic stupor. Thank God for the hardy perennials, led off by our baseball Muckdogs, who finished below .500, but who really cares about the score as long as one hears the crack of bat and sees the flash of glove? The game as gathering place is the thing.

For the second year, our daughter Gretel conducted a series of video interviews for thebatavian.com with the ballplayers, a likably cocksure lot. Her toughest question—"What's your favorite book?"—provoked one relief pitcher to respond, with boastful incredulity, "Yeah—like I *read*."

For those who do read, we finally installed a memorial bench this summer for Batavia's native son, the novelist John Gardner (*Grendel, October Light*). It's purple and yellow and sits outside the Pokadot, our unselfconsciously funky southside diner. Next time you're scudding along the New York State Thruway, Governor Dewey's soulless reprise of the Erie Canal, stop off at our fair town, grab a beef on weck at the Pokadot, and sit yourself down on the Gardner bench, which marks the literary-culinary epicenter of New York. (Elaine's and the White Horse Tavern are for poseurs.)

Hereabouts 'twas also a season of funerals, including two for nonagenarian great-uncles of mine: Uncle Johnny, an Italian who made the best dago-red wine that ever soused a toper, and Uncle Joe, the suave shortstop on the best town-ball team the tiny hamlet of Lime Rock ever fielded. How many times those dear men made me laugh....

I also lost a friend who dwelt in that most sleepless precinct of the demiworld, the outskirts of fame. I wrote several months ago about Bill Clune, the highest-paid male model of the Mad Men age. Bill's twin brother, Peter, an actor, died at age eighty-five this past July.

Peter was a raconteur, a wit (especially in the sense that a wit is someone who laughs at my jokes), the most prodigious consumer of gin this side of Nick and Nora, and a bon vivant who could take and keep a scunner—to use one of his novelist father's favorite words—as fiercely as any man I have known. Peter once angrily returned a Christmas card to us because my sloppy penmanship had obscured his middle initial (H) on the envelope. In the annals of Peter H. stories, this was virtually anodyne.

Yet Peter, unlike that relief pitcher, *read*. His father, Henry, had met or corresponded with a range of literary eminences, and Peter would refer with a respect bordering on awe to Mr. Maugham, Mr. O'Hara, Mr. (Samuel Hopkins) Adams, and their works. He paid genuine deference to talent, and so it nagged at him that in looking back upon his own career on stage and screen his accomplishments seemed few and paltry. They weren't, mind you, but theater performances are ephemeral. He insisted that he had been good in off-Broadway productions of *Born Yesterday* and *A View from the Bridge*, but how were we to know? The flickering images of Peter that endure consist of scattered B movies that range from dreadful to unlocatable (*Blue Sextet, Juke Box Racket, Dirtymouth*).

The first VHS release in which he had a sizable role was *Stigma* (1972), a lesser work of the soft-core/hard-gore auteur David (*I Drink Your Blood*) Durston. Peter, playing opposite the black guy from *Miami Vice*, is a New England sheriff who cheerfully spreads VD across his debauched domain. It's an infra dig role in a claptrap movie, and I didn't have the heart even to kid him about it.

But Peter had one brush with cinematic quality: *Blast of Silence* (1961), a low-budget, bleak film-noir much prized by connoisseurs of the genre, which recently was released as a Criterion Collection DVD and featured on Netflix. Peter, playing as always against his Hill School upbringing, portrays a low-life mob boss targeted for a hit. The assassin studies Peter's photo as the hardboiled narrator growls, "You know the type . . . a mustache to hide the fact that he has lips like a woman. The kind of face you hate." (In fact he had a big, beefy, drinker's face, neither feminine nor hateful, but a scenarist will have his license.)

I sometimes mused about organizing a Peter H. film festival for his friends, or at least that fraction thereof with which he was on speaking terms at any given time. Between *Blast of Silence*, the Italian gangster film *Anastasia Mio Fratello*, and various TV episodes, we'd have had three rollicking, gin-soaked evenings. Peter would've enjoyed the hell out of that.

It's the things we never do that we regret.

AT THE MOVIES

"That theme prevailed in all—except two—of my future films. It was the rebellious cry of the individual against being trampled to an ort by massiveness—mass production, mass thought, mass education, mass politics, mass wealth, mass conformity."

—FRANK CAPRA

Muskets and Misfires: The Revolutionary War on Film

Wall Street Journal, 2000

THE MAN WHO MADE Scottish nationalism bankable in *Braveheart* brandishes a thirteen-starred flag like a flintlock in the ubiquitous advertisements for what may be this summer's blockbuster: Mel Gibson's *The Patriot*. The movie, which opens later this month, is being sold as Mad Max fights the Revolutionary War.

Whether hit or flop, *The Patriot*'s very existence is a pleasant anomaly, for Hollywood has set more films in postnuclear holocaust wastelands than in the America of the 1770s. On those rare occasions when the War for Independence—or most any other episode from our eminently filmable history—has made the screen, it has been rendered risible.

The early moguls might be forgiven their timidity, for they were mindful of the remarkable case of Robert Goldstein. California native Goldstein was a costume supplier who had outfitted the cast of D.W. Griffith's *Birth of a Nation*. Bitten by the epic bug, Goldstein produced his one and only movie: *The Spirit of '76*, a lavish melodrama of the American Revolution that had the misfortune to open in May 1917, one month after the U.S. had entered—on the British side—Woodrow Wilson's war to end all wars.

Trying to tap into what he called a "Yankee Doodle, Wave the American Flag" vein, Goldstein filled his movie with stirring tableaux: Paul Revere's Ride, Washington at Valley Forge, Patrick Henry bellowing "Give me liberty or give me death." Several scenes depicted British soldiers killing Americans, as allegedly happened during the Revolution.

After its Los Angeles premiere, federal agents seized the movie. Goldstein was arrested for violating the Espionage Act. A federal court ruled, in a case deliciously titled *United States v. The Spirit of '76* , that the film could so "excite or inflame the passions of our people . . . that they will be deterred from giving that full measure of cooperation, sympathy, assistance and sacrifice which is due to Great Britain . . . as an ally of ours."

Goldstein was sentenced to ten years in prison, served three, and exited a broken man, embittered, impoverished, and a touch mad. His pathetic example was a cautionary tale right out of, well, Hollywood—and the industry noticed.

D.W. Griffith was not to make the same mistake as his costumer. In Griffith's *America* (1924), the Anglophilic director made his villain an American, the ruthless loyalist Capt. Walter Butler, whose band of Tories and Indians was notorious for its savagery. Robert W. Chambers, scenarist of *America*, emphasized that his intent was to remind Americans and Englishmen of our "common origin and of a common ideal and purpose." This trans-Atlantic lovefest flopped.

John Ford's first color film, *Drums Along the Mohawk* (1939), was based on Walter D. Edmonds's best-selling novel of the Revolution as fought in upstate New York's Mohawk Valley. War clouds were again gathering in Europe, and the filmmakers took Goldstein's lesson to heart: The enemies in *Drums Along the Mohawk* are redmen, not redcoats.

Settlers Henry Fonda and Claudette Colbert are harassed by eyepatch-wearing John Carradine and a band of marauding Mohawks. Fonda is lank and convincing in yet another of his American archetype roles. (His daughter Jane's unfulfilled ambition was to act with dad and brother Peter in a movie about the Revolutionary War.) Colbert, on the other hand, is ludicrous as a frontier wife who seems to be never far from a manicurist. The sight of her cradling a musket is one of those utterly incongruous moments—like Elton John singing "Saturday Night's All Right for Fighting"—that redeem pop culture.

The film's commitment to historical veracity was summed up by producer Darryl Zanuck: "We do not want to make a picture portraying the revolution in the Mohawk Valley." (More than fifty years later, I asked novelist Edmonds what he thought of Ford's adaptation. "I didn't like it very much," he said, politely.)

The "Golden Age" of Hollywood ignored the Revolution, as it did almost all of U.S. history. As Gore Vidal has written of his boyhood, "I recall no popular films about Washington or Jefferson or Lincoln the president." Shays' Rebellion, the Erie Canal, abolitionists and secessionists, titans of industry and Wobblies: So much of our history has never made the movies.

When America's war-birth was finally brought to the screen once more, it was by Brit Hugh Hudson in *Revolution* (1985), which may be the most grievously miscast film ever made. Perhaps atoning for the long-overlooked role of Sicilian-Americans in the Revolution, Hudson cast Al Pacino as a curiously accented New York trapper whose headstrong son leads him into the Continental Army. When Mr. Pacino tells his boy about a battle fought "unda da Brooklyn Heights," we can almost hear the thud of Joe Pesci's brass knuckles on the face of one of King George's grenadiers. (Redcoats, beware: don't mess with Yankee wiseguys.)

Equally miscast is Nastassja Kinski as the rebellious daughter of simpering Tory aristocrats. No matter how many bulky coats she wears as she makes her appointed patriot rounds, Kinski exudes a vampiric sexuality; she makes Claudette Colbert look like Ma Joad.

Revolution has the pacing of a Valley Forge winter, though it might have worked with a less ridiculous cast. In a nice touch out of Goldstein, the British, led by Donald Sutherland, are presented as effete sadists. Providing an "is that really her?" moment of eye-popping incredulity is singer Annie Lennox of the Eurythmics as "Liberty Woman." Sweet dreams, assuredly, are *not* made of these.

Kinski, Lennox, Colbert, the Englishman Howard Gaye as the American hero of *The Spirit of '76*: Films about our Revolution have usually featured foreign hams. Mel Gibson, though raised in Australia, was at least born in Peekskill, New York, on the strategically critical Hudson River. However, *The Patriot*'s director, Roland Emmerich, is German; his discredits include the witless and hardly patriotic *Independence Day*.

If *The Patriot* is a hit, we may yet see the rumored production of David Hackett Fischer's marvelous study *Paul Revere's Ride*. (With Hugh Grant as the midnight rider?) The travestying of Mr. Fischer's book was prefigured by Alan Alda's charming *Sweet Liberty* (1986). Mr. Alda plays a writer who watches as Hollywood vulgarizes his novel of the Revolution, most memorably in the lissome form of Michelle Pfeiffer as a foul-mouthed sexpot personating a demure goodwoman. When, a decade later, Demi Moore oozed Pilgrim pulchritude in *The Scarlet Letter*, bad art imitated movie life yet again.

The problem facing twenty-first-century moviemakers is that the standard villains of Revolutionary War films—pro-British Indians and campy periwigged British officers—are protected cinematic species in this age of *Dances With Wolves* and the Gay and Lesbian Alliance Against Defamation. Mel Gibson has exhibited a praiseworthy independence, but for most of Hollywood, our Founding presents an insuperable dramatic obstacle: There are no good guys. The all-purpose villains of today's mass-media culture—working-class white men with guns—are, after all, the ones who fought and won the Revolution.

How Not to Watch *Copperhead*: A Reply to Sidney Blumenthal

The American Conservative, 2013

I'VE BEEN WRITING BOOKS for twenty-five years now—I'm sure that silver anniversary festschrift is just around the corner—and I never reply to critics. I've had my say between the covers; let the reviewer have her say. Besides, life is too short and precious for squabbling with strangers. But Sidney Blumenthal's claim in the *Atlantic* that Ron Maxwell's film *Copperhead*, for which I wrote the screenplay, is "propaganda for an old variation of the neo-Confederate Lost Cause myth" is nonsense. (As recently as 2005 the *Atlantic*'s erstwhile literary editor, the great Benjamin Schwarz, was recommending my work to readers. Time doth fly.)

Mr. Blumenthal is so busy burning strawmen that he misses the point of the movie (and even misreports the ending, which he must not have seen). *Copperhead* does not reargue the Civil War, nor is it about the antiwar movement in the North. It measures the impact of the war on the Corners, one small settlement in Upstate New York. Abner Beech, the title character, does not even consider himself a Copperhead; he is, rather, an old-fashioned Jefferson-Jackson agrarian Upstate New York Democrat. (In contrast with the Democratic Party in New York City, the Upstate Democracy contained a large and noble faction that had long sought to bar slavery from the territories and limit the power of the slavocracy.)

The movie is about the effect of war on a community. It is about the way that wars tear families apart. It is about the challenge of loving one's neighbor. And it is about dissent, which is never exactly in robust condition in the land of the free.

Copperhead is based on a novella by Harold Frederic, who is not quite as obscure as Blumenthal believes him to be.

Harold Frederic, born in 1856, was a native of Utica, which though it is the eighth largest city in New York can fairly stake a claim to being, pound for pound, the literary capital of the state. Frederic lived a short but full—perhaps overly full—life. In brief, he began his career as a Utica and later Albany newspaper editor, in which capacity he was celebrated as a wit and bon vivant. He was a good friend of fellow Upstater and U.S. President Grover Cleveland, whose Jeffersonian Democratic political convictions Frederic shared. He left his native grounds—for good—in 1884 to become a *New York Times* foreign correspondent based in London. Between 1886 and his death in 1898, he published more than a dozen books, most famously *The Damnation of Theron Ware* (1896), a tale of a simple Upstate Methodist minister's loss of faith which is widely considered a masterpiece of late-nineteenth-century American realism. (F. Scott Fitzgerald called *The Damnation of Theron Ware* "the best American novel" written before 1920—the same year, coincidentally, that *This Side of Paradise* was published.)

The Copperhead—its title taken from the derisive serpentine epithet applied to Northern critics of the Civil War—was serialized in *Scribner's Magazine* in 1893 and published in book form that same year. The novel, or novella, or longish short story, as you prefer, would reappear in several collections of Frederic's fiction, most notably in *The Civil War Stories of Harold Frederic*, under the imprint of Syracuse University Press and with an introduction by Edmund Wilson.

In every incarnation it sold poorly, as Frederic's work usually did. But then *The Copperhead*, as with his other stories of the Civil War, hit none of the expected notes. It catered neither to "Battle Hymn of the Republic" Northern righteousness nor "Dixie" Southern romanticism.

Edmund Wilson, our greatest literary critic and a denizen of that magical literary ground surrounding Frederic's Utica, wrote that Frederic's "stories of New York during the Civil War reflect the peculiar mixture of patriotism and disaffection which was characteristic of that region. . . . Due to this, these stories differ fundamentally from any other Civil War fiction I know, and they have thus a unique historical as well as a literary importance."

There is an unblinking, unsentimental honesty to *The Copperhead*, as well as Frederic's other stories of the War. The fanfare and spangles, the soaring rhetoric and battlefield heroism: you'll find none of that on his York State homefronts. We are shown, instead, a little world pockmarked, drained of life, even, by what—and who—is absent. Young men leave communities of which they are essential pieces. Some return intact but irreparably altered; some stagger home shattered; others make the trip back in pine boxes. The normal rhythms of courtship are disrupted. The interdependence of small farms, crossroads shops, and little Protestant churches is unraveled, and we are given to understand that things will never be the same.

Stephen Crane, whose own *The Red Badge of Courage* is commonly regarded as the great American Civil War novel, said of Frederic's Civil War tales that they illumed "the great country back of the line of fight—the waiting women, the lightless windows, the tables set for three instead of five." This was the side of war that is most immediate for Americans yet which seldom interests our artists, let alone our politicians: The war at home. The domestic consequences of our crusades.

Frederic said that he based his Civil War stories on "my own recollections of the dreadful time—the actual things that a boy from five to nine saw and heard about him, while his own relatives were being killed, and his school-fellows orphaned, and women of his neighborhood forced into mourning and despair—and they had a right to be recorded"—however inconvenient these memories may be.

Typically, in a story of a dissenter, the author flatters himself and the audience. The deck is stacked; the cards are marked. Every right-thinking reader or viewer is confident that of course he or she would be at the side of this poor recusant who is being persecuted by narrow-minded peasants or by clerics who deny that the earth revolves 'round the sun or that man is a product of evolution or that the earth is older than six thousand years or that witches should not be hanged. But really: is there anything easier than standing—at a very safe distance of years—with Galileo or Scopes or the martyrs of Salem?

Harold Frederic does not let the reader bask in his own sanctimony. It's so easy to say that you're for free speech; that you honor the First Amendment; that though you may not agree with so and so who says such and such, you'll defend to the death his right to say it. Well, here's Abner Beech, an Upstate New York farmer of 1862. He thinks this war between the states—this hallowed war, this bloodletting out of which modern America was born—is an unconstitutional atrocity. He despises the soon-to-be martyred Abraham Lincoln, who by most twenty-first-century lights is the greatest American hero. Abner stands up and speaks his piece—his peace—during time of war.

Okay, Mr. Free Speech. Are you willing to defy the mob and defend Abner?

It's not so easy.

Copperhead is a subversive film. Its subverts narrative convention: Jee Hagadorn, the abolitionist who is absolutely right about the central question of the age, slavery, is a God-is-on-our-side zealot who has transformed a political/moral cause into an abstraction, thereby losing sight of those things nighest unto him—that never happens in real life, huh? The film's concerns—peace, community, rural Christianity, dissent—could hardly be more relevant in our age of placelessness, perpetual war, and the surveillance state.

In *Copperhead*, the abolitionist Esther (who with her pacifist brother is the moral center of the movie) suggests to the Irish farmhand and Copperhead Hurley that maybe poetry is more important than politics. I believe that; Jee and Abner, the abolitionist and the antiwar Democrat antagonists, do not.

Jee is of course right about slavery. If that were the only issue it'd be a pretty clear case of right and wrong. But that's *not* the only issue. From Abner's point of view, there's also the U.S. Constitution, which is being stretched and violated by things like the suspension of habeas corpus, the closing down of antiwar newspapers, and, ultimately, the draft, which many Democrats saw, ironically, as a form of slavery. And there's also the not-so-small matter—which is, bizarrely, often an afterthought—of 700,000 dead Americans. Millions of mothers and fathers, brothers and sisters, wives and girlfriends, have their lives shattered. The communities of which these young men are members are broken apart. From our distance of 150 years we accept this with equanimity; you can't make an omelette without breaking a few eggs, and they'd have died of something eventually anyway. But I find the enormous death toll a real obstacle to viewing this war as something glorious and wonderful. (Many of the slain were uneducated rural men and thus beneath the notice of moderns, but still, *seven hundred thousand*?)

I was born in (and repatriated to) the cradle of abolitionism, the Burned-Over District of Upstate New York. The Liberty Party was born a few miles down the road from me. My heroes include the abolitionists of the 1830s–'50s, brave men and women whose strategies of moral suasion and the passage of Personal Liberty Laws (defiance of the Fugitive Slave Acts) promoted the peaceful abolition of slavery. The great moral and political failure of American history is our failure to have freed the slaves not only many decades earlier but without bloodshed.

Yet if these early abolitionists are my ancestors, so are the antiwar Democrats, who upheld the Bill of Rights against Republican assaults, and so are the old Whigs who tried desperately to keep the union together. Like Whitman, we contain multitudes: Frederick Douglass and Robert E. Lee, Gerrit Smith and Horatio Seymour and Harriet Beecher Stowe . . . as an American, how are all these men and women not a part of me? Of us?

I write every day with a photo of Eugene V. Debs tacked to the wall on my left. Debs, the leading American socialist of the early twentieth century and, more importantly, a faithful citizen of Terre Haute, Indiana, was America's most famous martyr to wartime speech. In the photo, Debs is addressing an audience in Canton, Ohio, in June 1918, condemning U.S.

entry into the First World War and remarking, with wry prescience, that "it is extremely dangerous to exercise the constitutional right of free speech in a country fighting to make democracy safe in the world."

For this speech, Debs became one of 15,000 Americans jailed for violating President Woodrow Wilson's Espionage and Sedition Acts. As Judge Kenesaw Mountain Landis explained when handing down a twenty-year sentence in another such case, "In times of peace, you have a legal right to oppose, by free speech, preparations for war. But when war is declared, that right ceases." Strange, isn't it, how the Founders never got around to appending that footnote to the First Amendment?

Copperhead critics of the Civil War were often persecuted, too, though certainly not to the extent that dissenters from the First World War were. Newspapers were shut down, antiwar editors and speakers were imprisoned, habeas corpus took a holiday. War is always the enemy of liberty and free speech.

Those who wish to investigate the Copperheads further should read the works of the late historian and Marquette University professor Frank Klement, the dean of scholarly studies of Northern opposition to the Civil War. (Oddly, Blumenthal fails to mention Klement.) For more on such hobgoblins as the Knights of the Golden Circle—"I have here in my hand a list of half a million active conspirators!"—see Klement's *Dark Lanterns: Secret Political Societies, Conspiracies, and Treason Trials in the Civil War* (1984); for more on Ohio's Copperhead, see *The Limits of Dissent: Clement L. Vallandigham & The Civil War* (1970); for more on the geographical heart of the antiwar movement, see Klement's *The Copperheads of the Middle West* (1960); for a posthumously published collection of essays, see *Lincoln's Critics: The Copperheads of the North* (1999).

Frank Klement was a product of the University of Wisconsin's legendary history department and shared its populist-Middle American orientation. He demolished the myth that the Copperheads were disloyal pro-Southern traitors. By and large they were just Democrats: some rank partisans, others honorable dissenters.

Significantly, Frank Klement came of age as a historian during the Truman-McCarthy Cold War Red Scare, which he viewed as a witch-hunt. This surely colored his view of the Copperheads, for as Klement told an interviewer, "You can't separate a historian's philosophy of life or the era in which he lives from his scholarship." Ominously, in our own day, shadowed as it is by Bush-Cheney-Obama wars and see something/say something paranoia, the academy may be tilting back toward a view of the Copperheads as treasonous fifth columnists who ought to have been rounded up, a la the Japanese-Americans who filled FDR's West Coast internment camps, or the protesters of our day who are confined in Orwellian-named "free speech zones" if they dare grumble over Democrat-Republican policies.

We live in a time and in a country which finds principled dissent of the sort exercised by Eugene V. Debs and Abner Beech almost incomprehensible. In one sense, freedom of expression knows no bounds: Internet pornography, snuff-game videos, libelous tweets—laissez faire, man. But with respect to politics, art, culture ... seldom in American history have the limits of permissible speech been so narrow, so constricting. True, our Eugene Debses aren't usually thrown into jails, but nor do they become cause célèbres, like Debs. Their prison is the red state-blue state idiocy under which the limits of acceptable opinion are demarcated by Barack Obama and Mitt Romney, and writers live in the fear (which, I can tell you as one who has long worked with members of the DC punditocracy, absolutely paralyzes careerists) of saying the wrong thing and running afoul of the hall monitors and tattletales who police American discourse. Harold Frederic—and Edmund Wilson and pretty much any writer on American subjects who is worth a damn—does not fit the liberal-conservative straitjacket. The very premise of *Copperhead*—that some decent men of the North resisted Lincoln's call to arms, whether from commitment to Jeffersonian Democracy or wrongheadedness or pacifism or the awful presentiment that war would remake the country—enrages the enforcers of opinion orthodoxy, who insist that there is only one acceptable narrative (and a boring one at that) of American history: nationalist-consolidationist and social democratic at home, and world-saving-militarist abroad. There is no room in this carefully monitored and barren storyline for Abner or M'rye or Jeff Beech, or even Jee, Esther, and Ni Hagadorn. These men and women have been written out of American history. This film lets them back in.

Copperhead does not end with an affirmation of the Union, as convention would dictate. Nor does it end with an affirmation of *dis*union, as would a pro-Confederate film. Instead, it ends by affirming the Corners, the settlement of the Beech and Hagadorn families, as superior, in the lives of its inhabitants, to those larger countries. It reminds us that a patriot should never boast of the largeness of his country but rather should take pride in its smallness.

Peace, community, dissent, respect for rural Christianity: these are *Copperhead*'s themes. And they are as American as Crazy Horse, baseball, and Jack Kerouac.

Que Surratt, Surratt

The American Conservative, 2011

EVEN THE MOST DEDICATED cinephile may have blinked last spring and missed the brief visit of Robert Redford's *The Conspirator* to the suburban multiplex. The film had a shelf life shorter than a Ding Dong in Chris Christie's pantry. No, I take back that stupid joke. Not because I care about the hyperhyped Christie, but because one of our two obese presidents has been first-rate—Grover Cleveland, the Buffalo anti-imperialist—and the other—William Howard Taft—at least sired a statesman, his son Robert.

The Conspirator, recently released on DVD, deserves an audience, especially in these dark days of never-ending wars and "See it, Say it" government-stoked paranoia. The film's subject is the trial of Mary Surratt, the Maryland-born Catholic widow at whose Washington, D.C. boardinghouse bunked assorted members of the conspiracy responsible for the assassination of Abraham Lincoln. (John Wilkes Booth was a visitor, not a boarder.) "She kept the nest that hatched the egg," said President Andrew Johnson, whose failure to grant clemency to Mrs. Surratt was a low point of that drunken Tennessee tailor's rocky tenure at the top.

Mrs. Surratt was railroaded by a military tribunal for aiding and abetting Lincoln's murder. Although her son John was almost certainly implicated in the crime, Mary probably had no knowledge of the plot. "If I had two lives to give, I'd give one gladly to save Mrs. Surratt," said Booth associate Lewis Payne as he awaited the gallows. "She knew nothing about the conspiracy at all, and is an innocent woman." Mary's son, her priest, and even Union General Benjamin Butler would later proclaim her innocence. But by then the deed had been done. And hangmen don't do contrition.

The Conspirator, scripted by James Solomon, is refreshingly cant-free and without twenty-first-century red state–blue state simplemindedness. The luminous Robin Wright plays Mary as a woman of adamantine faith. "I am a Southerner, a Catholic, and a devoted mother above all else," she tells her lawyer. Three strikes and you're out, lady, one might think, but no, this film is respectful of Mrs. Surratt's loyalties. (Hostile reviewers, however, pointed out that Mrs. Surratt, even if innocent of any role in the assassination, was a Confederate sympathizer, and presumably deserved the noose. The sanctimonious are merciless.)

Maryland Senator Reverdy Johnson, the Lincoln pallbearer who was Mrs. Surratt's first attorney, is the film's voice of reason and constitutional fealty ("a military trial of civilians is an atrocity") in a time of panic. Secretary of War Edwin Stanton, played by an unrecognizable Kevin Kline, is the Dick Cheneyish villain of the piece. It's nice to see Stanton, a thoroughgoing bastard, get his. I expect he and Booth will meet Cheney soon enough in the sulfurous precincts of the afterworld.

The foreshadowing of post-9/11 America is deliberate but not clumsy or obtrusive. "The world has changed," the sinister Secretary Stanton tells Senator Johnson. "Abandoning the Constitution is not the answer," replies Johnson, sounding like, well, Ron Paul.

The Conspirator sits lonely in the almost empty sleeve of movies about spectacular violations of the Bill of Rights. So cheers for Robert Redford. As an actor, Redford projected an aloofness unusual in movie stars; he was emphatically *not* the kind of guy you'd like to have a beer with. 'Round here folks still talk about how unfriendly he was while filming *The Natural* (1984), in which the former University of Colorado pitcher made a convincing ballplayer in an unconvincing film.

He was at his best as a lone wolf, especially in the almost wordless mountain man tale *Jeremiah Johnson* (1972), directed by Sydney Pollack and adapted by John Milius from a Vardis Fisher novel.

Redford is an admirer of Edward Abbey, the late great anarchist voice of the desert Southwest. Making *The Conspirator* demonstrated Redford's indifference to the hall monitors of social-studies textbook history. Now how about filming Abbey's *The Fool's Progress* or *The Monkey Wrench Gang*? Cactus Ed makes Mary Surratt look like Betsy Ross.

The Hollywood (Ten)nessean
Chronicles, 1998

FIFTY YEARS HAVE PASSED since the orgy of squealing and sanctimony, of perfidy and posturing, that begat the Hollywood blacklist. What a cast of characters paraded before the House Committee on Un-American Activities: at this table, Communist screenwriters making $2,000 a week scribbling claptrap and convincing themselves that it was revolution; and at that table, stool pigeons betraying their friends, creating on the American Right the nauseating figure of the noble Judas, whose name has been Elia Kazan and Whittaker Chambers and Linda Tripp.

None of this would have happened if the film industry had been decentralized; if "local photoplayers in Topeka, or Indianapolis, or Denver" made the movies, as Vachel Lindsay once prophesied. But the coal shortages of the First World War drove movie production to Southern California, and the rest—alas, for those who love our country—is not history.

The HUAC hearings destroyed careers. One highlight of *Tender Comrades*, the new oral history of the Hollywood blacklist by Paul Buhle and Patrick McGilligan, is a lively chat with the feisty Abe Polonsky, writer-director of the commie-noir classic *Force of Evil* (1948). Cinephiles grieve over all those films that Polonsky & Co. never made.

But there are other Hollywood censorship stories that never get told: for instance, the tale of *Tennessee Johnson*.

Tennessee Johnson, an MGM biography of President Andrew Johnson, was released in January 1943. Directed by William Dieterle, whose credits include the phantasmal *The Devil and Daniel Webster* (1941), one of the finest movies ever made, *Tennessee Johnson* starred Van Heflin as the cussed tailor of Greeneville and Lionel Barrymore (one of Hollywood's great New Deal-haters) as Thaddeus Stevens, Johnson's radical Republican nemesis.

Tennessee Johnson received the sort of respectful notices often given earnest historical films. *Commonweal* judged it "a sincere visualization of American democracy"; *Time*'s reviewer thought it was "one of Hollywood's grown-up moments." It was also one of Hollywood's most craven moments.

AT THE MOVIES

The film originally was titled *The Man on America's Conscience*. The script, by John L. Balderston and Wells Root, took the Claude Bowers view of Reconstruction and Johnson's impeachment: that is, that Johnson "fought the bravest battle for constitutional liberty and for the preservation of our institutions ever waged by an executive" against Pennsylvania Congressman Stevens, the brilliant but hateful clubfoot who wished to mistreat the conquered Southerners like a vast peonage. (Stevens, rechristened Austin Stoneman, also played the devil to the archangel Abraham Lincoln in Thomas Dixon Jr.'s notorious KKK romance *The Clansman*, translated to the screen by D.W. Griffith as *Birth of a Nation*.)

Enter Walter White, secretary of the NAACP. White was annoyed, and understandably so, by Hollywood's depiction of blacks as scraping and bowing simpletons. When he learned that MGM was producing an anti-Reconstruction film, White complained to Lowell Mellett, director of the Bureau of Motion Pictures of the Office of War Information. The OWI, a propaganda agency created by one of FDR's executive orders, requested a copy of the screenplay from Louis B. Mayer. Mayer complied, piously assuring Walter White that "I live and breathe the air of freedom and I want it for others as well as myself."

When Mellett and White previewed the unedited film, they hit the roof. Mellett demanded that key scenes be reshot or removed. Thad Stevens, the screenplay's villain, was humanized; one new scene had him kissing and petting Andrew Johnson's grandkids. A scene in which Stevens plied Johnson with drink before his legendarily incoherent vice presidential inaugural address was left on the cutting room floor. Rewritten dialogue assured us that Stevens was "sincere" if a mite vengeful. The essential character of Lydia Smith, Stevens's mulatto housekeeper and probable mistress, disappeared.

Despite the changes, a gang of Hollywood liberals—Ben Hecht, Zero Mostel, Vincent Price—petitioned the OWI to *destroy* the picture, in best fascist fashion, in the cause of national unity.

Tennessee Johnson—the OWI demanded a conscience-less title—was released in its denatured form. It's a fairly standard biopic: Johnson, nicely played by Heflin, is the runaway tailor's apprentice and self-styled champion of "poor white trash" who is only trying to act upon his predecessor's wise policy of malice toward none and charity toward all. With the exception of Jefferson Davis, secessionists are depicted as huffy churls and hotheads.

Lionel Barrymore plays Thad Stevens as though he's rehearsing for the role of Mr. Potter. Growling, snarling, commanding a wheelchair as he would in *It's a Wonderful Life*, he seems to regard Johnson as a mere irritant who exists only to distract him from his real quarry: George Bailey and the Building and Loan.

(Nevertheless, *Tennessee Johnson* is far better than a contemporaneous "president movie," *The Remarkable Andrew*, which was written by the soon-to-be-blacklisted Dalton Trumbo. *The Remarkable Andrew* is a witless fantasy in which Andrew Jackson, played as a whiskey-swilling lout by Brian Donlevy, materializes to assist William Holden in rooting out corruption in a Colorado town. The film presents Jackson as the first New Dealer; think of it as a slapstick version of Arthur Schlesinger's *The Age of Jackson*.)

One consequence of Walter White's protest was the omission of Lydia Smith, a meaty role for a black actress. This part was recast as the corpulent "laws a mercy!" black maid of stereotype. The excision of Lydia Smith not only warred upon truth, it also made Stevens's Negrophilia less comprehensible. Love, after all, is always a higher afflatus than political principle.

Walter White's autobiography makes no mention of his role in altering Tennessee Johnson. The title is absent from a shelf full of recent books on censorship and the movies; censorship, it seems, only worked one way in Hollywood.

The most intelligent review of *Tennessee Johnson* was written by Manny Farber in *The New Republic*, of all places. "The picture looks to have been pretty thoroughly censored, so as not to rake up any coals still burning," wrote Farber, who concluded, "censorship is a disgrace, whether done by the Hays office and pressure groups, or by liberals and the OWI."

The bluenoses and red-baiters of the Hays office, HUAC, and the Legion of Decency have gotten their historiographical due. When, if ever, will Lowell Mellett and the OWI get theirs?

Go Home, Limey

The Spectator, 2000

FLEET STREET IS ALL a-twitter. In a forthcoming movie Tom Cruise is slated to escape from Colditz, although that feat was never performed by an American POW. Moreover, the hit film *U-571*, which opens in London next month, credits an American submarine with capturing the German Enigma cipher machine, an act of wartime heroism actually performed by the Royal Navy. The squeals of indignation have been so shrill that they may be heard even here in rural New York, drowning out the aggregate hum of all those television sets tuned in to that British gift to America, *Teletubbies*.

These American thefts of British derring-do cannot begin to alter the fact that American movies are obsessively Anglophilic. For starters, on those rare occasions when Hollywood makes a movie about American history, the historical personage is almost always played by an Englishman. Steven Spielberg's live-action cartoon *Amistad* featured Anthony Hopkins as ex-president John Quincy Adams, looking for all the world like a codfish Hannibal Lecter who can't wait to tear through the dull abolitionist speechifying and sit down to a meal of thick African flesh. Oliver Stone cast Hopkins as the title character in *Nixon*. (You will tell me that Hopkins is Welsh, and I will tell you, as a deep-dyed American provincial, that it is all the same to us.)

For decades, British actors have played quintessentially American roles: from Vivien Leigh and Leslie Howard as oddly accented lovers in *Gone with the Wind* to Emma Thompson imitating Hillary Clinton in *Primary Colors* and Daniel Day-Lewis roughing it as the frontiersman in Michael Mann's MTV version of James Fenimore Cooper's *The Last of the Mohicans*. Since the first goatish mogul molested the first ambitious starlet, Hollywood has been in love with England: truly, madly, deeply. True, whenever a part called for atrabilious superciliousness, George Sanders phoned in his English villain, but the incomparable Sanders was born in St Petersburg, not London. Brits used to play flits in slight American films, filling the bill whenever the role called for a mincing fairy, but that was before gays received the dramatic kiss of death. Today they are given the Sidney Poitier treatment, which means that the homosexual is either the flawless bore or the winning best friend. They have been flattened into nothingness by political correctness. Farewell to the arch British queens of cinema.

When it has really counted, Hollywood has been the handmaiden of the British Empire, transmitting English cultural imperialism and war-worship to the popcorn-munching masses. The American film industry's subservience to British interests began early, with one of the most outrageous freedom-of-speech violations in US history: during the First World War, the producer Robert Goldstein was sentenced to ten years in prison for making *The Spirit of '76*, a historical drama about the American Revolution that was deemed anti-British and thus a violation of President Woodrow Wilson's Espionage Act.

Well, yes, one supposes that a film depicting the American rebellion against the British would be somewhat anti-British. In any event, the number of movies made about the American Revolution over the next eighty-plus years can almost be counted on two hands. Before this summer's blockbuster-to-be, *The Patriot*, starring Australian-bred Mel Gibson and directed by the German Roland Emmerich, the last Hollywood stab at the spirit of '76 was the Brit Hugh Hudson's execrable *Revolution* (1985), memorable for its miscasting of Nastassia Kinski as a slinky Tory sexpot.

The next time the British Empire desired the military assistance of its quondam colonies, Hollywood signed on with the usual bellicose zeal of the pampered non-combatant. Winston Churchill even had his own man in Hollywood: the director-producer Alexander Korda. Korda—soon to be Sir Alexander for his espionage work in the trenches of sunny California—was sent to the United States by his handlers in British intelligence "to make major films that would subtly represent the British Point of view . . . in a way which would seem patriotic but not propagandistic," as his nephew Michael Korda has written.

Alexander Korda's *That Hamilton Woman* (1941), his account of the affair between Admiral Nelson and Lady Hamilton, featured a bit of bombast written by none other than Winston Churchill. ("You cannot make peace with dictators, you have to destroy them.") Never in those days of the censorious Hays Office was adultery presented so wholesomely. The film pushed the pro-intervention line with such epic seriousness that American moviegoers left the cinemas all afire to have their republic declare war on Napoleon.

A rash of such British-inflected pro-war movies led to a US Senate investigation of alien—read "British"—influence in Hollywood. The chief investigator was Senator Gerald Nye, a populist firebrand from North

Dakota who in the mid-1930s had made his name pillorying the "merchants of death," those arms-sellers who had profited from the carnage of World War One. In the months before Pearl Harbor, Nye set his sights on the spate of films "designed to rouse us to a state of war hysteria," particularly those movies "telling about the grandeur and the heavenly justice of the British Empire."

Hollywood "swarms with British actors," Nye told a nationwide radio audience in August 1941, and these tea drinkers had one common cause: to convince Americans to "make the world safe for British imperialism." Liberal muckraker John T. Flynn took aim at British agitprop in his testimony before Nye's Senate subcommittee: "Why is it that no picture is produced depicting the tyrannies and oppressions in India where at the moment there are 20,000 Indian patriots in jail? . . . [T]hink of the scenes in the jails and courts that could provide magnificent glamour." But "what we get are pictures . . . glorifying the magnificence, humanity and democracy of the British Empire." (When finally Hollywood did get around to visiting the Empire's misrule of its Indian subjects, the director was . . . Lord Attenborough.)

And then there was *Mrs. Miniver*. Director William Wyler called it "perfect as propaganda": shooting began one month before Pearl Harbor, and all involved conceded the intent of the film was to persuade American isolationists—that is, Middle Americans who would rather not send their sons halfway around the world to kill and die—to do just that for Great Britain. Forget the American Revolution, forget the War of 1812, forget the killing fields of the First World War—this time we were fighting for noble Greer Garson and the luminous Teresa Wright, and what red-blooded American lad wouldn't die for Miss Wright? (Put aside the fact that Wright was an American, beautiful English actresses being notoriously scarce at the time; Hermione Baddeley just wouldn't do.)

So British infiltration of the American film industry pulls us into two world wars, and you complain about Tom Cruise?

Certainly the English are right to resist, by any means necessary, the invasion of Gwyneth Paltrow, McDonald's, Microsoft, Starbucks, and *Friends*, but the insidious Anglicization of middle-class America is no less noxious. I do not mean the mannerly snoozers produced by Merchant and Ivory. The threat today comes not in movie theatres but on the field of sport. The indigenous American games, particularly baseball, are under assault.

Soccer, which one sports historian calls the British Empire's "most enduring export," is making inroads in our recalcitrant land of baseball. This is one of the more repugnant projects of global capitalism: Mastercard, Coca-Cola, and their ilk subsidized the World Cup, a colossal flop in the States, but now Nike is pumping $50 million into Project 2010, which seeks to soccerize the U.S. within the decade. How much easier marketing becomes when the entire world plays a single game.

Neither Britain nor the U.S. has a clean record when it comes to crimes of cultural imperialism. Perhaps the time has come for an alliance against the common foe; after all, as scriptwriter W. Churchill wrote, "You cannot make peace with dictators." It may be even more difficult, alas, to escape from the global economy than it was from Colditz.

Murder, Mayhem, and Meathead
Liberty, 1996

IT NEVER WOULD HAVE occurred to Franklin Pierce to denounce Walt Whitman's *Leaves of Grass*. William McKinley never called a press conference to vilify Theodore Dreiser for *Sister Carrie*. But that was then, and this is now, and Senator Robert Dole hopes to move into what blear-eyed sentimentalists risibly call "the people's house," aided by ghostwritten attacks on movies he hasn't bothered to watch.

Last year it was *Natural Born Killers* and *True Romance*; now it's *The Money Train*, which I have no doubt is deeply moronic, but *still* . . . isn't it odd to hear denunciations of fictional violence from a man who has rubberstamped a Clinton policy that will employ American men and tax dollars to kill real live Bosnian Serbs: people who have never so much as lifted a finger to harm us?

"We must hold Hollywood and the entire entertainment industry accountable for putting profit ahead of common decency," Dole thundered in his now-notorious campaign speech last year in Los Angeles. Disparaging those who take refuge in "the lofty language of free speech," he singled out *Natural Born Killers* and *True Romance* as "films that revel in mindless violence and loveless sex."

Natural Born Killers is a special case: for all of Oliver Stone's manifold talents as a writer-director, he lacks a sense of humor, which is more or less required when making a satire. But in re: *True Romance*, Dole's is the most inaccurate description of a movie since a critic called *Last Year at Marienbad* "entertaining." Anyone who finds the relationship between Patricia Arquette and her chivalrous husband Christian Slater "loveless" is the sort of guy who would dump an aging wife and take up with a powermad Beltwayette.

Dole praised such "friendly to the family" films as the cretinous *Flintstones* and the Arnold Schwarzenegger killfest *True Lies*. All of which called to mind Attorney General Janet "Burn Babies Burn" Reno's performance before the Senate Commerce Committee in October 1993. Fresh from her massacre of flesh-and-blood religious dissidents in Waco, Texas, the (h)AG scolded the TV networks for airing *make-believe* violence. She later offered her own mind-numbing idea for a movie-of the-week: a fourteen-year-old "helps raise his two siblings while his mother is recovering from crack addiction." Three years later, "she goes to law school and he graduates as valedictorian." (Dear old dad is nowhere to be found.)

Reno's hectoring paid off, not least in the seemingly endless parade of cute lesbians who pop up on television in non-threatening roles. And now comes the Rob Reiner-Aaron Sorkin valentine to Bill Clinton, *The American President*, which exhibits all the irreverence of Albanian *auteurs* in 1982 preparing a documentary on the life of Enver Hoxha. *(The American President* has been called "Capraesque," but Frank Capra was a bareknuckled populist, one of the great FDR-haters. He cut a treacly scene from the prologue of the *It's a Wonderful Life* script in which the angels gush over the newly deceased President Roosevelt.)

Be careful what you wish for, partisan movie-goers: you just might get it. In the 1970s, Responsibles hooted at a raft of lively films *(Sweet Sweetback's Baadassss Song, Shaft, Superfly)* about black characters who possess a more ambiguous morality than the usual Sidney Poitier cardboard cutouts; the resultant timidity gave us a handful of Noble Negro pictures and a long drought during which the only parts for black actors were as the white guy's bland sidekick (see: Glover, Danny, career of).

This was remedied by the Cinematic World On Its Head Act of 1991, which mandated that all judges in movies and TV be stern black females while the meaty criminal parts must go to white actors, preferably those who can affect Southern accents and play characters named Dean. Thus the silly "realistic" cop shows *NYPD Blue* and *Homicide* would have us believe that virtually every criminal in Baltimore and Gotham is a white guy, usually a skinhead, smarmy businessman, or working-class lout. "There are almost no ethnic villains on television," ABC executive Bruce J. Sallan told the *New York Times* a few years back. Nothing has changed, which may soothe liberal consciences but does not help black actors.

A Doleful Hollywood might have one or two surprises. A revisionist remake of *The Fugitive* in which the one-armed man is the hero? Or, if Reiner can apotheosize the dweeby George Stephanopoulos, will Glenn Close play Dole flunky Sheila Burke as the tigress of the Oval Office? (I don't suppose *I Was a Bag Man for Archer Daniels Midland* would be a viable project.)

Artists—even the fast-buck artists of Hollywood—are too useful to the state to ever be ignored. But is it too much to ask of the Beltway virtuecrats that they shut up and (for those who haven't abandoned spouse and children for trophy wives) tend to their own families?

Peckinpah Country

The American Conservative, 2012

I'M ON ONE OF my periodic Sam Peckinpah benders. ("You call *that* a bender?" I can hear Sam sneer, as he gestures scornfully to my beer bottle with way too little ullage.) The trigger this time was a visit with my in-laws in LA. I read James Cain and Raymond Chandler in preparation, not because I wanted to bump off a hapless cuckold but in order to see Glendale and Pasadena with 1930s eyes.

Peckinpah, a descendant of ranchers and lawyers from Fresno and the Sierra foothills, was California, Central Division. He was so Californian that his father was born on Peckinpah Mountain and his grandmother knew (and disliked) Calamity Jane.

Though sometimes caricatured as a nihilist for the balletic violence of his films, director Peckinpah was in fact "a desperate romantic at war with his own disillusionment," as biographer David Weddle writes.

Sam's grandfather, Denver Church, was a formative influence on the boy. Church, a four-term Democratic congressman who opposed U.S. entry into World War I, was described in John Wakeman's *World Film Directors* as "an American individualist of the old school" who "opposed all kinds of government control. Though a total abstainer himself, he voted in Congress against Prohibition and later abandoned his political career because of his disapproval of Franklin D. Roosevelt and the New Deal."

Romantic reactionaries tend to be born just as things they love are fading away. Sam recalled his foothills before the roads and developers invaded: "My brother Denny and I were in on the last of it. A lot of the old-timers dated back to when the place had been the domain of hunters and trappers, Indians, gold miners—all the drifters and hustlers. All that's left now are the names to remind you, and *what* names: towns like Coarsegold and Finegold, Shuteye Peak, Dead Man Mountain, Wild Horse Ridge, Slick Rock. Denny and I rode and fished and hunted all over that country. We thought we'd always be part of it."

They weren't. But the memory of that lost place—the pain of watching that which one loves disappear—informs his best movies: *The Wild Bunch, Ride the High Country, Junior Bonner, Pat Garrett & Billy the Kid.*

This last, with its elegiac score by Bob Dylan, is at once listless and haunting, as it treats Peckinpah's two favorite themes: men out of time and the imperative of loyalty. Its tersely poetical script is by the underrated novelist Rudolph Wurlitzer (check out his brutal and ethereal *The Drop Edge of Yonder*) of the jukebox family.

Queried why he doesn't kill his pursuer Pat Garrett, Billy the Kid (played by Kris Kristofferson) says simply, "He's my friend." No other explanation is necessary, or even possible. It's the same reason Peckinpah's Wild Bunch go on a mission perdu to rescue their compadre Angel from the sleazy *federale* Mapache.

"Aren't your losers and misfits conformists to outdated codes?" asked a *Playboy* interviewer in 1972. Peckinpah replied, "Outdated codes like courage, loyalty, friendship, grace under pressure, all the simple virtues that have become clichés, sure. They're cats who ran out of territory and they know it, but they're not going to bend, either: they refuse to be diminished by it. They play their string out to the end."

In my rare dark moods I wonder if this is our fate: to play out the string as best we can, even though the game was lost long before most of us were even born. During the nation's bicentennial, by which time Peckinpah was pretty well strung out, his best films behind him, the director said, "I feel I'm an American citizen. Dummy, I believe in all that shit. Mort Sahl called me a 1939 American. I still believe. But somebody better start waking up pretty soon."

I love Sahl's phrase: *1939 American*. Before perpetual war and suffocating bureaucracy, this used to be a helluva country, as Jack Nicholson mused through a haze of marijuana smoke in *Easy Rider*.

"1939 American" has nothing to do with ethnicity or national origin and everything to do with loyalty to one's place and love for one's country—the real country of flesh and bone and memory, not the televised "America" of Lady Gaga and the Pentagon. While in Southern California I spent several days in the company of Syrian-Armenians who didn't come to this country till well after 1939, and believe me, they are 1939 Americans.

They are also outraged that the effect, if not intent, of U.S. foreign policy is the systematic destruction of the Christian cultures of the Middle East. In our land of lost Angels, Mapache still has the guns.

Hoosiers Time
The American Enterprise, 2006

THE OTHER NIGHT I sat in the bandbox gym at Elba Central watching the girls play Notre Dame in the fiercest rivalry in local high-school basketball. The catercornered student sections traded taunts: not the hoary "We got spirit/Yes we do/We got spirit/How 'bout you?" but the terser "We Can't Hear You!" and, from Elba, the buoyantly populist "Sit Down, Rich Kids!"

You can bet that nearly every player on the floor has seen—and seen herself in—*Hoosiers* (1986), which is generally regarded as the best sports movie ever made and which is, withal, a deeply moving film about the centrality of a locally controlled school to a small town.

Hoosiers grew from the great mythic event in Indiana sports history: the 1954 state basketball championship won by the team from little Milan, which defeated Muncie in the title game, 32–30, on a last-second shot by its star player, the exquisitely named Bobby Plump. Indiana's tournament was open to all schools, regardless of size. Country boys, city boys, two-room academies and concrete blocks in the asphalt jungle: everyone competed in the same division.

Indiana schoolboys were raised on folkloric tales of mighty Milan. I recently traveled to the land of James Dean and James Whitcomb Riley to speak with one such Hoosier lad: Angelo Pizzo, the Bloomington native who wrote and coproduced *Hoosiers* and thereby apotheosized Milan (as "Hickory" in the movie) for the rest of us.

Pizzo and his college roommate, fellow Indianan David Anspaugh, had talked of making a movie "about the meaning of basketball to people in Indiana." The daydream started to take shape when Pizzo, home for Christmas from USC film school, dropped by a high school game at Bloomington South. "The energy in that place—it would blow away any rock concert," he recalled. "You have these guys in overalls, normally monosyllabic people, out of their seats, off the ground. I was just watching those people, feeling the energy, and I thought if I could ever capture this on film it would be special. Of course the state myth is Milan winning the championship so that's what I gravitated toward."

His early research was unpromising. "The essence of all drama is conflict. I went to interview the original [Milan] guys, and I said to the first person, 'Were there any problems, any adversities?' 'Nope, everybody got along real good.' I said, 'You didn't have one troublemaker?' 'Well, Bobby Plump used to show up late. Coach made him run laps.' I knew I didn't have a movie."

So Pizzo drew from his own Indiana boyhood. "I got in my mind five high-school buddies and I gave them form and voice."

The coach of Milan, Marvin Wood, was just twenty-six years old during that championship season. "I wrote it that way and the movie didn't work. If he had failed, he still had the rest of his life." Inspired by Horton Foote's *Tender Mercies*, with Robert Duvall's memorable performance, "I went back and made the character older, a guy with a last chance."

Consider the lineup that turned down *Hoosiers*. Robert Duvall passed on the role of the coach, Norman Dale, which went to Gene Hackman. The part of Shooter, the redeemable alcoholic ex-jock played by Dennis Hopper, was rejected by Harry Dean Stanton. John Mellencamp was asked to write the score, but according to Pizzo he said no because he thought "those guys don't know anything about basketball." (Pizzo adds, "John never played basketball. He was one of those kids who hated kids with letter jackets.")

Coach Dale, a volatile man getting a second chance in a movie about second chances, is based in part on Indiana University's legendary Bobby Knight. Pizzo says, "I wondered what would happen if Knight punched a player"—as the Hackman character had done. "I utilized Knight's offensive philosophy: four passes before a shot. I also created an arc for him where he actually listened to a player." (This last touch, admittedly, borders on science fiction.)

For two years, seeking financing for the film, Pizzo and Anspaugh were turned down by every Midwesterner and basketball fan they approached. Their savior was a foreign rogue who "had never seen a basketball game, never heard of Indiana." He was "an uneducated Cockney whose dad used to show up drunk and embarrass him when he was playing soccer." The relationship between Shooter and his son "made him cry. He said how much do you need? We got $6 million."

****

"I always felt that place in a movie is as powerful as a leading character," says Angelo Pizzo. "What is missing in a lot of movies is a sense of place: it becomes generic, it becomes Toronto through New York. With *Hoosiers*, David and I insisted that if we don't shoot in Indiana we don't shoot at all."

In a brilliant stroke of verisimilitude, "We determined not only to shoot in Indiana but to hire only real Indiana basketball players. We had open casting calls and reduced them not by reading but by basketball playing." (Art, of course, had the last word: the best basketball player in the cast, Wade Schenck, played the diffident team manager Ollie; the least-skilled, Maris Valainis, played star Jimmy Chitwood.)

The gamble paid off. The kids are utterly believable, and the film escaped the curse of such Hollywood sports movies as *Bang the Drum Slowly*, in which major league baseball catcher Robert De Niro throws like a girl. Pizzo adds, "The classic is Anthony Perkins in *Fear Strikes Out*," the story of psycho Red Sox outfielder Jimmy Piersall. "Talk about throwing like a girl—he was a girl!"

(In a tragic 2003 coda, Kent Poole, whose character Merle utters the most poignant line in the film—"Let's win this one for all the small schools that never had a chance to get here"—hanged himself from a tree in his Crawfordsville, Indiana, yard. "I got a call from him about a week before he killed himself," says Pizzo. "He said that he really needed to send me something and got my address. Then I heard he killed himself. Every day I went to the mailbox looking for whatever it was. I never got anything.")

In its sympathetic yet never bathetic understanding of rural life, *Hoosiers* avoids both mawkishness and smug anti-provincialism, the dominant keys in those rare cases when Hollywood has visited small town America. Coach Dale, who has been adrift—literally—in the navy for a decade, is greeted suspiciously upon his arrival in Hickory. "Real friendly town you got here," he wisecracks to the principal. "It can be," replies this old friend who has thrown out a lifeline. But Dale, who is placeless, must earn his place in settled Hickory. The nomadic coach, rather like *Shane* or Ethan Edwards in *The Searchers*, is unlikely to stay, though his sojourn in town effects a reconciliation between Shooter and his son and perhaps between the embittered schoolteacher Myra Fleener (Barbara Hershey) and the hometown she grudgingly inhabits. (Unlike Midwestern natives Hackman and Hopper, who by all accounts enjoyed the movie's making, Barbara Hershey, who grew up in Hollywood, was unhappy filming in Indiana—and it shows.)

Hoosiers also commits a refreshing crime against p.c. sensibilities. Hickory, like Milan in real life, defeats an integrated team for the state title. It's a jarring scene, since in Hollywood a "white team" can never defeat a "black team" unless the whites cheat, pay off the refs, or spit out racial epithets in cracker accents. "We tried to mirror what these kids experienced," explains Pizzo. "They didn't run up against any teams with black players—an unfortunate residue of the Klan in Southern Indiana. What we didn't show was that in the semifinals, they played Crispus Attucks, which had a young sophomore star in Oscar Robertson." In the film, the coach of the team that Hickory defeats in the finals is played by Ray Crowe, coach of the great Crispus Attucks teams.

Hoosiers is one of those rare movies that finds a larger audience with each passing year. "The fact that it's lived on blows my mind," says Pizzo. "The older the movie gets, the more popular it gets." You can't call it a cult movie, since every ninth-grade second-string point guard in America has seen it. The film is beloved but also genuinely good. It avoids schmaltz, cliché, cheapness. Its anchorage in Indiana myth, its respect for a place and a time, elevate it to that echelon of movies—*To Kill a Mockingbird*, *It's a Wonderful Life*, *The Grapes of Wrath*—that are widely cherished artistic successes.

The film was nominated for two Academy Awards (for Hopper's performance and Jerry Goldsmith's stirring score), but Pizzo and Anspaugh skipped the Oscars. You see, Indiana University was playing Syracuse for the NCAA championship coincident with the awards show, says Pizzo, "and I called David and said Indiana basketball is much more important" than the Oscars. Wise choice: Keith Smart's jumpshot won the game and title for the collegiate Hoosiers, and Pizzo's friendship with Bobby Knight resulted.

****

There's a wonderful moment in *Hoosiers* in which team manager Ollie recites the wonders of "progress," which include "school consolidation"—the kind of Progress that will swallow up and kill the Hickory Highs before the decade is out.

Milan survived because of the state title, but so many of the rural high schools which gave small communities a sense of identity were wiped out in the Cold War-fed school consolidation craze of the 1950s. "When Milan won the state championship, there were 756 high schools," notes Pizzo. "Last year, there were 265."

"Nobody had television," he says of the Milan of the early '50s. "They didn't have a movie house. Accents were different. The sense of pride and identity connected with your place was so different then. Now there's television and strip malls and Wal-Mart. They all play the same video games, they all have Play Stations."

Indiana's open tournament has been dismantled. Schools now play only schools of similar size. While this may seem "fairer" in some abstract sense, "it's ruined things," laments Pizzo. Teams "don't play their natural regional rivals" in the sectionals; instead, they travel long distances to play teams in their class. Disregarding geography, the sectionals "mean nothing. They've dissipated the excitement across the board."

Yet Hoosiers endure. "There is still a qualitative difference between people in Anderson, Indiana, and New Albany, Indiana," insists Angelo Pizzo, and that difference informs his work.

Pizzo and Anspaugh followed *Hoosiers* with two other feature film collaborations. In *Rudy* (1993), an ode to perseverance, a working-class Catholic kid from Joliet who dreams of Notre Dame and surmounts any number of obstacles to earn admittance and then a place on the football team's practice squad caps his career by finally getting into a game in his senior season. The film is treasured especially by Notre Damers, a twist because "growing up in Bloomington, I hated Notre Dame," laughs Pizzo. He saw in Rudy's tale "a metaphor for somebody from the middle of nowhere going into the film business and thinking he's going to make a movie, and people telling him he's crazy and a fool and he has no chance. It's a lonely pursuit, and this is a lonely guy."

Like *Hoosiers*, *Rudy* is notable for the respect with which it treats men of the cloth. The Protestant minister who drives the team bus in *Hoosiers*—a richly symbolic touch—emboldens the boys by reading from the story of David and Goliath; the priest in *Rudy* is a wise elder. In other films, the minister would have been a pharisaical prig and the priest a clammy child molester.

The Game of their Lives (2005), the story of the U.S. soccer team's astonishing 1950 World Cup upset of England, was the first failure for the Pizzo-Anspaugh team, and "a nightmare from start to finish," says Pizzo. The film flopped commercially and critically. But on the bright side, it forestalled the advance of the alien game of soccer upon American screens.

****

There is a fitting postscript to the *Hoosiers* story. Angelo Pizzo, the man who created Norman Dale and sent him to Hickory, Indiana, came home to Bloomington.

Pizzo's homecoming contradicts the typical pop-culture fairy tale, in which boys from Indiana dream of hightailing it to Hollywood or Manhattan and never looking back. As a handsome young guy with a hit film,

Pizzo was not exactly a bystander at the debauch, but marriage and children refocused his dreams.

"My wife [Greta] hated L.A.," he said. "Then we had two boys and she grew to hate it more. What we were looking for we didn't find: a sense of community. There was stratification, elitism, no mingling."

"I was coming back to Indiana ten or fifteen times a year, and it hit me that *Indiana was my community*. I always looked forward to coming back and I never wanted to get on the plane to Los Angeles, except to see my family."

The epiphany hit over eggs and coffee. A friend invited him to a weekly Wednesday morning breakfast at a Bloomington restaurant. The diners included a lawyer, a newspaper editor, a sports statistician, a pharmaceutical salesman, a retired principal, a hippie export-importer, a professor, and the ex-football coach at Indiana University.

"I had a profound sense of envy of my friend for going to those breakfasts," recalls Pizzo. "In L.A., you don't talk about anything other than the film business. I could never have a conversation that even remotely mirrored that one."

"He called me," says Greta, "and said, 'I want something like that.' Then that moved into, 'No, I want *that*!'"

They made the move to Bloomington in early 2004. "My only regret," says Pizzo, "is the month of March."

Greta, whom Pizzo met on the set of *Rudy*, says, "Angelo kept saying you can't go home again, but we've found that not only can you go home again but there's something about that experience that is essential. We're in a healthy community; our kids can walk a block and a half to their school; Angelo is connected to something."

He has not forsworn filmmaking, just the stifling assumption that one must live in the hive to make motion pictures. Pizzo has several projects on the tapis, including a semi-autobiographical film set in Bloomington. His hometown took its cinematic bow with *Breaking Away* (1979), the much-praised film about a band of townies winning Indiana University's Little 500 bike race, and while that film has a certain winsomeness, Pizzo was appalled by its inauthenticity: "I saw my hometown being depicted and I didn't recognize any of the people in it. Those people didn't belong in Bloomington. The director had never been to Indiana before; the parents were not Bloomington people." As for Dennis Christopher, the fey opera-singing hero, "What planet was he from? There's nothing Bloomington about that kid."

The lesson he drew from *Breaking Away* was that "in a movie called *Hoosiers*, you'd better get Indiana right."

Angelo Pizzo and David Anspaugh got it right.

Watch *Hoosiers*. Then get down to the high-school gym to watch the local team. Listen to the screams, the handclaps, the laughs, the shouts of encouragement. That noise you hear is the sound of community.

Wild (Warren) Oates

The American Conservative, 2009

NED BEATTY AND WARREN Oates, resplendent stars in a Kentucky-Hollywood zodiac that stretches from Tod Browning to Johnny Depp, were sitting by a pool in Houston when Beatty asked Oates, "How would you describe your politics?"

Oates screwed up his face and replied, "You know, I'm a by-god constitutional anarchist."

Of course. What else could he be? Warren Oates never could disappoint.

That conversation is recounted in Susan Compo's new biography *Warren Oates: A Wild Life*, which gave me a happy excuse to watch Oates again in the Westerns and road movies that put to such affecting use what John Doe of the great Los Angeles punk band X called Oates's "glare . . . the look of a shell-shocked soldier, broken lover or desert rat."

A drunken romantic, a self-described "total hick with a mountain accent," Warren Oates, a native of Depoy, Kentucky, was descended from a Revolutionary War major who fought under Francis Marion, the Swamp Fox. Oates praised Depoy as "a splendid place" with "real community spirit." He was proud to be a Kentuckian and he would frequently criticize Hollywood's anti-Southern bigotry.

He worked in TV Westerns and as a key member of the Sam Peckinpah ensemble in such films as *Ride the High Country*, *Major Dundee*, and *The Wild Bunch*, whose theme—"When you side with a man, you stay with him, and if you can't do that, you're like some animal, you're finished"—Oates could haul.

Then came a string of extraordinary performances in seldom seen films in which Oates was often heartbreaking and never cheaply so. He was the mute trainer of gamecocks in Monte Hellman's singular *Cockfighter* (1974) and, as the nomadic fabulist GTO, the only sign of life in Hellman's flat *Two-Lane Blacktop* (1971).

"If I'm not grounded pretty soon, I'm gonna go into orbit," GTO says by way of proposal to the hippie drifter known only as The Girl just before she hops on a stranger's motorcycle and takes off. Warren Oates had roots and he had the wanderlust, and that tension is palpable in many of his characters, footloose men of the border states or the South who have lost home and can't quite seem to find it again.

His best part was in Peter Fonda's dreamlike *The Hired Hand* (1971), beautifully filmed by Vilmos Zsigmond, a lovely meditation on friendship and responsibility, one of the least-known great movies of that richest of all cinematic eras, the early 1970s. Oates's films in these years, like those of Clint Eastwood and Jeff Bridges, were consistently interesting—soulful, often literate contrasts to the brain sludge for cretins that fills theaters today.

His response to the priggish carping at *The Wild Bunch* gives a taste of Oates the Goldwater voter from Depoy: "It shocked the hell out of a lot of moralistic weirdo pinko liberals." Yet he sympathized with the uncredentialed critics, saying that "some of the protest by Mexican-American groups is justified.... I feel it is the fault of the semi-intellectual community that writes about or makes films about Mexico, or hillbillies, or any specific group of people that does not belong to their semi-intellectual community. The clichéd Mexican or the clichéd southerner or the clichéd anyone is not a full man."

Oates was a prodigious consumer of booze, drugs, and available women. He was also, by all accounts, a helluva nice guy without a hint of movie-star hauteur. He displayed special kindness to waitresses, rural people, and those lacking a sophisticated veneer. Filming *Tom Sawyer* (1973) in Arrow Rock, Missouri, "Oates characteristically befriended the locals, inviting many of them to share a Coke or two." Shooting John Milius's *Dillinger* (1973), "Warren was very generous with the [Oklahoma extras]," said his knockout costar Michelle Phillips. "He was a kind of hillbilly; the people were a little like that too, and they loved him."

Susan Compo does justice to Oates, whom she obviously adores, and she has a style safely removed from that Forest Lawn of prose known as the celebrity biography. (Of the loosely screwed Laurie Bird, who played The Girl in *Two-Lane Blacktop*, Compo writes, "what did not kill her made her stranger.")

Oates was no saint, and the movie that was supposed to make him a star, *Bring Me the Head of Alfredo Garcia* (1974), was a splendid mess that marked the beginning of the end of Sam Peckinpah. But Warren Oates onscreen is enough to make you think that as bad and pernicious as the movies can be, once in a while, in the hands of an Oates, a Fonda, a Peckinpah, they really get this country right.

Thoroughly Anti-Modern Milius
The American Conservative, 2014

"I've been blacklisted as much as anyone in the '50s," says John Milius in the absorbing new documentary *Milius*, an aptly blusterous teddy bear of a movie directed by Joey Figueroa and Zak Knutson.

Milius, a self-described "Zen anarchist," scripted some of the best films of the 1970s: *Jeremiah Johnson* (adapted from a novel by the cranky Idaho Old Rightist Vardis Fisher), *Apocalypse Now* (its title taken, explains Milius, from a button he had minted in the 1960s to mock the hippies' "Nirvana Now" slogan), and *Dillinger* (starring the "constitutional anarchist" Warren Oates). His uncredited work includes *Dirty Harry*'s "Do you feel lucky?" street interrogation and Robert Shaw's selachian monologue on the fate of the *USS Indianapolis* in *Jaws*.

Milius was at once a central figure and also an outlier in the early '70s youth moment in Hollywood. Though personally close to the Midasian trio of Spielberg, Lucas, and Coppola, his firearm-based antics (such as bringing a loaded .45 to a meeting with a studio executive), as much as the masculine rite-of-passage motifs in his films, seemed to place him in that unpledged fraternity of directors with decidedly non-liberal politics: Michael Cimino, Walter Hill, Ron Maxwell, Clint Eastwood, Mel Gibson, Oliver Stone.

He completed the transition from colorful character to pariah, the documentary suggests, with *Red Dawn* (1984), which Milius cowrote and directed. *Red Dawn* is a *Boys Life* fantasy in which a gang of outdoorsy Colorado kids (nicknamed the Wolverines, after their high school mascot) resists the Soviet/Cuban occupation of their town. They run off to the mountains, sleep under the stars, play football, eat Rice Krispies for dinner, and draw up sorties in the dirt as if they were Hail Mary passes. It all sounds like a blast.

Despite the ludicrous premise, the film is filled with entertaining extended middle fingers (the occupiers use registration records to locate gun owners, among them the great Harry Dean Stanton, and throw them into re-education camps) that left conventional reviewers sputtering.

One of *Red Dawn*'s only thoughtful notices came from *The Nation*'s Andrew Kopkind, who saw it as a paean to insurgency, "a celebration of people's war." Milius, in this interpretation, is no jingo; he's on the side of indigenous people fighting an occupying army. Kopkind's essay is so good I can't help quoting at length: "Milius has produced the most convincing story about popular resistance to imperial oppression since the inimitable *Battle of Algiers*. He has only admiration for his guerrilla kids, and he understands their motivations (and excuses their naivete) far better than the hip liberal filmmakers of the 1960s counterculture. I'd take the Wolverines from Colorado over a small circle of friends from Harvard Square in any revolutionary situation I can imagine."

As the Wolverines are about to execute a prisoner of war, one teenage guerilla asks, "What's the difference between us and them?" To which the leader of the pack responds, "We live here." The line might just as well have been spoken by a boy in Vietnam or Afghanistan or Iraq or wherever else imperialist superpowers alight.

My favorite Milius movie is his magnum opus manqué, *Big Wednesday* (1978), in which three surfers (the trifecta of Jan-Michael Vincent, Gary Busey, and William Katt) confront Vietnam, adulthood, and monster swells. Elegiac, evocative, excessive, *Big Wednesday* was a box-office wipeout, but since when is that a demerit?

The Golden Age of American cinema, the first half of the 1970s, had room for—nay, welcomed—this asthmatic bombastic gun-crazy Jewish surfer from St. Louis who said, "The world I admire was dead before I was born." But today--Mistah Kurtz, he passé.

I despise Milius's hero, Teddy Roosevelt, and I'll bet we've never once cast a ballot for the same presidential candidate, but in our age of cringing yes-men and gutless herd-followers, who cannot admire a man who once explained himself to his fellow screenwriters: "I've suffered loss in my career for not being obedient. Believe me, the loss was little compared to the fear all you elite stomach every day. When the sun sets, I can sing 'My Way' with Elvis, Frank Sinatra, and Richard Nixon. What is your anthem?"

"To be a rebel is to court extinction," said the booze-addled and self-dramatizing silent-screen siren Louise Brooks. John Milius is an authentic rebel, a true son of liberty, and as he turns seventy, his work is as alive as ever. And hell, I haven't even mentioned *Geronimo*, *The Wind and the Lion*, or *Conan the Barbarian*.

"Why Not Have Stories Told From Where We Are About Who We Are?" Jay Craven Films Vermont

Orion, 2013

IN 1915, THE VAGABOND poet Vachel Lindsay, who had issued forth from Lincoln-haunted Springfield, Illinois (and would return there to die by drinking lye), delivered one of the most spectacularly wrong prophecies in the history of foretelling. In his book *The Art of the Moving Picture*, Lindsay predicted that soon enough, "every community of fifty thousand" would develop its own motion picture coterie whose films would express the genius and character of their places. Topeka, Indianapolis, Denver: each would find itself rendered upon the screen in the fledgling medium of the motion picture.

That sure didn't happen.

There have been, over the decades, rare filmmakers either based outside the smoggy environs of Los Angeles—think Pittsburgh's George Romero and his *Night of the Living Dead* zombies—or pursuing regionally themed films: e.g., the Indiana-bred writing-directing team of Angelo Pizzo and David Anspaugh, who collaborated on *Hoosiers* and *Rudy*, two of the best (and certainly most place-specific) sports movies ever made.

But overwhelmingly, American movies have been produced, directed, filmed, and financed in Hollywood, which largely explains why they have had so little connection to life as it has been lived in Butte or Bangor or Tulsa or Tallahassee.

Enter Jay Craven, stage left.

Jay Craven is a rara avis: a director with a solid body of feature-film work who lives and makes movies far from bright lights, big cities, or cocaine nose-jobs. He calls his work "place-based, indigenous cinema." His best-known films are based on novels by the acclaimed Howard Frank Mosher, his fellow resident of Vermont's sparsely populated and transcendently beautiful three-county area known as the Northeast Kingdom. Mosher is one of the best American novelists writing today. (Don't take my word for it: Richard Russo calls Mosher "the most natural storyteller around.")

"I grew up with a Texas grandmother who loved Westerns and Tennessee Williams pictures," Craven says as we chat in the library at Marlboro College in Vermont, where he teaches film when he's not—or even when he is—directing and producing movies and overseeing Kingdom County Productions, the arts organization he founded with his wife, documentary filmmaker Bess O'Brien. "While my peers were watching *Dumbo* I was watching *Red River* and *Cat on a Hot Tin Roof*." It was good training for a rural filmmaker, especially an adapter of Mosher's extraordinary novels.

Howard Frank Mosher's fictive terrain is Kingdom County, where the clock on the courthouse tower ignores daylight saving time, as do its citizens, who refuse to "adjust their clocks forward to accommodate someone else's notion of the way time ought to be kept."

Mosher's Vermonters are stubborn, whimsical, independent, brawling, and not excessively respectful of the law: they are ruggedly individualistic within a communitarian setting. Critics have called his novels "Easterns"; Craven praises their mixture of "hardscrabble social reality and larger than life characters," which endow them with "the mythic quality of the Western."

There are hints of magic, of ghostly intercessions, in Mosher's tales of moonshiners and hill farmers who are so suffused with the wild pioneer spirit that their material privations neither define nor confine them. Jay Craven has translated three—soon to be four—of these stories to the screen.

His debut, the powerful *Where the Rivers Flow North* (1993), stars Rip Torn as Noel Lord, a hook-handed logger fighting for the leased land on which his family has lived and loved and felled trees for generations. The ravenous Northern Power Company, which holds the lease, intends to flood the property to create the largest hydroelectric dam in the United States, as well as a "nature park"—the latter to be scenic, sterile, and stripped of inconvenient Vermonters.

But Lord refuses to budge. The choleric old man rejects an escalating series of monetary offers from the power company, growling, "I won't be bribed or forced off this land for any reason." His common-law wife (Native Canadian actress Tantoo Cardinal in a bravura performance) urges him to take the money and move into town. But Lord is adamant: "I won't work for any man. I'll starve first."

Where the Rivers Flow North is a fascinating character study. Noel Lord is not a flinty, cartoon, "a-yup" Vermonter hitching up his overalls while dispensing pithily cutting koans to befuddled flatlanders. He is a hard man, very much a product of a topography and a vocation whose stubborn nature is symbolized by the crude prosthetic protruding from his left arm.

Craven's next film was *A Stranger in the Kingdom* (1999), featuring Ernie Hudson as a black minister whose arrival in a small Vermont town coincides with a brutal murder. As with *To Kill a Mockingbird*, the aim was not to preach or demonize rural whites as vicious racists but rather to examine, with honesty and sympathy, small communities ripped apart by conflicting loyalties and prejudices. Seven years later, in 2006, *Disappearances* debuted, a supernaturally tinged tale set in 1932 about a bootlegger (Kris Kristofferson) who smuggles stolen whiskey from Quebec into the Northeast Kingdom. (I once disdained Kristofferson as the Mightiest Oak of wooden actors, but he's sure played some American parts, and played them well: Billy the Kid in Sam Peckinpah's *Pat Garrett and Billy the Kid*, Charlie Wade in John Sayles's *Lone Star*, and Quebec Bill Bonhomme in *Disappearances*.)

Craven has also directed one non-Vermont feature, *The Year that Trembled* (2002), exploring the reverberations of the Kent State shootings in a small Ohio town. If this is the least of his features, it is not without Buckeye resonances.

Place is essential to each of these films, and is manifested in the climate, flora, accent, pace, and even the faces of the background performers. These films are not only *about* their places, they are *of* them. They *breathe* Vermont: the blazing maples, the rutted roads, the ornery righteousness. Characters drop the regional quasi-curse "Christly" the way heavies in gangster movies spit the f-word. And they live with an astounding awareness of the history of their home ground. In Craven-Mosher films, time is fluid, and the past can flood the present as swiftly as the dam water threatens to overwhelm Noel Lord's ancestral lands.

You may have caught one or more of Craven's films on cable television; if you live in New England and haven't seen one at your local theater or Grange hall, it's not for lack of trying on Jay Craven's part.

Jay Craven came of age as a 1960s activist, and he never traded in the dream of a participatory democracy for a seat in the oligarchy. He speaks passionately of the potential of localist cinema, of "the idea that Vermont stories are worth telling. There is a population here that never sees its own culture, its own history, its own characters, validated in the mainstream cinema. When a Hollywood film uses the region it tends to caricature or stereotype the region. *Why not have stories told from where we are about who we are?*"

Why not? For one thing, explains Craven, "Like every huge industry," the movies are "concentrated and centralized." Southern California is the epicenter, from which Vermont—and Kansas and Mississippi and probably wherever you live—is invisible.

Craven recounts this exchange with the head of a major film distribution company about *Where the Rivers Flow North*.

> "You're talking about a kind of film that doesn't even register on our radar screens," he said. "A Vermont film won't play to our urban demographics."
>
> "How do you know?" I said. "And how can you characterize 'a Vermont film' without considering its own merits?"
>
> The distributor looked at a colleague, then at me. "Look," he said. "As far as I'm concerned, there's a brick wall eight miles outside of Manhattan. And I don't care what happens on either side of that wall. And I doubt [other] companies do, either."

Those of us who live beyond that wall are not without fault, however. "Maybe part of it," says Craven, "is that we accept our own marginalization. That can stop you before you start." We become inured to the effluvia of Hollywood, whose message is that unless we are Manhattan surgeons or LA lawyers or icy models or chiseled AK-47-wielding studs our lives are risible, trivial, unworthy.

"People like their regions but they don't necessarily view them as important in the larger scheme of things," says Craven. "Particularly when they are exposed to media that comes from a homogenized center." This is an old and discouraging story. From Flannery O'Connor of Milledgeville, Georgia, to Wendell Berry of Port Royal, Kentucky, the best modern American writers are almost invariably greatly undervalued by their neighbors. But then a certain book tells us that the prophet is always without honor in his hometown.

The possibilities of regional filmmaking were illuminated for Craven by *Northern Lights* (1978), a harsh and lovely independent film about the agrarian radicals of the Non-Partisan League of North Dakota. After meeting the Upper Midwestern makers of *Northern Lights* at an alternative cinema conference in 1979, Craven bought a print of the film and showed it in fifty towns across Vermont. He brought it to Grange halls and schools and wherever a screen could be set up. "I was really excited that here was a film made not only about a region but about farms. That's where I picked up this populist practice of touring my own films."

"That spirit of taking movies to people where they are—and who they are. That's been the most important part of my films." He adds, "Whether the economics work is another question."

Ah, yes, the economics.

Craven's early films had budgets in the $1.5–$2 million range. He put them together by hook or by crook—decidedly *not* by the book—from a combination of grants, nonprofit fundraising, bank loans, and investments sold in shares of $1,000, $6,000, and $10,000. Actors worked for scale: Hollywood veterans emoted in Vermont for perhaps $8,000 a picture, whether because they love Mosher's books or Craven's films or they just like to work. (In addition to the aforementioned actors, his casts typically mix Vermont players with established figures such as Michael J. Fox, Martin Sheen, and Carrie Snodgress.)

Only eighteen of Vermont's 236 towns and nine cities have theaters, yet Craven toured *Disappearances*, his most recent film, to an even 100 sites in Vermont, up from his usual schedule of sixty to seventy tour stops. He also brought *Disappearances* to Maine, New Hampshire, and Massachusetts, compassing a Northern New England cinema of place. In Craven's case, the prophet has been with honor—even profit—in his hometown. "*Where the Rivers Flow North* probably outgrossed *Men in Black* in Vermont," he laughs.

Outside New England, the commercial terrain is rougher.

"The film industry is brutal in terms of dealing with any independent film," he remarks, and "it has gotten progressively worse over the last twenty-five years." With *Where the Rivers Flow North*, "it was still possible to make individual connections with independent theater chains and independent theaters and art houses. We could talk our way into theaters" in cities like Chicago, Ithaca, and Charlottesville. That is nigh impossible today, as five chains own more than half of the almost 39,000 indoor theaters in America.

The big boxes are no more helpful than the theater chains. For instance, says Craven, *Where the Rivers Flow North* "sold 35,000 videos at $60 apiece." A dozen years later, *Disappearances* sold 120,000 DVDs retailing for $24.95 but which Wal-Mart, the main buyer, vended for $9.95, "providing very little revenue" for the filmmakers. Between those two releases, laments Craven, the industry had degenerated from the "thousands of video stores who purchased *Rivers*" to "basically eight buyers that accounted for nearly all the sales" of *Disappearances*. Consolidation, as is so often the case, was the enemy of the small and the local.

Yet Jay Craven keeps making films about his place and its people. He holds Vermont casting calls for all his films, and to the extent possible he uses Vermonters in the crew, though it is simply not possible, at this stage of Green Mountain cinema, to fill senior positions with local people.

When we met in October, Craven was doing postproduction on his next movie, *Northern Borders*, based on a Mosher novel. The budget for *Northern Borders* was half a million dollars, a sharp cut from previous productions. "I could not in good faith go forward to raise investment money" for a film that is unlikely to show a profit, he says. So under the aegis of Marlboro College, Craven brought thirty-four students and recent graduates from fifteen colleges together for a "film intensive semester" to top all film intensive semesters.

It started with a week at the Sundance Film Festival. Then came six weeks of academic work: reading Vermont stories and literature dealing with rural places; taking classes in cinematography, directing, and production design. And then, for the next seven weeks, these students, along with twenty production pros and a cast that included Bruce Dern and Genevieve Bujold as well as eight Vermont actors, made a movie. The students, drawn mostly from New England and New York colleges, had jobs that went well beyond fetching coffee for the stars. They filled such key roles as costume designer, script supervisor, boom operator, and best boy.

Northern Borders has a tentative release date of April 2013. You may not catch it at the local multiplex, but if you're within driving distance of Vermont you'll be able to watch a screening hosted by the director himself. Craven is already planning his next film, a New England seacoast drama (based not on a Mosher novel but a story by Guy de Maupassant) to be filmed with the same kind of straitened budget and hybrid crew as made *Northern Borders*.

Jay Craven is modest—real Vermonters don't brag—but he does allow that "maybe what's remarkable about my work is that I've been able to make as many films as I have." He has come closer than any other filmmaker to realizing Vachel Lindsay's dream of vital regional cinema that embodies the character and genius of a place in all its mystery and magnificence and even pain.

Our places will not flourish unless and until our artists turn their attention homeward, and paint on the canvases of their own backyards. Why conform to the cynical fashions or mimic the bloodless monuments to avarice of blockbuster-blinded Hollywood? Myth and drama, tragedy and farce: Every story we could ever hope to tell is waiting there on the streets where we live and the fields in which we work and play.

Young filmmakers: take heed. Your places, too, belong in the movies.

LOST HISTORY

"Denounce the government and embrace the flag. Hope to live in that free republic for which it stands."
—WENDELL BERRY

Dick & Julia
The American Enterprise, 1999

THE GENETIC JURY MAY still be out on Thomas Jefferson and Sally Hemings, but we don't need DNA detectives to determine whether a major figure of the Democratic Party of the 1830s—indeed, the Vice President of the United States—treated a black woman as his common-law wife and sired two children with her. He did it quite in the open, or as openly as mores would permit. And he even won the electoral votes of Mississippi and Alabama.

Richard Mentor Johnson was a Kentuckian who represented his state for more than twenty years in the House and Senate before serving as Martin Van Buren's Vice President from 1837–41. (His mother was named Jemima, but we shan't be Freudian about this, for by the sketchy accounts available Dick Johnson's beloved was no corpulent pancake-frying mammy.)

As an infant, Johnson's cradle was struck by a lighted arrow fired by attacking Indians. A born Indian fighter, you might say, a trait that came in handy when war broke out in 1812. Congressman Johnson became Colonel Johnson and led twenty frontiersmen in a "forlorn hope" charge against the legendary Tecumseh at the Battle of the Thames.

Fifteen of the twenty died in fierce battle; the badly wounded Johnson was smote in hip and thigh. An Indian rushed in to administer the coup de grace, but Johnson calmly aimed, fired, and down went Tecumseh—or so Johnson's friends claimed. (His enemies had their doubts about the slain Indian's identity.)

A hero was born: an unreluctant hero who liked to tear open his shirt and show off his scars while on the stump. For the next thirty years his admirers sang "Rumpsey Dumpsey, Colonel Johnson shot Tecumseh." Simple, but then so was "I like Ike."

Johnson was a classic picturesque Jacksonian Democrat—with one difference. For as the Louisville *Journal* declared, "The plain truth is that Colonel Johnson is the husband of a mulatto." Although officially a bachelor—miscegenation was against the law in Kentucky—Johnson's "mistress of the parlor" was his slave and lover, Julia Chinn. (They may have married sub rosa.) Richard and Julia had two daughters, Adaline and Imogene, whom he raised ... well, like daughters. Both married white men and were given considerable properties, including Johnson's grand manor.

Johnson's domestic situation was common knowledge. An opposition newspaper in Trenton, New Jersey, suggested that if the Colonel "expires in his wife's gentle embrace" his epitaph should read "Died in the Wool." The Washington *Spectator* predicted that a Johnson presidency would "be the means of an African jubilee ... throughout the country." (Johnson, as a good border-state Democrat, was no abolitionist, though he did emancipate many of his own slaves.)

Andrew Jackson was one Johnson mentor. Old Hickory, not exactly a *Guess Who's Coming to Dinner?* race-mixer, knew all about Julia Chinn. In 1835, Tennessee Justice John Catron wrote Jackson, "The idea of voting for [Johnson] is loathed beyond anything," for Johnson "had endeavoured often to force his daughters into society." Moreover, Julia and the girls "rode in carriages, and claimed equality." Catron denied that "a lucky random shot, even if it did hit Tecumseh, qualifies a man for Vice President."

It was a bereft Johnson who was elected Vice President in 1836. Julia had died of cholera three years earlier. In 1836 daughter Adaline—"a source of inexhaustible happiness and comfort to me"—passed away. Johnson's love life became erratic: He took up with a beautiful mulatto slave, who ran off with an Indian. Thus spurned, he turned to her teenaged sister. A Kentucky Democrat fretted, "He seems happy, but how can he expect his friends to countenance and sustain him, when he lives in adultery with a buxom young *Negro wench*?"

The Democrats dumped Johnson after one term, although he still received forty-eight vice presidential electoral votes in 1840. He returned to his old Kentucky home, where he served in the state legislature and played the role of Retired Great Man.

In 1929, one Kentucky old-timer recollected the "Colonel Dick Johnson" he had known as a boy. "I reckon he was the most popular man in the county," declared Judge James Y. Kelly. "He was the most polite man I ever saw. ... Old Colonel Johnson had a mulatto wife. ... His colored daughters got all the education they wanted. ... I heard men say they were treated so well by Colonel Johnson."

The Vice President's biographer notes, "Had Johnson sold his children on the slave market, as many men did in that day, no political exception would have been taken to it." But instead he did the right and honorable thing. He loved Julia Chinn; he loved his daughters as daughters.

One hundred sixty years later, in these morally superior times, can you name a prominent white politician—let alone a Vice President—with a black wife and children?

Just Deseret

The American Conservative, 2012

I can't say that some of my best friends are Mormons, but I've always had a soft spot for the Latter-day Saints. Their faith was founded about fifty miles to our east during the antebellum roil which gave to our region the appellation of the "Burned-Over District," as religious and reform enthusiasms (abolition, women's rights, spiritualism) set this land afire. I find the *Book of Mormon* implausible, but as an indiscriminate patriot of the Burned-Over District anything or anyone hailing from these parts is okay by me, from the free-love Oneida Community to Ann Lee and her celibate Shakers (and what a rotten perpetuation strategy *that* was: a no-sex sect).

My Mormon-friendliness (and no, I never experimented with LDS) is pretty much limited to rooting for BYU football, though in 1984, when I had quit the employ of Senator Pat Moynihan and wanted nothing more to do with politics, I rode the Hound to Salt Lake City, where I flopped for a couple of months at the New Grand Hotel, writing derivative Beat poetry and thinking on things. (I got a charge years later when I read in Wallace Stegner's novel *The Big Rock Candy Mountain* that his fictive alter ego's no-good father hung around the New Grand.)

Almost a score of years ago I published a travel book about rural New York (*Country Towns of New York*) in which I wrote up Palmyra, the Mormon mecca, in whose environs Joseph Smith claimed to have received a visit in 1823 from an angel named Moroni, who directed him to the west side of a glacial drumlin which the Mormons would call Cumorah. There Smith found a stone box containing a set of gold plates upon which was written (in an ancient language) the *Book of Mormon*.

For one week every July, tens of thousands of Mormons and Gentiles alike gather at sunset at the foot of the Hill Cumorah to watch a multimedia pageant of LDS history. As a waggish merchant said of the Mormons who descend upon Palmyra each summer, "They bring the Ten Commandments and a ten-dollar bill and never break either one."

The proselytizing at Hill Cumorah is low-key. Typically, the pageant's actors fan out through the crowd a couple of hours before show time. A cute

Mormon girl or earnest Mormon boy, dressed as a Lamanite or Nephite and soon to take the stage, will ask you where you're from, tell you that he or she has had an "awesome" time at Palmyra, and say something like, "I want you to know that all these stories you're going to see tonight are true, and reading the *Book of Mormon* has brought me more joy than I ever imagined."

And that's it for the evangelizing. I don't believe these stories are true, but for the life of me I can't understand why I'm supposed to despise these people.

Politically, though, it's a freefall descent from Joseph Smith to such wretched Mormon solons as the epicene Orrin Hatch or the bloodless (which is perhaps why his foreign policy is so bloodthirsty?) Mitt Romney.

Joseph Smith ran for president in 1844, at least until a mob killed him in Illinois. He was thus the first U.S. presidential candidate to be assassinated. (Those in the best position to win this toughest of all bar bets, however, are usually absent from the bar.)

Smith's supporters held a nominating convention in the Mormon settlement of Nauvoo, Illinois, on May 17, 1844. They declared themselves for "liberty and equal rights, Jeffersonian democracy, free trade, and sailor's rights." Hell, that beats anything that will come out of this year's late-summer covens in Tampa and Charlotte.

Smith issued a campaign document whose proposals ranged from the good ("Break off the shackles from the poor black man") to the bad (cut the size of Congress in half) to the ugly (grant the President "full power to send an army to suppress mobs," a presentimental plea for self-preservation).

Far and away the most interesting plank in Smith's platform was this: "Petition your state legislatures to pardon every convict in their several penitentiaries: blessing them as they go, and saying to them in the name of the Lord, *go thy way and sin no more.*"

Whaddaya say, Mitt?

Joseph Smith even broke into Whitmanesque rhapsody: "Restore freedom! Break down slavery! Banish imprisonment for debt, and be in love, fellowship, and peace with all the world."

"Love, fellowship, and peace with all the world"? For such heresies Smith would be reviled, if not maced and tasered, at Mitt's coronation. When it comes to Mormon politicos, give me that old-time religion.

Our (First?) Gay Vice President
The American Enterprise, 2003

VICE PRESIDENT WILLIAM RUFUS King of Alabama may have been a "prim, wig-topped mediocrity," as historian Roy F. Nichols judged him, but King was also about as flaming a queen as the 1840s would allow. As Steve Tally wrote in his popular account of the vice presidents, "King did nothing to dispel the stereotype of the effeminate homosexual. He was a flowing dandy who favored silk scarves, brilliant stickpins, and glittery accoutrements." The veep made Oscar Wilde in full flower look like Ernest Borgnine.

Rumor had it that King had carnal knowledge of his male slaves, but what inquiring minds have really wanted to know is just what, if anything, he did with his roommate, Pennsylvania Senator (and later President) James Buchanan.

While there is little question of King's proclivities, the matter of Buchanan's sexuality remains a mystery. His only serious courtship was of a rich Lancaster girl named Anne Coleman, who seems to have committed suicide after breaking off their engagement under murky circumstances. (Letters that might have illuminated the affair were burned by Buchanan's executors—at the President's request—after his death.) Historian Nichols argued that Buchanan used the "romantic legend" of Anne's suicide "to shield himself" from later suspicions that he lacked an interest in women. For fifty years his mourning gave him excuse to avoid female companionship.

Instead, he consorted with Democratic Senator King, with whom he roomed from 1836 until 1844. While same-sex cohabitation was common, their relationship clearly was not. Washingtonians called them "Siamese twins" and "Mr. and Mrs. Buchanan." King was widely referred to as "Aunt Fancy," while Andrew Jackson called him "Miss Nancy." Their household broke up when King was appointed minister to France, though he wrote "Dear Buchanan" from Paris, "I am selfish enough to hope you will not be able to procure an associate who will cause you to feel no regret at our separation."

Subtlety was shoved into the closet when opposition papers described either man. As one anti-Buchanan newspaper sketched him, "Mr. B has a shrill, almost female voice, and wholly beardless cheeks; and he is not by any means, in any aspect the sort of man likely to cut his throat for any Chloe or Phillis in Pennsylvania."

Uh, yeah, we get the picture.

The friends had but one serious political disagreement. Buchanan, stalwart of the imperialist wing of the Democratic Party, wished the U.S. to acquire Cuba and Central America, while King opposed expansion in any direction, even westward.

The roomies promoted each other's career with an avid mutuality. To no avail, Buchanan urged King upon his party in 1840 as a replacement for Van Buren's Vice President Richard M. Johnson, who had taken a series of black women as lovers. When Buchanan served as Secretary of State under Polk, he tried, unsuccessfully, to maneuver Polk into appointing King as his successor. For his part, King tirelessly boosted Old Buck for president. In 1852, after Buchanan had lost yet another Democratic nomination, he was appeased by the selection of King as Franklin Pierce's running mate.

King, sadly, was tubercular and dying. He sought recuperation in Cuba and by an act of Congress was allowed to take his oath of office on that island so coveted by Buchanan. He came home to Cahaba, Alabama, to die, and did so just six weeks into his vice presidency.

Four years later, Dear Buchanan became our only bachelor President. Though vilified as a weakling by conventional historians, Buchanan has had the posthumous good luck to fascinate his fellow Pennsylvanian John Updike, who has devoted a novel and a marvelous if obscure play (*Buchanan Dying*) to the Keystone State's only president.

As for William Rufus King, this gay slaveowning defender of the South's peculiar institution embodies a classic p.c. contradiction. In 1986, the sensitive solons of King County, Washington, approved a proposal to change their county's eponym from the Vice President to Martin Luther King Jr. But wait—was this not homophobia? A hate crime committed by Seattle liberals? So asserted one doughty gay-rights activist, who has launched a campaign to once more honor William R. King—or at least honor that half of him that loved men, not the half that owned them.

Mary Chesnut's View from the Plantation
The American Enterprise, 2005

"I WAS A SECEDER, *but* I dreaded the future," South Carolinian Mary Chesnut informs us early on in the remarkable diary she kept during the Civil War. For the next four years she will record conversations, table talk ("One more year of Stonewall would have saved us"), and rumors of war. But her prophecy of June 1861, frank and enigmatic, stands: "Slavery has to go, of course—and joy go with it."

Twenty years after joy's emancipation, Chesnut revised and recast her journals, imparting to them a literary quality that sets the diary in the first rank of Civil War writings. Edmund Wilson, in his classic study *Patriotic Gore*, called Chesnut's diary "an extraordinary document . . . a masterpiece," but its author did not live to see its publication. Her lifetime literary earnings totaled ten dollars, her pay for one article for the Charleston *Weekly News and Courier*.

Mary Chesnut was not born of the plain folk of the Old South. Daughter of South Carolina Governor Stephen Miller, who was "credited with launching the 'positive good' defense of slavery," in historian C. Vann Woodward's words, Mary was educated at Madame Talvande's French School for Young Ladies in Charleston.

Her husband, James Chesnut, was the first U.S. senator to resign after Lincoln's election, yet his refusal to jockey for office in the Confederacy tries Mary's always fragile patience: "I am certain of very few things in life now. This is one of them. Mr. C will never ask mortal man for any promotion for *himself* or *for one of his family*."

Mary is a little catty (she notices the dullness, plain Janeness, and embonpoint of other ladies) and a tad prideful: "It was a way I had, always, to stumble in on the *real* show." Her reading is vast, her style tart, and her opinions strong. She defends Jefferson Davis to the last ditch, and she takes special satisfaction in reading purloined Yankee letters: "What a comfort the spelling was. We were willing to admit their universal free school education put their rank and file ahead of us *literarily*. Now, these letters do not attest that fact. The spelling is comically bad."

Though Mary Chesnut is a loyal daughter of the South, "a rebel born," she is also something of an abolitionist: "God forgive us, but ours is a *monstrous* system and wrong."

In her hatred of slavery she is not, she insists, an anomaly: "not one third of our volunteer army are slave-owners," writes Chesnut, and "not one third of that third fail to dislike slavery as much as Mrs. Stowe or Horace Greeley."

But New England sanctimony rankles her: "On one side Mrs. Stowe, Greeley, Thoreau, Emerson, Sumner, in nice New England homes—clean, clear, sweet-smelling—shut up in libraries, writing books which ease their hearts of their bitterness to us.... What self-denial do they practice? It is the cheapest philanthropy trade in the world—easy."

Paranoia strikes deep when her cousin, Betsey Witherspoon, is strangled to death in her bed by "her own people. Her Negroes." Mary's mother-in-law declines to eat, fearing that her slaves have poisoned her soup. Even the formidable Mary is shaken: "Hitherto I have never thought of being afraid of negroes. I had never injured any of them. Why should they want to hurt me? ... Somehow today I feel that the ground is cut away from under my feet. Why should they treat me any better than they have done Cousin Betsey Witherspoon?"

The diaries darken as the months pass. "War cloud lowering," she reports in June 1861. Even sleep brings no respite, for "this horrible vision of the dead on the battlefield haunts me." By June 1862 she records, "All things are against us." And by September 1864, "The end has come ... We are going to be wiped off the face of the earth." Sherman burns South Carolina, and though the badly damaged Chesnut plantation is salvaged, Mary's world is ashes and dust. She calls it the "Grand smash." For consolation she puts down her English and French novelists and turns to Job. By February 1865, "Our world has gone to destruction."

Amidst the ravages of war, the desolation of defeat, Mary remains incapable of self-pity. She declares in May 1865, "If we are a crushed people, crushed to aught, I have vowed never to be a whimpering pining slave." That vow Mary Chesnut kept.

Poor Old Buck

The American Conservative, 2013

ONE DISADVANTAGE OF HAVING exiled our television for several years is that I'm counting on Rona Barrett and Mary Hart to relay this news, but if for some reason they are stuck in analog TV traffic, I must tell you that Ron (*Gettysburg, Gods and Generals*) Maxwell's new movie, *Copperhead*, which opens June 28, is from a screenplay I adapted from the novella by Upstate New York's greatest novelist. No, not James Fenimore Cooper (of whose *Deerslayer* Mark Twain said "its humor is pathetic; its pathos is funny; its conversations are—oh! indescribable; its love-scenes odious; its English a crime against the language") but Harold Frederic, the pride of Utica (along with Annette Funicello and Roscoe Conkling).

Ron and cast and crew did a marvelous job of making vivid the world and story of *Copperhead*, which concerns an Upstate farmer who in the sanguinary years of 1862–63 says *No* to the war for the Union. Abner Beech (Billy Campbell in a subtly powerful performance) is neither a doughface (i.e., a Northern man with Southern principles, a la Lincoln's predecessor, James Buchanan) nor a congenital contrarian: he is, rather, a Jefferson-Jackson agrarian in the Upstate New York Democratic tradition. His side will lose, his tradition almost disappear, but Abner will not be moved.

No spoiler alerts here; see the movie. I will say that *Copperhead* approaches the Civil War from an angle of vision unusual in American popular culture, though even there it might surprise you. Place and verism, after all, must always trump ideology. I despise "message" movies, or didacticism, or deck-stacking. Lord knows American movies are in need of alternative perspectives but the world can do without a libertarian Stanley Kramer or a localist Gene Roddenberry.

I mentioned the unlovable Buchanan, who has been on my mind since I recently reread *Buchanan Dying*, John Updike's imaginatively empathetic play about the despised fifteenth President, who on his deathbed revisits the people and the climacteric moments of his life in Lancaster and Washington.

James Buchanan was something of a cold fish, an inveterate office-seeker, and—typical of the decayed Democracy of that era—an expansionist/

imperialist who coveted Mexico, Cuba, and any other southerly territory that wasn't nailed down. He temporized—or played for time—as the Union ruptured during the interregnum between Lincoln's election and assumption of office, and Updike makes the best case he can for the wisdom of this course.

The play is an act of Pennsylvania patriotism. As Updike explained, "In my Pennsylvania childhood, I knew him to be the only President our great and ancient state had produced, but where were the monuments, the Buchanan Avenues, the extollatory juvenile volumes with titles like *Jimmie Buchanan, Keystone Son in the White House* or *'Old Buck,' the Hair-Splitter Who Preceded the Rail-Splitter*?"

In the tradition of such Middle Atlantic men of letters as Harold Frederic, Edmund Wilson, and Gore Vidal, Updike was something of a war skeptic, even a Copperhead, who referred to "the dubious cause of putting down secession with force." Writing in 1974 of "our hero," Updike noted hopefully that "it may be, in these years of high indignation over unbridled and corrupting Presidential power, that we can give more sympathy to Buchanan's cautious and literal constitutionalism than has been shown him in history books written by Lincolnophiles and neo-abolitionists."

Airball, John.

Vidal did not care much for Updike, whose books, he said, were surrounded by a "force field" that rendered them impenetrable. Vidal tamped his enthusiasm for *Buchanan Dying* because he thought Updike skirted the matter of Buchanan's ambiguous sexuality. Updike gives Buck an Ann Rutledge of his own, Anne Coleman, who takes her life in despair over her suitor's lack of ardency. He ignores the possibility—the *possibility*—that Buchanan had eyes instead for his erstwhile roommate, Senator (and Vice President) William Rufus King of Alabama, the silk-scarved dandy who was the most famous pre-Jim Nabors gay Alabaman.

As if playing his own devil's advocate, Updike quotes in his afterword Henry James: "The 'historic' novel is, for me, condemned ... to a fatal *cheapness*. . . . You may multiply the little facts that can be got from pictures and documents, relics and prints as much as you like—*the* real thing is almost impossible to do. . . . "

Buchanan Dying, like the historical novels of Gore Vidal and Thomas Mallon, among others, refutes James. On screen, I think *Copperhead* does too. But you be the judge of that.

Unfortunate Son

The American Enterprise, 2003

IF EXASPERATED SONS OF nutty mothers need a patron saint, why not call on poor reviled Robert T. Lincoln, son of Abraham and Mary?

The wild Bush girls, balletic Ron Reagan, awkward Chelsea: Posterity will little note nor long remember their foibles. Yet, as the sympathetic biographer of Robert T. Lincoln complains, "It seems to be an article of faith among those who admire Abraham Lincoln that his eldest son is to be criticized at every possible point."

Not that he didn't deserve it. He was a cold, snobbish lad grown into a money-grubbing corporate lawyer. "Robert T. Lincoln," sneered a contemporary, "was a man of mediocre attainments, puffed up with pride almost to the exploding point by the brilliance of his parentage, who, left to his own devices, never would have risen above the ranks of the commonplace."

The Lincoln home was famous for its lack of discipline. The children were uncontrollable, but Father Abraham "never reproved them or gave them a frown," said his law partner William Herndon. In the Lincoln Legend, Willie and Tad are lovably mischievous imps, while Robert is off at school, absorbing the worst traits of the upper class.

The "Prince of Rails," as Robert was dubbed, was the classic product of a twisted American tale. The father, wanting his son to have "everything that I never had," removed the boy from those healthy and earthy influences that had given the old man his hardihood.

Robert was hopelessly pompous. When the Lincolns entertained the newly-wed Tom Thumb and his miniature bride at the White House, Robert stayed upstairs in his room, spitting, "No, mother, I do not propose to assist in entertaining Tom Thumb. My notions of duty, perhaps, are somewhat different from yours."

Those notions of duty did not include dodging bullets in the war his father's government was waging. Robert was a shirker, a Harvard gentleman who sat out the war until February 1865, when he was given a resume-building captaincy.

After the war, Robert represented Eastern insurance companies and was eventually made president of the Pullman Company, maker of sleeping cars and breaker of strikes. As a "millionaire corporation lawyer and businessman of decidedly conservative views," writes Robert Goff, "Robert T. Lincoln does not fit well into the Lincoln legend."

Yet Pa had profitably represented railroads, and Son was very much the faithful Republican, serving as Secretary of War and Minister to Great Britain. His chief distinction, one newspaper reported, was in possessing the largest head in the Arthur cabinet. He was also honest, no common quality in the Gilded Age GOP.

Every quadrennium brought a modest Lincoln for President boomlet, but Robert scorned the office as a "gilded prison." In his final years he retreated to Hildene, his secluded Vermont estate, which he called, somewhat pathetically, his "ancestral home."

Robert might have lived out his life as a forgotten First Son had he not made the serious PR blunder of committing his mother to a nuthouse.

The deaths of her husband and three of four sons had unhinged Mary Todd Lincoln, not exactly a pillar in the best of times. A money-obsessed hypochondriac, she lived nomadically, consulted spiritualists, kept bonds sewn into her petticoat, and bought expensive clothing and jewelry which she refused to wear.

In March 1875, deluded that her hale son was deathly ill, Mary rushed to Chicago, where she wandered the halls of the Grand Pacific Hotel, partially clad, screaming at Robert, "You are going to murder me!"

Mother, meet Bedlam. Robert assembled a dream team of insanity declarers and had Mary packed off to a leafy sanitarium.

Mary was released within months, to Robert's dismay, for he feared that she would resume her shopping sprees and seances and make "herself talked of by everybody." Mary called Robert a "monster of mankind" whose concern was not for his mother's sanity but her securities. The public sympathized with the grieving widow. Yes, she was an eccentric shrew, but the Fourth Commandment must be obeyed. Mary fled to Europe to escape her only surviving child.

William Herndon, who clashed with Robert on occasion, wrote, "He has the insane rage of his mother without the sense of his father. Robert Lincoln is 'a wretch' of a man."

He wasn't that bad. But for all his riches, he was forever dwarfed by the face on the penny.

The Atheist Who Played in Peoria
The American Enterprise, 1998

BEFORE THE CIVIL WAR, he was a shrewd Illinois lawyer with corporate and railroad clients. A celebrated wit and gifted speaker, he entered politics, convinced that slavery was a wicked institution whose time was up. He was rumored to be a religious skeptic, even a scoffer. His heresy, he was told, would be a handicap in pursuing the political career he desired.

No, he was not Honest Abe. Indeed, this Illini lawyer, running his own congressional race in 1860, denounced Lincoln for being soft on the Fugitive Slave Law. But Abe won, and Robert Ingersoll lost, and while Abe went to Valhalla, Bob went to . . . well, millions would later come to have an opinion on *that* subject.

Robert Ingersoll gained renown for two activities that seem absurdly incompatible today: He was the nation's best-known propagator of the atheist creed, and he was the leading Republican orator of his age.

Robert G. Ingersoll was born in 1833 in the Finger Lakes region of New York, son of an itinerant Congregationalist minister. He loved his father but not his Father: "I have a dim recollection of hating Jehovah when I was exceedingly small."

As a Peoria lawyer, he rode the free-thinkers' lecture circuit in the early 1870s, ridiculing biblical inconsistencies, praising the serpent in the Garden of Eden, and predicting a glorious future in which "*Reason*, throned upon the world's brain, shall be the King of Kings, and God of Gods." (Think of him as Ayn Rand with a sense of humor. When a cigar manufacturer named one of its stogies the "Bob Ingersoll," the tobacco-mad eponym provided the slogan: "Let us smoke in this world—not in the next.")

Two years after declaring, "The Bible burned heretics, built dungeons, founded the Inquisition, and trampled upon all the liberties of men," Ingersoll delivered the most famous nominating speech in political convention history. He told the assembled Republicans in 1876, "Like an armed warrior, like a plumed knight, James G. Blaine marched down the halls of the American Congress and threw his shining lances full and fair against the brazen foreheads of every defamer of his country and maligner of its honor. For the Republican party to desert a gallant man now is worse than if an army should desert their general upon the field of battle."

Well, the Republicans did desert Blaine—"the continental liar from the state of Maine," as the unchivalrous called him—and nominated Rutherford B. Hayes, but Ingersoll's bizarre dual reputation was made: he hated G-O-D but loved the G-O-P. (As one wag noted, "A man who disbelieves in God may well believe in Blaine.")

It is inconceivable today that the nation's leading atheist would be the Republican Party's most popular speaker, but there you are. Ingersoll's political faith was ultra-orthodox: his trinity was gold, the tariff, and the GOP. By all accounts a kindly family man, Ingersoll was savage on the stump. He said of William Jennings Bryan, "His brain is an insane asylum without a keeper."

In our age, when bipartisanship is next to godliness, Ingersoll's waving of the bloody shirt could make a USA Today editorial writer faint: "The Democratic Party embraces within its filthy arms the worst elements in American society. . . . Every man that shot Union soldiers was a Democrat. Every man that denied to the Union prisoners even the worm-eaten crust of famine, and when some poor emaciated Union patriot, driven to insanity by famine, saw in an insane dream the face of his mother, and she beckoned him and he followed, hoping to press her lips once again against his fevered face . . . the wretch that put the bullet through his loving, throbbing heart was and is a Democrat. . . . The man that assassinated Abraham Lincoln was a Democrat. . . . Every man that raised bloodhounds to pursue human beings was a Democrat. . . . Soldiers, every scar you have on your heroic bodies was given you by a Democrat."

So, who you gonna vote for?

He was friendly with presidential candidates—James Garfield called him "Royal Bob"—but the usefulness of "Robert Injuresoul" always ended the day after the returns came in. A rumored ambassadorial appointment by President Hayes never materialized, for as the Washington Post jested, Ingersoll was already "plenipotentiary of his Satanic Majesty to the United States of America."

Ingersoll remained an unrepentant Republican and atheist to the end. His ashes are buried in Arlington Cemetery. As the Charlestown News and Courier reported his passing: "Robert Ingersoll died yesterday. Perhaps he knows better now."

Toledo's Golden Rule

The American Enterprise, 2005

TOLEDO, OHIO, HAS BEEN home to baseball-playing Mudhens, cross-dressing *MASH* corporals, and—stranger yet—the most colorful Tolstoyan anarchist ever to bear the honorific "Mayor."

Samuel "Golden Rule" Jones was a Welsh immigrant who made his fortune in the oilfields of Ohio and as the inventor of an oil-drilling implement manufactured in his Acme Sucker Rod factory. Jones experienced a religious awakening in 1894, which he announced by hanging a sign on the Acme wall reading "The Rule That Governs This Factory: 'Therefore Whatsoever Ye Would That Men Should Do Unto You, Do Ye Even So Unto Them.'"

He meant it. Jones abolished work rules and time clocks in his factory and instituted profit sharing, paid vacations, an eight-hour day, annual bonuses, and an adjacent Golden Rule Park, which featured fresh air, free concerts, and speakers preaching moral uplift. His goal, he said, was to show that "this fundamental rule of conduct, given us by the founder of Christianity, was a livable and practical thing."

The immensely popular Jones was elected mayor of Toledo in 1897 as a Republican but thereafter ran and won thrice as an independent whose platform called for banning political parties. Senator Mark Hanna (R-OH), the muscle behind President McKinley, called Jones "a crank, but he is a moral crank, and that makes the thing worse, for he believes what he says."

Golden Rule Jones's eccentricities were numerous and endearing. He stood on his head, sometimes speaking from that position. He gave away the better part of his fortune, often to strangers. He wore a flowing cravat and carried his heavily underlined copy of Whitman's *Leaves of Grass* into the prisons and workhouses whose inmates he visited. He paid court costs for the indigent out of his pocket.

Jones was often mistaken for a socialist, although the doctrinaire socialists derided him for his belief in Christian brotherhood and opposition to class warfare. He adorned his office with a portrait of Leo Tolstoy, not Karl Marx, and confessed, "I am indifferent to man-made laws."

In favoring public parks and municipal ownership of streetcars and utilities, Golden Rule Jones was a fairly standard, if unusually honest, Progressive mayor—except when it came to crime and punishment. "If I could I would open the penitentiaries," he said. "Anything which today separates me from the lowest soul in the penitentiary or tenderloin district is the very opposite of religion."

His psychobiographer and great-granddaughter Marnie Jones notes that Golden Rule "stands virtually alone among nineteenth-century reformers in his refusal to use municipal powers to repress vice." The state, he believed, could not abolish sin.

The teetotalling Jones would not enforce laws against boozing, gambling, or prostitution. He urged bluenoses to take ladies of the street into their homes until they got back on their feet, so to speak. His successor and friend, Brand Whitlock, said of Golden Rule: "He was an odd man, born so far ahead of his time that the sins of others never troubled his conscience."

Jones placed his faith in "the love of Christ" instead of the policeman's nightstick. "I believe the only way in which the saloon will finally disappear," he said, "will be through the growth of the loving spirit in mankind which will provide opportunity for people to lead decent lives."

When Mayor Jones sat in as Magistrate of the Police Court dealing with petty crimes, he routinely dismissed all cases. He explained: "I have done by them just as I would have another judge do by my son if he were a drunkard or a thief, or by my sister or daughter if she were a prostitute."

He paid no price at the polls for his heterodox views. The Golden Rule, it seems, was not bad politics. Mayor Jones died in office in 1904. "Toledo has my heart and my life," he said as the end drew nigh.

Albert Jay Nock called Golden Rule Jones "the incomparable true democrat, one of the children of light and sons of the Resurrection, such as appear but once in an era." As evidenced by the absence of an Anarchist Caucus within today's U.S. Conference of Mayors, our era has yet to find its own Golden Rule.

TR vs. the Dictionary

The American Enterprise, 2001

FROM BOYHOOD, THEODORE ROOSEVELT had been a notoriously bad speller, so as President he simply rewrote the rules of orthography—until a swarm of spelling bees stung him back to his senses.

The Spelling Reform Association had been founded in 1886 by Melvil Dewey, a dozen years after he had immortalized himself in the nation's libraries by siring the decimal cataloging system. America's spelling reformers advanced arguments ranging from the anti-colonialist (why shackle ourselves with sense-defying British spellings?) to the ridiculously practical: Lopping off superfluous letters would shorten books and save ink and paper, claimed the champions of "simplified spelling." Moreover, American schoolchildren could shave a full two years off their studies if liberated from spelling drills.

Defenders of traditional spelling occupied the high ground of poetry and custom, while the reformers trotted out the god of progressivism: efficiency. This Grate Debate wended its way down colorful byways. Mark Sullivan noted that the simplified spellers brandished a finding of an underemployed worker at the U.S. Pension Office, who had counted 1,690 different spellings of the word "diarrhea" in pension applications. To this, the mossback Librarian of Congress Ainsworth R. Spofford replied, "Is there any phonetic system which could bring about a uniform spelling of that word?"

The game was afoot—afut?—when the spelling reformers found a sugar daddy in Andrew Carnegie. The philanthropic steel titan bought naming rights with his subvention. Carnegie counseled a name change for the organization ("reform" scares people, he insisted), and so the Spelling Reform Association became the Simplified Spelling Board. It was studded with such eminences as Nicholas Murray Butler of Columbia, David Starr Jordan of Stanford, Mark Twain, and William James.

In March 1906, the SSB released a list of 300 words crying out for orthographic reform. Some of the recommendations had already slipped into accepted usage: "honor"without the u, "center" instead of "centre," "axe" with the e chopped off. But others looked bizarre: The SSB suggested replacing the "ed" in such words as "kissed and "missed" with a t. "Purr" would lose an r, and such words as "dullness" and "fullness" would be stripped of an l. "Through" would become "thru," and "thoroughly" would shrink to "thoroly." It all seemed so . . . mechanical. Rather like a metric system for words.

This was not phonetics, said literary critic Brander Matthews, chairman of the Simplified Spelling Board, but "simplification by omission."

Matthews had a friend in the White House, and in August 1906, with characteristic impulsiveness, President Roosevelt directed the Government Printing Office to adopt simplified spelling in all publications of the executive department. His order was not "far-reaching or sudden or violent," averred Roosevelt, but only a modest effort "to make our spelling a little less foolish and fantastic."

It may have been the worst miscalculation of TR's career.

The press heaped ridicule upon Roosevelt, who had a self-deprecating sense of humor but did not much like to be deprecated by others. The *Baltimore Sun* asked how the President's surname would be rendered in the new spelling: "Rusevelt" or "Butt-in-sky"? In best conspiracy-sniffing fashion, the Rochester *Post-Express* declared, "It is a scheme financed by Carnegie, backed by certain large publishing interests, and designed to carry out an immense project for jobbery in reprinting dictionaries and school books." Abroad, observers wondered just what had happened to the unruly and libertarian Americans. "Here is the language of 80 million people suddenly altered by a mere administrative ukase," marveled an English paper. "Could any other ruler on earth do this thing?"

The Supreme Court refused to folo soot, as did the House of Representatives, which voted 142–24 to overturn TR's order. The President withdrew his spelling edict and admitted defeat in this "undignified contest," though in a letter to Brander Matthews he deftly shifted the blame, asserting, improbably, that "the one word as to which I thought the new spelling was wrong—thru—was more responsible than anything else for our discomfiture."

Unbowed, Roosevelt vowed to use simplified spelling in his own correspondence, and he did so fitfully. As he would write a friend of his legacy, "I have succeeded in getting thru some things that I very much wisht, although not always in the form I most desired."

Roosevelt's crusade was carried on for some years by the *Chicago Tribune*, bastion of Midwestern Anglophobia, which between 1934 and 1975 used such spellings as "autograf," "ameba," "burocrat," and "rime," until finally its editors decided that enuf was enough.

Our First African President?
The American Enterprise, 1996

POOR WARREN HARDING. His administration gave us historic reductions in federal taxation and spending; a major naval disarmament treaty; and freedom for Eugene V. Debs and other political prisoners jailed by the original Red-baiter, Woodrow Wilson. Yet he is consistently rated a "failure" in polls of historians—polls which always deem the warmaking and state-building presidents "great."

If ever a black man has gotten a raw deal from a lily-white profession, it's Warren G. Harding.

Like so many American boys destined for greatness, Warren married rich. He was a handsome and amiable Marion, Ohio, newspaper publisher who took for his wife Florence Kling, the non-pulchritudinous daughter of Marion's wealthiest man. Her father, Amos Kling, would not allow Florence to cross his threshold for fourteen years—because he believed his son-in-law to have Negro blood.

So did many of the residents of Blooming Grove, Harding's birthplace. The President's partisans traced the mixed-blood stories to a pre-Civil War dispute between Ohio Democrats and Harding's abolitionist forebears, but some elderly locals said that for whatever reason, the Hardings had always been regarded as mulattoes in Blooming Grove.

It took a scholarly Harding-hater to give the rumor wings. William E. Chancellor was a professor at the College of Wooster (Ohio) and former superintendent of schools in Washington, D.C. He was a fanatical supporter of Woodrow Wilson, segregation, and the League of Nations, none of which Harding could abide. Throughout the 1920 presidential campaign, Chancellor published broadsides claiming that "Warren Gamaliel Harding is not a white man. . . . [He] was always considered a colored boy and nicknamed accordingly." Chancellor's evidence? Four notarized affadavits from Blooming Grove old-timers.

The style of the pamphlets was luridly racist—Harding's father was "obviously a mulatto; he has thick lips, rolling eyes, chocolate skin"—and they created a sensation in Ohio and beyond. In New York, operatives passed out photos of the White House labeled "Uncle Tom's Cabin?" As many as 250,000 circulars may have been printed. Yet editors refused to touch the story. As muckraker Samuel Hopkins Adams later wrote, "In the annals of American journalism there has never been another case where so much was left unpublished on a topic of major and sensational interest."

Republicans denounced "whispering campaigns" and "scurrilities" without mentioning their substance. (Though one GOP-produced poster reassured voters that "The Harding Stock" consisted of "the blood of English, German, Welsh, Irish, and Dutch.") The candidate himself said nothing. For as Pennsylvania pol Boies Penrose counseled, "Don't say a thing about it. From what I hear we've been having a lot of trouble holding the nigger vote lately."

Ultimately, Harding moved into the White House; Chancellor was summarily fired from Wooster. But the professor persevered.

In 1922, the obscure Sentinal (sic) Press published *A Review of Facts*, a bizarre agglomeration of Harding rumors compiled by Chancellor. "Our first Negro President," the book asserted, is "big, lazy, slouching, confused, ignorant, affable, yellow, and cringing like a Negro butler to the great." His boyhood nickname was "Nig"; he uses "cosmetics in order to make himself look more white than he really is."

The five-dollar book was sold door to door in Ohio and perhaps Washington, at least until Attorney General Harry Daugherty ordered the Bureau of Investigation into action. Bureau agents raided Sentinal Press, obtained a list of purchasers, and then ransacked Ohio, buying and seizing every copy of *A Review of Facts* they could find. They did a thorough job: only a handful of books are extant today, and they are among the greatest rarities of political Americana.

Investigator Gaston Means said that he burned "the entire edition" in a bonfire in "the rear grounds" of a Washington mansion. (Then again, the imaginative Means also maintained that Mrs. Harding poisoned her husband to save him from impeachment.)

President Harding died in 1923; Professor Chancellor outlived him by forty years, always denying authorship of the book that bore his name. Many black Harding families today claim kinship with the president. The Harding genealogy remains a mystery, though one that never seemed to trouble the easy-going Warren. As he once confided to an old friend who asked him about the rumor, "How do I know, Jim? One of my ancestors may have jumped the fence."

The Melodious Veep
The American Enterprise, 2004

THE ONLY U.S. VICE President to have written a tune covered by Van Morrison and the Four Tops knew something of the fickleness of fame.

Charles G. Dawes, the Chicago banker who served under Calvin Coolidge, had a great-great-grandfather who rode with Paul Revere (the patriot, not the guy who played keyboards for the Raiders). Yet legend has it that Henry Wadsworth Longfellow memorialized only the silversmith, and not Dawes's ancestor, because "the name Revere rhymed better."

A later poet, Helen F. Moore, would write sympathetically:

> 'Tis all very well for the children to hear
> Of the midnight ride of Paul Revere;
> But why should my name be quite forgot
> Who rode as boldly and well, God wot?
> Why should I ask? The reason is clear:
> My name was Dawes and his Revere.

Charles Dawes, descendant of the eclipsed rider, first made his mark rather less heroically, as a lieutenant in the Mark Hanna political machine that elected William McKinley President. Dawes's subsequent stint as comptroller of the currency led naturally into banking, but he was musical enough to stand out among the plutocrats. As one journalist wrote, "In the conformist Dawes there is bottled up an individualist. In the banker Dawes there is bottled up an artist."

Charles Dawes composed "Melody in A Major" in a single piano sitting in 1911. "It's just a tune that I got in my head, so I set it down," he said modestly. Dawes played it for a friend, violinist Francis MacMillan, who showed it to a publisher, and before he knew it, Dawes was a composer.

"No one told me it had been published," he recalled. "I was walking down State Street and came to a music shop. I saw a poster-size picture of myself, my name plastered all over the window in large letters and the window space entirely filled with the sheet music."

A phonograph recording of "Melody in A Major" sold briskly, to Dawes's amusement: "My business is that of a banker and few bankers have won renown as composers of music. I know that I will be the target of my punster friends. They will say that if all the notes in my bank are as bad as my musical ones, they are not worth the paper they were written on."

The banker-composer kept a hand (and wallet) in Republican politics. His ticket to national office was punched when in 1921, appearing before a Congressional committee investigating profiteering in the First World War, he bellowed, "Helen Maria! We weren't trying to keep a set of books; we were trying to win the war."

His Oliver North-ish outburst caught the voters' fancy, though with his martial swagger it was easy to forget that Dawes was chief of supply procurement, not a battle-grimed doughboy.

Running with Coolidge in 1924, Dawes entertained reporters with his "picturesque vocabulary, the odd collars, the strange pipes, the superficial don't-give-a-whoopness, the exaggeration of manner, the incoherence." And "wherever he went," as biographer Bascom Timmons wrote, "his 'Melody in A Major' was being manhandled by bands of every description."

Dawes complained, "General Sherman, with justifiable profanity once expressed his detestation of the tune 'Marching Through Georgia,' to which he was compelled to listen whenever he appeared anywhere. I sympathize with his feeling when I listen to this piece of mine over and over. If it had not been fairly good music I should have been subjected to unlimited ridicule."

In 1951, lyricist Carl Sigman supplied words to Dawes's music. They began:

> Many a tear has to fall
> but it's all in the game . . .

First recorded by crooner Tommy Edwards, "It's All in the Game" has been cooed, barked, purred, and growled by Dinah Shore, Sammy Kaye, the Four Tops, Cliff Richard, and Van Morrison. Edwards's soulful 1958 version made it to number one on the Billboard charts. His recording remains the standard, though rock writer Dave Marsh regards Van Morrison's 1979 rendering as "one of the most emotionally revealing travels through the history of pop music."

Charles Dawes died in 1951, the year his wordless melody took lyrical flight. If he is as forgotten as the ancestor who rode with Revere, well, Chuck, it's all in the game. . . .

O Say Can You Sing?
The American Enterprise, 2003

WHEN FRANCIS SCOTT KEY, a poetical lawyer, rendered in verse his account of American resistance to the September 1814 British assault on Fort McHenry, he saddled his stirring lines with the lumpish title "The Defence of Fort McHenry." Key quickly changed this to "The Star-Spangled Banner," which a Baltimore musician set to the tune of "To Anacreon in Heaven," an English tavern song. Within a fortnight, patriots far and wide were singing of dawn's early light, twilight's last gleaming, and the rockets' red glare—the poetry of the pre-game show.

History, as usual, smirked. As Irvin Molotsky noted in his book on the anthem, Key had opposed the War of 1812. Moreover, Key's grandson, pro-Confederate Baltimore editor Frank Key Howard, would be imprisoned for treason in Fort McHenry in September 1861.

We might think of the eventual designation of Key's poem as the national anthem as a case of Congressional constituent service run amuck. "The Star-Spangled Banner" was one of two pet causes of Maryland Democrat J. Charles Linthicum. (The other was the repeal of Prohibition.) Linthicum took up the issue during World War I after the importuning of an eccentric Baltimore matron named Ella Virginia Houck Holloway, described by the *Baltimore Sun* as "an imposing figure . . . [who] always appeared in public wearing a tall shako, a cylindrical beaver hat with plume, that rose a foot above her head."

Mrs. Holloway's ardor for the flag made her charmingly daft or a damned nuisance. She patrolled the streets of Baltimore, ever on the qui vive for violations of flag etiquette. If her portfolio was modest—chairwoman of the Committee on the Correct Use of the Flag of the United States Daughters of the War of 1812—her energy was boundless.

Rep. Linthicum pressed on. The United States needed an official anthem, or so he declared, and it had better have been written in Maryland. He brushed aside the numerous criticisms lodged against the "Banner": that it was beyond the range of shower-stall singers; that its imagery was militaristic, and thus unsuited for a peaceable nation; that it was Anglophobic (in the third stanza, the mother country tracks in "foul footsteps' pollution"); that it was Anglophilic, borrowing as it does an English tune; that the music of a "ponderous old English booze-song" was inappropriate since the Prohibition Amendment had banished the demon rum from sea to teetotaling sea; and that imposing an official song on Americans went far beyond the legitimate powers of the federal government.

Just why we needed a single national anthem was a mystery never quite explained by the Banner's supporters. In an exchange on the House floor during the anthem debate, skeptical Rep. Hatton William Sumners (D-TX) remarked, "I have never been so sure and I am becoming less sure of the wisdom of undertaking to give direction to the drift of public opinion by legislation rather than have that drift come up naturally." Rep. Sumners wondered if "the idea of a government guardianship of the people everywhere and all the time may not be involved here," but he was reassured by Rep. Emanuel Celler (D-NY) that "people want this song."

"There is nothing to keep them from singing it," shot back Sumners. But the Key fit. Impressed by the 5 million signatures the Veterans of Foreign Wars claimed to have acquired in support of "The Star-Spangled Banner," the House and Senate finally approved Linthicum's measure, and President Hoover signed the national anthem into law on March 3, 1931. The Great Depression did not lift, and partisans of the Banner's rivals were furious.

Its chief rival, "America the Beautiful," had been written by Wellesley professor Katharine Lee Bates, a Cape Cod native who was inspired by an 1893 trip to the summit of Pike's Peak. Her words, later joined to a melody by Newark church organist Samuel Augustus Ward, have lost none of their power due to Congressional inaction.

If "The Star-Spangled Banner" lacks the beauty of Bates's "America," the soul of Woody Guthrie's "This Land is Your Land," or even the nursery-rhyme sweetness of "My Country 'Tis of Thee," at least our national anthem isn't Irving Berlin's numbingly bland "God Bless America" or the truly execrable schlock-country number "God Bless the USA." And perhaps it does us good, at public occasions, to ask anew Key's question:

> O say, does that star-spangled banner yet wave
> O'er the land of the free and the home of the brave?

Quaker for Peace

The American Conservative, 2014

Robert Douglas "Bob" Stuart Jr., who died in May 2014 at the age of 98, helmed two of the 20th-century Midwest's flagship cultural enterprises: Quaker Oats and the America First Committee.

A dozen or so years ago, I helped Mr. Stuart assemble and write a private memoir for his family. What a strange and rewarding experience that was: I would spend mornings reading through boxes of old letters exchanged between his father and young Bob, away at the Los Alamos Ranch School (alma mater of Gore Vidal and William S. Burroughs) and Princeton; and then in the afternoon I would interview the bright-eyed and vigorous octogenarian who used to be that boy.

We had oatmeal at every breakfast. Never had I dreamed of that porridge's gustatory potential! But then the Stuart family knew oatmeal. Bob's grandfather cofounded Quaker Oats. His father was president and CEO of the family business, as was Bob. Both men also served as a U.S. ambassador: father (under Eisenhower) to Canada; son (under Reagan) to Norway.

Bob Stuart was an unpretentious Scots-Presbyterian ("I've always believed that I should work a little harder than the next guy and never show off") grounded in Lake Forest, Illinois. But as the obituaries noted, he played a signal role in American political history.

In September 1940, Bob Stuart and several Yale Law School classmates—including future President Gerald Ford and future Supreme Court Justice Potter Stewart—founded the America First Committee, the largest antiwar organization in American history. Their law professor Fred Rodell later wrote in *The Progressive*—before Vietnam—that America First was "the only important U.S. political movement ever sparked and kindled by youngsters." (Ford quit when he feared his involvement might jeopardize his position as assistant football coach at Yale. A profile in courage!)

Speaking of which, there were Kennedy footprints all over America First. Old lech Joe Kennedy kicked in a few bucks, and John F. Kennedy sent the AFC a check for $100, with a note reading "what you all are doing is vital." Mr. Stuart's long-time friend Sargent Shriver, Kennedy in-law and the last pro-life Democrat to run on the national ticket, was present at the creation.

Mr. Stuart said that the disastrous entry of the U.S. into the slaughterhouse of World War I was his motivation in founding the AFC. He saw the new European war as a continuation of the previous one, and he wanted no part of it for his country.

The America First story has been told well by historians Justus Doenecke and Wayne Cole. Its personalities ranged from Main Street Republicans to prairie populists, from pacifist novelists to Midwestern manufacturers. Behind its banner stood figures as various as Socialist Norman Thomas, American Legion commander Hanford MacNider, and Sears Roebuck chairman Robert E. Wood. And, of course, Charles Lindbergh.

As a boy, Bobby Stuart fantasized about Lucky Lindy making an emergency landing in his backyard. Flash forward to 1941: Lindbergh, who despite his decidedly non-jocular public demeanor "was actually very easygoing in private," according to Mr. Stuart, was flying with Bob throughout the Midwest, occasionally turning the controls over to the starstruck young man for a flying lesson.

I asked Mr. Stuart if Lindbergh, who in his famous Des Moines speech of September 11, 1941, said that "the British, the Jewish, and the Roosevelt Administration" were "the three most important groups" pushing the country into war, ever expressed anti-Semitic sentiments to him.

"Never," he replied. Mr. Stuart said that he asked Lindbergh after the speech why he had said what he had, and whether he understood the damage he had done to the antiwar cause.

"Bob, be realistic, I'm right," responded Lindbergh bluntly. "If it's right, I should say it."

And that was the end of that conversation.

After Pearl Harbor, America First disbanded. Bob Stuart reported to Fort Sill for artillery school while many of the interventionist polemicists who had baited America Firsters as dreamy peaceniks found that wartime journalism better suited their talents.

Postbellum, Mr. Stuart chose Quaker, because it "was in my blood." He was by all accounts a humane CEO, well-liked by employees, and saddened when in his retirement Quaker was swallowed up by PepsiCo.

Peace is usually a rotten career move for the ambitious, but the America First connection never came up in Mr. Stuart's ambassadorial confirmation hearing. Nor did it harm JFK, Shriver, or Stewart, for that matter. Their coevals had lived through that era, and they understood that the America First Committee was in the broad tradition of American political activism.

My background is small-town populist; Bob Stuart's was patrician business Republican. Yet we got on terrifically well—just as he had with my ancestors in 1940, before war became the permanent American condition.

Barry Goldwater, New Leftist
The American Enterprise, 1997

"When the histories are written," Barry Goldwater told his friend and speechwriter Karl Hess in 1968, "I'll bet that the Old Right and the New Left are put down as having a lot in common and that the people in the middle will be the enemy." After all, what self-respecting hippie wouldn't prefer his ornery libertarian grandfather to Robert Strange McNamara?

Observers marveled at the number of Goldwater kids who joined Students for a Democratic Society (SDS). If the liberals were going Clean for Gene, some conservatives got hairy after Barry. Carl Oglesby, former president of SDS, made the link explicit with his declaration that "the Old Right and the New Left are morally and politically coordinate."

Karl Hess and the ebullient economist Murray Rothbard were the jovial prophets of Left/Right convergence. As Rothbard memorably put it in 1968, "Twenty years ago I was an extreme right-wing Republican, a young and lone 'Neanderthal' (as the liberals used to call us) who believed, as one friend pungently put it, that 'Senator Taft had sold out to the socialists.' Today, I am most likely to be called an extreme leftist, since I favor immediate withdrawal from Vietnam, denounce U.S. imperialism, advocate Black Power, and have just joined the new Peace and Freedom Party. And yet my basic political views have not changed by a single iota in these two decades!" (Rothbard soon soured on the New Left for its "arrogant self-isolation from Middle America.")

The personification of this Left/Right agenda-bending was Karl Hess, a Republican ghostwriter who threw off his suit and tie and donned a workshirt, grew a beard, learned to use an acetylene torch, and took up welding and revolution. The sunny Hess, who remained an ardent admirer of his old boss Goldwater even as he marched on Fort Dix, argued that the American Right had been "individualistic, isolationist, decentralist—even anarchistic" until the Cold War reconciled conservatives to the leviathan state.

Why, Hess asked, should the Right lead cheers for a war cooked up in the university labs of New Frontier-Great Society liberalism? With utter sincerity, he published in the New Left journal *Ramparts* an audacious

"Open Letter to Barry Goldwater" in which he asked Mr. Conservative to join the New Left.

This was not as loony as it might sound. In his 1968 Senate campaign, Goldwater told University of Arizona students that he had "much in common with the anarchist wing of SDS," notably opposition to the draft and hostility to overgrown institutions. What with the interminable war, talk of wage-and-price controls, and the Nixon administration creating new government agencies every week, might the independent Arizonan break ranks?

Karl Hess thought so. Because you are "the most essentially honest and potentially radical major American political figure," he told the Senator, "you will find yourself on this side of the barricades."

Hess's pitch was a mixture of flattery and challenge. Hadn't the Senator ever wondered why "the largest corporations . . . so strenuously opposed you and supported Johnson. . . . Could it have been that you might not have played ball quite so well as he?"

Hess even fit Goldwater for a dashiki: "Senator, if you had been born black, and poor, you would now be a Panther or I seriously misjudge the strength of your character and convictions."

He concluded: "I will have to admit that there is not exactly a long line queued up on the New Left waiting to hear from you. But there's a hell of a lot more room for you over here . . . than in a Republican Party which regards Everett Dirksen as a hero and you as a maverick."

Goldwater stayed put.

But he also stayed Karl Hess's friend. There is an enduring image of Karl at his shaggiest, protesting the war outside the Capitol. Word was that the demonstration might turn violent, so even the putatively antiwar members of Congress stayed away. Only one politician showed up: Senator Barry Goldwater, who waded into the throng, parting the astonished crowd—"Is that really *Barry Goldwater*?"—and asking the demonstrators, "Where's Karl? Where's Karl Hess?"

They met. They shook hands in the midst of the tumult—two old friends, divided by politics, but wise enough to know that politics are ephemeral, and that the real thing, the lasting thing, is friendship.

The Ford Impeachment

The American Enterprise, 1999

ON APRIL 15, 1970, House Minority Leader Gerald R. Ford coined a lasting truism when he told his colleagues and a packed press gallery that "an impeachable offense is whatever a majority of the House of Representatives considers [it] to be at a given moment in history."

Ford was proposing that the House appoint a select committee to investigate whether grounds existed for the Great-1970s-Impeachment-Trial-That-Wasn't: that of the seemingly eternal Supreme Court Justice William O. Douglas.

Historians have penalized Ford several demerits for the episode: for his part, the ex-President maintains that his action was "politically ill advised, but it was not irresponsible."

The case against Douglas was not frivolous. A year earlier, Justice Abe Fortas had resigned from the Supreme Court after it was revealed that while on the bench he had pocketed a $20,000 retainer from the foundation of jailed financier Louis Wolfson. Justice Douglas was moonlighting in the same crooked fields. Newspaper reports had established that over the years Douglas had received $101,000 from the foundation of Albert Parvin, former co-owner of the Flamingo Hotel in Las Vegas and business associate of Meyer Lansky, "Ice Pick Willie" Alderman, and others not usually placed within the category of "nice Jewish boys."

"I can't for the life of me see what is the difference between what Fortas was doing and what Douglas did for a whole lot longer, except that Abe gave the money back when he got caught," Ford told aide Robert L. Hartmann.

(A secondary charge was that Douglas had failed to recuse himself from a libel case involving publisher Ralph Ginzburg even though *Avant Garde,* a Ginzburg magazine, had paid the justice $350 for an article about folk-singing. Douglas later conceded Ford's point, though he protested, plausibly, that he was unaware that Ginzburg owned *Avant Garde.*)

Ford's attack on Douglas was widely regarded as GOP payback for the Senate's rejection of Nixon Supreme Court nominees Haynsworth and

Carswell, but longtime Ford lieutenant Hartmann insisted otherwise. In his memoir *Palace Politics*, Hartmann wrote, "Ford disapproved of Douglas the way a Grand Rapids housewife would deplore the behavior of certain movie stars." The conflict was "not so much liberal vs. conservative as swinger vs. square." With four wives and a rumored sexual athleticism that belied his advanced years, Douglas's lechery made him a tempting target.

Luckily for Douglas, it diverted his pursuers from the Parvin trail. Minority Leader Ford fatally wounded his case by dwelling on the fact that *Evergreen*, a hybrid hippie-nudie magazine, had published an excerpt from a Douglas book. This was said to violate the "good behavior" requirement that the Constitution placed upon judges. Yet Random House had sold *Evergreen* the reprint rights without Douglas's knowledge; moreover, the justice's article consisted largely of an eminently sensible attack on the taxpayer-funded depredations of the Forest Service and "the powerful Highway Lobby."

The *Evergreen* charge was a disastrous red herring that allowed Ford's foes to paint him as a bluenose. It did, however, provide comic relief, in the improbable person of Ohio Democrat Wayne Hays, who soon would meet disgrace when his buxom employee Elizabeth Ray disclosed to the world that typing was not among her talents. Hays wryly—or should we say ryely, for it was cocktail hour—noted that Republicans were passing around the disputed issue of *Evergreen* and wondered if it was "available only to Republicans—or can some of us Democrats get it?" He brought down the House when he asked the rabid Rep. Louis Wyman, "Has anybody read the article—or is everybody over there who has a magazine just looking at the pictures?"

Justice Douglas's many admirers piled on Congressman Ford, who suffered the worst press of his career. How dare he impugn the integrity of one of the nine robed archons! Though Ford's resolution attracted fifty-nine Republican and fifty-two Democratic cosponsors, the House Judiciary Committee conducted a desultory investigation, sweeping the disturbing Parvin connection under the rug. The lesson of the Ford-Douglas debate: an impeachable offense is whatever the House of Representatives says it is.

The affair did have a postscript. On November 12, 1975, an enfeebled Justice William O. Douglas tendered his resignation from the Court to President Gerald R. Ford, who thanked him for his "firm devotion to the fundamental rights of individual freedom and privacy."

The Elector Defector
The American Enterprise, 2001

THE ELECTORAL COLLEGE HAS shut down for another four years. Gore-y fantasies of "faithless electors" escaping their ironclad lockboxes and bolting from Bush to Prince Albert have come to naught. Apparently the Republicans have learned something about vetting electors since 1972, when a GOP elector deserted—and did so quite predictably. For the '72 renegade, Roger Lea MacBride, had written a book twenty years earlier in which he praised the conscience-driven elector as a vital, if all too rare, feature of the Electoral College. Sometimes authors mean what they write.

As a lad of sixteen, Roger MacBride, a Coke-bottle spectacled son of a *Reader's Digest* editor, fell under the spell of a family friend, Rose Wilder Lane, daughter of Laura Ingalls Wilder of *Little House on the Prairie* fame. Rose, a libertarian globetrotter and popular journalist who once rejected a marriage proposal from King Zog of Albania, had become a *cause celebre* when she refused to accept a Social Security number. ("I will have nothing to do with that Ponzi fraud because it is treason; it will wreck this country as it wrecked Germany. I won't have it; you can't make me," she declared.)

The childless Lane made MacBride her "adopted grandson," a winning lottery ticket if ever there were one. He became heir to the *Little House* fortune, which is ample enough to build big houses from one end of South Dakota to the other.

As a young lawyer, MacBride wrote a little book titled *The American Electoral College* (1953) in which he proposed a "district system" similar to that now in use in Nebraska and Maine; electors would be awarded by congressional district, with two bonus electors given to the winner of the state. "The district mode was mostly, if not exclusively, in view when the Constitution was framed and adopted," explained James Madison, but largely abandoned as states sought to maximize their relative influence by delivering their electors as a bloc to the victor.

MacBride deplored deviations from the Founders' intent, for instance the fact that "Electors almost never exercis[e] independent judgment." They had become mere "mechanical men," drones who in some states are forbidden by law from voting their conscience.

MacBride urged an "attempt to restore to the members of the Electoral College some of the function of independent thinking and action assigned to them by the Federal Convention." In this he was echoing Madison, who in 1823 had endorsed the independence of electors: "altho' generally the mere mouths of their Constituents, they may be intentionally left sometimes to their own judgment, guided by further information."

MacBride's book disappeared without a trace, and in 1972 the champion of the faithless elector was chosen by the Virginia Republican Party as a Nixon-Agnew elector. It would seem that the fabled Nixon intelligence team, otherwise occupied at the Watergate, failed to do the necessary background check.

Meanwhile, at a much less pricey (if bug-less) hotel 2,000 miles westward—the Denver Radisson—the Libertarian Party was born. In that Watergate June of 1972, 100 devotees of laissez-faire—Ayn Rand readers, free marketeers disgusted by the Nixon administration's imposition of wage and price controls, and congenital rebels—nominated for President John Hospers, an eminent philosopher from USC who once almost flunked a football-swift but classroom-slow jock named O.J. Simpson. "Humbled, dubious, and a bit frightened," Hospers ran a thoughtful and low-key campaign; his name appeared on the ballot in just two states. When he told a colleague at USC that he was running for President, the impressed pedant replied, "President of the Faculty Council?"

But Hospers had a secret. Roger MacBride had phoned the philosopher to tell him that he intended to cast his electoral vote for Hospers and running mate Tonie Nathan, thus ensuring that the first woman to receive a vote in the Electoral College had no familial ties to organized crime.

The Hospers-Nathan ticket received just 3,673 votes, but the big surprise came one month after Election Day, when Vice President Spiro Agnew announced to a befuddled nation that one electoral vote had been cast for John Hospers of California, placing him just sixteen electoral votes behind George McGovern.

Roger MacBride's faithlessness—or was it fealty to a higher principle?—earned him the Libertarian Party's 1976 presidential nomination, but this time around there were no refractory libertarians lurking on the greensward of old Electoral College.

MacBride's bolt invigorated the newborn Libertarian Party, and it taught the older parties a valuable lesson: When appointing electors, stick with hacks. And never choose a man who has written in praise of the faithless elector.

Going to Mass

The American Conservative, 2011

ALMOST A QUARTER OF a century ago, my wife and I spent our wedding night in Salem, Massachusetts. It was not, despite my frequent and predictable jests to the contrary, an omen. Except in the sense that I was bewitched.

The following day we stopped at Edson Cemetery in Lowell, where Lucine left her wedding bouquet at the grave of Jack Kerouac: Catholic running back, Beat novelist, Taft Republican.

"Taxachusetts" clichés and Ellen Goodman aside, any state that gave us *On the Road* and Nathaniel Hawthorne, Shays' Rebellion and *Walden*, Sam and Henry Adams, and a goodly share of the best nineteenth-century American poets is welcome in my Union.

We had occasion to revisit Salem this summer, as we toured a New England university that left our daughter (and us) mightily unimpressed. But what citizen of the old America can endure the punishment of a college tour? Unless, perhaps, one turns it into a drinking game: a shot for every time the admissions officer says "kind of" or "sort of"—the *y'knows* of the degreed class—and a beer for every invocation of "diversity," a wonderful word that, like "tolerance," has been drained of meaning and is now used to enforce a grey and dreary uniformity of opinion.

We've heard eager student cicerones assure us that campus wiccans have access to the school chapel—boy, was that ever a load off my mind!—but I've yet to get the impression that the incessantly touted "diversity" includes, say, rural Christians or working-class Catholics.

This trip we returned to the agreeably hokey Salem Witch Museum, whose voice-over narrative, while hard on the Puritans, is delivered with stentorian, NFL Films-style gravity to a suitably eerie soundtrack. The museum's script takes the conventional, quite possibly accurate view that Salem's victims were innocents caught up in a frenzy of hysteria and untruths; it ignores the more interesting speculation (most famously proposed by historian Chadwick Hansen) that some of those hanged at Salem really *were* witches.

We skipped the museum's latest exhibit, which is devoted to contemporary witch-hunts such as "the McCarthy hearings on Communism and the persecution of the gay community at the start of the AIDS epidemic." When even glorified wax museums are infected by PC, what is left? Demolition derbies?

Joe McCarthy was a nasty character, but why should he so completely hog the devil's role in modern American history? Can't he share the part with someone with an infinitely higher body count: say, Nagasaki Harry Truman? (Tailgunner Joe, it must be remembered, ran as an internationalist and interventionist against the incumbent he defeated, antiwar isolationist Wisconsin Senator Robert La Follette Jr.)

Jack Kerouac rather liked McCarthy, but otherwise his political heroes were a helluva lot more tolerant than those supported by his poet pal, the irrepressible Allen Ginsberg.

Jack "believed in a conservative working-class America" and in "baseball, the Virgin Mary, Buddha, and apple pie," according to his friend, the Beat publisher John Montgomery. Naturally, he supported constitutional Republican Robert Taft for president in 1952. Ginsberg was avid for Senator Paul Douglas (D-IL), a smug statist who combined, in worst Cold War liberal fashion, passion for the warfare and welfare states.

Douglas began his career deprecating the senior Robert La Follette for his "ridiculous" respect for "the vanished days of small and independent business" and ended it hawking the Vietnam War. Hey, Mr. *Howl*, it was Douglas & Co. who destroyed the best minds of your generation! One man's witch is another man's wiccan.

Pedantic Paul Douglas—born, coincidentally, in Salem—displayed little tolerance for dissenters from the Cold War and the imperial presidency. He offered the rebuttal to Senator Taft's magnificent speech opening the Eighty-second Congress. "The principal purpose of the foreign policy of the United States is to maintain the liberty of our people," said Taft. "Its purpose is not to reform the entire world or spread sweetness and light and economic prosperity to peoples who have lived and worked out their own salvation for centuries, according to their customs, and to the best of their abilities."

Taft insisted that Truman—or any president—needed congressional authorization before sending troops to Europe or Korea. He reminded the Senate that war "promotes dictatorship and totalitarian government" and "is almost as disastrous for the victor as for the vanquished."

Senator Douglas denied that Congress had any real say in such matters. He charged Taft with "defeatism"—a favorite word of the prophets of deathism.

Back in Lowell, after a perfect balance of wrong turns and helpful locals, we found Jack Kerouac's modest grave once again. "He Honored Life," reads the epitaph. Would that we all did.

HOME, SWEET, HOME

"One day in Dipstick, Nebraska, or Landfill, Oklahoma, is worth more to me than an eternity in Dante's plastic Paradiso, or Yeats's gold-plated Byzantium."

—EDWARD ABBEY

The Last Gun Show? Not if Doc Spink of Attica, New York, Has Anything to Say About it

The American Enterprise, 1999

FOR NIGH THIRTY YEARS Dr. Bud Spink of Attica, a recently retired veterinarian known to man and beast as Doc Spink, has run the Alexander Gun Show in western New York. To yuppie editorialists and the fabled soccer moms—the women in these parts are *baseball* moms—gun shows are arms bazaars where Crips and Bloods stock up on Uzis. In fact—not that fact matters when there are focus groups to be analyzed—a gun show is a communal gathering of mostly rural men united by love of history, of the outdoors, and of place.

Doc Spink and the Attica Lions Club took on the Alexander show as a fundraising project. The Lions Club was broke: it had depleted its modest treasury organizing "a mass community sandwich- and soup-making campaign" to feed the hundreds of troopers and medics and nurses who flooded Attica in September 1971, during the prison riot that made the town's name a byword.

Doc and the Lions have since raised and donated over $100,000 to such noble causes as a burn-treatment center, the State School for the Blind in nearby Batavia, volunteer fire departments, and Mercy Flight (a helicopter that transports the badly injured to hospitals). "Much of what we do is quiet," says Doc. "The nurses in the schools pick some kid that needs a hearing aid or eyeglasses that their parents can't pay for," and the Lions play angel.

Doc Spink is Attican in a way that the prison is not. His family goes back several generations into the hills. "I was born with a bad set of lungs and allergies so I knew I'd never make it in farming," says Doc. "The old vets came to me when I was a kid and conned me into going" to Cornell. "With their help I got into vet school, and I promised 'em I'd always make sure people were taken care of, 'cause most of 'em are my relatives one way or another. Up in the hills, you go back far enough and we're all related."

His education was a matter of community concern. "I hitchhiked [to Cornell] and the first day I realized I was in trouble"—he hadn't even the money to cover tuition, let alone room and board. So "the local banker gave me a checkbook and just said, 'I'll cover it.'" Working three jobs, Bud Spink became a vet.

He came home, as he promised he would, and spent a career caring for the horses and cows of his neighbors and shirt-tail cousins. "I would be all strung out, and I'd unwind by taking an old gun apart." Doc is a black-powder-gun collector, a fan of early American firearms: "I don't think I've fired a modern rifle since I was a kid. I love history and that's how I got into running these shows."

Doc puts on three shows a year. His latest was June 20, the last day of spring, but this was different, for the menacing stench of prohibition was blowing in from Washington and Albany. Even the name had been changed to protect the innocent: The erstwhile Alexander Gun Show is now the Alexander Charity Show of Sporting & Military Collectibles. Was this a response to the anti-gun hysteria? "One hundred percent," says Doc. "I didn't want to wave a red flag in front of the media. We've had 'em show up, the Live Eye News with their cameras and a guy sticking a mike in my face as if he had a right to invade my privacy."

Sellers—about half licensed dealers and half private collectors—start setting up at seven a.m. Sunday morning, or "as soon as I can get the janitor out of bed," says Doc. As they lug their wares (shotguns and rifles and military uniforms and medals and ammo and tackle and books) into the Alexander Firemen's Rec Hall, the air is spiked with conviviality. "It's like old home week," says Spink. "Guys haven't seen each other in a year, they'll get to jawing. Everybody helps everybody out." Doc grabs the microphone every now and then to remind the assembled to bring their used eyeglasses and hearing aids to the next show, in October, so the Lions can distribute them to the poor.

Bleary eyes and industrial-strength coffee are the order of this early morning. Last night the Buffalo Sabres lost the Stanley Cup in a heartbreaking three-overtime game that ended at 1:30 a.m., and talk is of the lousy call that robbed the Sabres. Wisely, the vendor selling Sabres caps has slashed the price from $9.95 to $4.95.

Admission is four dollars a head. Doc rents the 104 tables that line the Rec Hall for thirteen bucks a pop, though a couple of the guys get special "rates"—for instance, Sol Sloan, a retired pawnbroker from Buffalo's tough East Side. But the eighty-five-year-old Sloan has seen tougher. A native of

Transylvania, his first wife and two children were murdered at Auschwitz on June 4, 1944. Sol's life was spared when he told the Nazis he knew a trade.

"I didn't even know how to hammer a nail," he admits. "The Hungarians rounded us up in the ghetto, June 1944, they took us to Auschwitz. My wife had to go to the left, I went to the right. They beat the hell out of us. The next morning there was an S.S. man. He says, 'who has a trade go on this side.' I walked over. I tried to convince my friends and father to come on this side, but they were afraid. They put us in another barrack. At night I was so lonesome, I said I'm going to go over to them the next morning. But I never saw them again."

After the war, Sol settled in Buffalo, where he worked in a slaughterhouse before becoming a peddler. He recalls his astonishment that in his new country firearms were sold freely; even an immigrant Jew could buy a gun. "I said, 'Everybody can buy guns?' I wanted a gun. If I had a gun I wouldn't have let my wife be killed."

Sol sold guns for thirty-eight years, and he has been making the forty-mile trip to Alexander for as long as anyone can remember. "These are good people," he says, surveying the crowd. His kindliness does not extend to New York's rabidly anti-Second Amendment senator, Charles Schumer. "That sonuvabitch!" he spits out. "I saw what happens when Jews don't have guns. That Schumer, if he would be there, he would be dead."

Doc Spink labors hundreds of hours setting up the shows; his payment is far richer than mere money. For one thing, he always takes the table next to Ed and Evelyn Tierson. Ed, seventy-six, ran a landing craft in the Navy during the Second World War. He came home to Rochester and built a successful sheet-metal company, which he has since handed to his son.

The Tierson table usually holds the show's finest antiquities and oddities. This time around Ed and Evelyn have brought Indian trading silver, pre-Civil War flasks, a powder horn, a Cree Indian wedding dress, a Ketland Indian Chief's gun—yes, there are a few firearms amid the Native Americana. Ed proudly wears an NRA cap.

"I like people to see the stuff," replies Ed when I ask why half his space is occupied by "Display Only" items not for sale. "Of course they can go to a museum, but here you can talk to the people, they can touch it." Old friends stop by to exchange greetings and admire the displays. Prized items are inquired after, grandchildren boasted of. Ed and Evelyn disdain city shows, which are "too big—they're overwhelming." Alexander is on the human scale—the perfect size.

Ed tells stories of old shows, of guns bought—but never of guns sold. He still regrets not buying a "Sharps carbine coffee-grinder" years ago. The coffee-grinder was emplaced in the stock of the Civil War rifle: "I've never seen once since," he marvels.

"It's horse-trading," says Doc Spink of a gun show. As if to illustrate, a fellow stops by the table, picks up an 1837 flask, and cooly lists its flaws. Ed takes in the disparagement with an amused smile.

"What's the best you can do?" the man asks.

"Six-fifteen," says Ed.

The man shakes his head. "Will you take an offer?"

Ed nods.

"Four hundred," says the man, a sum that seems extravagant for a flask whose condition had made it fit for the rubbish heap seconds earlier.

The deal is unconsummated. Ed is not crestfallen. "That's the trick of the trade," he grins. "When you own it, it's the best ever made; when you want it, it's the worst you've ever seen."

An old-timer stops by and mentions to Ed that he still likes to take his Henry Rifle out hunting.

"Lemme know if you ever want to get rid of it," says Ed.

"Whatta they go for? Ballpark," asks the old-timer.

"Twelve to twenty-four thousand."

"You're kidding," replies the old-timer. That's a lot of money to go traipsing around the woods with. Cards are exchanged. A deal pokes its head above the far horizon.

Down the aisle, John Cooper, fifty-two, a Seneca Indian from Le Roy, New York, is selling a Baker "Batavia Leader" twelve-gauge shotgun. The Baker company was a mainstay of the Batavia economy in the early years of our century, employing, among others, my ancestors. The gun, priced at $1,000, is a beautifully made local artifact, the handiwork of indigenous craftsmen. John is a coin dealer from whom I buy the occasional large cent, and it is a source of mutual disgust that urban and suburban politicians want to make my purchase of a Batavia Leader (if I had a thousand dollars) a federal case, as kids used to say. (Now that everything is a federal case, I assume the expression has lapsed into disuse.)

John is astonished that so basic a right as gun ownership is under assault: "To me, to be against the Second Amendment is treasonous."

"I've always wanted to keep it apolitical," Doc Spink says of his show, "but for the first time I told SCOPE they could have two tables in a side room." Mark Shephard, my oldest friend, is one of three guys manning the SCOPE (Shooters Committee on Political Education) table. Shep, Dave Kaufman (no relation), and John Susz sell chances on two Buck knives and also alert passersby to pending legislation that would bar gun shows from being held in any building that receives a dollar of federal or state aid (such as the Alexander Firemen's Rec Hall). The grapevine is abuzz: A gun show has been cancelled in Saranac Lake, and the weathervane Governor George Pataki has announced that no more shows may be held on state property.

"This might be the last gun show," warns Dave, and despite the sounds of trading, of laughter, of friendships renewed over coffee and donuts, an elegiac air perfumes the hall.

Mark Shephard has been coming to Alexander with his dad since he was eight years old, but he does not own a single gun. Rather, he collects political campaign items. (He owns no Schumers.) He became a local SCOPE leader after "seeing Clinton on TV mocking gun owners. I thought if I didn't act soon, someday it might be too late. We've become spineless in this country—we don't stand up anymore."

"There's a lot of fear" in the hall, Shep observes, for many gun owners "believe the government wants to make an example out of them." (Or as Evelyn Tierson says, "I used to enjoy [gun shows] before they made it so difficult. You're afraid to do anything.")

I don't see anyone clad in paramilitary gear or even innocent camouflage. The only eye-raising raiment belongs to Thomas J. Thompson, vice president of the Attica Rod & Gun Club, who is fitted as a captain in the Pennsylvania Regiments of 1779. For money, Thompson is a prison guard at Attica; for love, he is a Revolutionary War re-enactor who visits the V.A. hospital and local schools, carrying the message of 1776. The gun control battle is about "civil rights," Thompson insists, because the controllers are motivated by "bigotry and prejudice" against the largely rural and working-class men who make up the National Rifle Association.

Thompson is among the most vocally political men in the hall, but his attachment to the Bill of Rights is grounded in everyday life, not theory. "I took Doc out shooting the flintlock," Thompson smiles, for shooting is his hobby: Next Sunday afternoon his Attica Rod & Gun Club is sponsoring a rifle and pistol shoot—100 yards, ten rounds—to benefit the Wyoming County Wildlife Federation. Shooters do not vacation among trees and brooks and hills and meadows; they live there.

The men and women at Alexander understand that incrementalism is merely a strategy of the Schumers; the ultimate, always unstated goal is "gun confiscation," as dealer Ray Doan of Rochester says. Doan regards the proposals to jack up the age at which a lad can own a gun as a way to strangle the bond of responsible firearms use that connects father to adolescent son. "If you don't get a kid interested in guns between eight and thirteen," he says, "you've lost him. He goes on to girls."

Doc Spink views the war on guns as part of the professional class's war on rural life. "You're farming, you've got to have weapons. It's one way of eliminating suffering in a hurry. I've taken the rabies treatment twice. The quickest way to eliminate a rabies problem is everybody goes coon hunting and skunk hunting and fox hunting. This didn't used to be a problem when furs were popular, but the anti-fur people ruined trapping and hunting for furs, which used to be an added source of income for rural people. It's getting to be a lost art: Father and son don't go out trapping and hunting any more. Another chink in the armor of the father."

Demented children who shoot up their schools are never from healthy gun-owning families. "Kids no longer have a home base or neighborhood," says Ray Doan, pointing to the rampant mobility of the suburbs. Or as Evelyn Tierson asks, "How many of the school shooters were from families that belonged to the NRA?"

Terry Smith of Corfu, a licensed federal firearms dealer, says the proposed clampdown on gun shows "won't hurt me. It'll hurt private individuals, guys who have three or four weapons" they hope to sell to other collectors. But "I worry about private rights," says Smith, "not my dealer rights." For as John Susz of SCOPE warns, "They wanna disarm everybody so the only ones who have guns are the cops and the military."

The show lasts until 3:00, though things start winding down by about 1:30. Attendance has dropped from previous years. Perhaps 700 people walk through the doors; prior shows have been visited by as many as 1,000. "The legislation and fears have hurt," says Doc.

So how was the show? "Good for talking," says Ed Tierson. "Not for selling." Which is to say, given that fellowship trumps mammon in Alexander, New York, it was a good show. Will there be another in 2000? "Depends on the government," shrugs Doc.

I leave Alexander with the plaintive words of Evelyn Tierson ringing in my ears: "It's so wrong to take this away. How many of the politicians know anything about this? We look forward to this, to seeing old friends, to handing out pictures of the grandchildren. The wives, we get together at night. That's what this is about. It's so wrong what they're doing, what they've made it out to be. It really angers me. It's so wrong."

Consort of the Onion Queen
The American Conservative, 2008

I AM THE FIRST Man of Elba, New York, Onion Capital of the World, or so we claim, and who, really, is going to call us on it? The czarina, or technically town supervisor, of Elba, which borders my native Batavia, is my wife Lucine, whom I believe to be, since the retirement of Governor George Deukmejian, the highest ranking Armenian-American elected official in America. Or at least she will be until the voters of California elect Cher to the U.S. Senate.

This is one of the first things you learn upon marrying an Armenian: The List. "Famous Armenians" isn't like drawing up a catalogue of "Famous Irish-Americans" or "Famous Jewish-Americans": you're not picking and choosing, selecting Pat Moynihan and Hank Greenberg but leaving John O'Hara and Neil Diamond for the next draft. "Famous Armenians" begins with the sad sentimental poet of Fresno, William Saroyan, and goes on to include the guy who played Mannix (Krikor Ohanion, er, Mike Connors), Cher Sarkisian, Dr. Jack Kevorkian, mogul Kirk Kerkorian, Andre Agassi, and, for baseball fans, Steve Bedrosian. Well, diasporans, add to your list Lucine Andonian Kauffman, Town Supervisor of Elba, New York, El Dorado of the mucklands.

She was appointed to fill the uncompleted term of her retired predecessor, but when Lucine had to run her first race I took on the job of campaign manager, a post for which I had prepared a lifetime. Rudy can't fail, as they say, especially when the candidate is unopposed. Still, in order to minimize our vote, I had printed bumper stickers depicting onions against the colors of the Armenian flag and bearing the motto, "Ayo Gernank!" Antonio Villaraigosa had recently run for mayor of Los Angeles boasting "Si, se puede," or "Yes, We Can!" and so I asked my California father-in-law how to say that in Armenian. We lost the Turk vote, but principle has its price.

My role model as first spouse has been Pat Nixon, not Hillary Clinton, especially if the phone rings at three a.m. because a road hasn't been plowed. I declined to adopt a social cause or disease, a Just Say No campaign of my own, though one friend, mindful of his own affliction, urged the distribution of brown bracelets as part of an IBS awareness campaign. Opting, for once, for good taste, I just said no.

Lucine has largely and astutely ignored my advice on political matters. I wanted her to be the first elected Republican official in America to come out for Bush's impeachment, but she has instead promoted local agriculture and business and tried to ensure that revenues equal expenditures. Given the Palin Precedent, I'm touting my wife for vice president in 2012. She spent a hell of a lot less on the new salt storage shed than Sarah P did on the Wasilla ice rink.

The Republicans are indulgent of Lucine's non-Republican husband, but then in a healthy society politics plays so small a role in our lives that who really gives a damn how others vote? Cold ideologies melt in the warmth of daily communal life. I think of the local civic organizations in which, say, Assembly of God churchgoers and gays work side by side in the cheerful labor of neighbors. They can be friends because they are, to each other, rounded and fully dimensional. They are people, not cartoons. This is nigh impossible in larger places, where such disparate folk would never meet, and would exist to each other only on the flat screen of the TV set. Instead of Kate and Dave they would be "Religious Nut!" and "Fag!" How dreary. How lifeless. How very Red & Blue.

Elected officials are encouraged to stick campaign signs in their front yards, and we have reached an accommodation. We always put signs up for friends who are running. For higher (which is to say lower) office, we agree to one apiece: this year she chose the Republican state senate candidate and I stake my frame for the only old-fashioned patriot on the New York presidential ballot (Ralph Nader). The last Democrat sign I put up was for a Muckdogs booster who was on a mission perdu: running as a (D) for coroner in our lopsidedly (R) county. I proposed a desperate campaign promise—"No premature burials!"—but though she ran a fine race, her candidacy was DOA.

Given that the Republicans cede New York's carpetbag U.S. Senate seat to Hillary Clinton, a friend has urged me to start the rumor that Lucine is "exploring" a race as an antiwar, pro-organic farming, pro-Bill of Rights Republican against the militaristic liberty-shredding Democratic schoolmarm. Maybe Cher would do a benefit concert? Ayo Gernank, baby.

American Graffiti
The American Conservative, 2010

MY LOVELY LITERATE WIFE Lucine —"Armenian for Darlene," I type out of habit, and wince at the thought of the shoe flying across the room—recently reviewed for the local library one of those pop-anthropological books in which a big-city reporter spends a few weeks in a small town and lives to tell the tale.

I'll withhold the book's title, since Lucine said the author meant well, and besides, when a really egregious target waddles into my sights I've become like my dad hunting deer—I shoot wide and low and let it lollop away. When I was a mere stripling I'd blast the bastard, but I was so much older then, I'm younger than that now.

The latest Margaret Mead in Podunk committed this sentence: "It's easy to spot someone who grew up in a small town and got out: they have a breathless air about them, their expressions somehow startled and dreamy."

Talk about the shock of unrecognition: What the hell does that mean? My wife teased a few laughs from its sheer obtuseness. And if anyone can spot the startled dreaminess of exiles from Elm Street it ought to be Lucine, a Southern Cal gal turned rural Yorker who stubbornly resists my kindly efforts to compress her into the John Mellencamp line: "Married an LA doll and brought her to this small town/Now she's small town, just like me."

Actually, as town supervisor and emcee of the Onion Queen Pageant, she makes me look like a regular boulevardier, but I suppose as a native I can be identified by some hidden Lovecraftian nodule.

Where this latest tourist among the rustics goes wrong is in not crediting the stay-at-homes with the capacity to dream and in not noticing that some of those who "got out" dream of returning—a return barred, so often, by the poisonous assumption that success in America can be measured in the distance one has traveled from home.

My friend Patrick Deneen, who teaches political theory at Georgetown, has written on the decentralist website Front Porch Republic of interviewing at a college (much less prestigious than Georgetown) near his hometown in Connecticut:

> I was inordinately excited at this possibility, thinking that it might work out that my wife and I and newborn son might be able to settle close to family and childhood friends. When asked about accommodations, I proudly informed the college that I would be staying in my bedroom that night—my childhood bedroom, that is. During the two day interview I related in every conversation that I was native to the area and had a longstanding relationship to the campus, having attended its plays, movies, and used its library for many years. I believed my local connection would make me an especially attractive candidate, sure in the knowledge that a school would be attracted to someone who already had deep roots in the community and was likely to build a long life and career in that place.

In fact, Patrick writes, "this proud display of my nativeness went over badly." The American professional class does not just accept rootlessness as the cost of achievement—it positively fetishizes it. And so it is befuddled—startled, even—when confronted by a Deneen.

Levon Helm of Turkey Scratch, Arkansas, drummer for The Band and a great American, described a cotton-farming guitar player from Elaine, Arkansas, named Thurlow Brown: "He could have been famous, but he didn't like leaving his farm, so he never broke out of our area."

My hero!

Thurlow Brown of Elaine is worth every deracinated novelist who ever took a table at Elaine's. But how do we convince young Thurlow Browns to ignore the synthesized drumbeat that tells our children that to stay at home is the act of a loser, and that if you're not in NY, LA, or DC you're nowhere?

When another Front Porcher, the reprobate wit Jason Peters, cracked open the treasury of Augustana College a while back to have me out to hector his students, we did a little post-lecture proselytizing in the Quad Cities.

Midnight settled on Davenport, Iowa, home of the late-nineteenth-century local color novelist Octave Thanet. Fearing that her tones had been forgotten by the town she never forsook, and wondering just how I might interest the rantipole youths and roistering blades of Davenport in their native daughter, I took to decorating the men's rooms of that fair city with obscene graffiti about Octave's amative practices.

Forgive me, Octave, baby. I didn't know what else to do. Lacking the "breathless air" of those who "got out," you and Thurlow and I dream on.

Just My Type
The American Conservative, 2012

VAST LACUNAE DAPPLE THE landscape of my knowledge. As Sam Cooke sang, "Don't know much about . . ." Well, the list is as long as Sam's life was short. My nescience extends into neuroscience, jai alai, the novels of Anna Quindlen and William F. Buckley, and assorted arcana.

It also includes orchestral pop, which is why, when my friend Bob Knipe asked me to play the title instrument in the Genesee Symphony Orchestra's performance of Leroy Anderson's "The Typewriter," I said okay, in the way that we agree to engagements in the distant future, never realizing that our day will come.

But it always comes.

"The Typewriter" is a brief and lively piece that mimics the staccato strokes and clanging carriage return of what is now considered, I am sure, a charmingly primitive word processor. Typically, the miniature is performed with some hapless local writer sitting stage center and typing away while the band plays on.

An exceptional musician can type to the tune, but I am as arrhythmic as a toddler's rattle. At the first rehearsal I pecked merrily along to the music. When we finished, the conductor said amiably, "Great job—but don't actually type. Just fake it."

So I was to pantomime typing like some pop tart lip-synching the national anthem at the Super Bowl? Ah, jeez.

The comic potential of a guy pretending to type is limited, unless one goes the Professor Irwin Corey/Christopher Lloyd route and dons fright wig or clown makeup. I suppose I could have stepped out from the wings wearing nothing but a diaper—now *that* would be funny—but hey, I gotta live here.

Disinclined toward (and incapable of) slapstick as I am, my act was also constrained by the setting, which demanded a certain decorum. For the concert was hosted by St. James, the somberly beautiful neo-Gothic Episcopal church designed in the early twentieth century by a precocious architect and ex-St. James choirboy, Robert North. The grande dame of

Batavia, Adelaide Richmond Kenny, paid for young North's extended tour of the English countryside, from which he drew inspiration.

Mrs. Kenny was the daughter of Dean Richmond, our uncorrupt contribution to the nation's titans of industry. Richmond was president of the New York Central Railroad and chairman of the New York State Democratic Committee during the Civil War. He died while visiting the Gramercy Park mansion of future New York governor Samuel Tilden, the "Great Foreclose," as he was not so affectionately known, and the amasser, as Gore Vidal has written, of one of the nineteenth-century's largest pornography collections. I'm sure our Dean only sampled Tilden's library for the articles.

Richmond's survivors parceled out pieces of his fortune for the sort of good works (library, hospital, church) one associates with the better class of American plutocrats. Sure, the family sleeps in a Pharaonic mausoleum, but show me a modest railroad baron.

Come the first Sunday in December, I waited in the wings, looking out over the 600 or so concertgoers who packed St. James. In my mind I went over the sequence of weak sight gags I'd settled on: Limbering up my fingers before playing air-typewriter—yeah, that'll slay 'em!

I was supposed to look and act writerly, but I have neither corduroy jacket nor elbow patches, and I searched in vain for a preconcert martini. After the last notes of "March of the Toys" sounded, I shambled up to the lectern with the 1923 Underwood my wife picked up years ago for two dollars at a flea market. I scanned the churchful of faces, so many of them familiar. Narrative convention suggests that I say there was a note of expectancy in the air, but my dear wife and darling daughter were laughing already, anticipating the unfunny business. (Think Johnny Carson and Tommy Newsome.)

I spat on my hands, cocked an index finger at the conductor, and we were off. I can't recall much of the next ninety seconds. The musicians were superb; the percussionists used woodblock and ratchet to imitate the typing and carriage return sounds. After a mock hunt-and-peck routine, I typed the air in the manner of an intentionally asynchronous lip-synching singer. (Which Syd Barrett of Pink Floyd was said to have been on *American Bandstand*.) A bottle of white-out and a hip flask made serviceable props.

And then it was over. I basked in the applause meant for the GSO, which is one of the oldest, if not the oldest, community orchestras in the land. If you're going to make a fool of yourself, best to do it where everybody knows your name.

Commencement Address, Batavia High School

June 26, 2011

THIRTY-FOUR SHORT SUMMERS AGO I sat daydreaming in the shade of the spreading willow tree outside Batavia High while the class of '77's commencement speaker, a radio disk jockey from Buffalo, imparted words of Top Forty wisdom. I can't recall a single thing he said.

Commencement addresses have a bad reputation. They are endured, not enjoyed. They tend to be a series of creaky clichés clumsily fitted together. (For instance, I expect the DJ told us that our graduation was not an end but a beginning, and that while one door was closing another was opening.)

But the thing about clichés is that they're usually true, or at least partially true.

Oh, some commencement clichés are stretches—such as the old reliable "you can do anything you set your mind to." Well, no matter how I set my mind, I was never going to play quarterback for the Buffalo Bills. Heck, I was never going to play quarterback for the Batavia Blue Devils.

But the sentiment from which that cliché derives—follow your dreams—is sound advice. There are many ways of going, as a poet once said, and dreams take many forms. Unless our Hindu friends are right, this is the only life you're ever going to have on this earth. Don't spend it waiting for the weekend, living by that supremely depressing motto "Thank God it's Friday."

Discover what you enjoy doing; what gives you a sense of fulfillment, satisfaction, pride—whether it's carpentry or music or motherhood or coaching baseball or teaching math or fixing engines or painting.

The future is unknowable, so regard job-market forecasts as skeptically as you would a reading from a tarot card, or a promise from a politician. Pursue a craft, a calling, a trade, because you love it, not because some stranger says it will be a "hot job market" five years from now. In the mid-'80s I knew people working on Ph.D.s in the burgeoning field of Soviet studies—then in 1991 the Soviet Union disappeared in the blink of an eye. Gorbachev was out of a job, and so were they.

There are few things more yawn-inducing than some old guy telling you how much better things were when he was a kid. I shall resist that temptation—wisely, since I am a product of the heyday of leisure suits and the Captain and Tennille. But I am glad to see this generation questioning the false idols of materialism and mobility, and rediscovering the profound value of the local.

For success is not the accumulation of wealth—though sometimes that's a byproduct of success—nor is it the piling up of possessions. Success is not measured in the distance one travels from home, contra that silly phrase "he'll go far."

To be a good father or mother—a good teammate—a good neighbor—a good member of your church—a good friend—a good citizen—those are the things that count, that matter, that give life meaning and weight.

I had a friend named Henry Clune who lived to the age of 105. He was a well-known novelist and newspaperman. Until he was in his late nineties, Henry ran wind sprints on his front lawn every day. Even at 105 he still wrote in his diary every morning, read a favorite book every afternoon, drained a martini every day at five p.m. People would ask him, "What's the secret to living so long and so well?" It wasn't the martini. No, he answered, it was "curiosity."

Henry was interested. In the world. In his neighbors. In his own backyard. He participated. He listened. He engaged. He had found something he loved to do and he did it as well as he could, with joy and pride and always a sense of wonder and gratitude.

He wasn't jaded. He wasn't bored. His imagination had not been dulled by eight hours of television a day. He stayed in his hometown of Rochester for over 100 years yet it remained a source of endless fascination to him. Batavia, too, as I discovered after some years away, is in its own strange way a place of enchantment and mystery, if only we open our eyes to it.

Wherever you end up, you'll carry pieces of Batavia with you. You were shaped by this place, whether you love it or you hate it. And you have the power to help shape this place, or whichever place you choose to live. You can treat it with love; you can enrich it with your presence; or you can treat it as thoughtlessly as you would a used Big Mac wrapper. It's up to you.

Don't spend the years just skating on the surface—for as the end draws near, you'll be filled with regret at wasting this precious gift of life.

I don't usually preach, but since it's Sunday, and I have the pulpit, as it were, I'll dispense a little more free advice. Don't spend your life grousing, don't spend it sniping at others, don't spend it embittered, don't spend it—in this celebrity-obsessed culture—more caught up in the lives of people you don't know—vapid pop stars, fleeting images on a TV screen—than in the lives of the people who make up your world. Turn off reality TV; turn on the reality all around you.

The most poignant and undeniably true graduation cliché is that this is the last time this entire group will ever be gathered together. Some of these classmates you'll never see again for the rest of your life—even if you attend the class reunions, where, once you've reached the twentieth or twenty-fifth, you'll be shocked at all the old people who seem to have wandered into the room. There must be some mistake!

As the years go by and BHS recedes in memory, you'll be surprised at the things that stay with you. A line from a poem in English class; a joke someone told in study hall; a talk you had about life with a favorite teacher; an ambiguous, mysterious look from a girl or boy you barely knew; a perfect note you hit in band or a jump shot you made in basketball or just laughing as you walk down the hallway with your friends. These are the moments that make up a life—that give it substance, color, depth.

Each and every person is his own novel, her own book. Whether you're saddened to leave school or you're elated to get out, these scenes, these incidents, are already part of your book. You're writing it every day. The Batavia High chapter is at an end. But mark my words: you'll think about these days. You can go back and reread these pages whenever you like. But now there are new chapters to write. Go to it.

Thoughts for Your Penny?

The American Conservative, 2010

SENTIMENTAL SLOB THAT I am, I am a terrible bettor. If I drop by Batavia Downs to watch the horses run, I inevitably blow my dough on a hobbling longshot starting from the eighth post position. My March Madness brackets are filled with improbable victories by small Catholic colleges and schools from Upstate New York and the Rockies; my Final Four is liable to be Siena, Binghamton, Montana St., and Brigham Young. On Election Day, I predict impossible third-party upsets and dramatic rebukes to the Masters of War. I never win, but then what fun is winning?

So it was found money when I won a pile of "units" in my friend Steve's annual college football bowl pool. I bet this year like Dick Cheney ordering assassinations: grimly, ruthlessly, without a drop of human feeling. Competence is cold comfort.

Upon receipt of the loot I consulted my list of Stuff I've Wanted to Buy but Never Got Around to It: a poster of *Zabriskie Point* (Antonioni's ridiculously bad but mesmerizing "youth rebellion" movie), the collected albums of Tom Russell and Townes Van Zandt, a signed Sarah Orne Jewett *Country of the Pointed Firs*. As the tune goes, I'm not askin' for much.

My dad is an inveterate collector who is always picking up milk bottles from defunct dairies and old baseball gloves and railroad watches (befitting a New York Central man).

I have inherited the trait, albeit in desultory, sporadic fashion. I collect things for their evocations, their associations: programs and ticket stubs (1960s baseball, local theater, Canadian Football League); postcards (our street in 1910, Sinclair Lewis's home, nineteenth-century observatories); badges and banners from local fairs and rallies; hatboxes and shoehorns from the downtown stores of my boyhood; campaign pinbacks from the ones who had a notion, from Hiram Johnson to Norman Mailer.

In Candy's room there are pictures of her heroes on the wall. Thirty years ago I played that album so hard it skipped every other groove, and if I never got to Candy's room, my walls, too, are plastered with pictures I have collected. Scattered among my daughter's artwork and family photos on my office walls these real Americans look down on me, and I up to them: William Jennings Bryan, Gore Vidal, Randy Smith, Eugene V. Debs, George McGovern, Jack Kerouac, Walt Whitman, Batavia Clippers teams of the 1940s, Dorothy Day, Thomas Wolfe, Barber Conable, Al Smith, Burton K. Wheeler, Father Nelson Baker. Overseeing it all is the George Washington by Gilbert Stuart portrait that hung in my mother's one-room schoolhouse.

If some ungrateful descendant puts the contents of this room on ebay they won't fetch enough to cover shipping costs.

My dad collects coins, too, and I remember pressing 1910 and 1912-D Lincoln cents into the blue Whitman folders (using drinking glass bottoms to wedge them in). When my daughter was very young I did the same with her, and though she hasn't a half-cent of interest in coins today, she has inherited from me an affection for scraps and oddities. Like me, she's reluctant to throw out so much as a used Kleenex.

Coin collecting can be overly methodical, but I like its time-traveling quality. I marvel as I handle, say, an 1832 large cent: This disc was circulated by Americans who actually lived in a republic!

Feeling guilty that I had won this year's pool by betting against every team in the Mid-American Conference—isn't betting against Mid America how our oligarchs got rich?—I decided to convert my winnings into pennies. (Coin-wise, I never graduated beyond the penny, or should I say the school of common cents?)

I visited my dealer, John Cooper. John is a Seneca Indian, so he knows about ancestors. I love John's coin shop, which is on a side street in Le Roy, the birthplace of Jell-O. General Foods, the leviathan that swallowed Jell-O, vamoosed in 1964, so I don't mind telling you that I've heard face-scrunchingly gross tales about the human fluids workers used to flavor America's dessert.

Then again, my grandfather was a handyman for the First Family of Jell-O, the Woodwards, who in best seigneurial manner paid the doctor bills when employees had children, so thanks, lemonjello and orangejello, for my mother's duty-free entry into this world.

"Don't let your possessions possess you" seems inarguably true, but I don't know: I *am* possessed by certain possessions. They are tokens of the place and traditions to which I belong. I look up from typing this to see a photo of my uncle's 1950 football team, my daughter's painting of a bluebird, and a LaFollette for President pin. How do I not belong to them?

Clang, Clang, Go the Jail Guitar Doors
The American Conservative, 2012

I HAD DRINKS ONE night with an old friend who had spent the previous year in jail. Despite my entreaties, and my guarantee that it would provide rare cachet, he refused to loudly begin a sentence, "When I was in the joint . . ." In fact, he denied that prisoners ever called their domicile the joint, the rock, or the big house, and he confessed to not having met a single grizzled veteran of the pen who dispensed such gnomes as "Do time; don't let time do you."

You mean the movies lie about all this?

My levity shamed me. There's really nothing funny about having to live in a cage. My friend's fellow penmen ranged from the violent to the pathetic, from apparently unredeemable scumbags to the luckless and the dumb. *Innocent* was seldom an apt description of these men, but look hard enough and you can see the face of Christ in each one.

The prison-industrial complex depends upon the drug war for its seemingly limitless supply of bodies. (I write, by the way, as one so drug-averse that I don't even like taking Tylenol for a hangover—I much preferred Minor Threat to Johnny Thunders.)

Although we have reached a stage where the jock potheads of my boyhood have their avaricious little hands on the levers of power, the bong throng—including three consecutive deracinated ex-coke-sniffers in the White House—lack the guts even to take the gateway step of saying that to imprison men and women for buying and selling marijuana is an affront to personal liberty. (Not to worry: the empty cells can be filled with Thought Criminals.)

Who are the national political figures willing to say that marijuana ought to be legalized? The noble ascetic Ralph Nader, the heroic physician Ron Paul, and former New Mexico governor Gary Johnson, the triathlete running for president on the Libertarian ticket.

Governor Andrew Cuomo, no one's idea of a libertarian Democrat, has proposed decriminalizing the open possession of less than twenty-five grams of marijuana. This is the latest meliorative attempt by New York

Democrats to soften the state's drug laws, which took an infamous turn toward the draconian four decades ago under Governor Nelson Rockefeller.

I am chagrined, if not surprised, that rural Upstate legislators are the primary obstacles to reform. Keeping watch over the largely downstate prison population has become a staple of the regional economy, a degradation to which we have become accustomed. Prison jobs sure beat Wal-Mart.

Fifteen miles down the road sits Attica State Prison, damned site of the 1971 riot in which twenty-nine inmates and ten hostages were killed. Governor Rockefeller refused to come to Attica to negotiate for the release of those hostages. Sure, a bloodbath flooded D Yard, but hey, the dead were mostly rural working-class white guards and urban black prisoners. Probably not a one knew anything about abstract expressionism.

I don't suppose Rocky's sleep was ever troubled by nightmares of the families whose homes and small businesses he stole for his grotesque experiments in modernist urban renewal in Albany, or by the ghetto and shotgun-shack kids rotting away in his prisons for vending substances which the languid heirs of the ruling class consume with oligarchic immunity.

But God has a sense of humor. Rocky perished while—let's see; we must be discreet, as the sole witness to his tumbling off this mortal coil is with us still—let us just say that he died while in the company of a twenty-something-year-old female. The reliably fatuous *New York Times* courtier-journalist James "Scotty" Reston provided an unintentionally hilarious eulogy for the Butcher of Attica. Noting that Rocky expired "late on a Friday night" whilst laboring under "the consoling influences of art, beauty, and love," Reston gushed, "He was a worker, a yearner, and a builder to the end."

I'll say!

The great Mary Harris "Mother" Jones, matriarch of "the fighting army of the working class" and opponent of war, capitalism, and women's suffrage, once met with President William Howard Taft to plead for a pardon for labor radicals. (Imagine a modern President meeting congenially with a homegrown revolutionary.)

"Now, Mother," President Taft said pleasantly, "the trouble lies here: if I put the pardoning power in your hands there would be no one left in the jails."

"I'm not so sure of that," Mother Jones replied. "A lot of those who are in would be out, but a lot of those who are out would be in."

That's Mother Mary: speaking words of wisdom. Let it be.

Court is in Session

The American Conservative, 2012

IF IT'S LATE WINTER, it must be high-school basketball tournament time. Talk about a bargain: for a couple of bucks you can buy your way into a bandbox gym to sit on hard bleachers and listen to the glorious cacophony of community.

This year even my wife picked up her dribble. Inspired by our friend Amy's gnomic cry of "all ball," Lucine was ready to start yelling. Alas, she lacks even the most rudimentary knowledge of the game. I told her you can never go wrong bawling "Box out!" or "Three seconds!"

The first game we saw this season pitted the girls' teams from archrivals Elba Central and Notre Dame of Batavia. My dad was in Notre Dame's inaugural class but I'm a Batavia High boy so I always root against the Damers. Elba won the game but Notre Dame won the bantering battle by a knockout. The Elba student section's curiously Horace Mann-like chant of "Public Schools" was met, and overpowered, by the Fighting Irish's antiphon of "SAT Scores." Elite 1, Populists 0. I like Elba's signature agrarian incantation—"Eat Our Onions"—but at December's clash, Notre Dame met this alliaceous demand with the devastating "We Say Christmas." Outstanding!

High school sports shape and enrich a community's identity in a way that major league sports (with their mercenary players and subservience to the idiot box) and big-time college sports (ditto) do not. I stopped following the "local" cagers of Syracuse University when the Orangemen lost their Upstate New York accent, and the likes of Bug Williams, Roosevelt Bouie, and Hal Cohen were replaced by vagabonds from I Don't Care Where.

Sporting loyalties sorely vex those technocrats who would kill the small public school. Sitting with one's kith and kin and cheering for a quintet of young people to throw an orange ball into a hoop: How is this preparing the raw material of American Empire for their futures as cogs in corporate wheels or body-bag fillers in the next Middle Eastern war?

The outrageously undercatalogued massacre of little American schools occurred in two phases. The first wave was a product of the progressive movement of the early twentieth century. The "district schools" dappling the countryside—built, financed, and governed by parents and neighbors—were closed en masse, and their students fed into consolidated factories of education. The second assault on little schools was led by Cold Warriors who scorned smallness and the love of place as dangerous, even subversive weaknesses that the new empire could not tolerate.

The chief villain in this Gratingest Story Never Told was James B. Conant, Harvard president and a man who, having served the Army's Chemical Warfare Service in WWI and the Manhattan Project during WWII, had devoted the best years of his life to devising instruments of mass slaughter. A decent human being, having caused such incalculable suffering, would have spent the remainder of his days doing penance, perhaps by cleaning bedpans at a VA hospital. Instead, Conant produced a series of Carnegie-funded Cold War-era reports that demanded "the elimination of the small high school"—that is, schools with fewer than 100 students per grade. The extermination of human-scale and place-based learning was necessary because of "the struggle between the free nations and Communism." (Anti-communism did more to regiment and standardize America than the Reds ever did.)

The number of school districts in America has plummeted, from 127,531 in 1932 to 14,000 and change today. Yet long after media darling Conant and his Barbarians eradicated—"consolidated," in their corporate-speak—thousands of little schools, education researchers discovered the manifold virtues of these comfortably sized academies in which the student is more than just another brick in the wall. Frank Bryan, the soul of Vermont and author of the classic *Real Democracy*, learned this lesson from his 1959 class of seven students at Newbury High: "Keep it small. The basketball isn't good, but everybody gets to play."

The Angelo Pizzo-David Anspaugh collaboration *Hoosiers* beautifully depicts the centrality of a small public school and its basketball team to a community. The most poignant line in the film—"Let's win this one for all the small schools that never had a chance to get here"—is spoken by Kent Poole, who later hanged himself from a tree in his Crawfordsville, Indiana, yard.

We Americans are moved by *Hoosiers* yet we allow the Conants to push us around—to poison our organic institutions, to use our children as fodder. We might learn a lesson or two from the kids on the court. To steal from the great Steve Forbert: You cannot win if you do not play.

Revolt of the Provinces

The American Conservative, 2013

UNDER A SLATE SKY that mutes all that is glorious around us, I drive to the Alexander Gun Show, as I do on the first Sunday of most Octobers.

It is election season, though an off year—"off year" meaning we vote for the offices that ought to matter most (county legislature, city council, town supervisor) but, under our centralized dispensation, barely register. When 80 percent of the county budget is effectively drawn up in Albany, what does it matter?

Yard signs endorsing candidates dot the roadside, though they are vastly outnumbered by the red, white, and blue placards that have dominated rural New York for months now, and that read REPEAL NY'S SAFE ACT.

The SAFE Act was the panicked response to the Connecticut school shooting by Governor Andrew Cuomo (Mario without the intellect or introspection, which is to say a self-aggrandizing prick) and an urban-suburban controlled legislature. Drafted with appalling sloppiness—its definition of "assault weapons" is almost broad enough to include your kid's squirt gun—the SAFE Act is a suffocating welter of prohibitions, restrictions, and mandated background checks that severely constrict the historic liberties of my neighbors. (Whose violent crime rate, as is the case elsewhere in rural America, is minuscule.)

Fifty-two of the state's sixty-two counties have registered their opposition to the law, but these do not include the only counties that count in statewide politics: those containing New York City and its suburbs. Several county sheriffs, unlikely embodiments of Robert Frost's "insubordinate Americans," are refusing to enforce the act.

In the rusti-phobic imagination, gun shows are stygian gatherings of edentulous Junior Samples lookalikes, but they are really rural swap meets. This show, like most, is held in a volunteer fire department, an institution that is the modern analogue of yesteryear's militia. The dealers and browsers are the kind of men who serve in the wars that our liberal imperialists (Vietnam) and neoconservatives (Iraq I & II) design but never get around to shipping their own progeny off to. Absent is any glorification of the American Empire. My guess is that you'd find more vegans than Lindsey Graham fans here.

Walking the aisles I see Winchesters, fishing lures, knives, and ammo, interrupted by "National Instant Gun Background Check" signs, an ugly intrusion of the surveillance state.

The mood is alternately defiant and resigned; there is a frustration borne of powerlessness. While huffy displays of bravado are rare, some of these men—and women—have pondered the question once posed by The Clash:

> When they kick at your front door
> How you gonna come?
> With your hands on your head
> Or on the trigger of your gun?

Hardly a week goes by without a news dispatch about the rural outliers of some state—New York, Maryland, Colorado, California—seeking to take advantage of a legal anachronism (the U.S. Constitution) that permits new states to be formed out of existing ones. (Every such article includes a stern admonition from Professor So-and-So that the deluded hicks had better shut up.)

The quickening talk of state scission—of recalibrating governance more on the human scale—is a sign of hope, of an abiding faith in small-scale democracy, of, perhaps, the rekindling (or is it the last flicker?) of the old American ideal of local self-government. (I write about this at length in my history of American secession movements, *Bye Bye Miss American Empire*.)

I can't think of a time when rural and small town Americans were so disprized. That we have fed America, produced most of its enduring literature, and, politically, stood for peace and place—well, that was then. But rural America is still good for one thing.

Addressing Virginia farmers (including the great Joel Salatin) and agribusiness reps, Secretary of Agriculture Tom Vilsack noted that although the rural population of the U.S. has declined to just 16 percent, it makes up 40 percent of the nation's armed services. How can we occupy the world and destroy its traditionalist cultures, asked Vilsack, if the clodhoppers stop reproducing? (Okay, he didn't put it in quite *those* terms.)

During the First World War, the Kansas Socialist Kate Richards O'Hare was thrown into prison for sedition. Her crime? Telling a North Dakota audience that their rulers regarded farm mothers as "brood sows, having sons to be put into the army and made into fertilizer." A century later, Kansas Kate is confirmed.

From Western Maryland to the Southern Tier of New York to redwoods-and-weed Northern California, the brood sows are wondering if maybe they shouldn't have some say in the political arrangements under which they live. No man born with a living soul would deny them that right.

Home, Boys
Front Porch Republic (speech at Hope College, Holland, Michigan, 2012)

HOLLAND IS NOT A nether land. (They're only gonna get worse from here on in.) Holland matters, no matter what the corporate media tell us. Just as Iowa was "not a drab country inhabited by peasants, but a various, rich land abounding in painting material," as Grant Wood said, so too Holland. Its children are made in the image of God and meant to be something more than stupefied consumers of *The View* or body-bag fillers in the next unconstitutional war of aggression our rulers lie us into.

If American culture amounts to something more than Lady Gaga and Lee Greenwood—and it does—it depends upon a healthy and vital and self-confident Holland—and Saginaw and Mecosta and Detroit and Escanaba. What a bounty Michigan has produced over just the last half-century: Tom McGuane. Bob Seger. Russell Kirk. Jim Harrison. Tom Bissell. Iggy Pop. Levi Stubbs. Paul Schrader. Even Hope's own Sufjan Stevens.

Over the last decade I've reviewed a pile of books for the *Wall Street Journal*, and my sense is that we're in the early stages of a revival—a reflowering, I should say, being here in Tulipville—of regional literature. This walks hand in hand with the profusion of farm markets and CSAs and home brewing and homeschooling. No matter how often we are lectured by the political class and the placeless talking heads on TV that Baghdad is more important than our own backyards, the call of home—of a community in which you are known and in which you matter—is powerful. And salutary.

John Greenleaf Whittier poetized:

> He who wanders widest, lifts
> No more of beauty's jealous veil
> Then he who from his doorway sees
> The miracle of flowers and trees

"Locality gives art," said another ancient poet, Robert Frost, though that locality can be as loosely defined as "north of Boston" or as specific as "Boardwalk, Asbury Park, New Jersey." But what becomes of art when local idioms and neighborhood wisdom are supplanted by the rootless and artificial "culture" beamed—often, alas, welcomed—into our homes by the entertainment industry? "We look to Los Angeles for the language we use/ London is dead/London is dead," Morrissey sang some years ago. That's, like, real bad.

Los Angeles has not ripped out all our tongues yet, and in fact the resurgence of regional writing and art and music across America is among the many hopeful signs piercing the darkness of the early twenty-first century.

The regionalist dream has lasted a very long time—some of us have yet to wake from it.

Ignore the suffix. Regionalism is *not* an ism, or an ideology. Regionalism is the expression in artistic form of the particular character of a place. It has always been a feature of American writing, for "America" is not so much a single unit as it is the gorgeous welter of hundreds, nay thousands, of smaller places, from Sinclair Lewis's Sauk Centre to Elmer Kelton's West Texas.

Sang one antebellum New Yorker:

> Ere long, thine every stream shall find a tongue
> Land of the many waters!

That was Charles Fenno Hoffman, notable for three things: 1) He authored the best poem ever written about a dead dog; 2) He was the leading light in the 1845 movement to rename the United States of America "Allegania"; and 3) after a chambermaid accidentally used for kindling the manuscript of the nearly finished novel that he regarded as his masterpiece, he suffered a breakdown so complete that he spent the next thirty-five years in and out of lunatic asylums, writing no rhymes, the first forgotten mad poet in the Republic of Allegania.

The two great flowerings of regional literature were in the 1880s (the so-called "local color" school of Jewett, Freeman, Eggleston, Garland, et al.) and the 1930s, when a regionalist movement in art (Grant Wood, John Steuart Curry, Thomas Hart Benton) also flourished, and some sainted souls even attempted to fashion a regionalist economics.

The thirties were a fantastically fertile era in the provinces, producing everything from the Iowa poetry explosion to such historical fiction as Margaret Mitchell's *Gone with the Wind* (1936)—read it before you sneer—and the Upstate New York novels of the underrated Walter D. Edmonds. Prophets and holy fools evangelized for regional values not only in literature and politics but in art (Thomas Craven), classical music (Virgil Thomson), and architecture (Frank Lloyd Wright).

It died at Pearl Harbor. War kills places as well as people. But maybe everything that dies someday comes back. Maybe regionalism needs not a requiem but a revival.

Regionalism need not be rural—witness Brooklyn; oh, to go back and undo the Mistake of 1898 by which Brooklynites, by the narrowest of margins, forsook self-rule and threw in with the Vampire City!—and regionalism should never rely on the clichés found in Ford Truck commercials or political speeches. It is not studied quaintness. It is not an anthropological examination of "uneducated" people by a degreed interloper—though seeing through the eyes of the visitor to a settled community is a worthy narrative convention in regional fiction, as for instance in Sarah Orne Jewett's classic *Country of the Pointed Firs* (1896).

Regionalists do not deny or sugarcoat the ugly facts. We have often mistreated our places. In my memoir of my return to my hometown, *Dispatches from the Muckdog Gazette*, I lacerated the men who used federal urban renewal grants to knock down the core of my little city in the late '60s, early '70s, haughtily informing critics that You Can't Stop Progress. It's been forty years. I should forgive them. . . . I can't.

Regionalism never developed in the film industry, largely because producers, writers, actors, and directors were centralized in southern California. A novelist could live in Milledgeville, Georgia, or South Berwick, Maine; a film director—or screenwriter, for you detesters of auteur theory—almost had to live in Los Angeles and its environs. (Which is, perhaps, why the best films with a regional flavor are often set in Southern California—e.g., *Chinatown*). This is not as true today. Film production is dispersing. We await the golden cinematic age of Tulsa and Spokane and Holland.

Speaking of movies, I read that Frank Baum, author of the Oz books, had a summer home hereabouts. Our friend Caleb Stegall wrote a really fine essay a few years back contrasting Baum's populist vision of Kansas with Hollywood's depiction of a colorless tornado-denuded landscape from which a plucky girl can escape merely by closing her eyes and making a wish. With apologies to Buffalo's Harold Arlen, the gold that matters is found under the rainbow, not over it.

But to the impoverished of imagination, a life under the rainbow and away from *lights! camera! action!* is too dreary to contemplate. One Midwestern expat, actor Ronald Reagan, spoke disdainfully of "those sleepy old towns where generation after generation lived. And then the kids in the Midwest left; there was nothing in those towns—Lord, that's why I left! And they wanted to see the world, so they went to the cities."

Contrast Reagan with Booth Tarkington, Hoosier author of the masterpiece *The Magnificent Ambersons* (1918), which is today known primarily as the source of Orson Welles's studio-mutilated film. Says a character in Tark the non-shark's novel *The Gentleman from Indiana* (1899): "I was born in Indiana, and, in a way, the thought of coming back to a life-work in my native State appealed to me. I always had a dim sort of feeling that the people out in these parts knew more—had more *sense* and were less artificial, I mean—and were kinder, and tried less to be somebody else, than almost any other people anywhere. And I believe it's so."

Booth chose Indiana; Ronnie chose Hollywood and Washington. You tell me which man was magnificent.

In his novel *Remembering*, Wendell Berry describes a middle-aged writer: "Years ago, he resigned himself to living in cities. That was what his education was for, as his teachers all assumed and he believed. Its purpose was to get him away from home, out of the country, to someplace he could live up to his abilities. He needed an education, and the purpose of an education was to take him away."

Our schools do not offer a major in "home." When I was in college at the University of Rochester, there was not a single course about Rochester, about a culture that had produced George Eastman, Susan B. Anthony, the mature Frederick Douglass, and the Mangione family. The local was disparaged; no, even worse, it was ignored. It didn't exist. There was nothing of Rochester in the University of Rochester. What a huge, gaping shame. Hope College—I hope—is different.

In my state of New York, seventh grade was once the year in which our schoolchildren learned about the history under their feet: local history, the stories and legends of the places which they inhabit.

Public-school Yorker seventh graders no longer learn local history. No time for it, thanks to the standardized tests to which our children are increasingly subject in this age of fetishized testing, which reached its apex, or nadir, in George W. Bush's No Child Left Behind act. Anyone who thinks the Republicans are the party of decentralized government is not paying attention.

Now, whether Holland flourishes or becomes just another nether land is not entirely a matter beyond your control. We are not yet—actually, we never will be—wholly at the mercy of distant impersonal forces.

If we want our "culture" to consist of the cynical manufactures of deracinated coke-snorting imbeciles who sneer at Michigan as "fly-over country," then go sit gape-mawed in the Cineplex and supersize your fries so you can get a Batman plastic cup. If you want to help nurture a local cultural life that is expressive of Holland in all its multifarious glory, then get out and support western Michigan painters and craftswomen, punk bands and moviemakers.

The very fine Iowa novelist Ruth Suckow, who, like my neighbor of a century ago in Rochester, the cinquain poet Adelaide Crapsey, was one of those lady writers who really ought to have taken a husband's surname, called the Midwest "the seat of American complacency and the seat of American rebellion."

God knows we need a dose of rebellion in these complacent days. And every time you buy a peach at a farmer's market, every time you go cheer the local high school football team, every time you turn off the Kardashians and talk to a neighbor—you are not only living well, you are also committing an act of Suckowian rebellion and localist patriotism against the deeply un-American and anti-American Empire whose subjects no red-blooded son or daughter of the Midwest would ever wish or consent to be.

I'd like to recommend one other act of rebellion. Stay put. Don't sell yourself to the highest bidder like a whore. Consider—seriously—going back to your hometown. Or staying in Holland or whichever city you're attending college. Cast down your bucket where you are, as Booker T. Washington said. I offer this jarring advice in full knowledge of my own hypocrisy, since when I graduated I split for Washington, D.C., and later Southern California, and didn't come home till I was good and ready. So maybe I'm a bit like Lindsay Lohan telling you to save yourself for marriage.

Today, one-third of all Americans live outside their natal state. Twelve states are afflicted with a majority of immigrants, most fantastically Nevada, wherein 80 percent were born elsewhere. No doubt there are things to be said for Bugsy Siegel, Wayne Newton, and the UNLV Runnin' Rebels, but do we really want all of America to be as transient as Las Vegas?

The Tennessee novelist and agrarian Andrew Lytle said in 1980, shortly before he died: "The family is of first importance. It has to have location, has to be fixed somewhere. You can have a family without it, but location strengthens the family because you have gathered about a fixation on a spot of land, or even the inheritance of a business, the history of a family. Now, no family is any older than another, but the family that sees itself as older and has some inheritance that is worth passing on to the generations, is the family that is stable; such families make stable a society. You've got to have that old grandmother in the back room saying, 'have your tongue pulled out before you lie,' don't you see?"

That old grandmother ain't gonna be there if her sons and daughters are scattered across the fruitless plain, living in Myrtle Beach and Orlando and anywhere USA and nowhere USA.

A lot of the people I've written about over the years—Dorothy Day, Eugene McCarthy, Wendell Berry, Grant Wood, Edward Abbey—have this in common: they walked away from power, from the soulless capitals in which power is concentrated, and they went home, or they made new homes, in places far from the bright lights.

These people learned, as I learned, that healthy, life-giving parochialism exists in even the most dispirited or quotidian places, and that we—or at least I—can only ever really love the familiar. And even a justified anger or rage require the anchorage of love else they can become exhausting and pointless hatred.

American culture—indeed, America herself—is nothing without distinctive little towns and city neighborhoods. When the poets and painters forget Holland and Grand Rapids you're gonna end up with a vacuous national culture of Miley Cyrus, *Entertainment Tonight*, and Rush Limbaugh.

Oh, wait . . . that's what we have.

Not completely.

For we have within our hands, our wallets, our hearts, the power to revitalize our places. It's our choice.

The vagabond poet Vachel Lindsay, who at the end of all his wanderings came home to the state Reagan couldn't wait to leave—and killed himself drinking a bottle of lye—sang in "The Illinois Village":

> O you who lose the art of hope,
>
> Whose temples seem to shrine a lie,
>
> Whose sidewalks are but stones of fear,
>
> Who weep that Liberty must die,
>
> Turn to the little prairie towns,
>
> Your higher hope shall yet begin . . .

Read the authors of your place. Listen to its musicians, engage its artists. Teach your children. Write. Paint. Sing. Plant. Laugh.

SPACE

"I gaze in childish wonder at seven little stars that sparkle in a long-gone autumn sky."
—LESLIE PELTIER

Ohio's Backyard Scientist
First Principles, 2009

THE MOON'S MILD RAY has e'er bewitched me, but ne'er was a man more poorly suited to a life of science. Carbon, ions, gametes, the Doppler Effect: I can't think of a single chemical or physical phenomenon that I have ever really understood.

Yet we are often drawn to things we can't possibly comprehend, aren't we? I love to sit out back of a summer's eve, libation in hand, and watch the moon trace its slow and steady arc across the zodiac. I could not care less that a handful of government employees have bounded along its surface, and I abhor the thought that the American (or any other) Empire may one day deface our natural satellite with a military base. The moon, like the haggard ex-looker in the Raymond Chandler novel, is best seen at a distance.

So too believed Leslie Peltier (1900–1980) of Delphos, Ohio, whom Harvard College Observatory director Harlow Shapley called "the world's greatest non-professional astronomer." Peltier's memoir *Starlight Nights* (1965) is quite simply the best book ever written on the romance of the night sky, and how apt that the foreword to its latest paperback incarnation is by David H. Levy, a worthy heir to the great Peltier.

I had the pleasure several years ago of spending an April twilight interviewing Levy, the foremost comet-hunter of our age (he has twenty-two to his credit) at his home-based Jarnac Observatory in Vail, Arizona. After our chat we looked at Venus, Jupiter, and Saturn. This was like shooting baskets with Michael Jordan, trading obscene limericks with Jason Peters, or drinking with my friends the Sheehans. You don't belong on the same court (or bar) with 'em, but you're sure happy to be there.

Among Levy's books are a volume on astronomical poetry (*More Things in Heaven and Earth*/1997) and a fine biography of another small-town astronomer, Clyde Tombaugh of Burdett, Kansas, who discovered Pluto in 1930 at the Lowell Observatory in Flagstaff, that redoubt of poetical eccentricity and wide-eyed wonder endowed by the Brahmin Percival Lowell, who saw canals on Mars (and who am I to say he didn't?).

Leslie Peltier had no such illusions, but then he didn't need to conjure up superlunary utopias. He was, writes Levy, a "shy and retiring man who loved his Delphos, Ohio, home so much that he rarely left it."

Starlight Nights is as much about Peltier's life on Ohio ground as it is about his explorations of Ohio skies. "Blessed are those who are raised on a farm," is Peltier's addition to the Beatitudes. His family farm consisted of fifty acres of corn, wheat, oats, and clover, an orchard of fruit trees, and a few cows which young Leslie kept half an eye on whilst swimming in the Auglaize River, memorizing "Thanatopsis," playing his fife, and hunting English sparrows with his air rifle ("A plague on all these foreign imports!"). His room in the Peltier farmhouse was the outdoors brought inside, adorned with his collections of butterflies, Indian arrowheads, insects, and rocks. The social life of Delphos was defined by "Granges, Ladies Aids and country churches," though its economy, unhappily, was later distorted by "price supports, allotments, and controls."

At age fifteen a question occurred to Leslie that has occurred to many others who have looked upward into the night sky: "Why do I not know a single one of those stars?" A wise librarian in Delphos gave the curious boy Martha Evans Martin's *The Friendly Stars*, and within the year he had come to know Vega, Deneb, Antares, Capella, and the other stellar lights. Leslie Peltier was a classic American autodidact. He dropped out of high school to work on the family farm when his older brother went off to Europe to make the world safe for democracy, and Leslie never did return to school, for "life on the farm was so pleasant, so independent and so complete that I had no desire to give it up."

With eighteen dollars hard-earned from picking strawberries, Leslie purchased a little mail-order telescope for which he rigged up a mounting, the first in his series of do-it-yourself telescopic exhibitions of Buckeye ingenuity. A four-inch scope soon followed. As a teenager he began recording his observations of variable stars, compiled in the cow pasture in which he set up the instrument, his skywatching scored by crickets, owls, and bullfrogs. "Cows are friendly folk and have a great sense of curiosity," learned Peltier. "They often would come over and keep me company during my long hours at the telescope... slowly chewing their cuds and watching me thoughtfully with their big soft eyes."

Frost and dew and chill winds were among the inconveniences kept at bay when Leslie and his dad built an observatory (which the neighbors mistook for a chicken house), though he regretted that "I now had lost my common touch with all the other denizens of the night"—the fireflies, the chirping insects, and, to his sorrow, "my gallery of cows [which] deserted me completely."

This self-taught farmboy who sent in meticulous variable-star observations and wrote searching letters to famous astronomers was becoming known far beyond Delphos. The director of the Princeton Observatory sent him a six-inch refractor telescope, with which Leslie would seek out comets, emboldened by a passage in the *Beginner's Star Book*: "There is no weighty reason why any amateur astronomer should not be the discoverer of a comet. The requisites are a telescope of low power, large field, and generous illumination; a good store of pertinacity and patience, and a fair knowledge of the constellations."

Three years of hunting later, on Friday, November 13, 1925, Leslie Peltier, by now a stock clerk in a truck factory, finished his evening chores on the farm, bundled up in a heavy mackinaw, wool cap, and sheepskin gloves, and walked out to his observatory. While sweeping the sky he found a "small round fuzzy something" at the northern end of the constellation Bootes.

"Had I found a new comet or was it only new to me?" he wondered, if one can be said to wonder frantically. "Had I merely stumbled onto one that might have been spotted somewhere weeks before?"

Calming himself, Leslie "knew that I must make absolutely certain of everything and then get off a wire to Harvard College Observatory." He plotted its location, estimated its brightness and rate of motion, prepared a telegraphic message—NINTH MAGNITUDE COMET ONE FIVE TWO FIVE NORTH FORTY FOUR DEGREES RAPID MOTION SOUTH—and ran to the house to call Western Union. The office was closed. The operator informed Leslie that emergency telegrams could be sent from the signal tower at the railway depot, but it had no telephone connection. He would have to drive. Alas, his parents had the car and were out for the evening. So he took his old bicycle out of the garage, and raced several miles through a Delphic darkness, his only company the occasional barking of farm dogs. Finally he reached the tower, climbed its wooden steps, gave his message to the befuddled telegrapher ("This some sorta code?" "Sorta"), and pedaled home, alternately exuberant with the thrill of discovery and fearful that the haughty Harvardian who received his message would mock him ("I say, here's a good one, some chap out in Ohio has just found that comet that was reported about six weeks ago!").

A week later, the town druggist called to read a telegram from Harvard confirming the discovery. With a pride so movingly conveyed that only an automaton will not feel his heart swell, Leslie carved "Peltier 1925" into the mahogany tube of his comet-seeker. There would be eleven more comets over the years. How much more inspiring this achievement is than that of a later small-town Ohio boy, Neil Armstrong, who took a multibillion-dollar joyride to the moon.

Leslie Peltier didn't need taxpayer alms. I like his account of life during the Depression: "[O]nce again I became a full-time farmer. . . . Here on the farm life went on, basically, much as before. Turtlelike, we simply withdrew a bit into the shelter of our shell and waited." Their waiting should not be mistaken for torpor. Leslie and his doughty wife Dottie swam in the river, hiked, hunted fossils, cooked over a campfire, and watched the stars, which neither poverty nor tyranny could blot from the empyrean.

Starlight Nights limns a life spent among the stars, or "wandering aimlessly about the moon," yet Peltier's feet are always planted in Ohio earth. His love of Delphos is honest and generous. He does not approve of all he sees (as when, for instance, during the hysteria of World War One "some of the town's respected citizens caught the vigilante virus and forced their bewildered [German] neighbors to publicly kiss the flag"). Over the years Peltier and his observatory hosted thousands of schoolchildren. He and Dottie were "variously involved in church affairs, in Eastern Star, in garden clubs, and in a devious maze of Cub Scout work." They were citizens of their place, ordinary yet extraordinary, as famous astronomers made pilgrimages to Delphos to meet its resident high-school dropout with his Argus eye on the sky.

Like Thoreau, Leslie Peltier traveled widely in his own backyard. One of his few ventures outside Delphos was a charmingly described honeymoon trip he and Dottie took in the Southwest, camping their way across America while hunting gravestone epitaphs and rare minerals and spelunking in "old Indian caves." As a patriot of a place, he did not disdain other places: he loved them not in spite of their differences but *because* they were different, all part of this beautifully variegated world of which he and Delphos were a vital part.

A later Peltier book, *The Place on Jennings Creek* (1977), which I have never been able to lay eyes on, is said to be a rich account of the natural world, the flora and fauna, of his Delphos home. Leslie and Dottie finally bought their own home in 1948, the "old Moennig place" at the western end of town. "We made few changes and even those few were mostly in retrograde motion. What we found here was sound and good. It was a leftover bit of an earlier America and we had no desire to bring it up to date." He did, of course, move his observatory onto the grounds.

Peltier was unmoved by the glories of the sky when mediated by any technology much beyond two pieces of glass at either end of a tube. "No photograph has yet been made which is not cold and flat and dead when compared with the scenes that meet one's eyes when the moon is viewed through even a small telescope," he wrote.

The telescope, he stated "most emphatically," is "not essential to an enjoyment of the stars." Just stand 'neath the sky and gaze upward into the firmament. The enchantment, said Peltier, is the same. Without a scope, he concluded, "life for me would change but little. Telescope or not, I would still keep watch." (He did bemoan the artificial satellites traversing the sky: "mankind's latest pollution in the name of progress.")

Leslie Peltier, as a man firmly placed in Delphos, opposed the "conquest of the moon." The space program he regarded as just another act of "greedy pillage."

"I know that someday man will reach the moon but I sincerely hope this will not happen for a long, long time. He has a lot of growing up to do before he will be ready for the moon. . . . If man must meet a challenge he can find one here on earth. If he must conquer something let it be himself."

Night falls in my town somewhere east of Delphos, and I haul my eight-inch Dobsonian reflector out beyond the raspberry patch in our backyard. I bought the telescope several years ago when I finally received a payment I had long before given up on. I couldn't dust Leslie Peltier's eyepiece but that doesn't matter: the moon is there for me, too, rising over the hedgerow.

Leslie Peltier was right. The moon is just fine where it is. Leave it alone. Everything in its place, don't you know?

Earthling, Stay Home!
The American Enterprise, 2004

THE APOLLO VOYAGES TO the moon marked the triumph of the thirty-fifth president over the thirty-fourth.

Dwight Eisenhower had been a space skeptic who was "not about to hock my jewels" for vainglory. (The uncharitable might point out that Ike preferred his own massive public works project: the Interstate Highway System.)

In his extraordinary Farewell Address, Eisenhower warned of the "danger that public policy could itself become the captive of a scientific-technological elite." He viewed the rise of Big Science with republican alarm: "The prospect of domination of this nation's scholars by Federal employment, project allocations, and the power of money is ever present—and is gravely to be regarded."

President Kennedy, by contrast, seemed to welcome such domination. State and science were natural partners; JFK assured Americans that "every scientist, every engineer, every technician, contractor, and civil servant gives his personal pledge that this nation will move forward" into space.

And so it did.

Congressional foes of the space program consisted mostly of a few liberals who wished the money might be wasted on the Great Society, and a handful of parsimonious conservatives who objected to the astronomical expense. The incomparable penny-pincher H.R. Gross (R-IA) grumbled, "I hope that if we do get to the moon we find a gold mine up there because we will certainly need it."

Among maverick Democrats, Senate gadfly William Proxmire of Wisconsin denounced Apollo as just another instance of "corporate socialism," while Arkansas Senator William Fulbright called the moon landing a "nine-day wonder of history, a gaudy sideshow in the real work of the world."

More interesting were the Apollo critics who had neither D nor R affixed to their names.

The social critic Lewis Mumford found the space program "anti-human." Space travel, he argued, requires "the total mobilization of the megamachine, commanding to the point of exhaustion all the resources of the state: it is both a symbol of total control and a means of popularizing it and extending it as an ineffable symbol of progress."

Mumford urged the NASA-bedazzled to look homeward: "No comatose space travel, no millennial hibernation, however interminable, promise even a scintilla of what earthbound man has already accomplished."

The great amateur astronomer Leslie Peltier, author of the classic *Starlight Nights* (1965), which describes astronomy's lure better than anything ever written, detested Apollo.

Peltier, grounded in his native Delphos, Ohio, wrote, "The moon and I have been friends all these many years." He regarded Earth's invasion of this friend with dread: "I know that someday man will reach the moon but I sincerely hope this will not happen for a long, long time.... If [man] must conquer something let it be himself."

The moon, in this view, was to be just another conquered province of Earth. Robert Frost, who read the night sky as well as any poet, imagined himself exiled from modern America:

> They may end by banishing me
> To the penal colony
> They are thinking of pretty soon
> Establishing on the moon

Many Apollonians took from the moon landing a boundless faith in the efficacy of a centralized state. As *New York Times* columnist Tom Wicker mused, "If the same concentration of effort and control were applied to some useful earthly project, a similar success might be obtained."

Such government-directed "concentration of effort and control" struck other terrestrials as nightmarish. That poet of the American Middle, Bob Dylan of Hibbing, Minnesota, sang darkly:

> Man has invented his doom
> First step was touching the moon

A less talented versifier, military brat Jim Morrison of the Doors, saw escape from the Earth as futile:

> People walking on the moon
> Smog will get you pretty soon

The moonstruck had dimmer literary lights—Neil Armstrong couldn't even insert the article "a" in his muffed line about small steps and giant leaps—but hey, the Eagle landed.

Visit to a Small Planet

The American Conservative, 2010

FOUR SCORE AND ZERO years ago in Flagstaff, Arizona, Clyde Tombaugh, a bespectacled twenty-four-year-old just off the farm from Burdett, Kansas, joined an exclusive fraternity of merit from which he has been posthumously booted. Clyde found a planet which those costive bastards of the International Astronomical Union now say isn't a planet!

Our family rambled into Flagstaff a few years back, bunking in the downtown Hotel Monte Vista, a splendidly faded and haunted monument. We slept in the Clark Gable room, though Clark seems among the least likely Hollywood haints. (I wouldn't stay in a Sal Mineo room for nothin'!)

Flagstaff is also home to the Lowell Observatory, founded in 1894 by the Boston Brahmin Percival Lowell, who was convinced that he had seen with his own eyes Martian-made canals on the Red Planet.

Lowell was a rich man with a magnificent obsession and the integrity to pay for it himself rather than milk the taxpayers. If his astronomers never did find life on Mars, one found something even less expected—Pluto.

In contrast to the computerized robotism of astronomy today, everything about Pluto's discovery was fallible, painstaking, whimsical—human.

Discoverer Tombaugh was a classic American boy who spent his Kansas days in the wheatfields and his nights at the eyepiece of his homemade telescope. On cloudy evenings, he taught himself Greek and Latin; on Sunday afternoons, his pasture hosted the neighborhood touch-football game.

College was out of the question. So was a "career," until in one of those message-in-a-bottle tosses characteristic of bright and naïve provincial lads, Clyde sent his freehand drawings of Mars and Jupiter to the Lowell Observatory.

His timing was perfect. Observatory director Vesto Slipher was looking for a talented amateur to work long hours at low pay searching for the "Planet X" hypothesized by Percival Lowell. Vesto decided to give the kid a shot. So in January 1929, Muron Tombaugh drove his son Clyde to the train station at Larned, Kansas, whence the youth departed for Flagstaff with

Dad's parting words ringing in his ears: "Clyde, make yourself useful, and beware of easy women."

In his history of Great-Uncle Percy's colony of the starstruck, *The Explorers of Mars Hill* (1994), William Lowell Putnam writes that Slipher desired not a theoretician but a plodder for the "boring and tedious" planet search. Using a "blink comparator" microscope, Tombaugh spent up to nine hours a day comparing photographic plates of identical patches of sky taken at intervals of several days.

At about four p.m. on February 18, 1930, "I saw a little image popping in and out," Clyde told his biographer David Levy, himself a romantic comet-chasing poet of the Arizona sky. Clyde walked down the hall and into the director's office. "Dr. Slipher," he said, "I have found your Planet X."

The obscure Kansan, his era's version of an industrious office intern, had become the third person in recorded history to find a planet.

He became famous, in a "yes, but" way. In William Lowell Putnam's phrase, Clyde was Pluto's "fortuitous discoverer, the photographic technician Tombaugh."

Ouch! Bring me my tea, boy, and step lively!

Pluto—it's a good name, isn't it? Sure, it's no Uranus, that gift to generations of snickering schoolboys, but it evokes the underworld and honors with its first two letters Percival Lowell, whose batty and litigious widow asked Clyde, "Are you willing to have the planet named Constance?" (He was not, though Mrs. Lowell shared Pluto's iciness and highly irregular orbit.)

You might regard Tombaugh's story as a parable of the diligent clerk, the persevering drone, but there was an ardor in his arduousness. Bearing only a diploma from good old Burdett High—"Let each sheep wear his own skin," said Thoreau of such honors—Clyde seized the chance he was given by the outliers at Lowell, which was "virtually an outcast in professional astronomical circles," as Tombaugh later wrote. (Soon thereafter, the principal of Burdett High convinced the University of Kansas to award the planet discoverer a scholarship. Talk about a distinguished freshman! Clyde eventually taught astronomy at New Mexico State in Las Cruces, becoming that city's most famous resident since Billy the Kid-killer Pat Garrett.)

Eighty years after Clyde broke the news to Vesto, Pluto is in a categorical netherworld—more out than in. Those who expelled Pluto from the planet club are, in the main, credentialed astronomers employed by government-subsidized facilities in which a twenty-first-century Clyde Tombaugh would be wearing a hairnet and ladling mac and cheese in the cafeteria.

David Levy told me that Tombaugh, who died in 1997, was saddened in his final years by the suspicion that he and Pluto were in for a demotion.

"Dwarf planet" they call it now. But maybe that's okay. Pluto, Flagstaff, Clyde Tombaugh—small really is beautiful.

POLS

"Going into politics is as fatal to a gentleman as going into a bordello is fatal to a virgin."
—H. L. MENCKEN

Mr. Marrou Goes to Juneau

Reason, 1986

AT 8:00 A.M., REPRESENTATIVE Andre Marrou of the Alaska House of Representatives kisses his wife, Eileen, good-bye and skips down three flights of stairs at Juneau's Driftwood Lodge, gingerly stepping over a squashed banana and an empty bottle of beer. It's a five-minute walk to work, usually in the damp, gray weather for which Juneau, Alaska, is infamous.

The bearded Marrou, who looks like a cheerful Lenin, studies the day's legislative agenda from his sixth-floor office in the Court Building, overlooking downtown Juneau and the Gastineau Channel. At about ten minutes to 10:00, he trots across the street to the grim confines of the Alaska State Capitol (design: mid-century junior high school).

Wearing the standard legislative tweed jacket and tie, the forty-seven-year-old Marrou looks much like the thirty-nine other representatives converging on the House floor for today's 10:00 session. Except for his two lapel pins: an American eagle on the right chest, and on the left a skull, scarved in a red bandana, boasting the Hell's Angels motto "Ride Hard, Die Free."

As Marrou strides down the corridor leading to the House chamber, Finance Committee Chairman Al Adams throws him a mock-Nazi salute, bellowing "Liberty, Freedom!" Marrou ignores Adams, an Eskimo who is perhaps the most powerful man in the House, and takes his seat at the last desk in the last row, just in front of the table occupied by the press corps. (The location has its advantages—easy access to both the Fourth Estate and the bathroom.) A yellow Post-it note is stuck to Marrou's desk. It's his credo, scrawled in a particularly frustrating moment. It reads: "Statism Rules—But Liberty Should."

Marrou recites the morning Pledge of Allegiance loudly and with evident conviction. His eyes dart once or twice to liberal Democrat Peter Goll, who enrages some representatives by allegedly (ah, libel laws) refusing to salute the flag. A nervous, thin-lipped young man who could pass for a yuppie Frank Burns, Goll has a whiny voice, stirs coffee with his pinky finger, and is "the kind of guy people automatically hate," as one staffer puts it.

The legislature disposes of its routine business and takes up a bill to create a $1-billion Alaska Research Development Endowment, a bureaucracy whose purpose will be to subsidize natural-resources research and "unlock knowledge," in the words of Al Adams.

Marrou rises and is recognized to speak. (Which may be the most common occurrence in Juneau. "He's occupied more floor time than half these guys put together," marvels Democratic elder statesman Red Boucher.) Adams's plan to "unlock knowledge" is his target.

"Who says knowledge is locked up?" roars Marrou, heedless of his wife's plea earlier that morning to "talk a little quieter." He continues: "Is it in a chest somewhere, with a padlock? All we gotta do is just leave people alone and they'll do just jim-dandy. That's been the history of the world.... This bill appalls me. It's the worst bill we've had come before us. The vote should be 40–0 against."

The two members of the capital press corps present are smiling as Marrou sits down. It may be the speech (they know the bill will not be defeated 40–0), or it may be a drawing Marrou passed back minutes before, while an "art in public places" bill was being debated. It's a sketch of a screw driving into an IRS logo. "Screw the IRS," the rendering is titled, *"Art* by A.V. Marrou, Alaskan Artist." One reporter scribbles back, "What does the V stand for?" Without missing a beat, Marrou jots his answer. "Vicious."

The Speaker of the House wishes to close the debate and vote on the measure, but Marrou is up one more time. "Cooperation between state and industry," he says, his voice dropping, "is exactly how Nazi Germany operated." The Speaker is staring back at him, head resting on his chin, seemingly bored by Marrou's disquisition on fascist economics. The vote is taken. Twenty-three in favor, fourteen against. The measure passes. Marrou, at least, has improved on yesterday's showing, when he wound up on the losing end of 34–6, 33–6, 29–10, 32–6, 32–8, and 29–9 decisions.

When the papers report on Andre Marrou's speeches the next day, they'll designate him "L-Homer." It's jarring to non-Alaskans the first time they see it. For Marrou is neither Democrat nor Republican—he is a Libertarian. In fact, he is presently the only state legislator in the country from the Libertarian Party.

****

Like 80 percent of all adult Alaskans, Andre Marrou was born somewhere else. Southwest Texas, that is, which he left at age seventeen to study chemical engineering at the Massachusetts Institute of Technology. He stayed in Boston for seventeen years, until "in 1973 I came to Alaska with all my worldly possessions."

Marrou settled in Anchorage, a city of 250,000 that contains half the state's population (and is scornfully referred to as "Los Anchorage" by urbanophobe pioneer-types). He became a jack-of-all-trades, working as a cordwood salesman, disc jockey, and technical advisor on the Alaskan pipeline, before leaving the city and spending two years with his new wife, Eileen, in the woods. For those two years the Marrous lived what Alaskans call the subsistence life, chopping wood and picking berries in the solitude of Perl Island and Bear Cove.

The Marrouvian odyssey ended in Homer, a town of 2,500 located 200 miles down the road from Anchorage, at the tip of the Kenai peninsula. Actually, Homer is down the road from *every* city in the continental United States—it is the final stop in America's contiguous highway system. As Joe McGinniss described it in his fine "I survived Alaska" book, *Going to Extremes*: "If you got in your car in New York City and started to drive, Homer would be as far as you could go."

While living in Anchorage, Marrou discovered the fledgling Libertarian Party when a woman handed him a party brochure at a Small Business Administration seminar. "About two weeks later I read it," Marrou recalls, "and I was dumbfounded that this was *exactly* what I believed in." What he and the Libertarian Party believe is encapsulated in the Jeffersonian maxim that "that government is best which governs least." In practice, that translates into support for unfettered free enterprise and individual rights and opposition to government grants of favor and privilege.

Marrou soon became disenchanted with the Libertarians' incessant quibbling over fine points of doctrine—"there was a lot of philosophical debate going on and there was no attempt to bring people into the party." In his disgust, he and his wife fled into the woods, away from people and politics and everything else. Rustic reflection begat a new resolve. "I did a lot of thinking while chopping wood," remembers Marrou, "and I decided that I was not going to roll over and allow the establishment to run over me. I was going to do what I could to help the cause of liberty." Thus inspired, he and Eileen emerged from the woods and set their sights on entering the belly of the beast.

Marrou ran for the Alaska legislature in 1982, coming in second in a field of three. In 1984, he ran again, beat the incumbent by fifty-six votes out of some 11,000 cast, and set out for the old mining town of Juneau.

POETRY NIGHT AT THE BALLPARK

****

Juneau is a politician's dream.

Located in southeastern Alaska, in the chain of islands and inlets known as the Inside Passage, the city is inaccessible by road. Visitors arrive by ferry or by plane, the latter mode requiring a tricky descent through cloud-enshrouded mountains. (Travelers who are even a wee bit chary of flight are advised to booze it up well before landing.)

The preponderance of Alaska's population (read: constituents) is thus several hundred miles away from a capital that can't be approached except by the most expensive forms of transportation. No need, then, as a politician, to worry that the hoi polloi might take an undue interest in your actions.

Once a legislator gets to Juneau, he finds himself "isolated and surrounded by bureaucrats," in Marrou's words. Forty percent of the workforce of this city of 25,000 labor for some level of government, and the town's picturesque setting is sullied by a rash of ugly government buildings housing state agencies that perform functions you don't even want to think about. To keep his sanity in this sanctum of statism, the good Jeffersonian at least has recourse to a variety of fine drinking establishments: Bullwinkles ("For a Good Time in the Old Town Tonight"), Lucky Lady ("Juneau's Famous Irish Pub"), Red Dog Saloon ("Work Is the Curse of the Drinking Class"), etc.

There is considerable sentiment in Alaska to move the capital from Juneau to Willow, a tiny town north of Anchorage. Voters approved the move in a referendum several years ago, but funds for the move have never been appropriated. One fear is that the politicians would squander millions of dollars turning Willow into an arctic Brasilia, complete with lavishly appointed quarters for state officials and civil servants. Marrou, an ardent supporter of the move, envisions the capital of Willow as such: "You put up one Quonset hut for the Senate, one Quonset hut for the House, and one Quonset hut for the governor, and that's the capital." Not that he's unwilling to compromise with legislators who have more regal tastes: "You could give it a city name, if you like," he concedes.

****

But the "isolated little island of socialism" Marrou so despises is a political anomaly in Alaska. Voters in the rest of the state exhibit the healthy hostility to government one would expect from settlers on the final frontier. Hell, there's even a secession movement, Joe Vogler's Alaskan Independence Party, that advocates breaking away from the USA and declaring Alaska an independent country. ("It's a great idea that won't work," opines Marrou, noting that the matter was settled in 1865.)

The Libertarian Party has found Alaska far more hospitable to its message than any state in the Lower Forty-Eight. Two Libertarians, Dick Randolph and Ken Fanning, preceded Marrou in the legislature, and 1980 Libertarian presidential candidate Ed Clark carried 12 percent of Alaska's vote, including all twenty-nine votes cast in the town of Chicken. Randolph's spirited 1982 race for governor attracted 15 percent of the vote and inspired the Republican National Committee to broadcast anti-Libertarian radio ads around the state. This November, Marrou is up for reelection, running on a statewide slate with seven other Libertarians.

What explains the success of the antigovernment movement in Alaska? Marrou avers: "Alaskans generally came up here to get away from whatever they didn't like in the Lower Forty-Eight. By and large, when you ask them it turns out they didn't like the oppressiveness of government in the Lower Forty-Eight, so they came up here to get more *freedom*." He continues: "Things go fine for a year or two, until it finally dawns on them that Alaska is a very socialist state."

He's not exaggerating. In Alaska the "government owns almost everything," Milton Friedman has written, including the land. The percentage of Alaskan land that is in private ownership (under 5 percent) is less than the percentage of land devoted to private plots in the Soviet Union. Widespread resentment against the federal and state landlords has handed the Libertarians, who propose to allow individuals to homestead the land, a golden populist issue. Which they've exploited with some success: a Libertarian-sponsored "Tundra Rebellion" initiative, which instructed the state government to seize federally owned land as a first step toward privatization, passed overwhelmingly in 1982. (The initiative was subsequently deemed unconstitutional by the state attorney general.)

Complementing the virtual state monopoly on land is the embarrassment of riches hat has flowed into state coffers since the discovery of oil fifteen years ago at Prudhoe Bay, on state-owned land on the Arctic coast. Oil revenues account for over 85 percent of Alaska's budget, which has mushroomed from $100 million in pre-oil days to more than $3 billion today. "With $3 billion," sputters Marrou, "we ought to have our own navy, our own air force, and our own marine corps." Instead, they have an army of well-paid bureaucrats—50,000 state and local government workers whose average salary exceeds $32,000. The recent decline in oil prices may act as an oleaginous Gramm-Rudman, forcing cuts in state spending, but then again it may not. Democratic Governor Bill Sheffield and the usual cast of progressive thinkers are cautiously suggesting the restoration of a statewide personal income tax, which was repealed in 1979 after a tireless campaign by former Libertarian Representative Randolph.

****

There are no grizzled prospectors in the Alaska House of Representatives. Nor are there chair-tossing brawls; disputes are settled by the electronic tally board. No one carries a gun or drinks whiskey in the chamber, and the debate is no more raucous than a Young Republicans' Parcheesi party. There are fewer lawyers (six of forty) than in most legislatures, and more beards (ten of forty), but the Peter Golls far outnumber the Clint Eastwoods.

When the newly elected Marrou arrived in Juneau in January 1985, the first thing he did was meet with Speaker of the House Ben Grussendorf, a Sitka Democrat. "He said there were two things that he expected of me," remembers Marrou. "He said that he expected me to be the conscience of the legislature, and he expected me to generate a lot of ideas."

Marrou assured Grussendorf that he'd generate ideas, and he has—he introduced seventy-five bills in his first term, more than double the second most prolific legislator. But Grussendorf's other request took him aback. "The fact that the Speaker expected me to be the conscience of the legislature really stunned me. It brings up the next logical question: What the hell did they do for a conscience when there was no Libertarian there?"

Ask Marrou about the fortitude and character of his Housemates and he's off to the races. Other representatives have "come up to me and congratulated me and said things like, 'Andre, that was a great speech, I feel the same way, we've been needing someone to say that for years.' My answer is, 'Well, gee, you can do it too. I don't have to be the only hero around here. You can get up and say what you believe in.' But they're just afraid. Why they're afraid to stand up for what they believe I don't know. They're so afraid that sometimes they'll send me notes asking me to talk on various subjects for them, which I'm willing to do if it's pro-individual liberty and anti-government. But it astounds me that they're afraid to get up and talk for what they believe in."

No one has accused Marrou of being reticent. His practice of speaking on virtually every bill that restricts freedom or expands government has drawn mixed reviews. "He's a great speaker," allows *Anchorage Times* newsman James Wasserman. Another veteran capital correspondent is less kind: "I've had guys tell me that after a while they start to tune him out. . . . He makes some good points but they think he should be more selective."

Marrou has heard the criticism but shrugs it off. "I try not to talk on every bill," he says, "but they put up such garbage that I feel it's incumbent on me to do what I can to protect individual liberties by telling people what a ridiculous bill it is."

Other representatives have a far higher tolerance for absurdity. When Marrou dismissed a measure that would extend the life of a state board that regulates barbers, hairdressers, and cosmetologists as "another of those silly bills that shouldn't even see the light of day," Rep. Robin Taylor, a Wrangell Republican who sits at the desk in front of Marrou, rose to offer a persuasive dissent. "There are diseases in other states," Taylor pointed out, "that we haven't even heard of up here because we have licensed barbers." Taylor's argument carried; Alaska was saved from the unspeakable horror of unlicensed cosmetologists.

****

None of the seventy-five bills Marrou has introduced have become law. Two—a measure to deregulate concert promoters and a bill extending "good Samaritan" liability exemption to emergency medical technicians—passed the House and died in the Senate. His other seventy-three bills range the antistatist gamut, from repealing motorfuels taxes to transferring state lands to homesteaders to repealing a legislative pay raise.

As a minority of one, Marrou understands that he's no power broker. Rather, he acts as a sort of Ghost of America's Past, descending on the chamber each day to remind Alaska's legislators that the sentiments expressed in the Declaration of Independence have not been extirpated from this land, despite the best efforts of our governing class. He jokes and kids with his colleagues during recesses, but Marrou's passionate speeches sometimes have the quality of a jeremiad. "He's the conscience of the legislature," says Minority Leader Terry Martin with a smile. "He gets up there and says things we don't want to hear. Plays on our consciences, just like a priest. But this isn't church."

Nor is Marrou a miracle worker. But his influence seems to work in mysterious ways, as Minority Leader Martin recently found out when he asked the Minority Caucus (eleven Republicans and Marrou) to endorse a bill recriminalizing marijuana. (Alaskans may legally grow and own up to four ounces of the killer weed.)

When Martin brought the bill up, recalls Marrou, "I thought, 'Oh boy, here's where we separate the goats from the sheep. I'm going to be the only one out on this.' In fact, it failed. Out of twelve members, he got only five votes." That's right—a *majority* of conservative Republicans in the Alaska House of Representatives support legalized dope. In part, one suspects, because an eloquent voice for liberty haunts the chamber.

****

Marrou is having lunch at the Capitol Cafe with Walt Furnace, an Anchorage Republican who is perhaps Marrou's closest friend and ally in the House. Furnace is a burly, amiable black man, a Texas native who came to Alaska in 1963 with the Air Force and never left. Between bites of his liver-and-onions, Furnace discusses his colleagues' profiles in cowardice.

"Some of these guys have prostituted themselves so many times . . ." he shakes his head, voice trailing off. "Man, you *gotta* vote your conscience."

Much to Furnace's consternation, the whoredom is bipartisan. "The problem with Republicans," he says in a near-whisper, "is they don't have the *guts*" to vote against pro-government bills. "Most of the stuff we pass here," he leans back, chuckling, "the world wouldn't end tomorrow if we didn't pass 'em. There's just too many laws."

Marrou excuses himself from the table. Furnace is asked what his colleagues think of Marrou. He smiles, and offers the by-now standard refrain: "He's the conscience of the legislature—and people don't like that."

No, they don't. But watching Marrou wage his lonely battle for liberty, one can't help but admire him. Day after day, he defends the ideals of 1776 in the best way he knows how. He rises to speak on almost every bill, even though many of his colleagues wish he would just shut up. He loses almost every vote. He's involved in a tough race for re-election against opponents who attack him as "ineffective."

To the paternalists and the often venal, unprincipled types who dominate politics, he is the Randall "Tex" Cobb of Alaska, a fighter who hasn't a chance but refuses to hit the canvas so long as he has a breath to draw. But to the men who founded this country—the Patrick Henrys and Thomas Jeffersons and Samuel Adamses and the other patriots who valued freedom over power and the individual over the state—Andre Marrou would be as familiar and as welcome as the sunrise. He is a modern true Son of Liberty; that such a man is an oddity speaks volumes about the state of our union.

****

The House turns to consideration of "ice classics" legislation. Ice classics are a form of gambling wherein one purchases a chance to predict the exact moment that the ice breaks on several Alaskan rivers. The most popular such game, the Nenana Ice Classic, annually awards more than $100,000 to the winner.

Marrou is on his feet again, offering an amendment to the ice classics bill. This time his amendment, and speech, is scrupulously nonideological. He is proposing to allow the Kenai Chamber of Commerce to hold a "goose classic," in which bettors may predict the return of various types of geese to the area.

An amendment of this sort would pass most legislatures without much fuss. But most legislatures haven't consciences, men who stubbornly refuse to compromise and who insist on calling socialism, and authoritarianism, and statism, by their proper names.

The Speaker asks the members to cast their votes. The light next to Marrou's name flashes green, as does Furnace's and a batch of others, mostly Republican. An equal number of lights flash red. The vote is eighteen in favor, nineteen opposed. The renegade has got his comeuppance.

But then . . . preppette Drue Pearce, the glamorous Anchorage Republican, stands and is recognized. She asks that her vote be changed from no to yes. *Peripeteia!* Now Marrou has won, 19–18. Scattered applause breaks out in the chamber. Representatives wheel around on their swivel chairs, laughing, saluting. Red Boucher shouts, "Goose Marrou!" and everyone laughs some more. Marrou, beaming, passes a note back to the press table. "See. We *Can* Win."

****

The spring legislative session drones on into its last week. Legislators and staff are busy with moving plans, subletting apartments, and getting drunk at the Elks Club. The day before the first tourist boat of the season sails into the Gastineau Channel, Andre and Eileen Marrou will take the ferry up to Skagway, then drive home the scenic route, through Yukon Territory towns like Whitehorse and Dawson. Two weeks later they'll reach the end of the line, the dead end to end all dead ends, home sweet home, Homer.

Folky-Fakey Populists
Chronicles, 1992

DWIGHT MACDONALD, ONE OF our few perceptive political critics in that bleakest of decades, the 1940s, wrote of the Henry Wallace campaign of 1948: "Populism today is a shell which can be filled with any content, even Stalinism, and hence offers its prophet no guide to behavior. Compare Bryan's and Wallace's audiences. Bryan's favorite platform was the Chautauqua lecture: when he was secretary of state, he was criticized for continuing to appear on the Chautauqua circuit along with Swiss bell ringers and 'Sears, the Taffy Man.' The Chautauqua audience was composed of religious-minded, agrarian provincials who hated 'Wall Street' and detested the sophisticated, irreligious culture of the eastern seaboard. But Wallace's audience is drawn from liberals who are well-off and sophisticated. For them, populism is, culturally, a phony way of making a connection with the inarticulate masses (like Josh White's songs)."

Twenty-five years later, Macdonald added a musical footnote to his essay; he championed Country Joe McDonald over the "folkery-fakery" of Pete Seeger. Mr. Seeger is still with us, and ersatz Henry Wallace populism is back with a vengeance. Its latest standard-bearer is another son of Iowa, Senator Tom Harkin—or "Tom William Jennings Harkin," as the *New Republic* calls him. (This is supposed to be an insult.) Anyway, Harkin is pure counterfeit: a statist liberal, awash in PAC money, whose wife is a rich lawyer at Akin, Gump—one of Washington's high-octane firms. Harkin is abrasive and cruel, unlike the daffy idealist Wallace, a decent fool whom Westbrook Pegler dubbed "Old Bubblehead."

Like Bryan populism, rock and roll rings truest in the accents of the South or small-town Midwest. Yet rock critics, like pundits, are usually of affluent Eastern backgrounds; they prefer the mannered, the self-conscious, the safe. When confronted with the genuine article—George Wallace, Huey Long, Axl Rose—they flee to the illusory high ground of moral indignation.

Axl Rose, in case you don't know, is an insolent brat from Lafayette, Indiana, who sings for the most popular hard rock band in America, Guns

'N' Roses. He acts like any Main Street video arcade loudmouth, meaning he brags about his sexual exploits, calls homosexuals "faggots," and tells foreigners to "go back to Iran." Axl's a typical rowdy white-trash kid—smoking and drinking and not taking his SATs like a good Jason or Jennifer—yet the New York City-based press has demonized him as the smack-shooting reincarnation of Joe McCarthy. That he is the most pilloried figure in rock and roll—and, among working-and middle-class kids, the most adulated—suggests the enormous gulf between those who live in America and those who run it.

There's no chance of hearing Guns 'N' Roses at a Tom Harkin rally, but the musical tastes of faux populists have certainly improved since the Wallace campaign of 1948. Harkin's presidential campaign theme song is Bruce Springsteen's "Born in the USA," in which a jobless, womanless Vietnam vet finds himself with "nowhere to run, I got nowhere to go." Senator Harkin, happily, can run to a partnership with Akin, Gump should the voters desert him.

Nebraska Senator Bob Kerrey, whilom companion of the flighty actress Debra Winger, stumps to the accompaniment of Springsteen's "Born to Run." Great song, bad choice: "Baby this town rips the bones from your back/It's a death trap, it's a suicide rap/We gotta get out while we're young/'Cause tramps like us, baby we were born to run." The Senator, one gathers, has outgrown Omaha.

No one tried harder, or with less success, to co-opt Middle American rockers than President Reagan's handlers. In his 1984 campaign, Reagan's flunkies implored John Mellencamp to loan them use of "Pink Houses," a bitter, sardonic song by a man who has a healthy contempt for upward mobility. The irony was delicious: Ronald Reagan, paladin of modern conservatism, had spoken of the "sleepy old towns where generation after generation lived. And then the kids in the Midwest left; there was nothing in those towns—Lord, that's why I left!" John Mellencamp, by contrast, still lives in his hometown of Seymour, Indiana. You tell me who the conservative is.

In its dying weeks, the Dukakis campaign revved up its rallies with Creedence Clearwater Revival's "Fortunate Son," a wonderfully resentful song. ("Some folks are born silver spoon in hand/Lord don't they help themselves?/But when the taxman comes to the door/The house looks like a rummage sale/It ain't me, it ain't me, I ain't no millionaire's son/It ain't me, it ain't me, I ain't no fortunate one.") The fact that Dukakis, his parents, and his running mate were all millionaires vitiated the tune's effect somewhat.

Plenty of anthemic rock songs await a truly populist movement: Mellencamp's "Small Town," Springsteen's "My Hometown," Lynyrd Skynyrd's "Sweet Home Alabama," the Rainmakers' "Downstream," Neil Young's

"Keep on Rockin' in the Free World," and, best of all, the Iron City Houserockers' "Don't Let Them Push You Around."

Of course an authentic populist would be an America Firster who took on Wall Street, the military-industrial complex, newspaper chains, and the New York City-Washington-Los Angeles power axis on behalf of the Seymour, Indianas of this land. A Bryan for the '90s would be closer to John Mellencamp than to Tom Harkin. Alas, no Democrat in the current lineup fits that bill. Tracy Chapman, the Tufts graduate who is my generation's folky-fakey Pete Seeger, could—and probably will—sing for the lot of 'em.

Pat Buchanan: The Last American Leftist
The Independent, 1999

As Texas Governor George W. Bush saunters to the Republican presidential nomination like a complacent country-clubber strolling up the eighteenth fairway, wishing to God he could have a good stiff drink or three in the clubhouse, just like old times (but no: his days as a table-dancing, bimbo-banging scion are over, for he has become Compassionate Conservatism made flesh), a rude surprise awaits. That old hell-raiser Pat Buchanan is organizing a revolt of the caddies. Last week Buchanan's aides hinted that if—when—Buchanan is denied the Grand Old Party nomination, he may bolt and run as the candidate of Ross Perot's populist Reform Party.

Bush junior has raised the astonishing sum of $36 million from those corporations and investment bankers who seek to rent his services for the next quadrennium. No other Republican candidate has even a fraction of the Bush treasury, save the publishing heir Steve Forbes, who appears ready to expend tens of millions of dollars of the family wealth—whatever was not spent by his late father, Malcolm, in pursuit of leather-clad boys—in his own pursuit of Christian voters who believe the capital-gains tax to be unbiblical. The consultants who have lucked on to the Forbes gravy train seem to be enjoying themselves.

But sooner or later, whether in the grey February of New Hampshire, site of the first presidential primary in 2000, a state whose license plates read "Live Free or Die" and whose old Yankee residents mean it, or in November, as a renegade third-party candidate, Pat Buchanan and his populist band are going to block young Georgie's path to the presidency so recently occupied by his mediocre father. In best prep-school fashion, Bush will try to buy his way past the unruly townies. But this time, Roger Daltrey-like, the rabble are vowing that they won't get fooled again.

Patrick J. Buchanan receives the worst press of any American political figure since George Wallace, the southern firebrand of the 1960s. Wallace was crude, a poor white whom the educated Easterners of the press corps could feel superior to. But Buchanan is witty, engaging, and smart; he is

Washington-bred and Jesuit-educated. His father was an accountant who taught his sons to use their fists for fighting rather than gripping pencils. Young Pat learnt this lesson too well: he was suspended from Georgetown University for a year after brawling with police officers who had issued him a traffic ticket. Buchanan has spent most of his adulthood in the Imperial City, charming even the liberals he has so expertly baited.

So why does Pat Buchanan bear the mark of the beast? Because he is the only major American political figure to wake from the long Cold War nightmare and demand that his countrymen renounce empire. Buchanan is that rara avis in American public life: a politician who has sat back, examined the evidence, and changed his mind. He served as an advisor to two of the most internationalist presidents, Nixon and Reagan, and while he remains personally loyal to this dubious duo, his platform is a flat repudiation of their legacies.

He opposed the Gulf War. He denounced the recent war over Kosovo. He is for withdrawing U.S. troops from Europe and Korea. He has called his voters "anti-imperialist and anti-interventionist, disbelievers in Pax Americana." His forthcoming book is titled *A Republic, Not an Empire*, and the locution is instructive: he is the first American politician to use the e-word since Senator William Fulbright (the one honorable Bill that Arkansas has given the nation).

Buchanan is also the sole prominent politician (other than his kindred spirit, the ex-California governor and current Oakland mayor, Jerry Brown) who uses "capitalist" as an epithet. He speaks the language of the historically rooted American left, the noble left of Eugene V. Debs and prairie populists, who dreamt of a farmer-labor coalition against the forces of finance. "One day," Buchanan recently prophesied to unemployed steelworkers in West Virginia, "American workers will wake up and realize that their jobs [and] factory towns have been sacrificed—to save the bacon of the 'investment community.' When they do, the day of reckoning will be at hand."

It is quite impossible to imagine a Clinton Democrat using such language. Why, that's ... class warfare! Come, now: how about a federal retraining voucher instead? Just take a few computer courses and cram the kids into subsidized daycare and in no time at all you'll be a productive cog in the global economy. Lose that anger, pal: it'll eat you up inside. Here, have a healthy snack ... this is, by the way, a smoke-free environment.

There is no Left left in America. Pat Buchanan is it. The Democratic Party has crucified workers on its cross of globalism, justifying every nail (NAFTA, GATT, the periodic bailouts of Wall Street) as the inevitable and life-giving spikes of neoliberalism. American trade union bosses are terrified of Buchanan's appeal to their rank-and-file members. As well they ought to be: for fifty years the social democrats of labor have subordinated the interests of steelworkers and coal miners to the preferences of the chummy bipartisans of Washington.

Buchanan's program is frankly—foolishly—protectionist, less out of a philosophical commitment to tariffs than out of a sentimental attachment to the embattled America that exists far from the beach-front summer homes in which the bond traders and their anorexic partners are celebrating Independence Day by watching Wimbledon on TV and Merchant-Ivory snoozers on the VCR.

In its specifics, Buchanan's platform has a libertarian flavor—he would abolish far more federal agencies than the timorous Bush—but his rhetoric is fiercely communal: "I don't worship the market system. I don't worship at the altar of efficiency." His traditional Roman Catholic understanding of abortion and homosexuality scandalizes the yuppie liberals who run the Democratic Party (and who have battened on the Wall Street boom). He has successfully courted evangelical Protestants: the Pope may be the Antichrist, but Pat's their man. At the same time, however, the evangelicals' fervor on abortion and homosexuality makes Buchanan seem limply latitudinarian.

Buchanan the polemicist has always been a good read, but many people who were initially unsympathetic were drawn to him during the Great Vilifications of the 1992 and 1996 presidential elections. Among the most shameful aspects of American political life is the medicalization of dissent, which received its fullest treatment from the liberal historian Richard Hofstadter in *The Paranoid Style in American Politics* (1964). Hofstadter ascribed all dissent from the Cold War-Great Society consensus, whether on left or right, to mental illness. This was a gentler version of the Soviet strategy of committing dissidents to nuthouses, but the intent was the same: to strangle heterodoxy. The Hofstadterian diagnosis was revived in 1992, which in retrospect was an epochal election. Not because of the banal Bush and the crapulent Clinton, but for the electrifying presence of Buchanan, Jerry Brown, and Ross Perot, who revived a politics of populism that was hostile to concentrated power in all its forms: corporate, governmental, and cultural—in shorthand, Wall Street, Washington, and Hollywood. When the potential appeal of this revolt against giantism became clear, each of the three insurgents was quickly psychoanalyzed and pronounced "paranoid" or "crazy."

In 1996, running as the candidate of people who "feel alienated from Washington and the turbo-charged, two-tiered, go-go global economy," Buchanan stunned the pundits by defeating Bob Dole in the New Hampshire primary. A few independent voices on the left praised him—an admiring Norman Mailer asked him to run as a radical Democrat—but the

Republican hierarchs subjected Buchanan to a campaign of slander. After all, the GOP has been the party of big business since its very first president, the melancholic railroad lawyer A. Lincoln.

I once told Pat Buchanan that he should take Gore Vidal as his running mate in a third-party presidential bid. The anti-imperialist right meets the anti-imperialist left. He laughed at the idea; nothing, he seemed to suggest, could be crazier. Yet today he praises Vidal's writing. In post-republic America, the old straitjackets are being shed. Left and right give way to anti-imperialist and globalist. A new Party of the People is aborning. Take your time on that eighteenth hole, George. Something's got into these caddies. They won't be carrying your bag next round.

For Sick Willie, Washington is Worth a Massacre

The Independent, 1998

THE LATEST BOMBING OF Iraq could have been avoided had Bill Clinton fooled around the Republican way—that is, divorce wife number one when the old gal imploded into frumpiness and then take up with a lissome fashion plate who is sensibly coiffed in something other than the hooker hairdo favored by Clinton's conquests. House Speaker-never-to-be Bob Livingston notwithstanding, the party of family values is really the party of second wives; had Clinton tossed Hillary overboard, in the manner of Bob Dole and Newt Gingrich once their first spouses sagged, his dress-staining would not have constituted adultery, just good clean fun, and we would not be witnessing, from the comfort of our reclining chairs, remotes in hand, yet another mass murder of swarthy people who have committed no offense against American persons or territory.

In the mythology of the American right, Bill Clinton is the avenging devil of the 1960s, the hippie triumphant: once shaggy, now shorn, trading in his peace sign for the keys to the Oval Office. In fact, he is Lyndon Johnson redux: a maudlin cracker who avoided war when he was of draftable age yet, once his hair grays, wages it with a depraved indifference to human life and constitutional niceties. Just another oleaginous, tactile Southern Democrat with the hots for every woman not his wife.

Clinton's attack on Iraq, however immoral, is a bold political stroke that may yet save his presidency. He knows well the most pernicious maxim ever coined by our statesmen: "politics stops at the water's edge." For sixty years both parties have smeared foes of American intervention abroad—Charles Lindbergh, Senator Robert Taft, Students for a Democratic Society, Patrick J. Buchanan—as crypto-Nazis, commie symps, ignorant rubes, and various species of subhumanity, when they were simply old-fashioned anti-war Middle Americans.

In the halls of Congress and the lifeless editorial pages of American newspapers, bipartisanship is next to godliness: seldom is heard a dissident word once the cruise missiles start raining down on the New Hitler of the Month. (The current Hitler, Saddam Hussein, is a star turn who threatens to run as long as *Cats*. He replaced the unprepossessing Manuel Noriega and the tiresome Colonel Gaddafi.) Of course Bill Clinton struck Iraq to delay his impeachment. Of course this makes him (like his handmaiden Mr. Blair) despicable. But he's going after Adolf Hitler, for goodness sake, and besides, we've got to support our troops! Let's tie a yellow ribbon 'round the old oak tree . . . and there is no chance the Senate will remove a war president, however much Americans suspect Mr. Clinton's motives.

Like Richard Nixon, Clinton is thoroughly impeachable; like the Watergate-era Congress, the Republican House of Representatives ignored the administration's most grievous offenses and chose to wring its hands (and the President's neck) over comparatively venial sins—in this case, a lout's priapism.

In the summer of 1974 the House Judiciary Committee approved three articles of impeachment against Richard Nixon for Watergate-related acts; it rejected the one proposed article of unimpeachable constitutional soundness—namely, that Mr. Nixon had violated the U.S. Constitution by ordering, without congressional authorization, the bombing of Cambodia. Article 1, Section 8 of the Constitution reserves to Congress the power "[to] declare war," and although that musty old document has been shredded more thoroughly than the Clintons' Whitewater papers, the Founders were clear on this matter. Even Alexander Hamilton, co-author of *The Federalist Papers* and the best friend the executive branch ever had, wrote that "anything beyond [self-defense] must fall under the idea of reprisals and requires the sanction of that Department [Congress] which is to declare or make war." (In these final days of the American century any citizen who adverts to the Constitution—or, even more tactlessly, to any of our Founding Fathers—is suspected of being a militia member and probable Timothy McVeigh epigone.)

Like Nixon, Clinton has committed acts of war—the assault on Iraq; the groundless but convenient bombing of the Sudanese aspirin factory; the invasion of Haiti—without a formal declaration of war by Congress. If we want to be sticklers to the letter of the law, the imperial adventures of Ronald Reagan in Nicaragua and George Bush in Panama were also impeachable offenses—as a handful of lefties and pacifists insisted at the time, to general derision.

But then Reagan was of the Hollywood aristocracy and Bush was born to the Connecticut purple. Class—and not oral sex—is the great unmentionable in American politics. It has framed the entire Clinton-Lewinsky affair; it even illuminates the embers of Baghdad. The only Clinton quality I have ever found to be even mildly endearing is his white trashiness. His mother was a floozy and gambler, his stepfather an abusive drunk, his brother a cocaine-besotted buffoon. Young Bill may have made good grades in school, but at day's end he remains a classic example of white trash, with his indiscriminate rutting and comical refusal ever to take responsibility when something goes wrong. Clinton's failure to utter the simple truth about his grand jury testimony—"I lied"—sealed his fate in the House, yet this ornery refusal to own up was wholly consistent with the white-trash character. (As a rural American with populist sympathies, I hasten to distinguish white trash—slatternly, dishonest, lubricious women and brutish men—from poor whites in general.)

Yet white trash have a few admirable qualities: stubbornness, prickly pride, a lurking (and often correct) suspicion that those on top got there by foul means. Much of this was bred out of Mr. Clinton at Georgetown and Oxford and Yale, but his willingness to bomb a sovereign nation once his vote-counters had informed him that his goose was cooked is a classic white-trash reaction: when backed into a corner, bite, scratch, and gouge, but never surrender.

Arthur Schlesinger Jr., the superannuated Kennedy hagiographer and consummate Cold War liberal, was among those defending Mr. Clinton against impeachment in those misty days before the Clinton Phase of our Hundred Years War against Iraq. Schlesinger is the proud sponsor of those galling "rate the presidents" polls of historians. Oddly, those designated "great" or "near great" are usually the war presidents: Lincoln, Wilson, Roosevelt, Truman. The relative peaceniks—Van Buren, Harding, Hoover—are dumped into the "below average" or "failure" categories. The more blood they shed, the closer they get to the Pantheon.

Now, we all know that Mr. Clinton, when not groping zaftig interns, ruminates about his "place in history." Perhaps, in the dead of night, while avoiding Mrs. Clinton—"I'm gonna read, honey; don't wait up for me"—he has been inflicting Schlesinger upon himself. Thus the bombs, the carnage, the limbs and faces torn from innocent people. For if he keeps the war engines humming long enough, not only will Bill Clinton avoid conviction by the Senate, but future Schlesingers will adjudge him one of the truly great presidents in American history. Not bad for white trash.

At Least He Inhaled

The Spectator, 1999

WHITE MEN CAN'T JUMP, but they can raise large sums of money from other white men: witness the $12 million that former New York Knicks basketball forward Bill Bradley has amassed to fuel his challenge to Vice President Gore for the Democratic presidential nomination. (Gore has shaken the money tree for $18 million.) Bradley's teammates used to gibe that he couldn't leap over a Sunday *New York Times*, and the joke still works. Bradley has never transcended the sodden clichés that make the American newspaper of record so reliably dreary.

But whereas Albert Gore is widely—and rightly—derided, the equally wooden Bradley, a Wall Street Democrat who represented New Jersey in the U.S. Senate for eighteen years, is "the thinking man's politician," in the characteristically fatuous phrase of *Time*. (You could have fooled the staffer who tutored Bradley on tax policy when he joined the Senate Finance Committee: he once described his charge as "the dumbest Rhodes Scholar in history." Quite a distinction, really, when you consider the procession of numbingly "well-rounded" mediocrities who have taken Cecil Rhodes's blood money.) But not only is Bradley regarded as an intellectual, he is also a serious challenger to Gore—a poll this week showed that he was neck-and-neck with the Vice President in New Hampshire.

The legend of Bill Bradley, son of a Crystal City, Missouri, banker, was made on the basketball court at Princeton. He was the golden boy of sportswriters with literary pretensions. The great white basketball players tended to be unlettered hicks (Jerry West from Cheylan, West Virginia; Larry Bird from French Lick, Indiana; John Havlicek from Martins Ferry, Ohio). Suspicious of polysyllabic words, they lacked the student-council-president polish of "Dollar Bill" (an eerily prescient sobriquet, given Bradley's skill at coaxing millions of dollars from investment bankers and Hollywood moguls). When sportswriters discovered that Bradley could speak four consecutive sentences without a single "y'know," he was portrayed in breathless profiles as the Heidegger of the Hardwood. The believe-it-or-not treatment—a basketball player who reads books!—carried over to Bradley's Senate career, which he spent upholding the middling middle and being lauded as an independent, a man of conscience—even, absurdly, a maverick, despite his voting with Wall Street on NAFTA and GATT, and with the Cold Warriors on U.S. intervention in Nicaragua.

After a lifetime of having his banalities treated as pearls of sapience, Bradley has become insufferable in the fashion of a third-rate intellect convinced of his own genius. He is self-consciously aloof. He has mastered the art of answering questions haltingly, as though his forehead should be bannered "Cerebration in Progress."

Bradley's opinions are hackneyed. In the early '90s he said his priorities were "kids and the environment." Then Rodney King was beaten by Los Angeles cops and Bradley called for "an honest dialogue about race in America"—although "extremists" were to be barred from the dialogue, along with inconvenient facts (such as extraordinarily high black crime rates). In recent months he has taken up the gun confiscation cause much favored by the professional class. At each step he has merely mouthed the platitudes of the day, yet through it all his reputation as a cerebral stud with an independent streak endures. (There is one anomaly in the Bradley record: raised Presbyterian, he was active in the evangelical Fellowship of Christian Athletes—a serious *faux pas*, for proselytizing Christians are as marginalized a group as exists in the New York-Washington-Hollywood axis along which Bradley travels. He has been quiet on the God stuff throughout his career, but the Monolithic Middle has recently embraced "faith-based charity"—that is, funnelling welfare monies through religious organizations—and Bradley has picked up the tune.)

The Gore forces do not underestimate him. Bradley will receive adulatory press coverage. Unlike the Republican front-runner, he denies being a cokehead, though he has confessed to taking a few forbidden puffs on marijuana cigarettes. A genuine maverick would follow this admission with a call to legalize pot and call off the drug war, but have we mentioned that Senator Bradley cares deeply about children and the environment?

Bradley's greatest liability is his perceived weakness in the South, which was critical to the election of Democrats Carter and Clinton. Vice President Gore, after all, is technically a resident of the Upper South state of Tennessee, although he was raised in the Fairfax Hotel in Washington, D.C., and sent to ruling-class prep schools. Bradley's native state of Missouri shares a border with Tennessee: riven by the Civil War, the state was a hotbed of unregenerate Confederates, most famously Jesse James, no friend to Missouri bankers or their sons. Yet Bradley, whose Missourian qualities have long since eroded, has been written off in the South—unless, that is, there is no more South. For as the Bradley campaign chairman has explained hopefully: "Even in the South, you drive down the street and you see the same Blockbusters, the same McDonald's. Now, Wal-Marts are in the Northeast. There are both regional differences and huge commonalities."

These "huge commonalities"—the swamping of local idiosyncrasy by tyrannically homogeneous global capitalism—are what give a placeless person like Bradley a shot at winning this election. Appositely, one of the fat cats bankrolling Bradley is Howard Schultz, chairman of Starbucks, which operates on the premise that there is no real difference between Birmingham, England, and Birmingham, Alabama. Maybe the accents lack consonance, but television will take care of that soon enough.

"I have always preferred moving to standing still," Bradley began his memoir *Time Present, Time Past*, and it is this hypermobility, the refusal to stand in one place and defend its integrity, that is at the root of the "loneliness" that Bradley senses, correctly, among his countrymen.

Having lived his entire adult life on the run, without a sense of place, a President Bradley would be forever lecturing the dwindling band of rooted Americans on their "international responsibilities" to wage war on various swarthy renegades and, in general, to make the world safe for Microsoft. He calls himself a "citizen of the world," which means he is a citizen of no place in particular. But, then, isn't it time that Starbucks had a president?

Earl Dodge: He'd Rather Be Right than President

The American Enterprise, 2000

IN A FOURTH-FLOOR ROOM of the Bucks County Sheraton in Langhorne, Pennsylvania, perennial Prohibition Party presidential candidate Earl Dodge serenades me, in a church-choir baritone, with his party's theme song:

> I'd rather be right than president
> I want my conscience clear
> I'll firmly stand for truth and right
> I have a God to fear
> I'll work and vote the way I pray
> No matter what the scoffers say
> I'd rather be right than president
> I want my conscience clear

If the great third parties and their tribunes—the Socialists and Eugene V. Debs, George Wallace and the American Independent Party—are gone but not forgotten, the Prohibition Party is forgotten but not gone. Yet its sixty-seven-year-old embodiment, Earl Dodge, soldiers on.

"I could be called the moral Harold Stassen," he jokes.

Founded in 1869, the Prohibitionists are the oldest third-party in American politics. The party elected two congressmen and a governor of Florida early in this century; its high-water mark in presidential campaigns came in 1892, when reformed vintner General John Bidwell, having spurned the "drunkard-making business," won 271,058 votes, or about 250,000 more than Earl Dodge has received in four previous runs for the White House. No Prohibitionist has won election to office since 1978 (in the township of Lee in Maine, which was the first state to go dry, in 1851).

There is a charmingly anachronistic cast to Dodge and his party; the Eighteenth Amendment was repealed almost seventy years ago, but the party continues to demand "the prohibition of the manufacturing, distribution, and sale of all alcoholic beverages." They are still at it, a dwindling band of temperate ladies and male Sunday-school teachers in the only political party to address the question, "What About Those Bible Wines?" (They were probably grape juice.)

The indefatigable Earl Dodge is not delusive. "If I get to the White House it'll be on a public guided tour," he acknowledges. So why run? "It's important for people to have the right to vote for what they believe in. Everybody is going to be accountable to God. When I see God, He's not going to ask me if I belonged to the biggest party, but did I do what I know to be right?"

Earl joined the party in 1952, a Massachusetts teenager disillusioned by the failure of the Republican Party to nominate Robert Taft for president. His early work in a Boston rescue mission "gave me an education on how much damage booze does." The Baptist Dodge attests, "The Lord led me into this work when I was a young man because He knew that I would stick with it." The Lord was right. Earl became a one-dollar-a-year party field worker; he, his wife Barbara, and their swelling brood would spend twenty years moving from one prohibition headquarters to the next, living in Indiana, Michigan, California, and Kansas before settling near Denver in 1971.

The Dodges are the first family of temperance; think of them as the anti-Kennedys. Earl is Mr. Prohibition: He is party chairman, editor of its newsletter, and its quadrennial standard-bearer. Barbara runs the computer and mailing list and is one of her husband's electors. Two daughters and one son have run for office; of the seven Dodge children, "a majority votes the ticket." If the kids are not unanimous for dad, well, neither were the Reagans.

Earl has run for office at least twenty times, for everything from Massachusetts Secretary of State to governor of Colorado. He has never won, though he did come within hailing distance of being elected to the Kalamazoo City Commission in 1969.

Despite his labors in what we had best not call the political vineyards, Dodge has overseen the decline of his party. Whereas a century ago dissenters had easy access to the ballot, the "oppressive election laws" of post-World War II America have forced the Prohibitionists off the ballot in such erstwhile strongholds as Kansas and Alabama. This November, Dodge expects to be on the ballot in Colorado, Utah, Tennessee, Arkansas, Florida, New Jersey, and Mississippi. A vote total of 10,000 would be a windfall. "If you look at this from a cold, calculating political viewpoint, my wife's husband would be a blithering idiot for doing what he's doing," says the candidate. "The only excuse I can give is that I believe in it."

The Dodge campaign consists mostly of interviews with Christian radio stations and small-town newspapers and occasional visits to states with visible supporters. He is in Langhorne not to press the flesh but to exhibit at a political button show. "When I started working for the party all they had was two little pins in a drawer, so I started to build a collection," says Dodge. Thus he has become, poignantly, a party archivist as well: keeper of the dry flame, tender of a tradition that may not survive this recent recipient of a septuple bypass. For although the party has thirty-one national committee members from twenty-one states, there is no heir apparent to Earl Dodge. "I pray about that all the time," he says. "I don't know who would do it if I didn't."

******

Earl Dodge is amiable and garrulous—"my mother said I was vaccinated with a phonograph needle"—even after we establish that I would legalize marijuana and he would criminalize beer. While he is a True Believer, he does not routinely break out the Carrie Nation hatchet or subject stray wets to harangues on the Demon Rum. "Don't drive me to drink!" he jokes with wet friends. And no, he is not a reformed drunk out to scourge the liquor that put him in the gutter. "I've got many faults but I've never had a drink of alcohol in my life."

He defends the Eighteenth Amendment and the resultant thirteen-year dry spell as "a tremendous success"; he offers "$20,000 to anyone who can show that during prohibition, crime and diseases related to alcohol did not decline."

Dodge concedes that immediate prohibition today is impracticable: "There'd be no point in enacting a law without majority support because you couldn't enforce it, and drinking is an ingrained practice in America." So while "prohibition is the ultimate answer, in the meantime we favor education" and the semi-prohibitionist steps advocated by groups like Mothers Against Drunk Driving. "We are slowly going in the direction of a dry nation," says Dodge confidently. "If I live to eighty or eighty-five, I expect to see some form of prohibition."

Although Dodge doesn't "know of a single person in our party who smokes," the party takes a laissez-faire line on tobacco. "Unless they're blowing smoke in your face, they're not infringing on your rights," he says, while alcohol "takes good people and turns them into beasts. Marijuana, LSD, cocaine: all those drugs put together don't hurt a fraction of the people that booze does. The only parties that are honest and consistent on the alcohol-drug issue are the Prohibition Party and the Libertarians. They want to legalize it all; we want to ban it all." Pleased to find common ground, I steer the conversation back to the party's colorful past.

Dodge has a wonderful sense of history, of being part of an eccentrically American tradition. He calls the roll of Prohibitionists past: Isaac Funk published party magazines in addition to the dictionary he put out with Mr. Wagnalls. Grape-juice king Charles Welch ran for governor of New York in 1916 as a Prohibitionist. "Wrong-Way" Corrigan, the directionally challenged pilot who in 1938 aimed for California and wound up in Ireland, was the Prohibition candidate for U.S. Senate in 1946 from California. (He eventually did find his way there.) Astonishingly, the *New Yorker*-Hollywood wit Robert Benchley was a Prohibition activist before settling into a gin and rye haze during the 1920s: a Prohibitionist done in by prohibition!

The party's symbol has been various: once the white rose of purity, then the water fountain, then the one-humped camel—until "Camel cigarettes came out," whereupon the smoke-free party added a hump to make it Bactrian. "In our office in Denver we collect anything that's a camel," says Dodge. "We even have a small camel whiskey container—empty, of course."

****

Dodge's fifth nomination did not come without a fight. Meeting last summer in the dry Amish town of Bird-in-Hand, Pennsylvania, the Prohibitionists renominated Dodge over a surprise challenge from a Utahan who wanted to de-emphasize prohibition and play up less outré concerns. (If a century ago the party was progressive—woman suffrage and the income tax were second only to prohibition in its list of demands—today its platform is generally conservative-populist: pro-life, anti-foreign aid, pro-free enterprise, anti-immigration, pro-gun.) The convention chose Dodge by a vote of 9–8; he explains, "A lot of the traditional members were out having a late lunch; they didn't know there was going to be a contest." But even with his allies off at their no-martini lunch, Dodge's defense of tradition carried the day. "If we abandon or play down the booze issue, we don't deserve to exist as a party. We don't deserve to retain the name."

Earl Dodge wants the scoffers to remember something: "Even if people think we're a bunch of nuts, no one in the party has ever stood to make a nickel if what they were working for succeeded." It is this adherence to principle and ingenuous faith in American democracy that makes the Prohibitionists admirable, even to a beer-drinking libertarian. Dodge recalls a story that the wife of a one-time vice presidential candidate told at a convention long ago. "Her uncle grew peaches during a hard time in Kansas. The men were taking the peaches away in the truck, jostling the baskets, and he said, 'Don't do that—you'll bruise the peaches.' 'Don't worry about that,' they said. 'They're going to be crushed for brandy anyway.' He said, 'Not my peaches,' and he made them unload them. They sat there and rotted. He took the loss. You had that attitude once in this country: principle was important. Today people are primarily interested in their retirement benefits and the stock market. There's no other explanation for someone as despicable as Slick Willie being in office."

Earl Dodge "has quite literally given his life to our Party," salutes fellow Prohibitionist James Hedges. He knows that he will never be president. But he thinks he is right, and whether he is or not, his conscience is clear.

George W. Bush, the Anti-Family President
Counterpunch, 2003

BEHOLD THE PERVERSE AND heart-wrenchingly anti-family policies of Bush, Rumsfeld, and Cheney: Women reservists, young mothers of infants and small children, leave their families to go halfway 'round the world to act as cogs, expendable parts, in the machinery of the deeply anti-American Empire. And hearken to the silence of the courtiers and grant-grubbers of Establishment Conservatism, whose mingled nescience and cowardice testify to the gutlessness and wicked stupidity of what passes for the Right.

As a radical and a reactionary—a patriot of the old America—I am appalled by the violence done by the military-industrial complex at home as well as abroad. The images of families cleaved by the Iraqi War and occupation should outrage family-values conservatives—many of whom, especially at the grass roots, are sincere and decent, no matter how weasely the Bennetts and Bauers are. Here is yet another issue on which good people of the Greenish left and anti-imperialist right ought to unite: the first casualty of the militarized U.S. state is the family.

I once asked former Secretary of Defense Caspar Weinberger if the U.S. military wasn't "a government-subsidized uprooting of the population." He replied, shall we say, in the negative; I may as well have asked Caspar the unfriendly ghost if he preferred the Clash or the Sex Pistols. But I was dead serious: the single greatest cause of rootlessness—the great undiagnosed sickness afflicting America—has been our standing army. (If it really were standing it wouldn't be so bad; alas, it never stops moving.)

Benjamin Rush proposed in 1792 that two mottoes be painted "over the portals of the Department of War": "An office for butchering the human species" and "A Widow and Orphan making office." Rush was right. He might have added, "The Greatest Cuckold-Maker," for no government agency separates husbands from wives quite like the mendaciously renamed Department of Defense.

Absence may make the heart grow fonder, but love requires presence above all. The divorce rate more than doubled between 1940 and 1946.

The Second World War, by removing men from households and removing many of those households from the rural South into the unwelcoming urban North, waged its own mini-war upon the American family. Rosie the Riveter propaganda aside, the domestic face of the warfare state was sketched by an Arkansas social worker: "children's fathers go off to war and their mothers go to work, and thus the interests of parents is diverted from the home and the children."

Government-subsidized daycare was one offspring of the Second World War; thanks to the Lanham Act, over half a million children were cared for by strangers in these cold institutions. Today, Hillary Clinton and the corporate feminists point to the U.S. Army as the model daycare provider. And yet conservatives, who froth at the merest hint of the carpetbagger's name, are quiet, struck dumb by their worship of the widow-making bureaucracy. (The Middle American left should be anti-daycare. As Mother Jones said, "The human being is the only animal which is neglected in its babyhood. The brute mother suckles and preserves her young at the cost of her own life, if need be. The human mother hires another, poorer woman for the job." And: "The rich woman who has a maid to raise her child can't expect to get the right viewpoint of life. If they would raise their own babies, their hearts would open and their feelings would become human. And the effect on the child is just as bad. A nurse can't give her mother's love to somebody else's child.")

Authentic conservatives—those who defended the near and dear things against remote and abstract powers—used to understand the iniquity of militarism. In 1945, Mrs. Cecil Norton Broy, representing a ladies' study club in Arlington, Virginia, told a roomful of snickering U.S. senators that an interventionist foreign policy would lead to "the further disruption of normal American family life. . . . Our men would be like hired mercenary soldiers going forth to protect the commercial interests of greed and power. Our men thus forced into foreign service would see little if any of their native soil again. We would be working on the principle of scattering the most virile of our men over the face of the globe."

Tens of thousands of abandoned Amerasians who grew up without fathers shake their heads in assent. Yet in the unlikely event that a contemporary Mrs. Broy made it past the thought-crime detectors and into a Senate hearing room today, I expect that she'd be given a stern lecture by a GOP family-values fraud and be sent on her way with a minatory copy of the Patriot Act.

I could go on and on about the ways in which post-World War II militarism has eroded American family life. (I do go on and on elsewhere; see the chapter on the military vs. the family in my *With Good Intentions?*

Reflections on the Myth of Progress in America.) Divorce, dispersal, disruption of courtship patterns: ye shall know the warfare state by its rotten fruits. These include even the people-scattering Interstate Highway System, which was conceived during World War II by the top-down planner extraordinaire Rexford G. Tugwell and made concrete by a deracinated general named Dwight Eisenhower, who had admired Hitler's autobahn and got one of his own: the tellingly titled National System of Interstate and Defense Highways. Cohesive working-class neighborhoods in countless American cities were sacrificed to the Road Warriors.

The leadership of the family values Right is hopelessly compromised by its long-term adulterous affair with the Republican Party. But plenty of good folks who call themselves "conservatives" mean by that now-useless term that they believe in the integrity of families and small communities and detest the vulgar, home-wrecking, and even murderous intrusions of corporate capitalism and Big Government. As they watch this latest American diaspora, as young husbands and wives tearfully leave spouses and children and extended families to serve the Empire, we should remind them that the only foreign policy compatible with healthy family life is one of peace and non-intervention. Come home, America. Come home.

What a Country!
Wall Street Journal, 2004

EVERY FOUR YEARS THE national media rediscover those exotic entities known as the fifty states—or at least those states whose legislatures are savvy enough to schedule primaries and caucuses early in the bleak midwinter. For a frenzied month, even the smuggest cosmopolitan correspondent has an inkling that he has stumbled upon the great hidden strength of America, which is—not to sound like a college administrator—her diversity.

The worst reporters experience nothing and think it's America. Their time in the provinces is a flash of prison-like airports, chain hotels, and the monotonous Interstate Highway System (the first Republican monument to Big Government), all set to the soporific hum of CNN. They fall back upon the hoariest stereotypes, depicting Iowans as hearty, honest farmfolk (like Professor Harold Hill?) and New Hampshireites as flinty Yankees who say "A-yup" and give laconic directions to Laconia. If confronted by a genuine manifestation of regional pride—say, the Confederate flag in South Carolina—they squeal like six-year-old girls finding a snake.

Yet the persistence of regional clichés in the age of MTV gives reason for hope. Missouri is not indistinguishable from New Hampshire. Even Peter Jennings can sense this. Despite the ubiquity of pop culture, not every boy in Darlington, South Carolina prefers Britney Spears to the tramp next door. We are not a nation of interchangeable *Friends* watchers—yet.

Certain self-evident truths assert themselves as we watch the Men Who Would Be President hopscotch across the country. The most obvious is that our places are far more interesting than our politicians, who in their pursuit of power shed every oddity, mute every color, and efface every idiosyncrasy, until they achieve a state of nothingness that might be called Gephardtism.

The relentlessly uninteresting men who dominate American politics are poor reflections of our variegated states. Take Iowa, a place so rich in characters and loveliness that it gave us *Music Man* composer Meredith Willson, the Herbert Hoover-reverencing New Left historian William

Appleman Williams, and Donna Reed. Can such a glorious trio be distilled into, say, the faux-populist Senator Tom Harkin? I don't think so.

How did a bland New South ambulance chaser like John Edwards even dare show his face in Cedar Rapids, Iowa, artistic home of that sardonic painter of Middle America, Grant Wood, and birthplace of that iconic American company, Quaker Oats? (The recent absorption of Quaker Oats into Pepsi—over the heart-wrenching objections of loyal old Quaker employees—is a sign of these distressing times.)

Grant Wood was no diffident Midwesterner, deferential to coastal bosses. He loved and promoted the distinct culture of his region, urging a "revolt against the domination exercised over arts and letters and over much of our thinking and living by Eastern capitals of finance and politics." Iowans cannot achieve such a revolution by gathering in caucuses to vote for a boarding-school liberal like John Kerry, but the incongruity serves, again, to contrast the vitality of our places with the lifelessness of our candidates.

What can a rootless military bureaucrat like Wesley Clark think when he walks into a diner in Littleton, New Hampshire, whose patrons are bound to each other by a web of kinship, friendship, love and hate and secret histories that outsiders can never know? Clark can choke down the coffee and mumble platitudes about health care, but the encounter means nothing to anyone.

Unlike the placeless General Clark, Senator John Kerry at least secretes that New England preppie sense of entitlement that repels any townie with an ounce of pride. Odor of hauteur, we might call it. Thus Kerry does embody something of his region, albeit its least attractive aspect.

If, on the other hand, Howard Dean's candidacy heard its death knell in New England, perhaps it's because Dean was always more New York than Yankee. University of Vermont professor Frank Bryan, author of *Real Democracy*, the authoritative work on the New England town meeting, says that Governor Dean "was raised in an environment as completely estranged from town meetings as one can imagine . . . and [has] never participated as a citizen in a town meeting." Dean is about as "New England" as the Patriots, by which I do not mean Sam Adams and John Hancock.

In fact, the Super Bowl champs are a nice, if brutal, illustration of ersatz regionalism. Many of us vent our vestigial local loyalties by cheering for transient athletic mercenaries whose ties to the cities in which they play are no stronger than a free-agent contract.

The Patriots are as "New England" as Wal-Mart, and the Panthers are no more "Carolina" than Starbucks. For displays of authentic local pride in flyover America, drop by one of the high-school basketball tournaments getting underway later this month--and watch games in which the teams represent real communities and play without stopping for three-minute TV timeouts.

"Locality gives art," said Robert Frost, who as a Grover Cleveland Democrat would have scorned the statist vote-beggers swarming North of Boston every fourth winter. Alas for art's sake, Frost's road less traveled is filling up with Olive Gardens and Applebees. Concord, New Hampshire, and Columbia, South Carolina are looking too much alike for comfort these days. If the sameness is getting you down, join the club. (Not Sam's Club or BJ's, please.)

A great war rages in the forgotten—yet quadrenially headline-making—America of Iowa and New Hampshire and South Carolina. This battle pits locally based institutions against the grim forces of homogenization: it's *Sex and the City* vs. the Sadie Hawkins Dance; the Home Despot vs. mom-and-pop hardware stores; Justin Timberlake vs. the volunteer fire department. I haven't heard a single candidate even acknowledge the existence of this conflict. And I'm sure it's not uppermost in the mind of Teresa Heinz Kerry.

The more perceptive reporters left Iowa, New Hampshire, South Carolina, and the Groundhog Day-after primary states in a pleasant daze. They had seen a few pieces of America, pieces that weren't cut by the Washington jigsaw. And then it was back to the antiseptic newsroom or the TV studio, where the America that exists underneath the drone of Clear Channel and the witless smut of the Super Bowl halftime show is a half-remembered dream. There is still a mighty lovely country out here. Just don't look for it on CNN. At least not until midwinter 2008.

Hey, Ralph! Why Not Another Party of the People?

Counterpunch, 2004

THE CYNICAL ALABAMA POPULIST Governor George Wallace used to scoff that there wasn't a dime's worth of difference between the two parties. Thank God that manic cracker spent the bleak winter of 2004 in an otherworldly realm. For today there isn't a plug nickel's worth of difference between the Democrats and the Republicans. The parties of Jefferson and Lincoln have clearcut the redwood forests, drained the gulfstream waters, leveled the purple mountains and scalped the amber waves of grain only to come up with George W. Bush and John F. Kerry: Skull and Bones-dum versus Skull and Bones-dee.

God bless our meritocracy!

What a marvelous system we have in freedom's land. The Democrats, barely six weeks into the primary season, have disposed of the troublesomely frank Vermont Gov. Howard Dean and settled upon a presidential candidate who, but for his cadaverous countenance, might have skulked right out of the Bushes. Senator Kerry is a rich and haughty boarding-school boy, prolonged exposure to whom could turn the doughiest Tory into a raging Spartacist. At Yale he was tapped for Skull and Bones, the creepily macabre secret society whose possessions reportedly include the skull of the Apache chief Geronimo, stolen by President Bush's grandfather, Prescott Bush, in a bit of youthful deviltry. Despite Kerry's recent tergiversations, he was in favor of the U.S. war upon Iraq. A freespending statist, he is profligate with what only the most hopeless naifs still refer to as "the taxpayers' money."

The above description, of course, applies equally to the incumbent president. Lop six inches off Kerry's chin and a dozen points off his IQ and you've got President Bush II. Yes, there are niggling differences. Bush was a prep-school cheerleader and Kerry a decorated Vietnam veteran, but then Republicans have pretty much cornered the market on chickenhawks. To his credit, Bush married the literate Laura while Kerry dumped his first wife, a chronically depressed heiress, and traded up for Mrs. Croesus, the ketchup widow Teresa, who hit the jackpot when poor Senator Heinz splurted up to that great condiment table in the sky.

So what is the thickskulled boneweary voter to do?

As an old-fashioned decentralist antiwar patriot, my dream ticket would consist of Gore Vidal and Texas Congressman Ron Paul, noble lions of the Old Republic, of the America before MTV and WMD and ABC and all those acronyms buried my sweet USA, but they aren't going to be on the ballot. Ralph Nader is. And if Nader runs the antiwar, anti-corporate, pro-Middle America campaign he has previewed, we might finally hear the welcome echoes of the long lost William Jennings Bryan.

Funny, isn't it, that Bryan, the most popular and imaginatively radical major-party candidate of the post-Civil War Era—a populist so esteemed that he overcame the opposition of Wall Street to thrice serve as the Democratic candidate for president—has no heirs, no legatees, no annual dinners named after him? He exists for us only in the slanderous portrayal of him in that silly collection of clichés, *Inherit the Wind*.

Bryan, the Great Commoner, the windbag with a heart, tribune of the farmer and honest toiler, was a sort of anti-Kerry. Isn't one reason suburban Democrats nominate high-born stiffs like Kerry so that they can feel superior to white Southerners, born-agains, working-class Catholics, and the other gun-owning, church-going, war-hating homefolks who used to find a home in the Democratic Party of Bryan?

WJB called, in the mellifluous tones of his Plains, for a Jeffersonian dispersion of power—political, economic, and cultural. How he would have despised Clear Channel, Disney, and the *New York Times*. He'd have called for the restoration of local ownership of newspapers and TV and radio stations; he'd have understood that America's real enemies are the likes of Dick Cheney, *Sex and the City*, and the typewriter imperialists who know nothing of the real America but serve instead the deeply anti-American Empire.

Bryan, to be sure, would be passionately anti-Iraq War and anti-Patriot Act, but he would also be a stalwart defender of Mel Gibson's *The Passion of the Christ* against the hysterical condemnation of the anti-religious corporate media. (Bryan might regard Gibson's *Passion* as a wee bit Catholic for his tastes, but still. Many of us find it grotesque that one can win praise for making films glorifying serial killers, cannibals, and editors of the *New Republic*, but not our Lord. Jee-zus Christ!)

I do hope Ralph Nader speaks in the great Middle-American Bryanite accent. Defend—nay, champion—the small farm, the small merchant, the laborer, the homemaker, the dreamy poet. Bring the boys home—from Iraq, from Europe, from Korea, from everywhere. Slash the war budget. Cherish the Bill of Rights—including the Second Amendment. Dismantle the Clinton-Bush incipient police state. Attack corporate rule at its very roots: repeal corporate charters, break up the communications giants, eliminate corporate welfare. These are the causes of the America beyond the reach of HBO.

And please, Ralph, go after the folks who voted in 2000 for Bush (who was, you will recall, the candidate promising a "humble" foreign policy against the hawkish Gore).

My county in rural Western New York has been true-blue for the GOP since Abe Lincoln, and I have never heard my Republican neighbors express such doubt, such skepticism, even such open contempt toward a Republican president. These people are "conservative" in a way that the leaders of their party no longer are: that is to say, they prefer governmental powers to be limited and decentralized, and they do not wish to shoulder the burden of empire. The Bushies and their courtiers, who know as little of our history as Janet Jackson knows of Jane Austen, haven't the faintest idea that Republicans have often been the party of peace and non-interference in foreign wars. As President Benjamin Harrison once remarked, "We have no commission from God to police the world." Step outside the DC-NYC corridor and you'll find that millions of Americans agree. And we're supposed to choose from George W. Bush and John F. Kerry?

We have a choice, dammit.

Run, Ralph, run. Run left, run right, run as constitutionalist liberal, as antiwar patriot, as a man proud to stand in the Bryan-La Follette-Gene McCarthy-Paul Goodman tradition. You'd be surprised at how many Main Street conservatives, disaffected Republicans, and pissed-off libertarians wish you well. Hell, I probably disagree with half your platform but I wish you more than well. As night falls in what used to be America, the bedfellows get ever stranger.

The Candidates from Nowhere
Counterpunch, 2008

THE LAST THREE MAJOR-PARTY presidential candidates standing have this in common: the state abbreviations after their names—John McCain (AZ), Hillary Clinton (NY), and Barack Obama (IL)—are no more meaningful than the random pairings of letters in a spoonful of alphabet soup. These are the candidates from nowhere. Or in Obama's case, from everywhere. And this rootlessness has policy consequences.

Senator John McCain is a poster boy for the pathologies of the military brat. Born in the Panama Canal Zone, he attended twenty schools in his nomadic childhood. "The place I lived longest in my life was Hanoi," is how he shuts up critics of his carpetbagging, but he is making their point: Senator McCain's loyalty is not to any particular American place but rather to a bureaucratic institution (the military) and an abstraction (the American Empire).

After marrying his second wife in 1980, McCain alit in her home state of Arizona in 1981 and was elected to Congress in 1982. He was a classic political carpetbagger searching for a winnable congressional seat, but when a voter questioned his lack of roots he shot back:

"Listen, pal. I spent twenty-two years in the Navy. My father was in the Navy. My grandfather was in the Navy. We in the military service tend to move a lot. We have to live in all parts of the country, all parts of the world. I wish I could have had the luxury, like you, of growing up and living and spending my entire life in a nice place like the First District of Arizona, but I was doing other things."

An effective response, to be sure, but note the subsurface contempt for those who stay in one place. Not to worry: a President McCain, with his oft-quoted willingness to keep U.S. soldiers in Iraq for "a hundred years," won't let deep roots grow under our young people. His Army, always moving, is going to need bodies.

The Democrats are no more connected to particular places than is McCain. Hillary Clinton's rootlessness became a national joke in her 2000

U.S. Senate campaign to represent New York, a state in which she had never lived. Wearing a Yankees cap was about as far as she went to assert her ersatz New Yorkness.

Barack Obama, lauded as the "world candidate," was born in Hawaii, a state that is only in the union because of its military significance. Raised also in Indonesia and at various times resident in Los Angeles, New York City, and finally Chicago, Obama is a "cosmopolitan," which by some lights means a sophisticate but which I take to be a well-dressed homeless man.

Senator Obama has said that "We cannot afford to be a country of isolationists right now." Then again, cosmopolitans think we can *never* afford to leave other countries alone and mind our own business. Because their business *is* our business. Or as Obama says, American security is "inextricably linked to the security of all people."

Obama's limitless internationalism is encapsulated in his statement that "When poor villagers in Indonesia have no choice but to send chickens to market infected with avian flu, it cannot be seen as a distant concern." This is, quite possibly, the most expansive definition ever essayed of the American national interest. It is a license for endless interventions in the affairs of other nations. It is a recipe for blundering into numberless wars—which will be fought, disproportionately, by those God & Guns small-town Americans evidently despised or pitied by Mr. Obama. It is redolent of the biblical assurance that not even a sparrow can fall to the earth unnoticed by God. The congruence of the roles of the deity and U.S. foreign policy in Obama's mind is not reassuring to those of us who desire peace and a modest role for the U.S. military.

Why does this matter? What's wrong with electing competent but rootless people to public office? Because just as one cannot love the "human race" before one loves particular human beings, neither can one love "the world" unless he first achieves a deep understanding of his own little piece of that world. America is not, as the neoconservatives like to say, an idea: it is a place, or rather the sum of a thousand and one little, individuated places, each with its own history and accent and stories. A politician who understands this will act in ways that protect and preserve these real places. A rootless politico will babble on about "the homeland"—a creepily totalitarian phrase that, pre-Bush, was not applied to our country.

People lacking strong identifications with specific places—a block, a village, a city, a state, a region—will transfer their loyalties to abstractions. Woodrow Wilson, a displaced Southern minister's kid, renounced the traditional American practice of neutrality and tossed the First Amendment in the scrap heap in his crusade to "make the world safe for democracy." George W. Bush, the Texan-cum-Yankee prep-school cheerleader, has wasted astronomical sums and thousands of lives in a campaign whose ostensible purpose is to democratize the Middle East and "rid the world of evil." The costs of such grandiose schemes may be measured in billions of dollars and acres of corpses. In addition, political power is centralized, citizens are uprooted, and the economy undergoes wartime distortions. These are reckoned acceptable prices to pay for the achievement of mighty (if ultimately unachievable) abstractions. But democracy was no safer despite the First World War, and I daresay evil will exist long after U.S. troops come home from Iraq.

People with local attachments, by contrast, will ask the question that never quite gets injected into national debates over war and peace: What are the domestic costs of this crusade? Loving their block, they will not wish to bomb Iraq. Loyal to a neighborhood, they will not send its young men and women across the sea to kill and die for causes wholly unrelated to local life.

Losing sight of small and precious things, a president without roots will have no domestic or sentimental reminder of why foreign crusades, whose first casualties are the nearest and dearest things, should never be waged. But don't mind me: I'm just an isolationist.

The Republic Strikes Back
The American Conservative, 2009

AMERICAN POLITICAL DISCOURSE, DEFINED as it is by Arthur Schlesinger's ghost and Bill Bennett's ghostwriter, has contracted to such a pinpoint that I half expect a Big Bang to blow it all apart, as forbidden thoughts—Peace! Liberty! Localism!—bust loose from the thought prisons and the air is filled with the glorious cacophony of patriotic debate as free men and women relearn the language and habits of vigorous citizenship.

Ah, well: dare to dream.

I saw this dream last Labor Day weekend when Ron Paul threw a "Rally for the Republic" in Minneapolis as a Twin Cities counterpoint to John McCain's zombie dance in St. Paul.

I was a last-minute addition to the rally's roster of speakers and hellraisers. As I paced antsily, waiting to take the stage at the Target Center, it occurred to me that if my jokes bombed I would hear the sound of 10,000 people not laughing. (Happily, the crowd was terrific; you can find the speech on YouTube, though I must caution you: I am far better looking in person.)

The campaign put me up at a bed and breakfast in Excelsior, Minnesota, whose contribution to Top Forty culture was seeded when, in 1964, Mick Jagger, having played at the Danceland ballroom the night before, was standing in line to get his prescription filled at the Excelsior drugstore. Seems a local character named Jimmy Hutmaker started yapping about how he loved his cherry coke but that morning he was given a different flavor and y'know, Mr. Jagger, you can't always get what you want....

Call it a suburban legend, skeptic, but no man born with a living soul denies it.

At breakfast the morn of the rally, I sat across the table from a friendly dude wearing a peace-sign T-shirt and looking like an affable old surfer. He introduced himself as Gary Johnson, the former two-term governor of New Mexico. Over the next day, I spent a fair amount of time chatting with Governor Johnson: mountain-climber, triathlete, vetoer of 750 bills.

He told me that he may take a shot at the Republican presidential nomination in 2012 as an antiwar, anti-Fed, pro-personal liberties, slash-government-spending candidate—in other words, a Ron Paul libertarian.

South Carolina governor Mark Sanford seems to be carving out similar space in the GOP. While Sanford's stubborn parsimony within the spendthrift GOP is welcome—he is surely a stream of fresh air in a mephitic party—consider, if you will, Gary Johnson.

Yes, as a congressman Sanford opposed the U.S. intervention in Kosovo under a Democratic president; Gary Johnson opposed a Republican president's war upon Iraq. Sanford reluctantly endorsed McCain in 2008; Johnson emphatically endorsed Ron Paul. Sanford has potential on civil liberties; Johnson, like Paul, has the guts to call for the legalization of marijuana and an end to the drug war.

As this issue went to press, Governor Johnson told me that he was keeping his options open for 2012. Keep an eye out for him, will you?

Ron Paul started something. Or, rather, he revealed something: liberty has a constituency. I was heartened mightily by the crowd in Minneapolis, which was overwhelmingly young. What a rousing sight: bright and enthusiastic kids afire with the spirit of liberty, of resistance to regimentation and the tyranny of standardization. Homeschoolers, homebrewers, punk rockers, evangelical Christians, radical Kansans, and reactionary New Englanders. These were American girls and boys, beautifully stained in the American grain, hip to Republican lies and numbing Democratic statism. Hell no, they won't go. They'll not be cannon fodder for the wars of Bush-Cheney or Obama-Biden. They demand honesty and liberty and respect for all things small and smaller; they have nothing but scorn for the liars and whores who run the empire.

They reminded me of Emerson's description of the Loco Foco generation: "The new race is stiff, heady, and rebellious; they are fanatics in freedom; they hate tolls, taxes, turnpikes, banks, hierarchies, governors, yea, almost laws." (Spare me the mewling about "ordered liberty," please—fifty years of conservative pieties about "ordered liberty" led to Dick Cheney and a movement full of "men" who dared not open their mouths to defend liberty when she needed it most. Give me disorderly hinterland rebels any day.)

What I mean to say is that even if you can't always get what you want, I think the kids are all right.

Party Animus
The American Conservative, 2012

IN HIS MEMOIR *If You Don't Weaken* (1940), Oscar Ameringer, witty and humane radical from the erstwhile hotbed of American socialism, Oklahoma (it really was!), professed a "rule of never voting for a presidential candidate who had the slightest chance of election. The ballot is too precious lightly to be thrown away on candidates selected and financed by the 'angels' and archangels of the two historic old parties which have managed my adopted country into the condition it is in today."

Oscar's statute remains sound. We are facing in 2012 the worst Democrat-Republican twosome since, uh, 2008? 2004? 2000? I detect a pattern.

A state's electoral votes have never been decided by a single popular vote, so as history is our guide your vote for president *does not matter*.

Choose not between two evils: the candidate of crony capitalism and war with Iran or the candidate of crony socialism and smug anti-Catholicism. Groove instead to the old Prohibition Party hit: "I'd rather be right than president/I want my conscience clear."

Strategic voting is for Board of Education or City Council elections in which you and your franchise actually matter. As a citizen, you can play a role, even an essential role, in the affairs of your place. But as a subject of the Empire, you count for nothing. You're not even a brick in the wall in our quadrennial king-making charades.

So cast your ballot to satisfy your conscience. Obey the injunction of John Quincy Adams (whose son, Charles Francis Adams, bolted the Whigs to serve as Martin Van Buren's running mate on the 1848 Free Soil ticket): "Always vote for principle, though you may vote alone, and you may cherish the sweetest reflection that your vote is never lost."

I was born and bred in the cradle of minor partyism, so I suppose the blood—the ichor? the fever?—of electoral rebellion washes through my veins. Besides McGovern in 1972 and Goldwater in 1964, the last major-party candidate I might have voted for would have been Al Smith in 1928.

The nation's first third party, the Anti-Masons, arose in my backyard in 1826 after a footloose drunken apostate Mason, Captain William Morgan, spilled the secrets of the craft in his book *Illustrations of Freemasonry* and wound up missing in the Jimmy Hoffa sense. (Some local Masons long contended that the sot Morgan hightailed it to Canada and lived out a bibulous life. His ghost can be seen staggering about the stripjoints which stipple the Canadian side of the Niagara border.)

The first third party I'd have supported without reservation, the anarchist-tinged Liberty Party, was born twenty miles down the road in Warsaw, New York. (Reading a biography of John Greenleaf Whittier, who was forever whinging about his ailments as most poets do, I was amused to see him tell Gerrit Smith in 1840 that he planned to vote for Liberty Party candidate James Birney "if my life is spared" through November of that year. Like most hypochondriacs, Whittier lived forever, finally taking his leave fifty-two years later and entering the valetudinarian Hall of Fame.)

Why are the men with integrity and honor and courage so often found at the fringes of American political life? I think of Burton K. Wheeler (Progressive Party VP candidate in 1924) refusing to hand down a single sedition indictment as U.S. attorney for Montana during the First World War. Or Eugene V. Debs, five-time Socialist Party candidate for President, going to prison in 1919 for telling an audience in Canton, Ohio, that "the working class who freely shed their blood and furnish the corpses, have never yet had a voice in either declaring war or making peace. It is the ruling class that invariably does both."

Things sure have changed, huh?

Third parties have their share and more of frauds and kooks and backbiters (so unlike the Democrats and Republicans) but even at their meanest and most outré, a vote cast therefor serves as a gesture of protest, however ineffectual: an extended middle finger to the tank bearing down on you. Aaron Russo, the late Hollywood producer and manager of Bette Midler, tried and failed in the 1990s to launch a populist-libertarian party whose message to our overlords, in Russo's words, was "Fuck You! We're Not Going to Take This Shit!"

Much better than "Hope and Change," I'd say.

Me, I'm sticking with Oscar Ameringer. My default party in recent elections has been the Greens, but this time I'll vote for Gary Johnson, the Libertarian. I want my conscience clear.

New England Patriot

The American Conservative, 2014

THE ROVES AND AXELRODS who afflict American politics would run squealing from a man who in a 1992 fundraising letter for his gubernatorial campaign wrote, "If I don't raise $50,000 from this mailing I will be forced to drown my litter of Burmese rock pythons. And—get this—if your name is the one drawn from a large drum containing all my contributors' names YOU (fill in name) will win . . . ETERNAL LIFE. (Details to be announced later.)"

John McClaughry of Kirby Mountain, Vermont, penner of said letter, was trounced by Democratic incumbent Howard Dean, though the contest did yield a classic photograph of the Republican candidate presenting Governor Dean with the McClaughry campaign attire: a t-shirt bearing the image of a hooded executioner and an emblazoned NEXT.

For almost half a century, John McClaughry, kin of Tom and Frank McLaury of Gunfight at the O.K. Corral fame—Tom and Frank's "side of the family had a lot of trouble with spelling," says John—has haunted the GOP as an ornery, irrepressible, and gloriously untamable spirit of the vanished American Republic. If he has been too offbeat or too soulful to achieve success as it is measured by timeservers and lickspittles, he has embodied, in political form, the Jeffersonian persuasion. Now seventy-six, John has produced a characteristically free-swinging and self-deprecating memoir, *Promoting Civil Society Among the Heathen*, in which he recounts masterstrokes and misadventures while pushing measures to strengthen neighborhoods, small communities, and voluntary associations through such unlikely vessels as George Romney, Senator Charles Percy, and Ronald Reagan.

Years ago, John described his politics to me: "I am a 1700s Virginia republican, an 1800 Tertium Quid, an 1830s Loco Foco, an 1850s Republican, an 1890s western progressive, a 1930s agrarian distributist, and today a plain old decentralist agrarian Reaganaut." Given that I am wholly in sympathy with this list, Reaganautry excepted, I have wondered why John and I have so frequently disagreed on petty political matters. I've been aghast at his enthusiasm for the likes of Donald Rumsfeld and Pete du Pont; he's chided me for falling for Ross Perot and Jerry Brown. Well . . . strange bedfellows and all that.

John is that rare radical who has actually won elections. He served in the Vermont House and Senate, though he lost races for governor and U.S. Senate. He protests, however, that he is not a politician but a "tub thumper for public policies" designed to disperse political and economic power.

Some liberals saw him as the silver lining of the nascent Nixon administration. In late 1968, John Osborne in *The New Republic* wrote up McClaughry as "a remarkable white Republican activist" who was working with black-power leaders and believers in small-scale private enterprise "to promote black opportunity and black control of black communities." Nothing much came of this, says John, largely due to the "completely uncomprehending" nature of "many Republicans" in matters "relating to neighborhoods, minorities, or civil society."

Of Maurice Stans, the moneybag Commerce Secretary who oversaw Nixon's Office of Minority Business Enterprise, McClaughry writes: "Stans's familiarity with minority groups was apparently limited to ordering about the native porters on his many expeditions to decimate the animal population of Africa." This guy can write; imagine, had the voters of Vermont had the wit to elect McClaughry U.S. Senator in 1982, the trenchantly citric portraits he'd have sketched of Strom Thurmond, Joe Biden, Ted Kennedy, and other knaves he'd have known.

McClaughry has written under various names. He ghosted the best lines Ronald Reagan ever recited: his 1975 call for "an end to giantism, for a return to the human scale—the scale that human beings can understand and cope with." This was similar to the magnificent Karl Hess, Goldwater speechwriter cum Wobbly, scripting a 1968 talk by AuH2o in which the Arizona Cold Warrior told astonished students that he had "much in common with the anarchist wing of SDS."

Alas, a ghost leaves no footprints. McClaughry served a brief and unsatisfying stint on the Reagan White House policy staff, winning demerits from appalled careerists for such acts as leaving midweek to moderate the Kirby town meeting (which he has done since 1967).

McClaughry's most enduring work appeared under his own name: *The Vermont Papers* (1989), a blueprint for the radical decentralization of Green Mountain State government that he coauthored with University of Vermont political scientist Frank Bryan. The Vermont duo professed "values that are libertarian in the face of authority, decentralist in the face of giantism, and communal among our townspeople." *The Vermont Papers* is an idealistic and humane and neglected book, exuberantly contrary to the political spirit of its age.

Finishing John's sardonic and illuminating memoir, I was put in mind of Gloria Grahame's closing remark to Jimmy Stewart: John McClaughry, I'm glad I know you.

THE AMERICA THAT LOST

"Wasn't the whole country happier and in many ways wiser when it was smaller and cleaner and quieter and kinder?"
—BOOTH TARKINGTON

Who Needs a President?
The American Conservative, 2012

NO MATTER WHICH HOLLOW man occupies the bunker at 1600 Pennsylvania Avenue, the evidence from 225 years points to an inescapable conclusion: the Founders erred horribly in creating the presidency. To invest in one man quasi-kingly powers over the thirteen states then, 300 million people and half a continent today, is madness. And it didn't have to be this way.

Many Anti-Federalists proposed, as an alternative to what they called the "president-general," either a plural executive—two or more men sharing the office, a recipe for what a sage once called a wise and masterly inactivity—or they wanted no executive at all. Federal affairs would be so limited in scope that they could be performed competently and without aggrandizement by a unicameral legislature—that is, one house of Congress—as well as various administrative departments and perhaps a federal judiciary.

The New Jersey Plan, fathered by William Paterson of the Springsteen State, was the small-f federal option at the Constitutional Convention. It is the great decentralist what-might-have-been. The New Jersey Plan provided for a unicameral Congress with an equal vote for each state, and copresidents chosen by Congress for a single fixed term and removable by Congress if so directed by a majority of state governors.

This would have saved us from the cult of the presidency, the imperial presidency, the president as the world's celebrity-in-chief—the whole gargantuan mess.

One reason for the disastrous engorgement of presidential powers was that all parties at the Convention tacitly agreed that the first president would be George Washington, whom even the most suspicious Anti-Federalists admired. How much more protective of our liberties would the Framers have been, one wonders, if the putative first president was a man less universally respected than Washington: say, John Hancock?

Consider South Carolina delegate Pierce Butler's admission in a letter of May 1788 that the president's "Powers are full great, and greater than I was disposed to make them. Nor . . . do I believe they would have been so great had not many of the members cast their eyes towards General Washington as President; and shaped their Ideas of the Powers to be given to a President, by their opinions of his Virtue. So that the Man, who by his Patriotism and Virtue, Contributed largely to the Emancipation of his Country, may be the Innocent means of its being, when He is lay'd low, oppress'd."

The Framers, so often credited with farsightedness, saw no farther than the noble Washington. Only the Anti-Federalists, it seems, could envision Lyndon B. Johnson or George W. Bush. Well, I hate to break it to the demigods of the Philadelphia Convention, but George Washington had not discovered the elixir of eternal life. He was not going to live forever, let alone serve as president for the life of the republic. Lesser men would come along, and be granted those same powers, and the powers would expand, as the executive branch expanded, until you have men I'd not trust to serve as Exalted Rulers of the Batavia Elks Club being serenaded by "Hail to the Chief" and sending hundreds of thousands of American boys to the other side of the world to kill and die for . . . whatever it was and is that men killed and died for in Vietnam and Iraq.

The key vote of the Convention was not the famous Connecticut Compromise, approved on July 16, 1787, which provided for equality of representation in the Senate, but rather the vote of June 19 on Rufus King's motion that William Paterson's New Jersey Plan was "not admissible." By a vote of seven states to three, with Maryland divided, the Convention approved King's motion. James Madison's nationalizing Virginia Plan was to be the markup document.

A poet who wrote and lived just north of Boston, an Anti-Federalist of sorts, wrote about roads not taken.

What if delegates from the Anti-Federalist states of New Hampshire and Rhode Island had been present on June 19? What if the Anti-Federalist Mercer had been there to tip Maryland's vote? What if Connecticut had flipped? With a tweak here and epiphany there, and maybe a timely attack of gout thrown in for good measure, what if enough votes had shifted so that the New Jersey Plan had been the template of the new Constitution?

Would a monument (modest, naturally) to William Paterson greet the occasional visitor to the sleepy Federal City of . . . wait, there would be no Federal City. No Washington, D.C. Congress probably would meet in Philadelphia, where the presidents of the United States, whose names the citizens never can quite recall, also keep their spartan offices.

Maybe we shoulda taken that road. . . .

William Leggett: Manhattan's Agrarian
First Principles, 2009

WILLIAM LEGGETT—CONSUMPTIVE DUELIST, FEARLESSLY radical hero to New York City's working classes of the 1830s, theater critic turned *New York Evening Post* editor whose coruscant polemics made him the galvanizing editorialist of his age—ranks near the top of those unbiographied Americans most deserving of someone—preferably a non-nitwit—to write their life stories.

Even as a supporting actor in historical narratives, Leggett is always sharp and compelling, never a supernumerary.

He is the fiery and eloquent editor in Gore Vidal's novel *Burr* (1973), a writer with a "furious style," the thirty-two-year-old star of New York's literary empyrean, for "as a journalist he has taken all politics and literature for his field, and he is famous."

In Arthur Schlesinger Jr.'s *The Age of Jackson* (1945), Leggett is hymned for his "lucid, supple, and picturesque" style, his "irony and bloodcurdling invective. . . . His work had a penetration, a courage and, at the same time, a good humor and gusto, which make it memorable in American political journalism." (Apologies to the late William Appleman Williams for quoting AS Jr. respectfully.)

Historians have sung the praises of Leggett's purity of purpose, ardency of heart, and "romantic heroism." To Richard Hofstadter, who probably would have judged a Leggett of later times to be suffering from paranoia, the journalist "preached the bourgeois ideals of personal and property rights, freedom of contract, laissez faire, individualism, and private enterprise with as fine a sense for the needs and desires of the common man" as any figure in our past; to William Trimble, he was "one of the most sincere and brilliant apostles of democracy that America has ever known"; in *The Jacksonian Persuasion* (1957), Marvin Meyers devotes a chapter to Leggett, of whom he marvels, "There have been plenty of radical libertarians in the American past, but none, I think, surpasses William Leggett. . . . "

Who cannot love a man whose entry in the *Dictionary of American Biography* reads: "His chief characteristics as a writer were energy and absolute independence; his chief defect was violence."

William Leggett was a blazing comet who lit the New York sky in that most poetically fertile and politically fervent decade, the 1830s. This was the apex of literary New York, socially if not artistically, as the city's poets spoke as loudly and persuasively as would the city's businessmen of later generations. And none spoke so passionately as William Leggett.

The son of a Revolutionary War officer, William Leggett was born in Manhattan in 1801. He removed to southern Illinois in his ephebic years, at the conclusion of which he brought out his *Poems* (1822), the first piece of literature published in the Prairie State.

At twenty-one, Leggett went to sea, where he quickly became the most contumacious and quarrelsome midshipman in the U.S. Navy. He brawled; he dueled; he wrote naval poetry. He was court-martialed for a series of offenses that included hurling Shakespearean curses "of highly inflammatory, rancorous, and threatening import" at his martinet captain. William Cullen Bryant, who would hire, fire, and finally eulogize his hotspur friend, declared the court-martial a stiffening experience for Leggett: "There are some minds which despotism crushes and breaks; stronger natures find in it a discipline from which they gain new hardihood and energy."

Discharged, penniless, fair bursting with hardihood, brash as handsome young poets unvexed by doubt are wont to be, Leggett strode into the circle of the Knickerbocker literati as if Washington Irving were saving a seat for him. He published collections of stories and verse set on the frontier and the high seas; he bolted from newspaper to newspaper; he acted, and after failing on stage he founded *The Critic*, wherein he became one of the nation's first significant writers on theater. Leggett's naval stories, which burn with his contempt for authority, have been called the "American link between [Smollett] and Herman Melville"; his frontier fiction marks him as a pioneer realist. The notorious Rufus Griswold, arch-enemy of Poe (if not poesy) and the compulsive anthologist of antebellum American verse, deemed Leggett's naval and Illinois stories "probably the most spirited and ingenious productions of their kind ever written in this country."

Then the political bug bit. William Leggett, bellicose litterateur, discovered the cause of the Common Man. With verve, fanaticism, and style, he would spend the rest of his short life launching wit, calumny, and anything else that might stick against monopolists, English actors, and promoters of internal improvements.

In 1829, William Cullen Bryant, that erstwhile boy poet of the Berkshires, took Leggett on as an editor and partner of the *New York Evening*

Post, from which perch his incendiary editorials helped define the politics of his era.

Newspaper editorialists of the 1830s were not style-less hacks drooling hackneyed phrases onto their pages. They were often literary men, equally at home with the caucus or the canto. The wall separating distinguished prose from politics had yet to be erected. In the old America, writers and poets received diplomatic appointments (Washington Irving to Spain, John Howard "Home Sweet Home" Payne to Tunis, Nathaniel Hawthorne goin' down to Liverpool) that gave sinecure a good name.

Leggett was more than an agitated polemicist. He was, or so it has seemed to his readers then and even more so through the years, the last American revolutionary standing fast by the principles of 1776.

It was William Leggett's fate to hold high the banner of liberty in an age when finance capitalism was advancing upon the agrarian republic. He liked not what he saw.

"Walk through Wall Street," commanded Leggett, and you will "see a street of palaces." But if the tourist "investigates the source of their prodigious wealth, he will discover that it is extorted, under various delusive names, and by a deceptive process, from the pockets of the unprivileged and unprotected poor. These are the masters in this land of freedom. These are our aristocracy, our scrip nobility, our privileged order of charter-mongers and money-changers. Serfs of free America! Bow your necks submissively to the yoke, for these exchequer barons have you fully in their power."

The lords of Wall Street, he fumed, were "low-minded, ignorant and rapacious." They were "aristocrats, clothed with special immunities, who control, indirectly, but certainly, the political power of the state, monopolise the most copious sources of pecuniary profit, and wring the very crust from the hard hand of toil."

Early communists mistook Leggett for an ally, but in fact his economic view was that if we but "leave trade to its own laws, as we leave water to the laws of nature, both will be equally certain to find their proper level."

The problem, however, was that Wall Street was not on the level. It was the product of "special privileges" to the "opulent," especially charters of incorporation that gave favored corporations legal advantages—such as limited liability and perpetual life—not available to mere persons. Leggett was sure that one dose of radical liberty would fell Wall Street.

"Ostentatious luxury" and "this insane desire of acquisition and display," fed by chartered corporations and banks, were destroying the land even before the last of the Revolutionary veterans had died off. So in the midst of the most bustling and burgeoning city in America, a place "characterized by an unparalleled fierceness in money-chasing," as Leggett's fellow newsman and warm admirer Walt Whitman remarked, mercurial William Leggett was formulating the last-ditch theoretical defense of the republic of liberty.

Historians have been drawn to Leggett not least by the paradox he presents: how could a man who started from a laissez-faire philosophical base—whose strictures upon government regulation of the economy make Milton Friedman sound like a Swedish socialist—come to conclusions so harshly critical of capitalism? Leggett forces upon us an unsettling question: Was the flaming promise of the American Revolution really doused so quickly?

****

Leggett's libertarian sympathies made him an early advocate of (voluntary) labor unions, the abolition of capital punishment, and the enshrinement of restitution as a bedrock principle of criminal justice. Most strikingly, they brought about his conversion from an early indifference to, even grudging acceptance of, American slavery, to a position close to the prophetically bloody ground occupied by Nat Turner and John Brown.

For at a time when virtually all New York City Democrats sought conciliation with slave-owners, William Leggett was an abolitionist. This was no cheap moral posturing, no withdrawal from that bottomless reservoir of sanctimony Edmund Wilson charged the North with possessing; no, Leggett's stand came at the cost of an expected congressional nomination. Yet Leggett was also an anti-imperialist who denied that the federal government had any right to abolish slavery in the Southern states. Rather, he enthusiastically urged slaves to breathe deeply the spirit of '76 and rise in revolt, overthrowing their masters. If the enslaved Africans wanted freedom, they would have to seize it themselves.

Radical Democrats of libertarian bent, most of them young New Yorkers, were known as "Loco Focos," which would be spat as an epithet at equalitarians until the Civil War. Organized as a Democratic faction called the Equal Rights Party, the Loco Focos earned their name on an October night in 1835, when the Equal Rights men sought to take control of New York City's Democratic Party from Tammany Hall. Sensing defeat, the Tammany minions dimmed the gas lights, plunging the meeting into darkness. Responding to the shout "Let there be light!" the quick-thinking radicals struck Loco Foco matches, and the name stuck. The faction, like the matches, burned brightly, if briefly. (One of the Democratic oligarchs targeted by the Loco Focos bore the splendid name of Preserved Fish.)

William Leggett has been called "the prophet of the Loco Foco movement." In their pertinacious defense of the small producer, the neighborhood shop, and the self-employed artisan, Leggett and the Loco Focos represent the purest Jeffersonian response to the assaults of capitalism and its handmaiden state. They were "urban agrarians," in Carl Degler's aptly oxymoronic phrase. Their championship of the small against the big, the local against the national, the near-at-hand over the abstract, makes them an ancestor, albeit an unacknowledged and unknown ancestor, of those libertarians and greens of localist cast.

To the *New York Times*, chief organ of the Democratic establishment, the Leggett-inspired Loco Focos were "infidels," "scum," and "the Guy Fawkes' of politics." Leggett, no adept at cheek-turning, gave as good as he got. While remaining a Democrat, he became his party's most vituperative critic, damning other Democrats as "a set of creeping, dissembling creatures who have grown fat on the drippings of unclean bank legislation."

When Bryant left the *Evening Post* for Europe in June 1834, placing Leggett in charge, the Loco Foco unleashed a torrent of abuse that is still unmatched in New York journalism. Editors at rival newspapers he denounced, one by one, as "a detestable caitiff," "a craven wretch, spotted with all kinds of vices," and "a hireling slave." (You know, I think they're still working there....) Leggett's invective-laced editorials cost the *Evening Post* most of its friends among New York's ruling class and almost all its patronage and advertising. Mocked as "deranged" and ready for Bedlam, Leggett left the *Evening Post* and founded the New York *Plaindealer*, wherein he attacked banks, tariffs, Washington Irving (for his "unmanly timidity" in bowdlerizing a Leggett poem), and all who would discourage the flowering of a free, refractory, native American culture.

The *Plaindealer* folded. Leggett fell ill, despondent, suicidal. He survived for some months on the eleemosynary of his dear chum Edwin Forrest, America's premier actor and Leggett's beau ideal of the stage, a cultural patriot who was always somersaulting and playing lusty Indians and aiming to liberate American theater from prissy English conventions. (Forrest's partisans within the gangs of New York would later destroy the Astor Place Opera House in an anti-English riot that left twenty-two amateur theater critics dead.)

Hoping that a change of climate might revive Leggett's failing constitution, his friends lobbied President Van Buren to appoint the firebrand as diplomatic agent to Guatemala. Though Leggett had recently characterized the president as "cringing," "indecent," and other adjectives that job-seekers are usually advised not to apply to potential employers, the Red Fox of Kinderhook turned the other cheek and Leggett got his appointment. The shock of receiving a government post may have proved too much for the libertarian. Leggett died before going on Uncle Sam's payroll. Fittingly, "bilious colic" was the cause of death. He was thirty-eight.

Upon his death he was eulogized in verse by Bryant and Whittier, among others. Walt Whitman never ceased to praise "the glorious Leggett," the primary shaper of Whitman's laissez-faire political philosophy, avowing him the equal of "the great Jefferson."

William Cullen Bryant commemorated his deceased colleague:

> The words of fire that from his pen
> Were flung upon the fervid page,
> Still move, still shake the hearts of men,
> Amid a cold and coward age.

In our colder, even more cowardly age, as Americans forfeit traditional liberties as casually as a horseplayer discards a losing pari-mutuel ticket, may Leggett's "words of fire" light our deepening American night.

Who Can We Shoot?
Chronicles, 1996

WHO BETTER TO KICK off a discussion of American populism than Henry James? In *The Portrait of a Lady*, Sockless Hank had Henrietta Stackpole define a "cosmopolite": "That means he's a little of everything and not much of any. I must say I think patriotism is like charity—it begins at home." Likewise, a healthy populism must be grounded in a love of the particular, or else it is just a grab bag of (mostly valid) resentments.

James understood the consequences of the Spanish-American War to be "remote colonies run by bosses"; expansion diluted true patriotism and would "demoralize us." His diagnosis is still sound, though the American people are now cast in the role of the Filipinos. The alliances and friendships concreting as the American Empire staggers through caducity and hastens, one hopes, to a long-overdue demise are every bit as refreshingly meet as those spawned in the depths of Manila Bay: a backwoods hippie wearing a "Buchanan '96" button is descended from the sturdily Republican poet-editor Thomas Bailey Aldrich, who announced in 1899 that he would not "vote for McKinley again. I would sooner vote for Bryan. To be ruined financially is not so bad as to be ruined morally."

The dire predictions of the anti-imperialists came to pass: gentlemen such as James and Aldrich were no match for Teddy Roosevelt. A century later New Gingrich, TR's biggest fan, haunts our demoralized land. Gingrich may never have bagged an elk, but he is much like his heroes, the cousins Roosevelt and Harry Truman: a picked-on kid raised on war games who probably can't throw a baseball as far as Olive Chancellor could.

When asked about his provenance by a fellow graduate student, Gingrich replied, "I'm from nowhere." So were most of the blustery swindlers who disgraced the populist label while rising to prominence in the 1970s and '80s. They are the gasconading "populists" of the right who operate out of Northern Virginia post office boxes: Big Bad Foes of the New World Order who dwell in sprawling apartment complexes and could not name a neighbor if their lives depended on it. Anticommunist and pro-nothing, they cozened money out of credulous TV addicts for Ollie North and before him Jonas Savimbi—one of them dreamt of nominating his ebon god for President in 1988, if only that xenophobic native birth clause in the Constitution had not disqualified the Angolan. Today they trumpet "family values" from the mountain tops of junk mail, while down below in Chevy Chase their neglected children enter Riot Grrrl suicide pacts.

The populist "left" of the Dark Age was no better: it consisted of a few earnest student council presidents trudging door to door in strange neighborhoods gathering petition signatures to save the whales or the ozone layer, anything so long as it had nothing to do with the workaday lives of the lunkheaded proles who answered the doorbell.

But as Newt himself might crow, it's the beginning of a new age, and vascular American populism is resurgent. You can tell because *Newsweek* and that hoary and reliable enemy of the Old Republic, the *New Republic*, portentously invoke Richard Hofstadter's hilarious *The Paranoid Style in American Politics*—which ascribed all dissent from the Cold War Vital Center consensus to mental illness—and Alan Brinkley (Hofstadter born to a TV star) is trotted out to explain, like the girl in the Lou Reed song, why "down to you is up," and why anything smacking of popular rage is not really populism.

They want populism to be Rush Limbaugh and Common Cause, and I am very sorry to indulge in hate speech, but we are talking Daniel Shays and Tom Watson and Huey Long and their swelling band of offspring who are gathering under the Tree of Liberty. (If you can't beat 'em, co-opt 'em. How the corporate media clamored for an independent ticket of Colin Powell and Bill Bradley: at last, a third party Wall Street and the Pentagon can love!)

The post-Cold War populists—who are largely isolationist, decentralist, libertarian, ticked-off but sweetly naïve in a Frank Capra way—know that the enemy is not a Nicaraguan Marxist or a Compton rapper but a regime represented by the likes of William Bennett and Robert Rubin. We will not find succor in the Democracy—the party that effaced all regional distinctions in constructing our national security state—and as for the Republicans, can anyone name a single instance when Wall Street and Main Street lined up on opposite sides of an important issue and the GOP sided with Main Street? Don't two words—Wendell Willkie—say all that need ever be said about who owns the party of Reconstruction, TR, and the Gulf War?

Our forefather, William Jennings Bryan, had the varmints in his sight in a speech at Springfield, Ohio, in the summer of 1896: "My friends, remember that relief cannot come to you from those who have fastened this yoke upon you. You may go to New York or Boston and find financiers . . . that know more about Europe than they do about the United States. They go oftener to London than to the great prairies of the West and South. If because of their more intimate acquaintance with foreigners they have exaggerated ideas of the necessity for foreign aid, you people who live between the Alleghenies and the Golden Gate—you who are willing to trust your all upon the Republic and rise or fall with it—you have the power and the right to take the reins of government into your own hands and administer the law, not for foreign syndicates, but for the people of the United States."

The Wise Men who buried the republic were the children of those financiers. The fathers—robber barons and Wall Street sharks—shipped the sons from the hearthstone to exclusive boarding schools, where they spent their youths playing that epitome of boring internationalism, soccer, and learning a code of conduct which evidently countenanced the mass slaughter of one's countrymen in illegal wars, as long as the statesmen responsible knew which is the salad fork. The very best products of the prep schools became the patrician radicals who are among the greatest American independents (and the palladia of American independence), but for every Edmund Wilson at the Hill School there were fourscore Harrimans at Groton, boys stripped of attachments to particular American places or ancestors or anything beyond the plunderbund.

They came to form a deracinated ruling class which entangled us in the most quotidian affairs of Europe because London and Paris were, to them, closer than Abilene or Green Bay. There's nothing very jolly about what Skull and Bones did to my country, Roger.

Yet to oppose them—to say that Henry Stimson and Dean Acheson and their epigoni, George Bush and Strobe Talbott, are traitors who subverted an America of which they know nothing—is so far outside the pale of acceptable speech that merely to make the observation is to invite the eavesdropping of the ironically named Louis Freeh. (Who'd have guessed that the first client of the Empowerment Agenda would be the FBI?)

Again, I summon the shade of Bryan, "that Heaven-born Bryan/That Homer Bryan, who sang from the West," as Vachel Lindsay cried. In a campaign speech at Milwaukee, he said:

> I want to call your attention to what some one has said about the influence of foreign nations and foreign personages on the affairs of our nation: "Against the insidious wiles of foreign influence (I conjure you to believe me, fellow citizens), the jealousy of a free people ought to be constantly awake, since history and experience prove that foreign influence is one of the most baneful foes of Republican government." There is the language which I desire to press upon your memories. It is not my language. Whose language do you suppose it is? What man,

"trying to stir up the passions of our people against foreigners"; what demagogue "appealing to the mob to justify his course"; what anarchist do you suppose used those words? Those are the words of George Washington. . . . If it was true then, it is true now. My friends, I warn you against entrusting the destinies of this nation to legislative bodies which are beyond your control.

Note that Bryan did not say "beyond your ken" or "beyond your power of recognition" but "beyond your control." As Alexander Cockburn recently pointed out in the *Nation*, populists are fools to huff and puff at chimerical shadows (Jewish bankers! The Illuminati!) when the villains are hiding in plain sight.

Their creed was uttered a century and a half ago by Daniel Webster, who said, "There are no Alleghenies in my politics." This was a fib—the only time Webster lived down to this motto was in his disgraceful promotion of the Compromise of 1850, when he abjured New England interests and forced a hated Fugitive Slave Act on his people. But the ignoble sentiment underlying Webster's aphorism is shared by every knave and commissar of the New World Order (no matter if wifey collects folk art).

We are too versicolored a country to be embraced by a single American populism: our politics must be filled with Alleghenies. While patriots today share common foes—the whole *New York Times*-Heritage Foundation Vile Center—I should like to see, instead of an America First Party, a cluster of seventy-five or 180 smaller entities: a West Kansas First Party, a Rhode Island First Party, a Southern Oregon First Party, and so on, representing every nook and cranny of all forty-eight states. I say forty-eight because the revolution's got to start somewhere, so at our house we fly a forty-eight-star flag, honoring the contiguous United States, not those fruits of empire (Alaska and Hawaii) given statehood in that burst of insanity known as the Cold War.

The most thoughtful opponents of stitching the forty-ninth and fiftieth stars on the flag were Senator John Stennis, the courtly Mississippian, and Senator J. William Fulbright, the Confederate anti-imperialist. In the Alaska statehood debate, Stennis asked if, after admitting this frozen expanse to the Union, we would then have to "admit Hawaii? And then are we going to admit the Virgin Islands? Are we going to admit Puerto Rico? Are we going to admit Guam? Okinawa?" (In time, Senator, in time.) Stennis wondered "whether we shall take a disconnected area, whether it be in the Pacific, in South America, in Africa, or anywhere else . . . in the bosom of our nation? We are changing the pattern of our Union once we launch out on this program." And so Old Glory was defaced by the cosmopolites.

But lo and behold, a lively native nationalist movement has arisen in Hawaii (members identified by "Kingdom of Hawaii" license plates), and the crustier Alaskans have long favored secession, so to the dispossessed sons of Queen Liliuokalani and in atonement for my rapacious landsman William Seward I recommend the policy laid out by the New Zealand band Midnight Oil in its song about Maori land claims:

> The time has come
> A fact's a fact
> It belongs to them
> Let's give it back

And in what has become a hackneyed phrase—but one that can never really lose its tang—let's take back our own country.

There is a famous scene in John Steinbeck's *The Grapes of Wrath* in which a tenant farmer confronts the man evicting him from his shack:

> "It's mine. I built it. You bump it down—I'll be in the window with a rifle. You even come too close and I'll pot you like a rabbit."
>
> "It's not me. There's nothing I can do. I'll lose my job if I don't do it. And look—suppose you kill me? They'll just hang you, but long before you're hung there'll be another guy on the tractor, and he'll bump the house down. You're not killing the right guy."
>
> "That's so," the tenant said. "Who gave you orders? I'll go after him. He's the one to kill."
>
> "You're wrong. He got his orders from the bank. The bank told him, 'Clear those people out or it's your job.'"
>
> "Well, there's a president of the bank. There's a board of directors. I'll fill up the magazine of the rifle and go into the bank."
>
> The driver said, "Fellow was telling me the bank gets orders from the East. The orders were, 'Make the land show profit or we'll close you up.'"
>
> "But where does it stop? Who can we shoot? I don't aim to starve to death before I kill the man that's starving me."

We are not starvelings, and we know whom to shoot. (Figuratively speaking, of course—we should obey the example of Saint Dorothy Day and leave murder as an instrument of policy to the United States government.)

The new American populism has 1,000 offshoots, but a Southern League partisan in Alabama and an anti-nuclear dump activist in Allegany County, New York, are comrades in the nascent movement that is opposed, as Jerry Brown said in *Chronicles* (November 1994), to "a global focus over which we have virtually no control.... We have to force larger institutions to operate in the interest of local autonomy and local power.... Localism, if you really take it seriously, is going to interrupt certain patterns of modern growth and globalism."

Plenty of us do take localism seriously, not in its denatured form (block grants! expedited HHS waivers!) but in the way our fathers understood it, which is to say the octopus must be slain, starting with its most dangerous tentacles (abolish the FBI and CIA, slash the war budget, strip absentee owners of TV and radio licenses, and then in the second hour . . .). This train may not be bound for glory, but at least we're not going to Pyongyang or Port-au-Prince or Kuwait City.

What began with Henry James shall end with Pete Townshend. Hey you patriots of all bloodlines, you Tacoma sons of Wobblies and Nebraska sons of Grangers and Tuskegee sons of Washington and Chicago daughters of America Firsters: let's get together before we get much older.

Decline of the Planet of the Japes
The American Conservative, 2012

WHO IN HIS RIGHT (or left) mind wouldn't rather read H.L. Mencken than Joe Alsop, or Christopher Hitchens than Ellen Goodman, or Florence King than Cal Thomas? Wit, even vituperative wit, refreshes and restores, while sodden clots of clichés only drag you down, down, down.

Whene'er Mugwumps (and I am one, except when I am not) decry the incivility of political discourse, some pedant can be counted on to drag out those "mackerel by moonlight" insults that filled the partisan press back in the day when Americans lived in a republic.

Amidst the unzoned sprawl of my files is a folder containing favorite examples of political invective I've collected over the years. I'll instance three:

—Massachusetts Federalist Josiah Quincy described Henry Clay and his fellow warhawks of 1812 as "sycophantic, fawning reptiles, who crowded at the feet of the president, and left their filthy slime upon the carpet of the palace." Quincy later served as president of Harvard, where he no doubt made a fuller study of sycophantic, fawning reptiles.

—The *St. Louis Globe Democrat*, looking askance at the Democratic Party's 1880 standard bearer, the eminently respectable war hero Winfield Scott Hancock, editorialized that the nomination "no more changes the character of Democracy than a figurehead of the Virgin on Kidd's pirate craft would change it into an honest ship." I like the backhanded Catholic reference, lest readers forget that the Democracy is the party of rum, Romanism, and rebellion.

—When the unloved Theodore G. Joslin became President Hoover's press secretary late in Hoover's term, a wag described it as the "first known instance of a rat joining a sinking ship." Maybe Michael Chertoff climbing aboard George W. Bush's Cabinet was the second?

These go on and on, some barbs directed at scoundrels and others at sages, but the vitriol is animated and made memorable by wit. One takes pleasure in reading a good sentence, even if one's paladin is speared by it.

"Irreverence," as Mark Twain remarked, "is the champion of liberty and its only sure defense."

In this winter of American discontent the political invective is flowing, all right, but in the manner of a busted latrine. It spews. The target is Ron Paul, who has committed the thought crime of "isolationism"—that is, he wishes neither to kill nor be killed by foreigners. Most Americans are instinctively isolationist, which is why Paul is denounced so hysterically by the hall monitors of acceptable opinion: the belligerent bootlickers of Beltway Conservatism, or the neutered progressives who flee from an unconventional thought like Victorian spinsters from a penis.

Significantly, Paul's critics never cite the two leading scholars of American isolationism, Wayne S. Cole and Justus Doenecke. But then the Fox shouters are ignorant of pre-Reagan America, and harrumphing NY-DC editorialists suspect that nothing good ever came from places like Idaho or Iowa anyway.

So Rep. Paul is gouged, not with slashing style *a la* Mencken but with blades of prison-grey dullness. The attacks on Paul are as crude and witless as the infamous lines in the candidate's old newsletters. (I readily concede that he should not be elected national editor-in-chief.) The collective sputum has a party-line, un-American quality to it. It's about as funny as a copy of *The Daily Worker*. In fact, it is redolent of the way the journalistic defenders of FDR, Truman, and Joe McCarthy went after antiwar and anti-Cold War critics of the 1940s and '50s. (Read the New York City tabloid *PM* or early *National Review* for the depressing evidence. Be prepared to not laugh.)

Those traduced critics were often censored for good measure. William Saroyan was called "sinful" in the *New York Times* and threatened with a court-martial by the Office of War Information for writing the antiwar novel *The Adventures of Wesley Jackson*, which ends with the commie sentiment, "Human beings must not murder one another. They must wait for God to take them in His own good time." Poet Robinson Jeffers was denounced by his own publisher for his volume *The Double Axe*, which *Time* called a "necrophilic nightmare." Lippincott ordered novelist-folklorist Zora Neale Hurston to remove her "international opinions"—which favored peace over war, and deplored Western imperialism and colonialism—from her autobiography *Dust Tracks on a Road*.

Saroyan, Jeffers, Hurston: that crazy old America of dreamy Armenians and anarchist anchorites and black farmers—that's my country. We don't really need a president, to tell the truth, but if we've got to have one make mine Ron Paul.

Heil to the Chief:
Philip Roth versus My America

The American Conservative, 2004

PHILIP ROTH'S *THE PLOT Against America* is the novel that a neoconservative would write, if a neoconservative could write a novel.

In 1940, as in 2004, voters faced a choiceless presidential election between pro-war interventionists, with a noble antiwar socialist (Norman Thomas then, Ralph Nader now) the best man in the field.

In Roth's what-if world, we the people have an actual choice in 1940. Instead of a third term for President Franklin D. Roosevelt, America Firster Charles Lindbergh is elected president, whereupon all hell breaks loose—which is to say America is at peace, a condition never again to be permitted, apparently, in the United States of Armaments. The horrific consequences of electing an antiwar Midwesterner are seen through the eyes of young Philip Roth, son of an insurance agent, and his Jewish family in Newark, New Jersey.

In our world, Wall Street operatives steered the 1940 GOP nomination to the hawkish utilities executive Wendell Willkie, as Gore Vidal describes with wit, artistry, and panache in *The Golden Age* (2000). That novel also pivots on the 1940 election, although Vidal regards Lindbergh as "the true white knight through and through," and "the best that we are ever apt to produce in the hero line, American style."

Vidal is a proprietary patriot, utterly comfortable with our history because it is his history. Roth is ill at ease in the American past; his research seems to have consisted of a quick flip through the courtier histories of James MacGregor Burns and Arthur Schlesinger. He bristles with contempt for the benighted denizens of "the working-class heartland of isolationist America"—that is, mothers and fathers who would rather not send their boys to die in foreign wars. Their parochial and pacific instincts point the way to a Middle American fascism.

Roth writes in sodden clichés: for instance, FDR "inspired millions of ordinary families like ours to remain hopeful in the midst of hardship."

This is *Time-Life* prose. There is not a felicitous sentence in this book; nor is there a spark of wit or a single subversive thought. The literary critics of the Department of Homeland Security will pronounce it fit for best-sellerdom.

Charles A. Lindbergh was a classic product of Upper Midwest populism. His congressman father, a fierce foe of U.S. involvement in World War I, was dubbed the "Gopher Bolshevik" by the *New York Times*. Lindbergh is easily understood in a Minnesota tradition that stretches from the Gopher Bolshevik and Sen. Henrik Shipstead through Bob Dylan and Eugene McCarthy. He was no more a Nazi than FDR was.

But not since the Spanish-American War have honorable Americans been permitted to criticize a war without being slandered as traitorous lackeys for the enemy. Just as Eugene V. Debs was calumnied as a Kaiser-lover and Martin Luther King Jr. as a communist, so must Charles Lindbergh be a crypto-Nazi. Given the current climate, Roth's book is especially odious. Or perhaps *The Plot Against America* is meant to serve as the writing sample in Roth's application for a speechwriter job in the Bush administration.

The Plot Against America is the sort of novel a bootlicking author might write to curry favor with a totalitarian government. The author puts a fictive gloss over the officially sanctioned history. Thank God things happened as they did! The alternative to the regime was madness, chaos, murder. Dissenters must be demonized, so Roth saddles his America First villains with positions exactly opposite those they actually took.

The America First Committee was the largest (800,000 members) antiwar organization in U.S. history. Its members ranged from patricians to populists, from Main Street Republicans to prairie socialists. John F. Kennedy was a donor; his future brother-in-law Sargent Shriver was a founder, as were Gerald Ford, Potter Stewart, and Kingman Brewster. Many of the finest writers in America sympathized with (or joined) America First—Sinclair Lewis, Edmund Wilson, Robinson Jeffers, e.e. cummings, and William Saroyan—while the leading pro-war authors were such toadies as Archibald MacLeish (or macarchibald maclapdog macleish, as cummings called him). Aviator Lindbergh was the AFC's most popular speaker, though he never formally joined the committee.

The antiwar movement of 1940–41 was essentially libertarian: in favor of peace and civil liberties, opposed to conscription. Rather than accept this complexity, Roth opts for inversion: his isolationists are the party of repression and conscription, while his warhawks are the party of liberty. War is Peace. Freedom is Slavery.

And so Montana Senator Burton K. Wheeler, running mate of "Fighting Bob" La Follette on the 1924 Progressive Party ticket and an early supporter of the New Deal who went into opposition over FDR's attempt to pack the Supreme Court, emerges as Lindbergh's wicked vice president, a despoiler of the Constitution and declarer of martial law. Never mind that the real Burton K. Wheeler was an anti-draft, antiwar, anti-big business defender of civil liberties: in Roth's world, this great American—a "brilliant, incorruptible, courageous man," in La Follette's glowing tribute—must be depicted as pro-fascist. (The closest thing to a real live fascist in American politics in 1940 was FDR brain-truster Rexford G. Tugwell.) Vice President Wheeler is portrayed as a "combative" snarler whose job is to "attack and revile" foes—a role actually played by Rothian hero Harold Ickes, the FDR hatchetman so memorably described by Clare Boothe Luce as having "the soul of a meat axe and the mind of a commissar."

Roth's Lindbergh is laconic to the point of simplemindedness. The real Lindy was a fine writer who composed his own speeches, but Roth suggests that these were written in Germany. The Lindbergh of *The Plot Against America* declares, "My intention in running for the presidency is to preserve American democracy by preventing America from taking part in another world war. Your choice is simple. It's not between Charles A. Lindbergh and Franklin Delano Roosevelt. It's between Lindbergh and war." This is an eminently fair summation. But of course the American people were presented no such choice in 1940, nor really in any other quadrennium since World War II except, perhaps, 1972.

The Lindbergh nomination is engineered by North Dakota Sen. Gerald P. Nye, whom Roth dismisses with the lazy adjective "right-wing." Oh really? In fact, Nye criticized the New Deal from the Left for its timorousness. Nye had made his name as the scourge of the "merchants of death" who profited from the disastrous U.S. entry into the First World War, and he always feared a replay.

Campaigning in "the remotest rural counties," Lindbergh wins in a landslide, the Republicans take Congress, and the threat of peace, no conscription, and full enjoyment of the Bill of Rights darkens the Rothian sky. To young Philip's parents, America is good only insofar as it sends its sons to die in foreign lands. The family's favorite presidents are Wilson and FDR, who shipped more Americans to die overseas than any other chief execs. Unwashed Americans, who live in places like North Dakota or Minnesota or Montana, mean harm to the Roths; their reluctance to send their sons to transatlantic graves is presented as a particularly insidious symptom of anti-Semitism.

In Roth's flip-flopped universe, President Lindbergh institutes a peacetime draft—which in fact FDR did, over the ardent objections of the isolationists, who argued against conscription on libertarian grounds.

President Lindbergh cozies up to the Nazis while pursuing a domestic policy that might be stamped "Made in Germany." He is wildly popular, even with "the highly assimilated upper echelon of German Jewish society," whose cultured members are depicted herein as craven social climbers.

Among the turncoat Jews is Rabbi Lionel Bengelsdorf of Newark, a South Carolina native with a "courtly Southern accent"—always the tip-off to knavery when a mediocrity is at the typewriter. The Rabbi opposes women's suffrage, not exactly a hot topic in 1940, but then Roth is limning character, don't you see? The scene in which Rabbi Bengelsdorf vivisects FDR's Scottie Fala must have been excised by a wise editor.

Lindbergh and Rabbi Bengelsdorf create an Office of American Absorption, whose centerpiece is the "Just Folks" program, under which Jewish youth are shipped out to the "Gentile heartland" to become real Amerrykuns. Philip's brother spends the summer with a "Kentucky tobacco farmer." He returns with an accent, respect for farm life, a taste for ham and bacon, and a dose of the fascist clap that Philip Roth imagines lurks everywhere in that darksome forest of fear west of the Hudson. To Roth, a small farm in Kentucky is the perfect training ground for a fascist. Tell it to Wendell Berry, Philip.

"Just Folks" is yet another Roth reversal: FDR's Civilian Conservation Corps was the actual (if benign) means of rusticating urban boys in the 1930s. In the 1940s, it was urban politicians who tore rural boys from their native ground and sent them to war. The dislocating effects of militarism meant that 15 million Americans lived in a different county in March 1945 than they had in December 1941—and that doesn't count the 12 million-plus in uniform. A disproportionate number of the displaced, by the way, were from Kentucky. As an anti-hillbilly joke of the time went, America lost three states in the early 1940s: Kentucky and Tennessee had gone to Indiana, and Indiana had gone to hell. But to Roth, the Gentile heartland is hell.

If *The Plot Against America* sounds like Roth's savage satire on Jewish paranoia, it is not. For the rural folk eventually run riot as a kind of cornfed, baccy-smokin' Khmer Rouge.

Under the Office of American Absorption, Metropolitan Life offers Philip's father a transfer to Danville, Kentucky. He refuses, probably because novelist Roth has no idea how to describe life in a Klan-Nazi hotbed like Kentucky, but it is in resisting relocation that the Roth family attains a certain nobility. "A child of my background had a sixth sense in those days, the geographic sense, the sharp sense of where he lived and who and what surrounded him," writes Roth. The faces, the voices, the ejaculations (because, after all, this is Philip Roth): these people are Newark, and we are made to understand the enormity of their unmooring. Dislocation exacts a terrible human cost. A pity that Roth does not mind uprooting the hicks he so obviously hates—for war is the most pitiless uprooter of all.

In the real 1940–41, antiwar entertainers were blacklisted for daring to speak their minds. (The case of Lillian Gish was notably disgusting.) In Roth's world, the pro-war radio gossip Walter Winchell is fired by Jergens Lotion when he denounces President Lindbergh. Winchell then declares his candidacy for president and barnstorms the black heart of America. He is baited and mocked in South Boston, Little Italy, and wherever papist brutes foregather. (In fact, it was America First speakers who were harassed in 1941, heckled by warhawks and denied permits in jingo towns.)

It is here that Roth's loathing of Catholicism, with its "witchy" nuns and "creepily morticianlike priests," reaches a fever-swamp pitch. Winchell's taunting of the antiwar wafer-eaters brings "the Lindbergh grotesquery to the surface." He is assaulted in South Boston and greeted with chants of "Kike Go Home!" in Upstate New York, Pennsylvania, the Midwest—all sewers "notorious for their bigotry."

Working-class Catholics erupt in anti-Semitic riots in Detroit: "shops were looted and windows broken, Jews trapped outdoors were set upon and beaten, and kerosene-soaked crosses were ignited" on the lawns of Jewish homeowners. Jewish schools are bombed and synagogues trashed in America's first-ever pogrom. Anti- Jewish riots also break out in Cleveland, Cincinnati, Indianapolis, St. Louis, Buffalo, Pittsburgh, Scranton, Akron, Syracuse—all across the hate-filled heartland, for the "menace of anti-Semitism" stretches "from one end of America to the other." Our heroes make a mad dash across "rural West Virginia," where "Ku Klux Klansmen had to be lying in wait for any Jew foolhardy enough to be driving through." Almost Heaven? Not in this book.

Walter Winchell is killed in Kentucky by "an American Nazi Party assassin working in collaboration with the Ku Klux Klan." Roth takes an especial scunner to poor Kentucky, his locus of American evil. A Jewish lady from Newark, exiled to Danville, is set upon by a mob of Klansmen, which is to say ordinary Kentuckians; she is beaten and burned to death in the state that provides "a nightmarish vision of America's anti-Semitic fury." To add insult to fatal injury, her son, "the smartest kid in our class" in Newark, is "stunted" and mentally "stopped" by his exposure to the aments of Kaintuck.

Coincidentally, I slogged through Roth right after reading three Kentucky novels: Berry's *Watch With Me* (1994), James Still's *River of Earth* (1940), and *The Time of Man* (1926) by Elizabeth Madox Roberts. Each is set within a decade or two of 1940. The characters are remarkably unlike

Nazis, though perhaps Mr. Roth knows the true heart of Kentucky better than Kentuckians themselves.

The Winchell funeral is the winch that turns the cranks out of office. Lindy disappears in flight, probably a victim of the Nazis who orchestrated the antiwar movement all along. (Just as Saddam Hussein's hidden bank accounts are enriching today's peace movement.) Acting President Wheeler declares martial law—quite a trick for a civil libertarian to pull off—anti-Semitic riots stain America red with the blood of Jewish martyrs, till FDR comes out of retirement . . . oh, I don't want to spoil the ending for you. Suffice to say that Roth, in his dotage, displays all the imagination of an assistant censor in the Office of War Information. Franklin D. retakes the White House and promptly gets us into the world war, wherein all those louts from Kentucky either die as fodder or walk tall as members of the Greatest Generation. All's well that ends well.

This is a repellent novel, bigoted and libelous of the dead, dripping with hatred of rural America, of Catholics, of any Middle American who has ever dared stand against the war machine. All that is left, I suppose, is for the author to collect his Presidential Medal of Freedom.

The Other Eisenhowers
The American Conservative, 2011

DWIGHT D. EISENHOWER'S MOTHER was a pacifist, a breed common in the Middle America of yore, before war became the national religion. Her son left Kansas to climb the martial ladder of the Department of War, whose motto, suggested Declaration of Independence signatory Benjamin Rush, should have been "A Widow and Orphan making office." It was also the greatest deracinating force in American history; Dwight, unlike Dorothy and Toto, never returned to the Sunflower State.

Old men grow sentimentally pensive, and one wonders if President Eisenhower's sober and remarkable Farewell Address counseling vigilance against the "military-industrial complex"—delivered fifty years ago over the televisions that even then were addling America—echoes, however faintly, Ida Eisenhower's Mennonite convictions. It surely is redolent of his older brother and frequent correspondent Edgar, the Tacoma attorney who in most Eisenhower biographies gets a walk-on as the crusty reactionary pestering the moderate Ike to repeal the New Deal and support the Bricker Amendment, that last gasp of the Old Right.

The president's son John, in his memoir *Strictly Personal*, writes affectionately that Uncle Ed "considered President Roosevelt a work of the devil." No jingo chickenhawk of the sort whose squawk dominates today's Right, Ed tried to talk John out of a career in the military: "he declared that I should forego any ideas of becoming a 'professional killer' and go to law school at his expense, later to join his law office."

This language—"professional killer"—marked Edgar Eisenhower as an anachronism among the placeless technocrats who were busy engineering the Empire of Euphemism. Organization men like Robert McNamara and McGeorge Bundy could no more understand Edgar Eisenhower than they could dig Jack Kerouac or Paul Goodman.

In his new study of Ike's valediction, *Unwarranted Influence*, James Ledbetter places the Farewell Address within a thematic range that stretches from North Dakota Senator Gerald Nye's 1930s investigation of the "merchants of death" to the power-elite analysis of C. Wright Mills and his idealistic admirers in Students for a Democratic Society. Speechwriters Malcolm Moos and Capt. Ralph Williams—perhaps younger brother Milton Eisenhower, too—crafted much of the address, but its concerns were those of the president, who later wrote in *Waging Peace*: "During the years of my Presidency, and especially the latter years, I began to feel more and more uneasiness about the effect on the nation of tremendous peacetime military expenditures." (How many Republican members of the 112th Congress would nod assent: ten, at most?)

The somber dignity with which Eisenhower left office ought not to obscure his administration's disgraceful interventions abroad (Iran, Guatemala) and at home (the Interstate Highway System, the National Defense Education Act). For those who preferred the American Republic to the American Empire, Ohio Sen. Robert Taft was the GOP choice in 1952.

Yet Ike was the last president confident enough to name, and even sometimes take on, the military-industrial complex. He lamented the "appalling costs" of the war machine and worried that a "garrison state" might arise in freedom's erstwhile land. He was justly furious to be reproved as soft on defense by such hawkish Democrats as the Pulitzer Prize-winning PT boat hero and devoted husband John F. Kennedy.

In his twilight, my old boss, Sen. Pat Moynihan, a Kennedy loyalist, was unsettled in Eisenhower-like ways by the seeming permanence of the national-security state, enshrouded in its miasmic secrecy. The new collection *Daniel Patrick Moynihan: A Portrait in Letters of an American Visionary*, contains a September 8, 1990, letter to Erwin N. Griswold, former dean of Harvard Law School, in which Moynihan grandiloquently—that is, characteristically—announces, "I have one purpose left in life; or at least in the Senate. It is to try to sort out what would be involved in reconstituting the American government in the aftermath of the cold war. Huge changes took place, some of which we hardly notice."

Two months later, in a letter to constituents—which Moynihan, unlike most members of Congress this side of Tennessee's Jimmy Duncan and my late friend Barber Conable, wrote himself—the senator "wondered . . . whether we any longer knew how" to be a "nation essentially at peace with the rest of the world."

We do not. Since 1941, war has warped American life. Only the doddering and the dotards among us have lived in an America that is not armed, aggressive, and perpetually at war. If you would seek those who know what an America at peace is like, visit the nursing home. If you would hear the sounds of America at war, walk the corridors of a veterans' hospital. Listen to the shrieks and sobs—the keening for the lost America of Ida and Edgar Eisenhower.

What Was Right About the New Left? Or, We Haven't Had That Spirit Here Since 1968

The American Conservative, 2008

THE GHOSTS OF 1968 are haunting Barack Obama, which is tremendously unfair, I say as his coeval, given that our cohort spent the Chicago Democratic Convention sticking baseball cards in our bicycle spokes rather than pelting Mayor Daley's finest with porcine epithets. But guilt by association is ironclad in these days when American political discourse is controlled by hall monitors and tattletales. Obama's friendship—acquaintance?—with Bill Ayers and Bernadine Dohrn is about to get an extended play, as the Republicans contrast Obama's Weatherfriends with their nominee's stint in the Hanoi Hilton. (To his credit, Obama has refused to act like a neocon and denounce his friends, whether Bill Ayers or Reverend Jeremiah Wright.)

By his own account, John McCain lived in North Vietnamese captivity longer than he had lived anywhere else in his itinerant life. This deracination and the resultant military-brat pathologies on display in McCain will go unexploited by the Democrats, whose nominee-in-waiting and maid-of-dishonor are just as placeless as Carpetbag John. And besides, the entire political class of Washingtron has all the indigenous flavor of the Crystal City metro station. It would never occur to an attack-ad maker that there was anything wrong with rootlessness.

If Obama bears the standard, the revolutionary posturing of Bill ("kill your parents") Ayers and Bernadine ("bring the war home") Dohrn will serve as the synecdoche of '68 in Republican minds. Prepare for another aphasiac episode in what Gore Vidal calls the United States of Amnesia. But I say to hell with Ayers and Dohrn: Let us remember the other New Left—a humane, decentralist, thoroughly American New Left which regarded socialism as "a way to bury social problems under a federal bureaucracy," in the words of Carl Oglesby, president of Students for a Democratic Society in 1965–66 and a key figure in its Middle American wing, which extended from independent anti-imperialist liberals to trans-Mississippi "Prairie Power" radicals. ("Texas anarchists," sneered the elite East Coast-schooled red diaper babies at the hell-raising directional state college Prairie Power kids.)

As Old Right historian Leonard Liggio wrote in 1970, "Since there was little official SDS ideology, and what there was was populist and libertarian, it was attractive to the large numbers of American students who were growing conscious of their opposition to the educational factory system, the bureaucracy, the draft and the war." This libertarian Middle American tendency faded as humorless Marxists and violent fanatics a la Ayers and Dohrn blew SDS apart, but even as it decomposed the New Left was an olio of old-fashioned American rebellion, naïve idealization of Third World revolutionaries, and the bomb-happy Marxism of groups such as Weatherman. The sager figures in the New Left, however, rejected television, IBM, nomadic corporate culture, and the Cold War—all profoundly anti-conservative forces—and I wonder just what is so "left" about that?

The Port Huron Statement, 1962 manifesto of SDS, was drawn up in large part by the Michigan Catholic baseball fan Tom Hayden. The Statement is a mixed bag: denunciations of racial bigotry, bureaucracy, and the militarization of American life bump into simultaneous calls for national health care and an expanded welfare state. Yet the Port Huron Statement, and SDS, emphasized the core principle of "decentralization," of breaking overly large institutions (and even cities) down to a more human scale, "based on the vision of man as master of his machines and his society."

"We oppose the depersonalization that reduces human beings to the status of things," declared the authors, and the line might have been written by another Michigan lad, Russell Kirk of Mecosta. Kirk was no New Leftist, though he did later befriend (and in 1976 voted for) Eugene McCarthy, the peace candidate of the 1968 Democratic primaries, the Distributist-inclined Catholic intellectual who befuddled his conventional liberal supporters with talk of a salutary "depersonalizing" of the presidency, of reducing that office to its constitutional dimensions, shorn of the accreted cult of personality.

Left and right mostly hurled anathemas at each other in 1968, but not always, and the rare friendly exchanges over the phantom barriers were rich with promise—a promise fulfilled, in a way, one year later, in the 1969 New York City mayoralty campaign of Norman Mailer, who campaigned as a "left conservative" on a platform of power to the neighborhoods.

But SDS president Carl Oglesby was the New Left figure who first saw the potential of a left-right linkage.

Oglesby was the son of rural working-class Southerners who had joined the diaspora north, where his father worked in an Akron rubber factory. Said Dad to his radical son: "Damn it, you ought to get yourself a real job where you can settle down and take care of your family and quit all this unpatriotic horseshit." Carl did not follow his father's advice, but just the hearing of it matters, too.

Oglesby was a playwright (he had written a well-received work on the Hatfield-McCoy feud) toiling within the military-industrial complex at Bendix Aerospace Systems when, fresh off the composition of an anti-Vietnam War position paper, he was elected president of SDS in June 1965. He was, at once, both more radical and more conservative than Hayden and the organization's leftist activists. As he writes in his recent memoir, *Ravens in the Storm*, "I believed that America's 'small-r' republicans would also have to get engaged if the antiwar cause were to have the least chance of succeeding."

Taking up his predecessor Paul Potter's challenge to "name the system," Oglesby made his own name with a November 1965 speech in Washington in which he fingered "corporate liberalism" as the "system that creates and sustains the war in Vietnam." He named names: not Goldwater or Kirk but Truman, Eisenhower, Kennedy, Bundy, McNamara, Rusk, Lodge, and Goldberg.

Through Professor Richard Schaull of Princeton Theological Seminary, Oglesby was introduced to the writings of Murray Rothbard, the antimilitarist libertarian economist whose long and winding and yet somehow consistent road had taken him from anti-New Deal isolationist Robert Taft supporter into friendship with the quasi-pacifist Nebraska Republican Congressman Howard Buffett (father of a much less interesting man) then over to the League of [Adlai] Stevensonian Democrats and, by 1968, into tentative comradeship with the anarchist factions of the New Left. While other young radicals read Marcuse or Fanon, Carl Oglesby dug Murray Rothbard.

In his essay "Vietnamese Crucible" (published in the 1967 volume *Containment and Change*), Oglesby rejected the "socialist radical, the corporatist conservative, and the welfare-state liberal" and challenged the New Left to embrace "American democratic populism" and "the American libertarian right."

Invoking Senator Taft, General Douglas MacArthur, Rep. Buffett, and *Saturday Evening Post* writer Garet Garrett, among other stalwarts of the Old Right, he asked, "Why have the traditional opponents of big, militarized, central authoritarian government now joined forces with such a government's boldest advocates?" What in the name of Thomas Jefferson were conservatives doing holding the bag for Robert Strange McNamara?

After explicating the Old Right to a readership that must have been, at the least, nonplussed, Oglesby connected the dots: "This style of political thought, rootedly American, is carried forward today by the Negro freedom movement and the student movement against Great Society-Free World imperialism. That these movements are called leftist means nothing. They are of the grain of American humanist individualism and voluntaristic associational action; and it is only through them that the libertarian tradition is activated and kept alive. In a strong sense, the Old Right and the New Left are morally and politically coordinate."

Oglesby did not predict an alliance; he merely pointed out the kinship of dissenters. Whether the twain would ever meet was another matter. (They might have met, come to think of it, via Mark Twain, in the person of an anti-imperialist Tom Sawyer.)

"The New Left," warned Oglesby, "can lose itself in the imported left-wing debates of the thirties, wondering what it ought to say about technocracy and Stalin." (It did lose itself, though Uncle Joe was not the cause—more like Leninism and an unmooring from those American roots.) "The libertarian right," Oglesby continued, "can remain hypnotically charmed by the authoritarian imperialists whose only ultimate love is Power, the subhuman brownshirted power of the jingo state militant, the state rampant, the iron state possessed of its own clanking glory." Well, yes, that and the need to kiss the asses of foundation presidents who doled out the money on which the organized right became just as dependent as any puling mendicant from the National Welfare Rights Organization.

(Among those captivated by this essay was a former Goldwater Girl named Hillary Rodham, who became friendly, for a while, with Oglesby. Alas, she entered her own crucible and came out mistress of the iron-maiden state.)

The Marxists and conventional leftists within SDS had no idea what to make of this stirring call for a prison break from the left-right bastille. Consider Bernadine Dohrn, the bloodlusting ex-cheerleader and pinup girl of Weatherman. Dohrn, a self-declared "revolutionary communist," was perplexed by Oglesby's fondness for right-wing isolationists.

"I'm not sure I know where you're coming from," Dorhn said to Oglesby, as he recounts in *Ravens in the Storm*.

Oglesby's reply was simple, brilliant, and no doubt baffling to Dohrn: "Ann Arbor, Kent, Akron, Kalamazoo."

For Oglesby understood, as that landmark druggy paean to youth culture and the pioneer virtues, *Easy Rider* (1969), had it, that for all their surface differences and rote hostility the hippies and rednecks, the small farmers and shaggy communards, were on the same side: that of liberty, of locally based community, of independence from the war machine. Billy

Joe Smythe, LeRoy Washington, and Luis Chavez were as one to McGeorge Bundy: interchangeable body-bag fillers. Hello, Big Muddy; Hello, Fodder.

Oglesby was in '68, and remains today, an admirer of Bobby Kennedy as the only pol who might have gathered the dispossessed in a hopeful democratic movement. Scoff if you will—he's used to it. After all, Oglesby once tried to convince Dohrn that an SDS-organized volunteer band of sugarcane cutters defying the travel ban to Cuba should include such "good, old-fashioned regular Americans" as PTA members and "Rotarians and Elks."

"Carl, you're getting a bit wild-eyed," replied the woman who responded to news of the Manson family's murder spree by ejaculating, "Dig it. First they killed those pigs, then they ate dinner in the same room as them. Then they even shoved a fork into a victim's stomach. Wild!" The only good Elk, it seems, is a dead Elk.

Oglesby was drummed out of SDS in a 1969 star-chamber trial. A harridan named Arlene Eisen Bergman arraigned him for being "trapped in our early, bourgeois stage," and for not progressing into "a Marxist-Leninist perspective." Oglesby's sins, as enumerated by Bergman, included "that bizarre last chapter in your book . . . where you actually propose an alliance with what you call, let's see, 'principled conservatives.'"

"SDS is not trying to reach the readers of *Life* magazine," Dohrn shouted at Oglesby. Carl was expelled; he went on to record two fine albums of folk-Beat Americana, and one supposes that his vision came closest to being realized in the music of Bob Dylan, the Minnesota-bred Goldwater-admiring scourge of the masters of war who wrote in the liner notes to his 1993 album *World Gone Wrong*, "give me a thousand acres of tractable land & all the gang members that exist & you'll see the Authentic alternative lifestyle, the Agrarian one."

What Oglesby called the "freewheeling participatory democracy" of SDS was dynamited by the likes of Ayers and Dohrn, representatives of the very worst of the anti-American left, who have settled into their sixties in comfortable prosperity while Carl Oglesby, lacking inherited wealth, battles illness as best he can. Life ain't fair. The cheerleaders and the rich boys always win, don't they?

Black Panther Eldridge Cleaver asked Oglesby to run as his vice presidential candidate on the 1968 Peace and Freedom Party ticket; Carl, in a hiccup of realpolitik, said no. But there had been common concerns. Cleaver had sharply assayed the demise of federalism: "There aren't any more state governments. We have these honorary pigs like Mayor Alioto . . . presiding over the distribution of a lot of federal funds. He's plugged into one gigantic system, one octopus spanning the continent from one end to the other, reaching its tentacles all around the world, in everybody's pocket and around everybody's neck. We have just one octopus. A beast with his head wherever LBJ might be tonight."

Yeah, the Panthers were thugs, the least imaginative of them had been infected with the Marxist-Leninist virus, and Cleaver committed some horrendous crimes. But the Panthers, unlike John McCain, came from neighborhoods, and the best of them were groping toward a Marcus Garvey-Malcolm X philosophy of community self-reliance. You've also got to admit that they were solid on Second Amendment issues. (Lynn Scarlett and I interviewed Cleaver for *Reason* in 1985. His place was easy to find: 'twas the only front porch in his Berkeley neighborhood flying an American flag.)

Okay, so maybe Eldridge isn't your cup of hallucinatory nutmeg tea. What about the only other 1968 general election presidential candidate worth a look: Governor George Wallace of the right-wing American Independent Party?

If you can get beyond Wallace's reprehensible race-baiting (which soon gave way to active courtship of black voters), certain of his policies overlapped with the humane left. He proposed decentralizing industries because "I don't think God meant people to be all jammed up in cities. No courtesy, no time, no room—that's all you get in cities." He called for removing the tax exemption from foundations and emitted a class-war cry— "the rednecks are coming"—that frightened the hell out of New York Times readers and William F. Buckley Jr., who called him a "country and western Marxist." Listen to Wallace and tell me if this isn't also the spirit of the New Left: "The biggest domestic issue for 1968? I'll tell you. It's people—our fine American people, living their own lives, buying their own homes, educating their children, running their own farms, working the way they like to work, and not having the bureaucrats and intellectual morons trying to manage everything for them. It's a matter of trusting the people to make their own decisions."

One of the few journalists who heard Wallace in '68 was Pete Hamill, who wrote in the New Left monthly *Ramparts* that "Wallace and the black and radical militants . . . share some common ground: local control of schools and institutions, a desire to radically change America, a violent distrust of the power structure and the establishment. In this year's election, the only one of the three major candidates who is a true radical is Wallace."

George Wallace and the New Left despised each other: "fascist" and "dirty beatniks" were about as sophisticated as the badinage got. Only a hopeless romantic—and what other kind is there?—would ponder the cross-pollinating possibilities: Creedence Clearwater Revival playing "Fortunate Son" at Wallace rallies, or the Guvnah's supporters (Chill Wills,

Walter Brennan, George "Goober" Lindsay) joining Phil Ochs in the chorus of "I Ain't Marching Anymore" at a rally outside the Opelika draft board.

Sigh. Maybe the closest we got to this sort of hybrid was the flat-out racist Asa Carter, who penned Wallace's disgraceful 1962 "segregation now, segregation tomorrow, segregation forever" inaugural address, and later wrote, under the name Forrest Carter, the novel *Gone To Texas*, which became the Clint Eastwood masterpiece *The Outlaw Josey Wales*.

Compared to Humphrey and Nixon, George Wallace was the peacenik in the '68 race. (Apologies to the aborted Cleaver-Oglesby ticket.) If the Vietnam War was not winnable within ninety days of his taking office, Wallace pledged an immediate withdrawal of U.S. troops. As his aides told Pete Hamill about Vietnam, "The hell with it."

Wallace also called foreign aid money "poured down a rat hole" and demanded that European and Asian allies pay more for their defense. The relative prudence of the Alabama governor's foreign policy was obscured by his disastrous selection of General Curtis "bomb them back into the Stone Age" LeMay as his running mate. LeMay thought himself a "moderate Republican," which may have been true: the most hawkish figure in American politics in 1968, after all, was that moderate Republican and Picasso-collecting warmongering New York Governor Nelson Rockefeller. (Oh, what might have been: before LeMay, Wallace reportedly had asked Colonel Sanders, Mr. Kentucky Fried Chicken, to join the ticket. Extra crispy chicken or extra crispy Vietnamese children: therein lies the Sanders-LeMay difference.)

Maybe "the Devil's got a Wallace sticker on the back of his car," as the Drive-By Truckers sing, but ol' George sure had trust-fund Weatherboy Billy Ayers's number: "It's the damn rich who turn Communist. You ever see a poor Communist?"

Wallace traditionally ran strong primary campaigns in Wisconsin, stronghold of Upper Midwest populism, but as he was running in '68 the state was losing one of its great patriots, William Appleman Williams, the favorite historian of the Middle American New Left. Williams was from Atlantic, Iowa—legend has it, says Paul Buhle, coauthor of an excellent biography of Williams, that the highway sign welcoming visitors to Atlantic bore "the Jeffersonian motto 'The Government Which Governs Least, Governs Best.'" Bill Williams, who left Atlantic for the U.S. Naval Academy (and remained proud of the fact) and later rehabilitated those defenderless conservative presidents, John Quincy Adams and Herbert Hoover, fit perfectly within the American populist tradition of the University of Wisconsin. But in 1968, Williams left Madison for Oregon State to, in Buhle's words, "teach undergraduates, live by the ocean, and live in a diversified community of 'ordinary' Americans."

As he moved off-center, taking his stand in the hinterlands, Williams called for a return to the Articles of Confederation and a radical decentralization of political and economic power—a decentralist socialism that probably looked better in cooperative theory than it would have in barbed-regulation practice. He decried the American Empire as unworthy of us; he, too, was of the left yet speaking to the right, trying to find that little egalitarian village where the shopkeeper and the jazz musician and the carpenter might live in liberty and fraternity.

I recently asked Williams's biographer Buhle, a Madison SDSer, publisher of the New Left journal *Radical America*, and editor of the recent *Students for a Democratic Society: A Graphic History* (Hill & Wang), about the prospects for cashing in on the missed chances of 1968. "The spirit at large in the US now reminds me more of the later 1960s New Left/Old Right dialogue or encounter than anything since then," he says. "Consequently, I find myself more in dialogue with old-fashioned conservatives than I have been, and I suspect that this is widely true."

The Bush Wars have brought together anti-imperialists of left and right, but their coalescence is being forged not so much overseas as in our backyards. A "wonderful example," says Buhle, "is conservation, small-town life, and the bird population. All kinds of conservatives and small-town Republicans find themselves fending off new demands for exploitation of public resources (threats to water supplies and such)." Farm markets are another meeting ground, he notes, as the organic and Eat Local and community-supported agriculture movements introduce folks who look homeward rather than into Baghdad suns. Left? Right? What difference does it make? The model organic farm in my neck of the woods, a truly inspiring extended-family venture, was begun by a former college hockey player and active member of the New York State Conservative Party. I know greens, right-to-lifers, NRA members, and just plain apolitical farmers who are re-localizing life, brightening their little corner of the world, in their daily acts.

The imperialists, the depersonalizers, the warmakers are with us still. But look around and you'll see that the seeds planted by the New Left have not all fallen on hard ground. I think maybe they're ready to flower.

I Love My Country.
But Perhaps Not This One

The Independent, 2001

THE OFFICE OF HOMELAND Security. Has a nice retro-Soviet ring to it, eh? Or how about Operation Infinite Justice, the Orwell-by-way-of-Madison-Avenue moniker that Pentagon image-makers first hung on our nascent World War Three? When the propagandists adopt phrases plucked from dystopian novels, we're in trouble.

We are not yet living in a police state; not even close. But neither are we quite living in America any more. Erstwhile civil libertarians endorse national ID cards. The ominous whisper of a military draft is in the air. When in the privacy of the family homestead I ventured the opinion that the September 11 attacks were a wicked response to wrong-headed US intervention in the Middle East, a dear family member counseled, "Don't say that too loud, Bill. Someone will report you to the police." She was serious.

The American precepts of individual rights, local self-rule and avoidance of foreign wars are so deeply buried under the rubble of empire that to mouth what once was a commonplace ("let's keep our noses out of others' business") is now a virtual act of sedition.

"Our calling" has become the eradication of terror from the world, according to President Bush. We are to "rid the world of evil," vow his speechwriters: mad and hubristic guff from callow thirtyish policy geeks who don't know a gun's stock from its barrel.

As an ardent patriot I love my country because it is mine. I suppose I should be pleased by the ubiquity of the red, white and blue banner. Flags fly from pizza shops, porches, car antennae.

Those whose knowledge comes from the idiot box will believe America to be the sum of *Friends* and Madeleine Albright and the preppies of the Family Bush, and they will hate us—understandably. But there is an untelevised America, a land of Iowa poets and rural volunteer fire departments and villages of faith and neighborliness and the continuity of generations.

This is the America I love, one that the keyboard bombardiers of DC would destroy in a New York minute.

Patriots—by which I mean Americans who love their untelevised country—despise war, not least for its catastrophic domestic consequences. In time of war, power flows to the center. Regional culture withers, idiosyncrasies are smothered, young men are sent across the globe to serve as armed employees of the central government. People shift their loyalties from the local and immediate to the abstract and remote; already, local charities are reporting huge shortfalls as generous souls send their donations to the bureaucracies of New York and Washington. Through it all, the belligerent eggheads of the militaristic right and world-reforming left piss their pants with glee.

I defer to no one in my desire that the homicides who orchestrated the evil acts of September 11 be given their measure of justice, thrice over. But I will not watch silently as my country disappears. Empire is not worth a single American (or Afghan) life; defending Israel is not worth sacrificing what remains of our traditional liberties; overthrowing the Taliban is not worth bleaching the color out of regional America.

The time for dissenters to keep quiet out of respect for the dead is over. Simple patriotism demands that we take up the plaint of a peaceable statesman from the Vietnam era: Come home, America. Come home now, while there is still a recognizable America.

Bringing it All Back Home
First Principles, 2011

REPUBLICAN MEMBERS OF CONGRESS—NIGH lockstep supporters of the Wall Street bailout, the Iraq War, and the Patriot Act when their party controlled the executive branch—profess to have rediscovered the Constitution during the first two years of the Age of Obama. Those of us who were not swept away by the Francophobia of 2003 might say we are experiencing déjà vu. For the first Clinton administration provoked a similar fit of GOP "constitutionalism," which peaked—or reached its nadir—when in 1996, future Viagra spokesman and Republican presidential candidate Bob Dole took to carrying in his (shirt!) pocket a copy of the Tenth Amendment, that paper guarantor of the rights of the states. (No one ever bothered to ask Senator Dole what he thought of his wife's leadership, as Secretary of Transportation under Ronald Reagan, in forcing the fifty states to adopt a uniform minimum drinking of age of twenty-one.)

I am a notoriously poor forecaster—every year I pick the Buffalo Bills to win the Super Bowl—but I can with unshakeable confidence predict that Republican invocations of constitutional limits on the powers of the national government will cease as soon as another Republican wins the keys to 1600 Pennsylvania Avenue.

(Allow me to raise, and then drop, a possible problem with these "constitutionalists" that is far more fundamental, even intractable, than my somewhat shopworn charge of hypocrisy. That is, what if the Anti-Federalists, those often prescient opponents of the new Constitution in 1787–88, were correct in asserting that the Constitution would lead, inexorably, to a centralized national government that would levy extortionate taxes, wage shameful wars, and usurp the powers of state and local governments? Was disregarding George Mason, Patrick Henry, and Luther Martin, and scrapping the Articles of Confederation, a fatal mistake?)

Let us, for the sake of this short essay, assume the possibility of a limited government that stays within constitutional bounds. A decent respect for Senator Dole's Tenth Amendment would deprive the federal government of its current role in education, for instance, as well as the provision of healthcare. But no single act would have a more profound and far-reaching effect than reorienting U.S. foreign policy along the lines of the advice given in George Washington's Farewell Address: to reject "foreign alliances, attachments, and intrigues" (goodbye, NATO); to avoid "excessive partiality for one foreign nation and excessive dislike of another" (goodbye, Middle East); and to beware "those overgrown military establishments which, under any form of government, are inauspicious to liberty, and which are to be regarded as particularly hostile to republican liberty" (goodbye, military-industrial complex).

With a handful of noble exceptions—I think of Representatives Ron Paul (TX), John Duncan Jr. (TN), and Walter Jones (NC)—Republicans have placed the $700-billion "defense" budget off-limits. I put defense within quotes because relatively little of this money is spent on the defense of the North American continent. In fact, an artless Republican congressman once described the abominable Department of Homeland Security as a "Defense Department for the United States"—which makes one wonder what the job of the actual Defense Department might be.

The baneful ramifications of an overgrown military establishment and promiscuous intervention in faraway lands go well beyond the budgetary. Edwin Starr once asked: "War—what is it good for?" And the answers should please no one who values liberty, small-scale community, republican governance, and a culture of life. War centralizes culture, displaces young adults, and tramples domestic liberties. (In time of war "the Constitution is just a scrap of paper to me," John J. McCloy, FDR's designated jailer of Japanese-Americans, once observed.)

In my book *Ain't My America: The Long, Noble History of Antiwar Conservatism and Middle-American Anti-Imperialism* (2008), I included what some reviewers thought to be an anomalous chapter detailing, in typically discursive form, the many pernicious byproducts of the warfare state and that military-industrial complex against which President Eisenhower so eloquently and ineffectively warned. I didn't cite Tang, but I did write about government-sponsored daycare (the "Total Army Family," in Pentagon 1984-speak), the Interstate Highway System, school consolidation, daylight saving time, and even the wretched metric system.

Rootlessness, divorce, children being raised by strangers: the military has contributed more than its share to social maladies that once troubled conservatives—and that, in ways direct and indirect, nurture the growth of the central state. The return of American soldiers to their homes and their families would be the most pro-family policy a family-values conservative could propose—and it would please fiscal conservatives, too, as deep and healthy cuts in the war budget would return American tax dollars to those who earned them.

John Randolph, the Virginia statesman and subject of Russell Kirk's magnificent biography, explained, "The Government of the United States was not calculated to wage offensive foreign war—it was instituted for the common defence and general welfare; and whosoever should embark it in a war of offence, would put it to a test which it was by no means calculated to endure." Isn't it time we started tending to our own backyards? We might begin to restore the health of our families, our local communities, our economy, and our Constitution—things worth conserving.

I Laughed—and I Was Ashamed
The Independent, 2001
(one week after September 11)

LIKE MOST AMERICANS, I spent Tuesday morning sitting with slack jaw and moist eyes in front of our TV set, stupefied by the enormity of it all and fantasizing revenge upon the Mohammedans responsible. But the corporate media are expert at wringing bathos out of tragedy, and of making risible the ineffably sad, so by noontime we had switched off the idiot box. The blandly handsome anchormen and pert anchorwomen were so histrionic and moronic that my wife and I found ourselves laughing, and we felt ashamed of our irreverence.

We live at the rural western end of New York State, 400 miles and several cultures distant from New York City. As a rule I am skeptical of vicarious grief, of the distressing modern practice of sobbing for strangers who die on the television whilst one's neighbors pass away unnoticed, but this is that rare time when the usually factitious "national community" of TV watchers has substance. People remain mesmerized by the admixture of sheer evil and staggering woe; at intervals, they issue from their homes to condole with one another.

The corporate media speak to, but never for, Middle America. The fatuous ABC host Charlie Gibson claims that Americans are enraged because "a symbol of America has been defiled," even though most Americans outside the New York City area had never heard of the World Trade Center, let alone venerated this symbol of global capitalism. What enrages them is mass murder. The NBC newsreader Tom Brokaw, glib peddler of World War II nostalgia, declared that the attack demonstrated the folly of "Fortress America isolation," whereas in fact it did just the opposite: if our foreign policy had reflected Middle American indifference to the Middle East, our troops would be home, Israel would be on its own, Muslims would not hate us, and uncounted thousands of unfortunate souls would still be alive. Such truths are unsayable in time of war, but there you are.

In his Farewell Address, which is the American version of the Ten Commandments—a sacred injunction serially violated—George Washington advised posterity to respect our "detached and distant situation" and to avoid foreign entanglements. This pacific counsel is today derided as "isolationism," fit only for indurated knuckle-draggers. American isolationists—who oppose killing foreigners—are tagged xenophobes, while those ordering the missile launches and inviting suicide attacks are the humane internationalists. Go figure.

The real lesson of this unspeakably awful Tuesday is that empire has a cost. It's not worth it, not by a long shot. But we the people will continue to pay the taxes and supply the corpses to the American Empire, never really sure just why in hell we're Over There.

The world is shrinking, and nothing will ever be the same, pundits insist in phrases trite and repellent. In the days after the carnage, we bought the first cider of the season, tossed around the football, and hunted new-fallen chestnuts. In the margins of empire, the world is as wondrously large as it ever was. I pray that it remains so.

Decentralism

The Encyclopedia of Libertarianism
(SAGE/Cato), 2008

"SMALL IS BEAUTIFUL," DECLARED economist E.F. Schumacher in his 1973 book of the same title, and the epigram encapsulates the spirit of decentralism. There is a poetic quality to decentralism, rooted as it is in a love of the particular. The British writer G. K. Chesterton noted in his novel of local patriotism, *The Napoleon of Notting Hill*, that the true patriot "never under any circumstances boasts of the largeness of his country, but always, and of necessity, boasts of the smallness of it."

A decentralist believes that political power (and, in some but hardly all cases, wealth) should be widely dispersed. He or she believes that concentrated power is the bane of liberty; its very remoteness insulates the wielder of power from the citizen—or, perhaps more accurately, the subject. As the most literary of modern decentralists, the Kentucky poet-farmer Wendell Berry, has warned, "Everywhere, every day, local life is being discomforted, disrupted, endangered, or destroyed by powerful people who live, or who are privileged to think that they live, beyond the bad effects of their bad work." Decentralists would cite as specific examples the 1970s federal policy of requiring cities to bus children to schools outside their neighborhoods, which virtually destroyed cohesive ethnic enclaves in American cities; the siting of public-housing projects and nuclear-waste facilities over the objections of residents of the affected areas; and the deracinating effects of an interventionist foreign policy which sends young men (and now women) hither and yon, far from their home places.

From the founding, American political debate has pitted advocates of a strong central state against partisans of decentralism. While James Madison, writing as Publius, assured readers in *Federalist* 45 that "The powers delegated by the proposed Constitution to the federal government are few and defined," the Anti-Federalists, who opposed ratification, saw in the Philadelphia compact the scaffolding of empire. Republican government "is only suited to a small and compact territory," argued Maryland Constitutional

Convention delegate Luther Martin. Within a unitary government spread over a wide territory, citizens would have little opportunity to know those whom they might elect; lawmakers would govern in ignorance of local conditions, and tyranny would be necessary to enforce their laws.

This argument has continued throughout American history: are liberty, property, and the integrity of small places best secured by local government or by national (or, increasingly in the age of globalization, international) authority?

In American politics this has often been rendered in shorthand as the Jefferson-Hamilton debate. Thomas Jefferson, though his presidential administration sometimes overstepped constitutional bounds (for instance, with his Louisiana Purchase) and though he was essentially neutral on the matter of the Constitution's ratification, is regarded as the founding father of American decentralism. Sketching his ideal in a letter from Monticello in 1824, Jefferson wrote that even the county was too distended a district for meaningful citizenship; he favored the creation of smaller "wards." In Jefferson's description, "Each ward would thus be a small republic within itself, and every man in the State would thus become an acting member of the common government, transacting in person a great portion of its rights and duties, subordinate indeed, yet important, and entirely within his competence. The wit of man cannot devise a more solid basis for a free, durable, and well administered republic."

The wit of man, at least in the United States, had other plans. The centripetal force of three major wars—the Civil War and the two world wars—consolidated extraordinary power in the national government; decentralists were relegated to the political fringe, for as the liberal historian Arthur Schlesinger Jr., cautioned in his manifesto of Cold War liberalism, *The Vital Center* (1949), "One can dally with the distributist dream of decentralization," but "you cannot flee from science and technology into a quietist dreamworld. The state and the factory are inexorable: bad men will run them if good abdicate the job."

The "distributists" whom Schlesinger dismissed as airy dreamers were the most visible decentralists in the years 1930–1950. Drawing inspiration from Catholic social teaching and from such figures as G.K. Chesterton and Dorothy Day, founder of the anarchist Catholic Worker movement, the distributists promoted the Catholic principle of subsidiarity: that is, the management of affairs ought to devolve to the lowest possible level of society—individual, family, block, village, and only in the rarest cases to the national government. In 1936 the American distributists, in league with agrarian and libertarian allies, published a widely heralded programmatic guide, *Who Owns America?*, which had little practical effect on the drift toward centralization.

In post–World War II American politics, decentralist themes can be found in such disparate groups as the New Left (especially Paul Goodman, Carl Oglesby, and Karl Hess), the libertarians, the Greens (see Kirkpatrick Sale's encyclopedic *Human Scale*), the Democratic left (former California Governor and Oakland Mayor Jerry Brown), Southern agrarian intellectuals (Thomas J. Fleming, Clyde Wilson, Donald Livingston), and such Republican Party figures as Senator Robert Taft of Ohio and Vermont State Senator John McClaughry.

In 1975, Ronald Reagan declared, in words ghostwritten by McClaughry, "I am calling for an end to giantism and for a return to the human scale—the scale that human beings can understand and cope with. . . . In government, the human scale is the town council, the board of selectmen, the precinct captain. It is this activity on a small human scale that creates the fabric of community, a framework for the creation of abundance and liberty."

If the Reagan administration seldom honored this vision—imposing a national drinking age of twenty-one, ordering state National Guard units to Central America over the objections of governors—recent years have seen a revivification of decentralist thought. The post-Cold war fissioning of overlarge states is the realization of Leopold Kohr's exhortation, in *The Breakdown of Nations* (1978), "Instead of union, let us have disunion now. Instead of fusing the small, let us dismember the big. Instead of creating fewer and larger states, let us create more and smaller ones."

Decentralism is a motive force in the early twenty-first-century secession movements in Quebec, Scotland, Northern Italy, and elsewhere, as well as in proposals to divide such American states as California, New York, and even Kansas into two or more states. The Nobel laureate Russian novelist Aleksandr Solzhenitysn made a lyrical, if largely ignored, plea for a "democracy of small areas" in *Rebuilding Russia* (1991). There was also in the 1990s a renewed emphasis, in popular if not yet in legal circles, on the Tenth Amendment to the U.S. Constitution, which provides that "The powers not delegated to the United States by the Constitution, nor prohibited by it to the States, are reserved to the States respectively, or to the people."

Decentralists insist that the love of the local and particular need not exclude a love of the national or even universal. In his essay "Provincialism," the early-twentieth-century philosopher Josiah Royce emphasized that "the tendency toward national unity and that toward local independence of spirit must henceforth grow together": the national culture of the United States was to be the sum of a thousand and one distinct and vibrant local cultures. (The cultural implications of centralized government ought not to be discounted: the two great flowerings of American letters, in the 1850s and 1920s, came during eras of much-derided "weak" presidents and a relatively inactive national government.)

In the formulation of the Iowa painter Grant Wood, "when the different regions develop characteristics of their own, they will come into competition with each other; and out of this competition a rich American culture will grow."

Political decentralists would extend the same principle to governance: permit each polity to adopt laws suited to local conditions; let San Francisco be San Francisco, and let Utah be Utah. Or in the remark of Supreme Court Justice Louis Brandeis, "The United States should go back to the federation idea, letting each state evolve a policy and develop itself. There are enough good men in Alabama, for example, to make Alabama a good state."

Critics of decentralism demur. They point to the numerous instances in which local authority has been exercised unwisely or even repressively, most notably in the Jim Crow laws and state-sanctioned segregation in the states of the Deep South. The federal government, through the Civil Rights Act of 1964 and the Voting Rights Act of 1965, secured the basic rights of American blacks—though decentralists would reply that the very same government was sending those same young black Southern men across the world to fight and die in Vietnam. The central state giveth, and the central state taketh away.

Dorothy Day's Catholic Worker movement, which drew localist and anarchist lesssons from Christianity, held that bigness "is not only impersonal, but also makes accountability, and, therefore, an effective political forum for redressing grievances, next to impossible." If my town council passes an ordinance that I regard as silly or oppressive, I can remonstrate, face-to-face, with men and women who are my neighbors. If the federal government enacts a law to which I object, I can do little more than write a letter to a federal office-holder, who will respond with a computer-generated reply, or cast a vote in the next federal election: impersonal and probably futile acts.

The devitalizing, dispiriting effect of centralization was captured by novelist Norman Mailer, who in his 1969 campaign for the mayoralty of New York City proposed that the city become an independent state and that this new state devolve all political power to the neighborhood level. Mailer wrote: "Our authority has been handed over to the federal power. We expect our economic solutions, our habitats, yes, even our entertainments, to derive from that remote abstract power, remote as the other end of a television tube. We are like wards in an orphan asylum. The shaping of the style of our lives is removed from us—we pay for huge military adventures and social experiments so separated from our direct control that . . . our condition is spiritless. We wait for abstract impersonal powers to save us, we despise the abstractness of those powers, we loathe ourselves for our own apathy."

From Thomas Jefferson to Norman Mailer: the faces change, the styles too, but decentralists endure.

BIBLIOGRAPHY

Herbert Agar and Allen Tate, editors, *Who Owns America? A New Declaration of Independence* (Wilmington, Delaware: ISI Books, 1999/original publication 1936)
Berry, Wendell, *Home Economics* (San Francisco: North Point Press, 1987)
Bryan, Frank, and John McClaughry, *The Vermont Papers* (Colchester, Vermont: Chelsea Green, 1989)
Chesterton, G.K., *The Napoleon of Notting Hill* (Mineola, NY: Dover, 1991/originally published 1904)
Davidson, Donald, *The Attack on Leviathan* (Chapel Hill: University of North Carolina Press, 1938)
Hess, Karl, *Dear America* (New York: Morrow, 1975)
Jefferson, Thomas, *Writings* (New York: Library of America, 1984)
Mailer, Norman, "An Instrument for the City," *Existential Errands* (Boston: Little, Brown, 1972)
Naylor, Thomas, and William H. Willimon, *Downsizing the U.S.A.* (Grand Rapids, Michigan: Eerdmans, 1997)

Anarchism

American Conservatism: An Encyclopedia
(ISI Books), 2006

PERHAPS NO POLITICAL TERM is quite so misunderstood as "anarchy." In the popular press, it is a synonym for disorder and chaos, not to mention looting and pillage: countries like Haiti are always being "plunged into anarchy." The anarchist, meanwhile, is frozen into a late-19th-century caricature: he is furtive, hirsute, beady-eyed, given to gesticulation, gibberish, and, most of all, pointless acts of violence.

Yet anarchy, according to most of its proponents through the years, is peaceable, wholly voluntary, and perhaps a bit utopian. The word means "without a ruler"; anarchy is defined as the absence of a state and its attendant coercive powers. It implies nothing about social arrangements, family and sexual life, or religion; and in fact the most persuasive anarchists, from Russian novelist Leo Tolstoy to Catholic Worker founder Dorothy Day, have been devout Christians.

Under anarchy, wrote its advocate Prince Peter Kropotkin in *The Encyclopedia Britannica* (1910), "the voluntary associations which already now begin to cover all the fields of human activity would take a still greater extension so as to substitute themselves for the state in all its functions." From alms to arms, "an anarchist is a voluntarist," explained Karl Hess, the speechwriter for Barry Goldwater who chucked it all to live as a husband, neighbor, and welder in rural West Virginia. Anarchists would separate state from church, state from education, state from welfare, even state from justice. (Murray N. Rothbard and David Friedman, among others, have explored how courts and policing might work in a stateless society.)

The word anarchism was not popularized until 1840 (by Pierre-Joseph Proudhon), but its practice predates its philosophical defenders. In many ways, the American settlers and citizens of the early republic were, in their daily deeds, living anarchism. As Ralph Waldo Emerson explained, "Massachusetts, in its heroic day, had no government—was an anarchy. Every man stood on his own feet, was his own governor; and there was no breach of peace from Cape Cod to Mount Hoosac."

"The new race is stiff, heady, and rebellious," said Emerson of his confreres in the 1830s, the heyday of American anarchism. "They are fanatics in freedom; they hate tolls, taxes, turnpikes, banks, hierarchies, governors, yea, almost laws." Emerson's handyman, Henry David Thoreau, expressed his anarchism aphoristically, altering the maxim of Thomas Jefferson to read "that government is best which governs not at all."

The abolitionist ranks included a number of anarchists, among them the wealthy New York Congressman Gerrit Smith, who made an exception to his anti-statism by advocating the prohibition of alcohol. Smith might appear a hypocrite, but with a nod to Emerson's counsel about hobgoblins and little minds, the inconsistency of American anarchists has been one of their charms.

Systematic anarchists weaving their elaborate schemes have usually been bores, men just as trapped in webs of abstraction as the statists against whom they rail. Their influence within the broader culture has been nil. American anarchism has been more a tendency than a philosophy; the most appealing anarchists have been literary men deeply dyed in the American grain.

Anarchists acquired the twin taints of violence and alienness in the late nineteenth century. Although a handful of "individualist anarchists," most prominently Benjamin Tucker, editor of the publication *Liberty*, have attracted scholarly attention, the "anarchist-communists" of the era were far more visible, vocal, and execrated. While most American anarchists have agreed with Dorothy Day that "property is proper to man," the anarchist-communists generally sought collective ownership of property, including land. As the Russian-born Emma Goldman, America's most noted anarchist-communist, explained her ideal: "Voluntary economic cooperation of all toward the needs of each." (Despite her collectivism, Goldman was a fierce critic of the Soviet Union's denial of individual liberties.)

The anarchist-communists, largely foreign-born, acting outside any local or even identifiably American context, were persecuted by the Wilson administration for their opposition to the First World War and disappeared, leaving few traces.

Yet echoes of native anarchism may be heard throughout American history: in the warnings of the Anti-Federalists about the centralizing thrust of the new Constitution; in the Garrisonian abolitionists who reviled any government that countenanced slavery; in the Populists of the 1890s, with their attacks on chartered corporations and paper wealth; in the Old Right of the 1930s, which saw the New Deal as potentially totalitarian; in the

New Left of the 1960s, which denounced the military, the university, and the corporation as dehumanizing; and among contemporary libertarians, especially those influenced by the economist and anti-imperialist Murray N. Rothbard. But except for the anarchist-tinged Industrial Workers of the World, the radical labor union that reached its zenith in the early twentieth century, anarchists have never been adept organizers. For the most part anarchy in the USA has been a literary-political tendency. A very partial list of American men and women of letters who have described themselves as anarchists include Henry Adams (a "conservative Christian anarchist"), Paul Goodman, Norman Mailer, Robinson Jeffers, e.e. cummings, Lawrence Ferlinghetti, Ursula Le Guin, William Saroyan, Dwight Macdonald, and Edward Abbey.

Abbey's novels, especially *The Brave Cowboy* (1956), *The Monkeywrench Gang* (1975), and *The Fool's Progress* (1988), feature merry anarchist heroes who live by Abbey's anarchist creed: "Be loyal to your family, your clan, your friends, and your community. Let the nation-state go hang itself."

Literary anarchists often display an intense localism, reflecting Ernest Hemingway's belief that "No larger unit than the village can exist without things being impossible."

They are anti-political in that they deny that politics, or the demands of state, have any claim to our time, or families, our lives. In *Notes of a Neolithic Conservative* (1970), Paul Goodman, sometime guru of the New Left, wrote, "As a conservative anarchist, I believe that to seek for Power is otiose, yet I want to derange as little as possible the powers that be; I am eager to sign off as soon as conditions are tolerable, so people can go back to the things that matter, their professions, their sports, and friendships."

Ernest Crosby, who succeeded Theodore Roosevelt in the New York State Assembly in 1887, was a fervent admirer of Tolstoy and something of an anarchist himself. Crosby is remembered for *Captain Jinks: Hero* (1902), his satirical novel of American imperialism, but his poem, "The State," might serve as a stark summation of the anarchist view:

> They talked much of the State—the State.
> I had never seen the State, and I asked them to picture it to me, as my gross mind could not follow their subtle language when they spake of it.
> Then they told me to think of it as of a beautiful goddess, enthroned and sceptred, benignly caring for her children.
> But for some reason I was not satisfied.
> And once upon a time, as I was lying awake at night and thinking, I had as it were a vision,

And I seemed to see a barren ridge of sand beneath a lurid sky;
　　　And lo, against the sky stood out in bold relief a black scaffold and gallows-tree, and from the end of its gaunt arm hung, limp and motionless, a shadowy, empty noose.
　　　And a Voice whispered in my ear, "Behold the State incarnate!"

FURTHER READING

Charles A. Madison, "Anarchism in the United States," *Journal of the History of Ideas* (Vol. VI, No. 1, January 1945): 46–66.

James J. Martin, *Men Against the State: The Expositors of Individualist Anarchism in America, 1827–1908* (Colorado Springs: Ralph Myles Publisher, 1970/first published DeKalb, IL 1953)

William O. Reichert, *Partisans of Freedom: A Study in American Anarchism* (Bowling Green, OH: Bowling Green University Popular Press, 1976)

Eunice Minette Schuster, "Native American Anarchism," *Smith College Studies in History* (Vol. XVII, Nos. 1–4, October 1931–July 1932): 1–202.

Boulder Rocks

The American Conservative, 2009

I ALWAYS FIGURED THAT if ever I got to Boulder, Colorado, it would be as a student at the Jack Kerouac School of Disembodied Poetics, namesake of the Taft Republican novelist from Lowell, Massachusetts, at whose gravesite my wife left her bridal bouquet.

But instead, I rolled into Boulder to debate—a most un-Kerouacian act, although for all his shyness, Saint Jack had a knack for the non sequitur to which there is no reply. He once halted the verbigeration of a strange episode of *Firing Line* by barking a line from a tune by Slim & Slam: "Flat foot floogie with a floy floy."

How do you answer *that*?

My worthy opponent in Boulder was my friend Gary Gregg of the University of Louisville, able debater and genial post-debate drinking companion. We had a grand old time of it and the college kids didn't seem overly bored . . . hell, we probably ought to take this show on the road as a slightly more highbrow version of the WWF.

Our subject? Whether or not the Constitution ought to have been ratified. Now that's a debate that has grown cold in 220 years, eh?

Poised as ever on the cutting edge of antiquarian irrelevancy, I took the Anti-Federalist side, arguing for liberty and self-rule within a small and modest republic and against the designing men who scrapped the Articles of Confederation for what Patrick Henry called "the most fatal plan that could possibly be conceived to enslave a free people."

Yet I was no epicene Oxonian willing to argue it either way. *I mean it man*, as a Ron Paul admirer once spat onto vinyl. The Constitution was our first mistake.

I channeled the bibulous Maryland Anti-Federalist Luther Martin, whose dubious fortune it was to attract me as a biographer (*Forgotten Founder, Drunken Prophet: The Life of Luther Martin*). Sartorially, we are equally disheveled, but my man Luther, whose bile rode on a rummy wave, could've drunk under the table every fratboy in Boulder. I was sipping water, so my impersonation lacked the necessary alcoholic verisimilitude.

In America, the losers in history's debates either grow devil's horns or disappear into the grey cloud of consensus, while the winners acquire absurd haloes. Never was this more the case than in the struggle over the Constitution.

The primary architects and defenders of the document were grandiose universalists who believed, as Gouverneur Morris told the Constitutional Convention, that they "came here as . . . representative[s] of the whole human race." The placeless land speculator James Wilson explained that the consolidators had "to form our calculations on a scale commensurate to a large portion of the globe." These men saw a forest but no trees.

This disorder extends to the *Federalist Papers*, wherein local attachments and local knowledge are belittled throughout. James Madison argues in *Federalist* 10 for a "large over a small republic" because the former will have "representatives whose enlightened views and sentiments render them superior to local prejudices and to schemes of injustice." The staggering inaccuracy of this observation has not in the least detracted from the éclat accorded this essay by students of American government.

Yet the Anti-Federalists, prophetic on matters ranging from the imperial presidency to the emasculation of the states, also misread the future. "[C]an it be supposed," asked Luther Martin, that people who had so recently fought a revolution for independence "would ever submit to have a national government established, the seat of which would be more than a thousand miles removed from some of them?"

Well, they did. And after the steady nationalization not only of political power but of culture and financial decisionmaking, today we the people submit to any depredation from distant authorities. Our rulers in Washington send kids from Boulder across James Wilson's globe to die for nothing, their blood seeding faraway sands—and Colorado meekly submits. The Anti-Federalists thought we'd fight back. Maybe they thought too much of us.

I am sorry to say, Dr. Franklin, that we did not keep the republic. We blew it. Luther Martin warned us that this was going to happen. The conservative shibboleth when objecting to egregious acts in Washington has long been "It's unconstitutional!" The Anti-Federalists would have told you that such "unconstitutional" interventions were inevitable.

If we cannot undo 1787 at least we can cut the Constitutionolatry and acknowledge as ancestors the Anti-Federalists, those forgotten localist patriots who stood for small things, for liberty, for their homes, against the assault of centralization.

"Happiness is preferable to the Splendors of a national Government," said Luther Martin, in vain, to a Constitutional Convention whose delegates, forgetting modesty, aimed at glory and grandeur.

Martin may as well have told Madison, "Flat foot floogie with a floy floy."

In A Cause That Will (Or Won't) Triumph
The American Conservative, 2009

IN EDWARD ABBEY'S AFTER-THE-COLLAPSE novel *Good News* (1980), Sam the Shaman tells the valiant anarchist cowboy Jack Burns that "There's one thing wrong with always fighting for freedom, and justice, and decency, and so forth."

"Only one thing?" replies Burns. "What's that?"

"You almost always lose."

In deference to Edgar Lee Masters, *Spoon River Anthology* poet and anti-imperialist states' rights Democrat, I shan't quote Clarence Darrow's line about lost causes being the only ones worth fighting for. Masters had been Darrow's law partner, and he disdained the Chicago loudmouth as a headline-hogging welsher.

Still, there is the matter of the lostness of our cause. Peace, it seems, often passeth understanding.

Is *The American Conservative*—to cite one sign of life—a contrail in the sky of a dying America or the bright harbinger of revival—of a better, more humane Little America? I do not say this better America would be a more conservative America because for half a century, "conservative" has been a synonym of—a slave to—militarism, profligacy, the invasion of other nations, contempt for personal liberties, and an ignorance of and hostility toward provincial America that is Philip Roth-ian in its scope. The conservative movement, like the empire whose adjunct and cheerleader it is, is a daisy chain of epicene dissemblers and vampiric chickenhawks who feast on the carrion of our republic. The c-word is quite simply beyond reclamation. The anarchist founder of the Intercollegiate Studies Institute, Frank Chodorov, had the right idea, even if it did contradict his pacifism: "Anyone who calls me a conservative gets a punch in the nose." If we have to play Name that Tendency I'd opt for Little American, Front Porch republican, localist, decentralist, libertarian, or, to borrow Robert Frost's term, plain old Insubordinate American—anything but C! (With a nod to Shel Silverstein.)

Be not deceived that a few opportunistic Republicans who said absolutely nothing in defense of our America during the Bush octennium are now sending up false flags of state sovereignty and the Tenth Amendment. Their Contract with America doppelgangers pulled the same stunt a decade ago before signing on, without any apparent qualms, to the brutally consolidationist Bush-Cheney regime. Recall that Bob Dole carried a copy of the Tenth Amendment during his flaccid 1996 presidential campaign, presumably in the same pocket that held the pills he needed to gulp in order to entertain the gracious Liddy. If these people were anything other than cynical party hacks I would be enthusiastic, but for God's sake, Charlie Brown, how often does Lucy have to yank the football away before you wise up?

The national "conversation," to misuse that word, is and has been limited to belligerent neoconservatives and liberal imperialists for many years now. Ed Abbey's Jack Burns is sooner to wind up on a Department of Homeland Security watch list than he is on CNN. But so what? We dishonor our forebears if we whine that the rulers and their lackeys are nasty, tyrannical, and placeless. Of course they are—they're rulers and lackeys!

The great John Randolph once explained his contumacy: "I found I might co-operate, or be an honest man. I have therefore opposed them and will oppose them." This is even truer today, though mere opposition is a debilitating condition for all but the most friendless crank. Standing athwart things is a good way to get neutered. Luckily, we are *for* things—a restoration of the republic, the rebirth of citizenship, social and political life on a human scale, a peaceful America that minds its own damn business. These goals will confound those who mimic the attitudes (never the Beatitudes!) blared from the rectangular soul-stealer in the living room, but among those who think up their own notions and sign their own names, to borrow Edmund Wilson's phrase, we have company. Anyone who engages in authentic civil or social life—ref in a pickup basketball game, drummer in a cowpunk band, secretary of a ladies' study club, rhubarb-cutter in a community garden—is acting upon the healthy, voluntaristic, small-is-not-always-beautiful-but-at-least-it's-human impulses that animate the first, last, and best alternative to the empire.

Whether we ever get together politically remains an open question. Protest politics is mostly boring street theater overseen by puppet-master choreographers in service of the two parties. True dissenters who undertake national campaigns—Ron Paul, Ralph Nader—are mocked, libeled, or ignored. Words are stripped of their meaning, even inverted, so that a vote for change produces Joe Biden, and a cheer for family values brings forth Newt Gingrich. I used to be disgusted but now I try to be amused, though how much, really, can one take? And for how long? Sixty-plus years ago the disgusted but amused H. L. Mencken covered his last campaign, which pitted the double atom-bomb dropper Harry Truman versus the little man on the wedding cake, Thomas E. Dewey. Was Obama v. McCain really that much worse a choice?

Our decline predates the Bushes, the Clintons, even the Kennedys. Trace it, if you like, back to the overthrow of the gentle Articles of Confederation and the triumph of Hamilton, Madison, and James Wilson over Patrick Henry, Luther Martin, and Melancton Smith in 1787–88. We have a helluva losing streak going, but there is a value in showing up for a game and taking your swings even if you have no chance. To give in is a sin.

So many of the vital and flavorful American political traditions go utterly, offensively, incredibly unrepresented in national discourse: the Anti-Federalists, the Populists, Brahmin anti-imperialists, independent liberals, prairie socialists, Old Right libertarians. It is our ennobling duty to keep these fires burning, even in the present darkness. For they illuminate the hopeful signs in our midst: homeschoolers, community-supported agriculture, independence movements from Vermont to Hawaii, the kids fired up by Ron Paul.

"Be joyful though you have considered all the facts," advises Wendell Berry. Excellent advice!

Our country is that same Wendell Berry, Townes Van Zandt, Mavis Staples, Ken Kesey, Cormac McCarthy, Levon Helm. . . . How can one despair with these by our sides, at our backs, in our heads? Editorialists in the *New York Times* and *Washington Post*, shouters on the television, sallow callow master bloggers who jerk out their vitriol over dissenters: they aren't worth the scorn in a thumbnail vial. Their depressing and ephemeral work dissipates with the air it befouls, the paper it poisons, the screen it scars. The real country endures. It produces whatever books and songs and films and paintings add up to American culture. It is where sandlot baseball and farm markets come from; it is where peace dwells in this nation of perpetual war.

Sursum corda, pals. We ain't dead yet. Turn off the TV. Reject the chains they have fashioned for you. Live as if in a free country. Look again at the things nighest unto you. That's America. That's worth saving.

www.ingramcontent.com/pod-product-compliance
Lightning Source LLC
Chambersburg PA
CBHW021927290426
44108CB00012B/751